MW01133922

SAMUEL JOHNSON IN CONTEXT

Few authors benefit from being set in their contemporary context more than Samuel Johnson. *Samuel Johnson in Context* is a guide to his world, offering readers a comprehensive account of eighteenth-century life and culture as it relates to his work. Short, lively, and eminently readable chapters illuminate not only Johnson's own life, writings, and career, but the literary, critical, journalistic, social, political, scientific, artistic, medical, and financial contexts in which his works came into being. Written by leading experts in Johnson and in eighteenth-century studies, these chapters offer both depth and range of information and suggestions for further study and research. Richly illustrated, with a chronology of Johnson's life and works and an extensive further reading list, this book is a major new work of reference on eighteenth-century culture and the age of Johnson.

JACK LYNCH is Professor of English at Rutgers University. His publications include *The Age of Elizabeth in the Age of Johnson* (Cambridge, 2003) and, as editor, *Anniversary Essays on Johnson's "Dictionary"* (Cambridge, 2005).

SAMUEL JOHNSON IN CONTEXT

EDITED BY

JACK LYNCH

CAMBRIDGE UNIVERSITY PRESS
Cambridge, New York, Melbourne, Madrid, Cape Town,
Singapore, São Paulo, Delhi, Tokyo, Mexico City

Cambridge University Press
The Edinburgh Building, Cambridge CB2 8RU, UK

Published in the United States of America by Cambridge University Press, New York

www.cambridge.org
Information on this title: www.cambridge.org/9780521190107

First published 2012

Printed in the United Kingdom at the University Press, Cambridge

A catalogue record for this publication is available from the British Library

Library of Congress Cataloguing in Publication data
Samuel Johnson in context / Jack Lynch.
p. cm.
Includes bibliographical references and index.
ISBN 978-0-521-19010-7 (hardback)
1. Johnson, Samuel, 1709–1784–Criticism and interpretation. 2. English literature–18th century–History and criticism. 3. Great Britain–Intellectual life–18th century.
I. Lynch, Jack (John T.)
PR3534.S26 2011
828′.609–dc23
2011029845

ISBN 978-0-521-19010-7 Hardback

Contents

Illustrations

Contributors

BARRY BALDWIN is Emeritus Professor of Classics, University of Calgary, and Fellow of the Royal Society of Canada. He has published *The Latin and Greek Poems of Samuel Johnson* (1995) as well as articles on Johnson and other eighteenth-century topics. He is editing Johnson's school and college Latin prose for Yale University Press.

LISA BERGLUND is Associate Professor of English at Buffalo State College and the executive secretary of the Dictionary Society of North America. She has published numerous articles on Johnson, Piozzi, Boswell, teaching eighteenth-century literature, and book history.

O M BRACK, JR. is Emeritus Professor of English at Arizona State University. He is the editor of two forthcoming volumes of *The Yale Edition of the Works of Samuel Johnson*: *Biographical and Related Writings* and *Miscellaneous Writings*, and the textual editor of *The Parliamentary Debates* and *A Commentary on Mr. Pope's Principles of Morality, or Essay on Man*. He has written and edited Sir John Hawkins's *Life of Samuel Johnson, LL.D.* (2009), *The Early Biographies of Samuel Johnson* (1974), and *Samuel Johnson's Early Biographers* (1971), with Robert E. Kelley. He is also founding editor and textual editor for *The Works of Tobias Smollett.*

BRYCCHAN CAREY is Reader in English Literature at Kingston University, London. He is the author of *British Abolitionism and the Rhetoric of Sensibility: Writing, Sentiment, and Slavery, 1760–1807* (2005) and the editor (with Peter Kitson) of *Slavery and the Cultures of Abolition: Essays Marking the British Abolition Act of 1807* (2007) and (with Markman Ellis and Sara Salih) of *Discourses of Slavery and Abolition: Britain and its Colonies, 1760–1838* (2004). He is completing a book on the origins and development of Quaker antislavery rhetoric in the seventeenth and eighteenth centuries.

PETER CLARK is Professor of European Urban History at the University of Helsinki. Previously, he was a professor at the University of Leicester. He has published or edited nearly twenty books on urban and social history, including *British Clubs and Societies, 1580–1800* (2000) and *European Cities and Towns, 400–2000* (2009). He is currently editing the *Oxford Handbook on Cities in History.*

GREG CLINGHAM is the John P. Crozer Chair of English Literature and Director of the University Press at Bucknell University, author of *Johnson, Writing, and Memory* (Cambridge University Press, 2002), and editor of *The Cambridge Companion to Samuel Johnson* (Cambridge University Press, 1997).

D'MARIS COFFMAN received her MA and PhD in history from the University of Pennsylvania and her BSc in Economics from the Wharton School. She is the Mary Bateson Research Fellow at Newnham College, Cambridge, and the director of the Winton Centre for Financial History there. She co-manages the European State Finance Database.

THOMAS M. CURLEY, Professor of English at Bridgewater State University, is the author of *Sir Robert Chambers: Law, Literature, and Empire in the Age of Johnson* (1998), which was nominated for a Pulitzer Prize and won the Choice Outstanding Academic Book Award. His most recent study is *Samuel Johnson, the "Ossian" Fraud, and the Celtic Revival in Great Britain and Ireland* (Cambridge University Press, 2009).

ROBERT DEMARIA, JR. is the Henry Noble MacCracken Professor of English at Vassar College, where he has taught all of his career. He is the author of three books and many articles on Johnson and general editor of *The Yale Edition of the Works of Samuel Johnson*. In that series, with Gwin Kolb, he edited *Johnson on the English Language* (2005) and he is editing, with O M Brack, Jr., the final volume in the series, *Miscellaneous Prose*. He is now at work on *British Literature 1640–1789: Keywords.*

HELEN DEUTSCH, Professor of English at UCLA, is the author of *Resemblance and Disgrace: Alexander Pope and the Deformation of Culture* (1996) and *Loving Dr. Johnson* (2005). She is working on a book on the literary afterlife of Jonathan Swift.

CATHERINE DILLE has written on various aspects of early modern literature and culture, including eighteenth-century educational practice and the literary legacy of Samuel Johnson. She has most recently published an edition of Hester Thrale Piozzi's *Observations and Reflections Made in the Course of a Journey through France, Italy and Germany* (2009).

ROBERT FOLKENFLIK, Edward A. Dickson Emeritus Professor of English at the University of California, Irvine, is the author of *Samuel Johnson, Biographer*, has coauthored *Samuel Johnson: Pictures and Words* with Paul Alkon, and has published numerous essays on Johnson and eighteenth-century literature. For his work on Johnson portraiture he received a grant from the Paul Mellon Centre for Studies in British Art, and he has given lectures on the topic at the National Portrait Gallery (London), Harvard University, Haverford College, and Bryn Mawr College (The Center for Visual Studies).

JACLYN GELLER is Associate Professor of English, Central Connecticut State University. She is the author of *Here Comes the Bride: Women, Weddings, and the Marriage Mystique* (2001) and essays on Samuel Johnson, Samuel Butler, and Jonathan Swift.

DUSTIN GRIFFIN, Professor of English Emeritus at New York University, retired in 2009 after forty years of full-time teaching. He is the author of a number of books on the long eighteenth century, including *Literary Patronage in England, 1650–1800* (Cambridge University Press, 1996). His most recent book is *Swift and Pope: Satirists in Dialogue* (Cambridge University Press, 2010).

SHARON HARROW is Professor of English at Shippensburg University of Pennsylvania. She is the author of *Adventures in Domesticity: Gender and Colonial Adulteration in Eighteenth-Century British Literature* (2004) and of articles and reviews on eighteenth-century women writers. She is at work on a book about the literature and culture of eighteenth-century British sport.

CLEMENT HAWES is Professor of English and History at the University of Michigan. His publications include *Mania and Literary Style: The Rhetoric of Enthusiasm from the Ranters to Christopher Smart* (Cambridge University Press, 1996), *Christopher Smart and the Enlightenment* (1999), and *The British Eighteenth Century and Global Critique* (2005).

NICHOLAS HUDSON, Professor of English at the University of British Columbia, is the author of two monographs on Johnson, *Samuel Johnson and Eighteenth-Century Thought* (1988) and *Samuel Johnson and the Making of Modern England* (Cambridge University Press, 2003).

He is also the author of *Writing and European Thought, 1600–1830* (Cambridge University Press, 1994) and of many essays on eighteenth-century British literature, culture, and thought. He most recently coedited, with Aaron Santesso, *Swift's Travels: Eighteenth-Century British Satire and Its Legacy* (Cambridge University Press, 2008), and has completed a new monograph, *A Long Revolution: Social Hierarchy and Literary Change in Britain, 1660–1832*.

ALLAN INGRAM is Professor of English at the University of Northumbria. His works include monographs on Boswell, on Swift and Pope, and on madness and writing (*The Madhouse of Language*, 1991), as well as two collections of source material, *Voices of Madness* (1997) and *Patterns of Madness in the Eighteenth Century* (1998). His most recent book is *Cultural Constructions of Madness in Eighteenth-Century Writing* (2005, with Michelle Faubert). He is coeditor (with Stuart Sim) of *Melancholy Experience in Literature of the Long Eighteenth Century: Before Depression, 1660–1800* (2011), and co-general editor (with Leigh Wetherall-Dickson) for *Depression and Melancholy 1660–1800*, 4 vols. (2012).

H. J. JACKSON, who teaches English and Book History at the University of Toronto, writes mainly on eighteenth-century and Romantic literature. She served as editor or coeditor of six volumes in the *Collected Works of Samuel Taylor Coleridge* and is the author of two recent books about readers' notes in books, *Marginalia* (2001) and *Romantic Readers* (2005).

FREYA JOHNSTON is University Lecturer and Tutorial Fellow in English at St. Anne's College, Oxford. She is the author of *Samuel Johnson and the Art of Sinking* (2005) and of various chapters and essays on Johnson, Austen, and their contemporaries. She is coediting, with Matthew Bevis, *The Cambridge Edition of the Novels of Thomas Love Peacock*.

JONATHAN LAMB is Mellon Professor of the Humanities at Vanderbilt University. Most recently he is author of *The Evolution of Sympathy* (2009) and coeditor, with Vanessa Agnew, of *Settler and Creole Reenactment* (2009). *The Things Things Say* is in press with Princeton University Press.

JACK LYNCH is Professor of English at Rutgers University–Newark. He is the author of *The Age of Elizabeth in the Age of Johnson* (Cambridge University Press, 2003) and *Deception and Detection in*

Eighteenth-Century Britain (2008). He is also the coeditor, with Anne McDermott, of *Anniversary Essays on Johnson's "Dictionary"* (Cambridge University Press, 2005) and editor of *The Age of Johnson: A Scholarly Annual.*

PAULA MCDOWELL is Associate Professor of English at New York University. She is the author of *The Women of Grub Street: Press, Politics and Gender in the London Literary Marketplace, 1678–1730* (1998) and *Elinor James: Printed Writings* (2005). She is completing a book titled *Fugitive Voices: Print Commerce and the Invention of the Oral in Eighteenth-Century Britain.*

LEE MORRISSEY is Alumni Distinguished Professor of English at Clemson University, and author, most recently, of *The Constitution of Literature: Literacy, Democracy, and Early English Literary Criticism* (2008).

LYNDA MUGGLESTONE is Professor of History of English at the University of Oxford and a Fellow of Pembroke College, Oxford. She has published widely on language in the late eighteenth and nineteenth centuries, and has written a number of books on dictionaries including *Lexicography and the OED: Pioneers in the Untrodden Forest* (2003), *Lost for Words: The Hidden History of the Oxford English Dictionary* (2005), and *Dictionaries: A Very Short Introduction* (2011). She edited *The Oxford History of English* (2006, 2007) and is now working on a book on Johnson.

T. JOCK MURRAY is Professor Emeritus, Dalhousie University, Halifax, Nova Scotia. A neurologist recently retired from research and practice with multiple sclerosis patients, he has had a parallel career as an educator, Dean of Medicine, and as Professor of Medical Humanities. Over the last thirty years he has published on Johnson's illness, his knowledge of science and medicine, and the physician circle around Johnson.

NORA NACHUMI is Associate Professor of English at Yeshiva University and author of *Acting like a Lady: British Women Novelists and the Eighteenth-Century Theater* (2008) and several articles on eighteenth-century theatre and fiction.

MELVYN NEW, Professor Emeritus, University of Florida, has been writing about eighteenth-century literature for more than forty years. He is General Editor of the *Florida Edition of the Works of Laurence Sterne*, volumes 7 and 8 of which, *Sterne's Letters*, appeared in 2009. Recent essays on Sterne include contributions to the *Cambridge Companion to Laurence Sterne* (2009) and the *Cambridge Companion to English Novelists* (2009).

FRED PARKER is a Fellow of Clare College, Cambridge, and author of *Johnson's Shakespeare* (1989), *Scepticism and Literature: An Essay on Pope, Hume, Sterne, and Johnson* (2003), and *The Devil as Muse: Blake, Byron and the Adversary* (2011).

MURRAY PITTOCK is Bradley Professor of English Literature, Head of College, and Vice-Principal (Arts) of the University of Glasgow. His work on Jacobitism and Romanticism has redefined aspects of our understanding of the eighteenth century in books, including *The Myth of the Jacobite Clans* (1995, 1999, 2009), *Poetry and Jacobite Politics in Eighteenth-Century Britain and Ireland* (Cambridge University Press, 1994, 2006), and *Scottish and Irish Romanticism* (2008). His current projects include an edition of the *Scots Musical Museum* for the Oxford Collected Burns and the Yale edition of the *Political Correspondence of James Boswell.*

DAHLIA PORTER is Assistant Professor of English at Vanderbilt University; her research focuses on the intersection of science and literature in the eighteenth century and Romantic period. She has published articles on Robert Southey, Charlotte Smith, Erasmus Darwin, and the theory of the novel, and coedited *Lyrical Ballads 1798 and 1800* (2008, with Michael Gamer). She is completing a book, *Composite Orders*, on empiricism and formal innovation in the Romantic period, and beginning a project on inventory and the classification of knowledge.

MARTIN POSTLE is Assistant Director of the Paul Mellon Centre for Studies in British Art, Yale University. He has published extensively on aspects of eighteenth-century British art, and is an authority on Sir Joshua Reynolds.

JOHN RICHARDSON is Professor of English Literature at the National University of Singapore. Since the publication of *Slavery and Augustan Literature: Swift, Pope, Gay* (2004), he has been working principally on the representation of war in the eighteenth century.

JOHN RICHETTI is A. M. Rosenthal Professor of English (emeritus) at the University of Pennsylvania. His most recent book is *The Life of Daniel Defoe: A Critical Biography* (2005). He has also edited *The Cambridge Companion to Daniel Defoe* (2008). He is at work on a history of English eighteenth-century literature, part of the Blackwell History of English Literature.

FIONA RITCHIE is Assistant Professor of Drama and Theatre in the Department of English at McGill University. She is the author of several articles on women and Shakespeare in the long eighteenth century and is currently writing a monograph on that topic. She is also the coeditor, with Peter Sabor, of an essay collection entitled *Shakespeare in the Eighteenth Century*.

PAT ROGERS is Distinguished University Professor and DeBartolo Chair in the Liberal Arts at the University of South Florida. His recent work includes *The Cambridge Companion to Alexander Pope* (2007); *Edmund Curll, Bookseller*, with Paul Baines (2007); *Producing the Eighteenth-Century Book: Writers and Publishers in England, 1650–1800* (2009); and *A Political Biography of Alexander Pope* (2010).

ADAM ROUNCE is Senior Lecturer at Manchester Metropolitan University. He has written on Dryden, Johnson, Churchill, Cowper, Akenside, Warburton, Joseph Warton, and Godwin. His main ongoing research is with the *Cambridge Edition of the Complete Works of Jonathan Swift*, for which he is coediting one volume, as well as contributing a chronology. He has also recently written a book about literary failure, concerning the unsuccessful careers of writers that were known to Samuel Johnson.

J. T. SCANLAN teaches eighteenth-century literature at Providence College, where he is also the Pre-Law Advisor.

STEVEN SCHERWATZKY is Professor of English at Merrimack College and author of numerous articles on eighteenth-century literature and culture.

PHILIP SMALLWOOD was for many years Professor of English at Birmingham City University and is now Visiting Fellow in the English Department at the University of Bristol. He has written widely on Samuel Johnson and eighteenth-century literary criticism.

JENNIFER ELLIS SNEAD is Assistant Professor of English at Texas Tech University. She has published articles on Johnson, Pope, book history, and the eighteenth-century evangelical revival. She is at work on a book about early Methodism and popular literacy.

JOHN STONE is a Canadian-born lecturer in English at the University of Barcelona, with a keen interest in the use of English as a language of culture in eighteenth-century Spain. He has published a scholarly edition of Samuel Johnson's *Preface to Shakespeare* in Catalan (2002), as well as articles on Johnson in the collections *Anniversary Essays on Johnson's "Dictionary"* (Cambridge University Press, 2005) and *Cultural Transfer through Translation: The Circulation of Enlightened Thought in Europe by Means of Translation* (2010).

MICHAEL F. SUAREZ, S.J. is Director of Rare Book School, Professor of English, and University Professor at the University of Virginia. He coedited (with Michael Turner) *The Cambridge History of the Book in Britain*, vol. 5, *1695–1830* (2009) and is co-general editor (with H. R. Woudhuysen) of *The Oxford Companion to the Book* (2010).

PAUL TANKARD is Senior Lecturer in English at the world's southernmost university, the University of Otago, Dunedin, New Zealand. He has published dozens of scholarly articles and reviews about Johnson, and edits the Papers of the Johnson Society of Australia. His other work concerns marginal genres, the future of literacy, and the Inklings. He has prepared the first edited selection of Boswell's journalistic writings, forthcoming.

KATHERINE TURNER is Associate Professor of English at Mary Baldwin College, in Staunton, Virginia. She has published on eighteenth-century travel writing and poetry, and has coedited (with Francis O'Gorman) *The Victorians and the Eighteenth Century: Reassessing the Tradition* (2004), to which she also contributed an essay on Johnson's Victorian reputation. She has recently edited Sterne's *Sentimental Journey* for Broadview Press, and several volumes of Women's Court and Society Memoirs for Pickering & Chatto.

DAVID F. VENTURO, Professor of English at The College of New Jersey, author of *Johnson the Poet: The Poetic Career of Samuel Johnson* (1999), and editor of *The School of the Eucharist* (2006), has written extensively on British literature and culture, 1640–1830. He helps edit several journals and is working on projects on ambiguity and indirection in Milton, Dryden, and Swift, and on baseball and American culture. He teaches courses on Shakespeare, the eighteenth century, modern poetry, baseball and American culture, and The Beatles.

CYNTHIA WALL is Professor of English at the University of Virginia. She is author of *The Prose of Things: Transformations of Description in the Eighteenth Century* (2006, Honorable Mention for the James Russell

Lowell Prize) and *The Literary and Cultural Spaces of Restoration London* (Cambridge University Press, 1998). She is an editor of Defoe, Pope, and Bunyan.

JOHN WILTSHIRE's most recent books are *The Cinematic Jane Austen*, with David Monaghan and Ariane Hudelet (2009), and *The Making of Dr. Johnson* (2009).

Preface

PRE′FACE. *n.s.* [*preface*, Fr. *præfatio*, Lat.] Something spoken introductory to the main design; introduction; something proemial.

> This superficial tale
> Is but a *preface* to her worthy praise. *Shakesp.*

Perhaps no English author gains more from being set in context than Samuel Johnson. "The Age of Johnson" – the phrase has been used since at least 1834 – suggests that he stands at the center of "his" age in a way few writers do. Studies of Johnson, therefore, almost always turn into studies of his age: it is impossible to discuss him without also discussing his intellectual, literary, and cultural contexts. His uniquely encyclopedic mind somehow stands for his entire world. Finding one's way through that world, though, can be daunting, because the volume of accumulated scholarship on the subject is vast. *Samuel Johnson in Context* therefore serves as a kind of *vade-mecum* to eighteenth-century British culture. The contributions from forty-seven leading experts in the field explore the state of the art in recent thinking about eighteenth-century British life.

The collection is divided into three parts. The first, "Life and works," focuses on Johnson himself: his biography and his most important biographers, the works he wrote for publication, and the letters he wrote for private consumption. The second part, "Critical fortunes," gives a broad overview of the way Johnson has been discussed, analyzed, studied, and mythologized during his lifetime and since: the collected editions of his works, the translations of his writings into other languages, the critical reception of his works from his death to the present, the portraits and caricatures that appeared during and shortly after his lifetime, and his transformation into the legendary character "Dr. Johnson."

The third, and longest, part, "Contexts," contains thirty-eight chapters, arranged in alphabetical order, not so much about Johnson himself as about the culture in which he lived. So copious was Johnson's mind, and so wide-ranging his interests, that he is one of the very few writers whose name can be paired with almost any noun in the language to produce a promising research subject. There are good articles waiting to be written on Johnson and agronomy, Johnson and numismatics, Johnson and navigation, Johnson and calculus. But space is necessarily limited, and I have therefore focused on the contexts that best illuminate Johnson's life and writings.

Some of those contexts will be obvious: a chapter on essays makes sense for one of England's greatest essayists; a chapter on clubs helps to illuminate the co-founder of The Club; a chapter on literary criticism is a must for the age's greatest critic. Others, though, may be less expected. When A. S. Turberville published *Johnson's England: An Account of the Life and Manners of His Age* three-quarters of a century ago, he found no room for any discussion of women authors, empire, anthropology, nationalism, or slavery. Putting that volume next to this one can be enlightening, since it shows how much the Johnson of the early twenty-first century differs from that of the early twentieth. Subjects once thought peripheral are now at the center of Johnsonian studies. It is telling that the most frequently quoted sentence in this volume is Johnson's indictment of slavery: "How is it that we hear the loudest yelps for liberty among the drivers of negroes?" (*Works*, 10:454).

A chronology lays out the major events of Johnson's lifetime and the years that followed; after that, each chapter opens with a short selection from Johnson's famous *Dictionary of the English Language* (1755): the etymology, a single definition, and a single quotation. Several dozen illustrations from eighteenth-century sources allow readers to experience something of the visual culture of the age that Johnson made his.

JACK LYNCH

Chronology

Jack Lynch

CHRONO'LOGY. *n.s.* [χρόνος, time, and λόγος, doctrine] The science of computing and adjusting the periods of time as the revolution of the sun and moon; and of computing time past, and referring each event to the proper year.

Where I allude to the customs of the Greeks, I believe I may be justified by the strictest *chronology*; though a poet is not obliged to the rules that confine an historian. *Prior.*

1709	
September 7	Samuel Johnson born in Lichfield (after Britain adopted the Gregorian calendar in 1752, Johnson observed his birthday on September 18).
1710	The "Act for the Encouragement of Learning," the world's first copyright law, comes into effect.
1711	
March	Addison and Steele begin publishing *The Spectator* (through December 1712).
1712	
March	SJ taken to London to be touched by Queen Anne.
October	SJ's brother Nathaniel born.
1717	
January	SJ starts at Lichfield Grammar School.
1720	
August	South Sea Company stock prices begin to fall, prompting the South Sea Bubble.

1721	
April 3	Robert Walpole appointed First Lord of the Treasury.
	Nathan Bailey publishes *An Universal Etymological English Dictionary.*
1723	
July 16	Joshua Reynolds born.
1728	
October 31	SJ begins at Pembroke College, Oxford.
1729	
December	SJ leaves Oxford without a degree.
1730	Nathan Bailey publishes *Dictionarium Britannicum.*
1731	
January	Edward Cave begins publishing the *Gentleman's Magazine.*
December 7	Michael Johnson, SJ's father, dies.
1732	
March	SJ works as an usher at Market Bosworth Grammar School, leaving after a few months.
1733	SJ contributes to the *Birmingham Journal.*
1734	
August 5	SJ publishes proposals for an edition of the poems of Politian.
1735	*A Voyage to Abyssinia*, SJ's first book, published.
July 9	SJ marries Elizabeth ("Tetty") Jervis Porter.
	Thomas Dyche and William Pardon publish *A New General English Dictionary.*
1737	
March 2	SJ's brother Nathaniel dies.
March 2	SJ and David Garrick leave Lichfield for London.
July 12	SJ writes to Edward Cave, offering to contribute to the *Gentleman's Magazine.*
1738	
March	SJ writes "Ad Urbanum" to Edward Cave.
May 13	*London*, SJ's first major poem, published.
June	"Debates in the Senate of *Magna Lilliputia*" begin appearing in the *Gentleman's Magazine.*

Summer	SJ at work on *The History of the Council of Trent.*
1739	
Spring	*Marmor Norfolciense* and *A Compleat Vindication of the Licensers of the Stage* published.
July	Richard Savage leaves London.
August	SJ leaves London to return to Lichfield.
1740	
Spring	SJ once again moves to London.
1741	
January 27	Hester Thrale born.
June 24	SJ writes proposals for Robert James's *Medicinal Dictionary.*
July	SJ becomes the sole writer of the parliamentary debates (through March 1744).
1742	
February 11	Robert Walpole resigns.
Autumn	Thomas Osborne hires SJ to catalogue the Harleian Library.
1743	
August 1	Richard Savage dies in debtors' prison.
1744	
February 11	*The Life of Richard Savage* published.
May 30	Alexander Pope dies.
1745	
April 6	*Miscellaneous Observations on the Tragedy of Macbeth* published; the proposed edition comes to nothing.
July 23	Charles Edward Stuart, descendant of the deposed James II, lands with a Jacobite invading force.
October 19	Jonathan Swift dies.
1746	
April 16	The Jacobites are defeated at the Battle of Culloden.
June 18	SJ signs a contract to produce a dictionary in three years.
1747	
August	*The Plan of an English Dictionary* published.

September 15 — SJ's "Drury Lane Prologue" delivered by Garrick to mark his management of the theater.

1748

April 7 — SJ contributes a preface to *The Preceptor.*

1749

January 9 — *The Vanity of Human Wishes* published.

February 6 — *Irene* first performed at Drury Lane.

1750

March 20 — The first *Rambler* essay published.

Francis Barber brought from Jamaica to England by his owner, Richard Bathurst.

1752

March 14 — The last *Rambler* essay published.

March 28 — SJ's wife, Elizabeth, dies.

1753

March 3 — SJ begins contributing to the *Adventurer* (through March 2, 1754).

1755

February 20 — SJ awarded an honorary Master of Arts by Oxford University.

April 15 — *A Dictionary of the English Language* published.

1756

March — SJ arrested for debt.

April — SJ becomes editor of the *Literary Magazine.*

May 18 — England declares war on France, entering the Seven Years' War.

June 2 — SJ signs a contract to edit Shakespeare's plays, promising to deliver them by Christmas 1757.

SJ meets Sir Joshua Reynolds.

1757

January 1 — The first number of the *London Chronicle* appears with an article by SJ.

1758

April 15 — The first *Idler* essay published (through April 5, 1760).

1759

January 20	Sarah Johnson, SJ's mother, dies.
April 20	*Rasselas* published.
September 13	General James Wolfe dies in the Battle of Quebec, Britain's greatest victory in the Seven Years' War.

1760

May 1	SJ attends a meeting to promote the education of black Americans with Benjamin Franklin.
October 25	George II dies; George III assumes the throne.

1761

Winter	SJ visits Lichfield for the first time in twenty years.

1762

July	SJ awarded a pension of £300 a year.

1763

February 10	The Treaty of Paris ends the Seven Years' War.
May 16	SJ meets James Boswell.

1764

January	SJ and Reynolds form the Literary Club with Oliver Goldsmith, Edmund Burke, John Hawkins, Topham Beauclerk, Anthony Chamier, Bennet Langton, and Christopher Nugent.

1765

January 9	SJ meets Henry and Hester Thrale.
July 23	SJ awarded an honorary doctorate by Trinity College, Dublin.
October 10	SJ's edition of Shakespeare's plays published.

1766

October	SJ begins his collaboration with Sir Robert Chambers on *A Course of Lectures on the English Law.*

1767

February	SJ meets George III, who urges him to continue writing.

1768

August 25	Captain James Cook leaves England, to arrive in Tahiti on April 13, 1769.

1769

January 2	Reynolds delivers the first of his *Discourses* at the Royal Academy.
	SJ appointed Honorary Professor of Ancient Literature at the Royal Academy.

1770

January 17	*The False Alarm* published.

1771

March 16	*Thoughts on the Late Transactions Respecting Falkland's Islands* published.

1772

June 22	The Mansfield decision renders slavery unenforceable in Britain.

1773

March	The revised fourth folio edition of the *Dictionary* published.
August	SJ leaves London to join JB on a tour of the Western Islands of Scotland.
December 16	The Boston Tea Party shows the extent of American discontent with British policy.

1774

February	*Donaldson v. Becket* declares copyright is not perpetual.
July 5	SJ and the Thrales travel to North Wales, returning in September.
October 12	*The Patriot* published.

1775

January 18	*A Journey to the Western Islands of Scotland* published.
March 8	*Taxation No Tyranny* published.
April 1	SJ receives his honorary doctorate granted by Oxford University.
April 19	The Battle of Lexington and Concord marks the beginning of the War of American Independence.
September	SJ travels to France with the Thrales and Giuseppe Baretti, returning in November.

1776	
May 15	JB arranges for SJ to meet John Wilkes.
July 4	The Continental Congress adopts the Declaration of Independence.
1777	
March	SJ meets Frances Burney.
March 29	SJ agrees to contribute "little Lives, and little Prefaces, to a little edition of the English Poets."
1779	
January 20	Garrick dies.
March	The first four volumes of *Lives of the Poets* published.
June	SJ witnesses the Gordon Riots.
1781	
April 4	Henry Thrale dies.
May	The last volume of the *Lives of the Poets* published.
1782	
January 17	Robert Levet dies.
1783	
June 17	SJ suffers a stroke and is unable to speak for two days.
September 3	The Treaty of Paris officially ends the War of American Independence.
September 6	Anna Williams dies.
December 8	SJ founds the Essex Head Club.
1784	
June 22	SJ attends the Club for the last time.
June 30	SJ and JB meet for the last time.
July 23	Hester Thrale marries Gabriel Piozzi.
December 8	SJ makes his final will.
December 13	SJ dies in London.
December 20	SJ buried at Westminster Abbey.
December	Thomas Tyers's *Biographical Sketch of Dr. Samuel Johnson* published.

1785

February 1	SJ's dedication of Charles Burney's *Account of the Musical Performance in Westminster Abbey* published posthumously.
August	SJ's *Prayers and Meditations* published posthumously.
October 1	JB's *Journal of a Tour to the Hebrides* published.

1786

March 26	Hester Piozzi publishes *Anecdotes of the Late Samuel Johnson, LL.D.*

1787

March 20	Sir John Hawkins publishes *The Works of Samuel Johnson*, including *The Life of Samuel Johnson*.

1791

May 16	JB publishes *The Life of Samuel Johnson, LL.D.*

1795

May 19	JB dies.

1796

February 23	A monument to SJ erected in Westminster Abbey.

Abbreviations

Boswell, *Life*	James Boswell, *The Life of Samuel Johnson, LL.D.*, ed. G. B. Hill, rev. L. F. Powell, 6 vols. (Oxford: Clarendon Press, 1934–64)
Boswell, *London Journal*	James Boswell, *Boswell's London Journal, 1762–1763: Now First Published from the Original Manuscript*, ed. Frederick A. Pottle (New York: McGraw-Hill, 1950)
Dictionary	Samuel Johnson, *A Dictionary of the English Language*, 2 vols. (London, 1755)
Gleanings	*Johnsonian Gleanings*, ed. Aleyn Lyell Reade, 11 vols. (London: privately printed, 1909–52)
Hawkins, *Life*	Sir John Hawkins, *The Life of Samuel Johnson, LL.D.*, ed. O M Brack, Jr. (Athens: University of Georgia Press, 2009)
Letters	*The Letters of Samuel Johnson*, ed. Bruce Redford, 5 vols. (Princeton, NJ: Princeton University Press, 1992–4)
Lives	Samuel Johnson, *The Lives of the Most Eminent English Poets: With Critical Observations on Their Works*, ed. Roger Lonsdale, 4 vols. (Oxford: Oxford University Press, 2006)
Miscellanies	*Johnsonian Miscellanies*, ed. G. B. Hill, 2 vols. (Oxford: Clarendon Press, 1897)
Prefaces & Dedications	*Samuel Johnson's Prefaces & Dedications*, ed. Allen T. Hazen (New Haven, CT: Yale University Press, 1937)

Thraliana	*Thraliana: The Diary of Mrs. Hester Lynch Thrale (Later Mrs. Piozzi)*, ed. Katharine C. Balderston, 2nd edn., 2 vols. (Oxford: Clarendon Press, 1951)
Works	*The Yale Edition of the Works of Samuel Johnson*, 18 vols. to date (New Haven, CT: Yale University Press, 1958–)

PART I

Life and works

CHAPTER I

Life

Lisa Berglund

LIFE. *n.s.* plural *lives.* [lifian, to live, Saxon.]
13. Narrative of a life past.

Plutarch, that writes his *life*,
Tells us, that Cato dearly lov'd his wife. *Pope.*

Samuel Johnson lived one of the most thoroughly documented lives of the eighteenth century, and he was the subject of what many consider the greatest biography ever written, James Boswell's *Life of Samuel Johnson, LL.D.* To understand that life, however, we need to pay attention to a wide range of biographical materials, including not only the biographical works of Johnson's contemporaries – Sir John Hawkins and Hester Lynch Piozzi above all – but also the more scholarly tradition of Johnsonian biography that has run through the twentieth century and continues to thrive in the twenty-first.

EARLY LIFE

Samuel Johnson was born in the cathedral town of Lichfield, in the West Midlands of England, on September 7, 1709. (After England changed its calendar in 1752, Johnson observed his birthday on September 18.) His father, Michael, owned a bookshop, and his mother, Sarah, was of a prominent local family. From his wet nurse the infant Samuel contracted scrofula, a tubercular infection that affected his eyesight and his hearing and left his face badly scarred (see chapter 29, "Medicine"). It was to be the first in a long catalogue of physical and mental maladies that would torment Johnson throughout his seventy-five years. When Samuel was two years old, Sarah Johnson took her son to London to be "touched for the King's evil," a folk remedy for scrofula. Queen Anne was the last British monarch to "touch" her subjects and, though the ritual did nothing to improve his health, Johnson wore the amulet he received from her for the rest of his life.

Johnson attended Lichfield Grammar School, but much of his education came from the shelves of his father's bookshop, where he read omnivorously. A small inheritance enabled his family to send him to Pembroke College, Oxford, but after thirteen months financial pressures obliged him to withdraw. (He never graduated from university; his title "Doctor" comes from an honorary degree, awarded by the University of Dublin in 1765.) After working unsuccessfully as a schoolmaster in Lichfield, Johnson moved to Birmingham to live with a schoolfriend, Edmund Hector. In 1735, the twenty-six-year-old Johnson married Elizabeth ("Tetty") Porter, a well-off widow twenty years his senior, with a daughter nearly Johnson's age.

Hawkins and Boswell treat his marriage gingerly, with embarrassment tinged by contempt. Yet Elizabeth Porter must surely have been a perceptive woman: even Boswell notes that she recognized in the ugly and peculiar Johnson "the most sensible man that I ever saw in my life" (Boswell, *Life*, 1:95). A more balanced portrait is offered by Hester Thrale (later Piozzi). Thrale did not meet Johnson until long after Elizabeth's death, but she certainly understood the emotional demands that Johnson could make on his female friends. One of her anecdotes records Mrs. Johnson's riposte when her husband repeatedly "huffed his wife about his dinner." Johnson told Thrale, "at last she called to me, and said, Nay, hold Mr. Johnson, and do not make a farce of thanking God for a dinner which in a few minutes you will protest not eatable" (*Miscellanies*, 1:249–50).

The money that Elizabeth Johnson brought to the marriage was invested in setting up a school at Edial, near Lichfield – and once again Johnson failed as a schoolmaster (see chapter 20, "Education"). Without other prospects he was "obliged," as he would write of his friend Richard Savage, "to seek some other means of support; and, having no profession, became by necessity an author" (*Lives*, 3:124). While Tetty remained unhappily in Lichfield with her mother-in-law, Johnson, joined by one of his few remaining pupils, David Garrick, walked to London.

ARRIVAL IN LONDON

Penniless and occasionally homeless, struggling to find employment in the metropolis, Johnson contracted an important friendship. Richard Savage was a talented, irresponsible poet famous for both his conversation and a tendency to stick his friends with the bar bill. Hawkins, who knew Johnson in these early London years, records that the friendship was cemented by the fact that Savage and Johnson "had both felt the pangs of poverty and the want of patronage" (Hawkins, *Life*, p. 33). The nights spent roaming the streets with Savage indelibly shaped Johnson's thinking about both poverty and patronage. Piozzi observed that he refused to take seriously any distress less acute than "*want of necessaries*," as Johnson put it (*Works*, 17:406). Witnessing Savage's disappointments, Johnson also became acutely conscious of the difficulty of carving an independent way as a writer (see chapter 13, "Authorship").

Savage was a paradoxical catalyst for Johnson's successful literary career. Savage may have inspired Johnson's first important poem, *London*, and *The Life of Mr. Richard Savage* established Johnson's reputation as a perceptive and compelling biographer. In the meantime, Johnson had secured regular work with Edward Cave, founder and editor of the *Gentleman's Magazine*. This employment enabled Johnson to bring his wife to London, and during the next few years he published poems, book reviews, biographies, translations, and occasional journalism (see chapter 2, "Publication history").

DICTIONARY JOHNSON AND BEREAVEMENT

Johnson's definitive work, and the turning point of his career, was the *Dictionary of the English Language*. In 1746, bookseller Robert Dodsley encouraged him to prepare *A Plan of a Dictionary*, and shortly thereafter Johnson signed the contract. Nine years later, the *Dictionary* appeared. The first really comprehensive dictionary in English, and the first to make extensive use of illustrative quotations, Johnson's *Dictionary* is arguably the single most astonishing achievement in the history of lexicography – and it had been completed virtually single-handed, save for the help of six amanuenses (see chapter 18, "Dictionaries"). Even more remarkably, during this period Johnson also published an important essay series, the *Rambler*, his play *Irene*, and many other literary projects.

The success of the *Dictionary* was overshadowed, though, by the financial difficulties and frequent separations that strained Johnson's marriage. Elizabeth Johnson's later years, Dr. Robert Levet said, were marked by "perpetual illness and perpetual opium" (*Miscellanies*, 1:248). Her death in 1752 hit Johnson hard, as he must have been aware that he had contributed to her loneliness and despair. He wrote bitterly in the preface to the *Dictionary* that "I have protracted my work till most of those whom I wished to please, have sunk into the grave" (*Works*, 18:113). He thereafter observed the anniversary of his wife's death by composing a prayer each year: in 1770, for instance, he wrote, "This is the day on which in –52 I was deprived of poor dear Tetty … when I recollect the time in which we lived together, my grief for her departure is not abated, and I have less pleasure in any good that befals me, because she does not partake it" (*Works*, 1:127). Despite emotional and physical attraction to several other women over the course of his life, he never remarried.

Four years later, Johnson's mother died at the age of ninety-one. As with the death of his wife, Johnson's mourning seems tinged with guilt: he was aware of his mother's declining health, yet forbore to visit her on her deathbed. Johnson reflects on her loss in *Idler* 41:

> such is the course of nature, that whoever lives long must outlive those whom he loves and honours. Such is the condition of our present existence, that life must one time lose its associations, and every inhabitant of the earth must walk downward to the grave alone and unregarded, without any partner of his joy or grief, without any interested witness of his misfortunes or success. (*Works*, 2:130)

In that same year, 1759, he also wrote his philosophical tale *The History of Rasselas, Prince of Abissinia*. According to the publisher William Strahan, Johnson wrote the book "in the evenings of one week, and sent it to the press in portions as it was written … that with the profits he might defray the expense of his mother's funeral" (Boswell, *Life*, 1:341).

THE 1760S AND 1770S

In the 1760s Johnson contracted two enduring friendships with his future biographers, James Boswell and Hester Lynch Thrale (later Piozzi).

Bozzy and Piozzi, as they were dubbed by satirists, were both diligent diarists who developed a cordial competition with one another, which became a vicious rivalry after Johnson's death. Their relationships with Johnson were very different. With Boswell, who practiced law in Edinburgh and visited London occasionally, Johnson spent intense periods of time – hours, days, even weeks during their 1773 trip to the Hebrides. Boswell could be amazingly charming but also irritating, and his inquisitive scrutiny was sometimes infuriating: "Sir," an exasperated Johnson once snapped, "you have but two topicks, yourself and me. I am sick of both" (Boswell, *Life*, 3:57). But his steadfast attention could also be rewarding.

Hester Thrale, by contrast, was the wife of a prosperous brewer and the mother of a large, sickly family. Concerned for Johnson's health and impressed by his conversation, Henry and Hester Thrale invited him to stay with them at their country house in Streatham, south of London.

The Thrales surrounded Johnson with physical and social comforts, and included him on their trips to Paris and Wales. For Johnson, Hester Thrale seems to have combined the attractions of a nurse, a mother, and a courtly love object; when they were apart he bombarded her with letters, and when they were together he confided in her, monopolized her, and teased her. Her kindness, Johnson acknowledged in his last letter to her, had "soothed twenty years of a life radically wretched" (*Letters*, 4:343).

In 1762, the government awarded Johnson a pension of £300, which ensured financial security if not affluence. Johnson was able to retire from constant literary labors, and he founded the famous Literary Club (see chapter 16, "Clubs"). Still, his prominence created a certain pressure, most famously articulated by King George III, who sought out Johnson when the latter was visiting the royal library in 1767. The king encouraged Johnson to continue writing, but Johnson demurred, saying that "he had already done his part as a writer. 'I should have thought so too, (said the King,) if you had not written so well'" (Boswell, *Life*, 2:35). In the 1770s, Johnson completed a few projects: a series of political pamphlets and a major revision of the *Dictionary*. The climax to his literary career, however, was the monumental *Lives of the English Poets*, a large collection of biographical and critical prefaces ranging from a few pages to book-length. These biographies, together with the *Dictionary* and the edition of Shakespeare, completed Johnson's reputation as the authority on English literature and language, a reputation he retains today.

HEALTH

Johnson's childhood illness had left him significantly nearsighted, so much so that he recalled having to kneel down to feel the curb in order to find his way safely home from school:

> he was then so near-sighted, that he was obliged to stoop down on his hands and knees to take a view of the kennel before he ventured to step over it. His school-mistress, afraid that he might miss his way, or fall into the kennel, or be run over by a cart, followed him at some distance. He happened to turn about and perceive her. Feeling her careful attention as an insult to his manliness, he ran back to her in a rage, and beat her, as well as his strength would permit. (Boswell, *Life*, 1:39)

Johnson's critical thinking also was shaped by his poor eyesight, as in his famous observation in his preface to Shakespeare that "a play read, affects the mind like a play acted" (*Works*, 7:79), or in his dismissive comments on landscape and painting. He "was almost as deaf as he was blind: travelling with Dr. Johnson was for these reasons tiresome enough," Piozzi reports. "Mr. Thrale loved prospects … But when he wished to point them out to his companion: 'Never heed such nonsense,' would be [Johnson's] reply: a blade of grass is always a blade of grass, whether in one country or another. Let us, if we *do* talk, talk about something; men and women are my subjects of enquiry" (*Miscellanies*, 1:215). Johnson's need to hold books close to his eyes also shaped his social behavior: "he would be quite lost to the company, and withdraw all his attention to what he was reading, without the smallest knowledge or care about the noise made round him. His deafness made such conduct less odd and less difficult to him than it would have been to another man" (*Miscellanies*, 1:319).

More dramatically, Johnson suffered from convulsive tics and other peculiar habits – he muttered to himself, rolled his body from side to side, and ritualistically touched every fence post he passed. Boswell observed that "he never knew the natural joy of a free and vigorous use of his limbs: when he walked, it was like the struggling gait of one in fetters; when he rode, he had no command or direction of his horse, but was carried as if in a balloon" (Boswell, *Life*, 4:425). Modern biographers theorize that Johnson suffered from Tourette's syndrome, but in the eighteenth century no diagnosis was available.

Suffering from inexplicable compulsions, Johnson not surprisingly was anxious about his mental as well as his physical health, and his life is marked by episodes of lethargic depression or "melancholy" (see chapter 30, "Mental health"). Boswell records that Johnson "felt himself overwhelmed with an horrible hypochondria, with perpetual irritation, fretfulness, and impatience; and with a dejection, gloom, and despair, which made existence misery"; he often "strove to overcome it by forcible exertions. He frequently walked to Birmingham and back again [a thirty-two-mile round-trip], and tried many other expedients, but all in vain" (Boswell, *Life*, 1:63–4). While at Oxford he had undergone a serious deepening of his Christian faith, but his beliefs also contributed to his worries about his sanity and his future state.

Fortunately Johnson also had a gift for making and keeping friends, who were attracted by his brilliance, his impressive moral force, even his neediness. Those friends sustained Johnson through his episodes of melancholy. In 1734, for example, Edmund Hector found Johnson too depressed to get out of bed; the result was Johnson's first publication, a translation of Father Jerome Lobo's *A Voyage to Abyssinia*, which Hector genially bullied him into dictating. In 1765 the Thrales called on Johnson, found him sunk in misery, and insisted he come home with them; Johnson lived with them, off and on, until Henry Thrale's death in 1781.

FINAL DAYS

With the death of Henry Thrale, Johnson's comfortable life at Streatham came to an end. Some in their circle thought Johnson should marry the brewer's rich widow (thirty-two years his junior). It was not to be: Hester Thrale fell in love with her daughter's Italian Catholic music teacher, Gabriel Piozzi; defying family opposition and social ostracism, she married him in 1784. Johnson felt betrayed, and lashed out with a cruel, insulting letter: "You are ignominiously married … If You have abandoned your children and your religion, God forgive your wickedness; if you have forfeited your Fame [reputation], and your country, may your folly do no further mischief" (*Letters*, 4:338). The newly married Mrs. Piozzi responded with a dignified request that their correspondence cease. They never met again.

Despite his long list of illnesses, Johnson was physically robust, a large, active man, whose recollections of a year at Oxford University dwelled as much upon "sliding in Christ-Church meadow" as on his studies. On his arrival in London, his muscular frame led one bookseller to recommend that the would-be author instead buy himself a "porter's knot" (*Miscellanies*, 1:380), the strip of cloth used to carry heavy loads. In his seventy-fifth year his health was inevitably in decline, but Johnson remained remarkably vigorous, visiting old friends at Lichfield and Oxford, renewing the stones on his family graves, and maintaining a wide correspondence. He expressed a firm confidence in his salvation, and wrote a codicil to his will leaving an annuity to his black adopted son, Frank Barber. He died in London, on December 13, 1784, and was buried in Westminster Abbey.

BIOGRAPHIES

In the six years after Johnson's death twelve biographies were published, and he has remained a fascinating subject for biographers ever since. A series of brief pieces appeared in the weeks and months after his death, including Thomas Tyers's *Biographical Sketch of Dr. Samuel Johnson* (1784), but the first book-length biographical account was Boswell's *Journal of a Tour to the Hebrides with Samuel Johnson, LL.D.* (1785). Boswell had been planning a full-length biography for many years, and had been

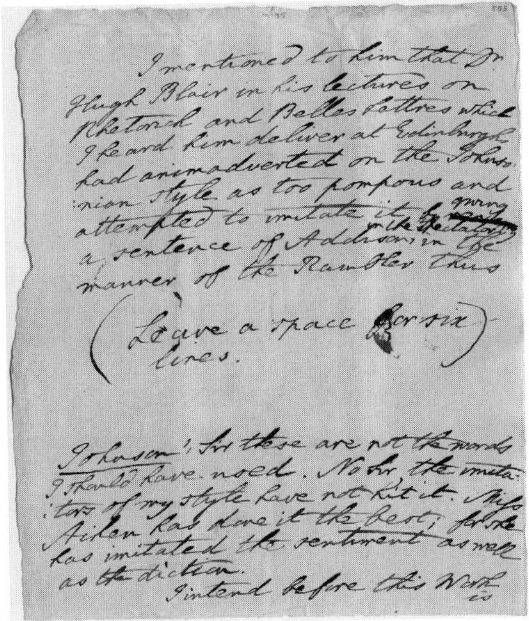
I mentioned to him that Dr Hugh Blair in his lectures on Rhetorick and Belles Lettres which I heard him deliver at Edinburgh had animadverted on the Johnso:nian style as too pompous and attempted to imitate it by giving a sentence of Addison in the Spectator in the manner of the Rambler thus

(Leave a space for six lines.)

Johnson: Sir these are not the words I should have used. No Sir the imita:tors of my style have not hit it. Miss Aiken has done it the best; for she has imitated the sentiment as well as the diction.

I intend before this Work is

Figure 1 Boswell, manuscript of *The Life of Johnson*, "Papers Apart." Courtesy of the General Collection, Beinecke Rare Book and Manuscript Library, Yale University.

assiduously collecting material; he delivered this account of the tour the two of them made in 1773 as a kind of down-payment on the *Life* he had begun writing.

Hester Lynch Piozzi followed Boswell's *Journal of a Tour* with her *Anecdotes of the Late Samuel Johnson, LL.D., during the Last Twenty Years of His Life*, which appeared in 1786. Drawn from her diaries, it recounted many of Johnson's conversations and witty observations. The first full-dress biography to appear, though, was Sir John Hawkins's *Life of Samuel Johnson, LL.D.* Hawkins was well positioned to write Johnson's life: he had known him longer than anyone else, and he was the executor of Johnson's will, so it is only natural that the booksellers who commissioned a collected edition of Johnson's works in 1787 asked Hawkins to devote an entire volume to a biography. Hawkins's tendency to depict Johnson unfavorably and his occasionally awkward style, though, did little to promote the book's popularity, and only in 2009 was Hawkins's *Life* finally made available in a carefully edited and annotated edition.

Figure 2 Hester Lynch Piozzi, from *Johnsoniana*, ed. Robina Napier (1884).

The most important of Johnson's lives is Boswell's *Life of Samuel Johnson, LL.D. Comprehending an Account of His Studies and Numerous Works, in Chronological Order; a Series of His Epistolary Correspondence and Conversations with Many Eminent Persons; and Various Original Pieces of His Composition, Never Before Published: The Whole Exhibiting a View of Literature and Literary Men in Great-Britain, for Near Half a Century, During Which He Flourished*, published in two volumes in 1791. Boswell began his great work by asserting that he was the most qualified of Johnson's friends to write his life: "I had the honour and happiness of enjoying his friendship for upwards of twenty years," he writes, and "I had the scheme of writing his life constantly in view … I flatter myself that few biographers have entered upon such a work as this, with more advantages." He then turns on the competition. "Since my work was announced," he writes, "several Lives and Memoirs of Dr. Johnson have been published." These, he informs his readers, are inferior to his own. Hawkins, for instance, was "a man, whom, during my long intimacy with

Dr. Johnson, I never saw in his company, I think but once, and I am sure not above twice." Piozzi is dismissed even more bluntly when Boswell vows to defend Johnson from the "aspersions of a lady who once lived in great intimacy with him" (Boswell, *Life*, 1:25–8).

The resulting biography, though, however marked by occasional pettiness and many inaccuracies, remains a literary masterpiece. Beginning not long after the *Life* appeared, the English language acquired a new noun, a *Boswell*, defined by the *Oxford English Dictionary* as "a constant companion or attendant who witnesses and records what a person does." Even Sherlock Holmes, paying tribute to his friend Dr. Watson, admitted that "I am lost without my Boswell."[1] Boswell's *Life* was so successful that, for more than a century, it succeeded in displacing not only all the other biographies of Johnson, but even most of Johnson's own writing.

Beginning in the middle of the twentieth century, though, the discovery of Boswell's diaries and the handwritten drafts of the *Life* have made clear just how much he worked to reshape his material. Most scholars now recognize Boswell's work as a brilliant work of art, but consider it unwise to depend on him for reliable facts about Johnson's life – too many things were either unknown to him or molded to suit his own purposes.

Piozzi, Hawkins, and Boswell remain important sources of information, but those interested in a reliable account of Johnson's life may be better served by more scholarly modern biographies, of which the most important are James L. Clifford's *Young Sam Johnson* (1955) and *Dictionary Johnson* (1979), W. Jackson Bate's *Samuel Johnson* (1977), and Robert DeMaria, Jr.'s *Life of Samuel Johnson: A Critical Biography* (1993). The recent tercentenary of Johnson's birth brought three more biographies: Jeffrey Meyers's *Samuel Johnson: The Struggle* (2008), Peter Martin's *Samuel Johnson: A Biography* (2008), and David Nokes's *Samuel Johnson: A Life* (2010).

NOTE

1 Arthur Conan Doyle, *The Adventures of Sherlock Holmes*, ed. Richard Lancelyn Green (Oxford: Oxford University Press, 1993), p. 10.

CHAPTER 2

Publication history

O M Brack, Jr.

> To PU'BLISH, *v.a.* [*publier*, Fr. *publico*, Lat.]
> 2. To put forth a book into the world.
>
> If I had not unwarily too far engaged myself for the present *publishing* it, I should have kept it by me. *Digby.*

The Yale Edition of the Works of Samuel Johnson, when it is complete, will comprise twenty-three stout volumes, roughly 10,000 pages, of Johnson's writings – and that does not include the two huge volumes of the *Dictionary*, the eight volumes of his Shakespeare edition, the five volumes of his catalogue of the Harleian Library, the five volumes of his letters, or many of the other uncollected writings. Johnson's oeuvre is not only extensive but stunningly diverse: in those dozens of volumes we find fiction, poetry, a play, journalism, biographies, essays, and pamphlets on subjects as diverse as politics, psychology, religion, sociology, travel, literary criticism, linguistics, even science, medicine, and music. Simply to list those works in their various editions – as J. D. Fleeman did in his magisterial *Bibliography of the Works of Samuel Johnson, Treating His Published Works from the Beginnings to 1984* (2000) – fills 2,000 pages. It is impossible to do justice to the full range of Johnson's publications in an essay of this size, or even one many times larger. We can, however, put his major publications in the context of his career.

EARLY YEARS

After the failure of Johnson's school at Edial Hall, near his hometown of Lichfield, in 1736, his prospects looked bleak. Johnson decided to try his fortune in London, and in March 1737 he set out with a tragedy he had been writing, *Irene*, in his pocket. When he failed to have this play produced and his funds were running low, he turned to Edward Cave, founder in 1731 of the first magazine, the monthly *Gentleman's Magazine* (see chapter 25, "Journalism"). It was the beginning of Johnson's life as a published author.

Johnson wrote to Cave on July 12, 1737, within months of arriving in London, and before they had met: "Having observed in your papers very uncommon offers of encouragement to Men of Letters, I have chosen, being a Stranger in London, to communicate to You the following design" (*Letters*, 1:12–13). The design was a translation of the *History of the Council of Trent* (1619), a famous criticism of the Counter-Reformation, by Father Paolo Sarpi, Venetian patriot, scholar, and Church reformer. Cave initially rejected the proposal. Johnson, however, did not give up.

In March 1738 he arrived at Cave's editorial offices at St. John's Gate with the poem "Ad Urbanum," an ode in Latin praising Cave, whose pen name was Sylvanus Urban. Cave was flattered, and published the ode in the March number. Johnson followed with a letter to Cave offering him his poetic satire, *London*, although he pretended it was written by another, remarking, "I believed I could not procure more advantageous terms from any person than from you, who have so much distinguished yourself by your generous encouragement of poetry" (*Letters*, 1:14). Cave was again impressed, and arranged for Robert Dodsley, a leading bookseller of the day, to publish *London* anonymously on May 13, 1738. Johnson received ten guineas for the poem, a fair price for an unknown poet (see chapter 31, "Money"). More important, though, it earned him the respect and friendship of Cave, who was to be his major source of income until 1745, and of Dodsley, who was to be the force behind the *Dictionary*.

Dodsley was to prove a steady friend, inviting Johnson to write the preface to *The Preceptor* (1748), an early textbook for home instruction. It was one of Johnson's most important early writings. To the same work he contributed a short allegory, "The Vision of Theodore, the Hermit of Teneriffe," his earliest fiction and one of his own favorite works. Dodsley also published Johnson's greatest poem, *The Vanity of Human Wishes* (1749), paying him fifteen guineas, and his tragedy *Irene*, after it finally reached the stage in February 1749, for which Johnson received £100. He was later to receive a guinea from Dodsley for his excellent introduction to the first number of the *London Chronicle* (1756), and Dodsley, along with William Johnston and William Strahan, paid Johnson £100 for *Rasselas* (1759). On January 9, 1759, Johnson wrote to his friend Bennet Langton, "Doddy, you know, is my patron" (*Letters*, 1:173), and he gave the meaning of this statement in a conversation in St. Andrews in 1773: "We have done with patronage. In the infancy of learning, we find some great man praised for it." Now, Johnson, explains, "A man goes to a bookseller, and gets what he can" (Boswell, *Life*, 5:59; see chapters 13, "Authorship," and 15, "Book trade").

BY NECESSITY AN AUTHOR

Johnson, when first employed by Cave, had little to recommend him. Apart from the unpublished *Irene*, he had written a few poems not for publication, contributed an unknown number of essays to Richard Warren's *Birmingham Journal* (none of which have survived), and for the same printer had translated and epitomized Father Jerome Lobo's *Voyage to Abyssinia*.

He therefore began as any other professional writer did, performing booksellers' jobs for low pay, always living on the edge, hoping to find enough work to stay alive. Like his friend Richard Savage, Johnson "was therefore obliged to seek some other means of support; and, having no profession, became by necessity an author" (*Lives*, 3:124). Many of the writers with whom Johnson associated in the world of Grub Street fell into drink and poverty; most never escaped, often dying at a relatively young age. They are described by Sir John Hawkins: "Of these men it may be said that they were miners in literature, they worked, though not in darkness, under ground; their motive was gain; their labor silent and incessant" (Hawkins, *Life*, p. 134).

Cave, whose manner Johnson described as slow and deliberate, nevertheless came to recognize that Johnson had talent and ambition superior to those hack writers surrounding him. He befriended Johnson, encouraged him, and made him editor of the magazine. In return, Johnson did his share of translation from the French, and to the *Gentleman's Magazine*, from 1738 to 1745, he contributed a dozen biographies, including lives of Herman Boerhaave and Thomas Sydenham, two famous physicians; Admiral Robert Blake, Oliver Cromwell's general-at-sea; and the explorer Sir Francis Drake. He contributed several important essays, "Remarks on John Gay's Monument" and "An Essay on Epitaphs," prefaces to the collected volumes of the magazine, poems, and journalistic squibs. For three years he also wrote a half-million words of the parliamentary debates, though *created* may be the better word, since he worked only from scant notes supplied to him by others. They were widely believed at the time to be verbatim reports of the debates in Parliament.

STARVED TO DEATH IN TRANSLATING FOR BOOKSELLERS

How was it possible to escape this world? A professional author typically became involved in large projects to provide income over a number of years, which would allow time to be spent on works for which the pay was less certain. This strategy undoubtedly had an appeal for Johnson, but he had a more ambitious goal. He wished to establish himself as a man of letters – a scholar – not just in England, but on the Continent. Johnson had tried to join this "circle of European scholar-poets that he most admired" well before he traveled to London.[1] He had printed proposals dated August 5, 1734, for publishing by subscription an edition of the Latin poems of Politian (Angelo Poliziano), a fifteenth-century Italian poet, humanist, and scholar, for which he was to furnish a life, a history of Latin poetry from Petrarch (a century before) to Politian, and notes. The project, however, failed for lack of interest.

Johnson's next attempt at establishing a reputation was the translation, *The History of the Council of Trent*. Although Cave had initially rejected the project, Johnson was at work on it by summer 1738. The French edition he was to translate had appeared in two large quarto volumes of 200 sheets – 1,600 pages. With the translation of this work Johnson hoped to establish his reputation as a scholar. It was not to be anonymous, like his work for the *Gentleman's Magazine* or *London*; his name appeared in large letters on the proposals. Then, on October 20, a letter appeared in the *Daily Advertiser* announcing that a rival edition was already under way. Johnson tried to maintain his claim on the project by publishing a brief "Life of Father Paul Sarpi" in the November 1738 number of the *Gentleman's Magazine*, signed "S.J." Nevertheless, the translation was abandoned, but not before Johnson received forty-seven guineas (£49 7*s*.) for his work. If he was paid a half-guinea a sheet, he must have completed translating roughly half of this huge work. If he was paid a guinea a sheet – at the upper end of the pay scale – he would have translated a quarter of the work. None of it survives.

Johnson was so discouraged by the failure of this work that he left London in autumn 1739 and returned to the Midlands. He was reported to have said that he would rather "die upon the road, *than be starved to death in translating for Booksellers*, which has been his only subsistence for some time past."[2] He even tried to secure a teaching post, though he hated teaching. He had written earlier to Edmund Hector, his old friend from Lichfield Grammar School, about his life as a teacher, saying, "it was hard to say whose difficulty was greatest He to explain Nonsense, or they to understand it."[3] When he returned to London in the spring of 1740, though, he had reconciled himself to being a professional author, and once again immersed himself in the world of the *Gentleman's Magazine*.

The work did not keep him fully occupied, and with his wife, Tetty, in declining health and requiring separate maintenance, he needed additional money. In 1739 he had published two political pamphlets attacking Sir Robert Walpole's administration in the House of Commons, *Marmor Norfolciense* and *A Compleat Vindication of the Licensers of the Stage*. Both were published anonymously; they brought him no fame and, probably, only a few pounds. In the same year he translated a sizeable work from the French for Cave, Jean Pierre de Crousaz's *Commentary on Mr. Pope's Principles of Morality, or Essay on Man*.

When, in autumn 1742, the bookseller Thomas Osborne purchased the vast library of Edward Harley, second Earl of Oxford, Johnson was hired to write advertisements for selling the library, to catalogue it, and to choose a number of scarce pamphlets to publish in an eight-volume *Harleian Miscellany*. Although his extensive work in one of the great private libraries provided him with abundant information for his later writings, it was grinding work. Only one piece of his own choosing seems to have been written during this entire period, a life of the poet Richard Savage in 1744. For writing it Johnson received only fifteen guineas, and once again his name was not on the title page.

Cave, however, remained convinced that Johnson was capable of great things. Around this time he decided – no doubt persuaded by Johnson – that there was a market for an inexpensive edition of Shakespeare's plays. Because his contributions to the *Gentleman's Magazine* virtually cease in the winter of 1744–5, Johnson seems to have been paid by Cave to spend the time making preparations for the edition. In April 1745 Cave published Johnson's *Miscellaneous Observations on the Tragedy of Macbeth*, along with the proposals for the complete edition, clearly demonstrating Johnson's literary, critical, and linguistic skills. But yet again Johnson was balked. Jacob Tonson, one of the leading London booksellers, claimed that he and his associates owned the copyright to Shakespeare's works, and wrote to Cave threatening a lawsuit in the Chancery court if his rights were invaded (see chapter 15, "Book trade"). Cave wisely withdrew. Johnson was still a poorly paid writer, little known except to a small group of booksellers. They at least recognized after *Miscellaneous Observations on Macbeth* that he had considerable skills as a scholar and a linguist but, after eight hard years in London, his career had hardly begun.

THE *DICTIONARY*, *VANITY*, AND THE PERIODICAL ESSAYS

In the spring of 1746, though, when Johnson was thirty-six, his life began to change. Dodsley, who had published *London*, suggested that he write a dictionary. It was not by any means the first English dictionary, but it would be on an unprecedented scale, a comprehensive dictionary along the lines of those produced by the French and Italian academies (see chapter 18, "Dictionaries"). Dodsley thought Johnson had the ability; it would also provide him with a steady income. To spread the financial risk of such an undertaking, Dodsley assembled a group of seven booksellers representing five different firms. On June 18, 1746, Johnson signed a contract to be paid £1,575 (1,500 guineas) to complete the dictionary in three years. Complications and delays kept him from meeting his deadline; it took nine years instead of three. But *A Dictionary of the English Language*, published on April 15, 1755, was an amazing feat for one man.

Though he finally had a project worthy of his talents, his problems were not entirely behind him. The money paid him to write the *Dictionary* had long since been spent, and in the next few years he was arrested twice for debt. Partly, perhaps, as a relief from the drudgery of working on the *Dictionary*, and certainly to earn extra money, Johnson published his most famous poem, *The Vanity of Human Wishes*, in 1749. On March 20, 1750, he began to write the *Rambler* essays, published every Tuesday and Saturday until March 14, 1752. He was paid two guineas apiece for the 203 essays he wrote. Although he continued to struggle financially, these essays earned him the sobriquet "Mr. Rambler" and the reputation as the "great moralist." From early 1753 until early 1754 he also contributed an occasional essay to the *Adventurer*, edited by John Hawkesworth. Then, for two years beginning April 15, 1758, he contributed the bulk of the *Idler* essays to a newspaper, the *Universal Chronicle*.

THE *LITERARY MAGAZINE*, SHAKESPEARE, AND *RASSELAS*

By the time the *Dictionary* appeared, Johnson's career had begun in earnest, and he achieved fame as "Dictionary Johnson." In 1756 he edited an edition of Sir Thomas Browne's *Christian Morals*, for which he supplied a life of Browne and annotations. He also put his magazine experience to good use by becoming editor of the *Literary Magazine*. Over a period of about a year and a half he contributed, in addition to editorial commentary, the "Memoirs of the King of Prussia" and more than three dozen book reviews, including his two most famous: one on Soame Jenyns's *Free Inquiry into the Nature and Origin of Evil*, with its devastating attack on Jenyns's confident take on the nature of evil, and another on Jonas Hanway's *Journal of Eight Days' Journey*.

Johnson's next major project began on June 2, 1756, when he signed an agreement to edit the *Plays of William Shakespeare*, to be published by subscription. As with the *Dictionary*, he missed many deadlines; the volumes were promised for Christmas 1757, but were not delivered to subscribers until October 10, 1765. Once again, though, as with the *Dictionary*, Johnson showed himself capable of taking on large-scale scholarly projects and completing them virtually single-handedly. The Shakespeare edition, with its famous preface and incisive annotations, also established his high reputation as a literary critic.

The subscription money taken in for the Shakespeare edition must have provided a good deal of income, as the number of works identified as by him published from 1757 into 1763 are so few it is hard to imagine how he lived. In 1759, however, to defray the cost of his mother's funeral and pay her debts, he published his short fiction, *The Prince of Abissinia*, now known as *Rasselas* – perhaps his best-known work.

LATE WORKS

In July 1762 Johnson was awarded a £300-a-year pension by George III, allowing him for the first time in his life, at age fifty-two, not to have to write for a living. Johnson continued to write, but now he could afford to do so largely at his own pace. In the 1770s he wrote four political pamphlets on issues that concerned him – *The False Alarm* (1770), *Thoughts on the Late Transactions Respecting Falkland's Islands* (1771), *The Patriot* (1774), and *Taxation No Tyranny* (1775) – and he extensively revised his *Dictionary* for the fourth edition (1773). After a trip with Boswell to the Hebrides in 1773, he published *A Journey to the Western Islands of Scotland* in early 1775.

On March 29, 1777, to the surprise of even his closest friends, Johnson agreed to write "little Lives, and little Prefaces, to a little edition of the English Poets" (*Letters*, 3:20). These "little Lives" were to grow into the ten-volume *Prefaces, Biographical and Critical, to the Works of the English Poets* (1779–81), given the title *Lives of the Most Eminent English Poets; with Critical Observations on Their Works* for the second London edition (1781), and since then widely known as the *Lives of the Poets*. Johnson's great contribution to English literary criticism is succinctly summed up by Edmund Wilson:

> The *Lives of the Poets* and the preface and commentary on Shakespeare are among the most brilliant and most acute documents in the whole range of English criticism, and the products of a mind which, so far from being parochially local and hopelessly cramped by the taste of its age, saw literature in a long perspective and could respond to the humanity of Shakespeare as well as the wit of Pope.[4]

In spite of Johnson's well-known insistence that "No man but a blockhead ever wrote, except for money" (Boswell, *Life*, 3:19), he was "at the call of almost any one, to assist, either by correction, or by a preface, or dedication, in the publication of works not his own" (Hawkins, *Life*, p. 235). For which of these acts of kindness he was paid, or the amount, is known in few cases. He contributed paragraphs to the proposals for Robert James's *Medicinal Dictionary* (1741), and he wrote for Zachariah Williams *An Account of an Attempt to Ascertain the Longitude* (1755). For James Bennet he wrote proposals (1757), a life, and annotations for the *English Works of Roger Ascham* (1761), published under the distressed schoolmaster's name for his benefit. Beginning in December 1766, and for several years thereafter, he collaborated with Robert Chambers to produce the second Vinerian law lectures. He also contributed either a dedication, corrections, or assistance with publication in one form or another to most of the publications of his friends Giuseppe Baretti and Charlotte Lennox. It is fitting that what seems to be Johnson's final writing for the public was for a friend, a dedication to George III for Charles Burney's *Account of the Musical Performance in Westminster Abbey, and the Pantheon … in Commemoration of Handel*, published February 1, 1785.

NOTES

1 Robert DeMaria, Jr., *The Life of Samuel Johnson: A Critical Biography* (Oxford: Blackwell, 1993), p. 32.

2 *The Early Biographies of Samuel Johnson*, ed. O M Brack, Jr., and Robert E. Kelley (Iowa City: University of Iowa Press, 1974), p. 25.

3 James Boswell, *The Correspondence and Other Papers Relating to the Making of the "Life of Johnson,"* ed. Marshall Waingrow, 2nd edn. (New Haven, CT: Yale University Press, 2001), pp. 132, 133 n. 7; see also Boswell, *Life*, 1:84.

4 Edmund Wilson, "Reëxamining Dr. Johnson," in *Classics and Commercials* (New York: Farrar, Straus and Company, 1950), pp. 244–9 at p. 247.

CHAPTER 3

Correspondence

Freya Johnston

CORRESPO'NDENCE, CORRESPO'NDENCY. *n.s.* [from *correspond.*]
2. Intercourse; reciprocal intelligence.

> It happens very oddly, that the pope and I should have the same thought much about the same time: my enemies will be apt to say, that we hold a *correspondence* together, and act by concert in this matter. *Addison's Guardian*, N°. 116.

If the impression persists of Johnson as an "*épistolier malgré lui*," as Bruce Redford has called him (*Letters*, 1:ix) – a letter-writer despite himself – Johnson himself is partly to blame. During an age of prolific correspondence, in which letters were usually celebrated for their spontaneity and candor, Johnson instead stressed their tendency to deceive: "There is, indeed, no transaction which offers stronger temptations to fallacy and sophistication than epistolary intercourse" (*Lives*, 4:58). It is also the case that two Johnsonian monuments have obscured the range and variety of his private correspondence. Two of his most famous letters, the vigorous denunciations of Lord Chesterfield and James Macpherson, are necessarily unrepresentative; they triumphantly declare to the world both the author's independence and his antagonist's impudence: "I hope it is no very cinical asperity not to confess obligation where no benefit has been received"; "I will not desist from detecting what I think a cheat, from any fear of the menaces of a Ruffian" (*Letters*, 1:96; 2:169).

NO INTELLIGENCE IS COMMUNICATED

Around three quarters of Johnson's surviving correspondence dates from the last twelve years of his life. The usually businesslike notes he sent between his twenties and his fifties give little indication of the late flowering of subtle, teasing, and allusive letters to Hester Thrale and her family, letters which he sensed might one day appear in print. In *Rambler* 152, he regretted that none of the tribe of writers who "excelled in the art of decorating insignificance" had published their familiar correspondence. The remark about "art" suggests that he valued not so much the frankness as the elegance of letters written about nothing in particular. In works of his own in which "no intelligence is communicated, or business transacted" (*Works*, 5:44, 47), he enjoyed playing the role of a mock-heroic narrator: "This, Madam," he wrote with *faux* solemnity, "is the history of one of my toes" (*Letters*, 3:186). He told Thrale that "To sit down so often with nothing to say, to say something so often, almost without consciousness of saying, and without any remembrance of having said, is a power of which I will not violate my modesty by boasting, but I do not believe that every body has it" (*Letters*, 3:89).

This kind of letter really is a display of "power," in the sense that it translates "nothing" into "something." Like a paradoxical encomium, it is generated from the slightest of materials, resulting in a perilously comic style that always threatens to collapse into laughter. It is an exercise in entertaining a friend and in settling a debt: during the eighteenth century, the person who paid for the delivery of a letter was usually its recipient. The fact that the reader typically shouldered the cost suggests that the letter-writer's task was akin to that of any author in the marketplace. Then again, Henry Thrale, as a Member of Parliament, did not have to pay for his letters, which gave Johnson license to write to Hester Thrale more frequently, at greater length, and about more trivial topics than he could to other correspondents.

NOTHING DISTORTED

Johnson always remained on guard against Alexander Pope's claims, in letters to friends, to have casually unmasked his heart to the world. So it is appropriate that one of the least personally revealing of his letters to Hester Thrale is that in which he claims to reveal everything:

> In a Man's Letters you know, Madam, his soul lies naked, his letters are only the mirrour of his breast, whatever passes within him is shown undisguised in its natural process. Nothing is inverted, nothing distorted, you see systems in their elements, you discover actions in their motives.
>
> Of this great truth sounded by the knowing to the ignorant, and so echoed by the ignorant to the knowing, what evidence have you now before you. Is not my soul laid open in these veracious pages? do not you see me reduced to my first principles? This is the pleasure of corresponding with a friend, where doubt and distrust have no place, and every thing is said as it is thought … These are the letters by which souls are united, and by which Minds naturally in unison

move each other as they are moved themselves ... I have indeed concealed nothing from you, nor do I expect ever to repent of having thus opened my heart. (*Letters*, 3:89–90)

In this parodic version of epistolary exchange, there is a magic, even mechanical, correspondence between one mind and another: the writer has only to feel moved in order to transport his reader; he has nothing but pure, transparent ideas. Johnson truly cannot "expect ever to repent of having thus opened my heart," because his heart remains utterly inscrutable. Yet most of his letters to Hester Thrale, although he may emphasize their studied elements, do beg to be read as openings of his heart and mind; they are full of professions of continuing, undisguised regard for his "dear mistress" and her family (e.g., *Letters*, 3:78–85). They ask her to write just as she would speak to him. The flagrant irony of his epistolary parody both shields and displays a wish for the plainest communication between them, just as Johnson's theatrical insistence that Thrale neither cares where he is nor knows what he does both shields and displays his genuine terror – eventually well-founded – that she really has lost interest and patience.

CALM AND DELIBERATE PERFORMANCE

Four years after his "undisguised" epistle to Thrale, when he came to examine Pope's correspondence, Johnson concluded that "a friendly letter" was a calculated transaction, "a calm and deliberate performance" (*Lives*, 4:58). He recognized in Pope the same powerful, contradictory impulses towards self-exposure and imaginative disguise that characterized his own letters. But where Pope dwelt on the fidelity of his self-portraits, Johnson insisted on finding in letters evidence of self-concealment. Hester Thrale complained that he was "often scrupulous of opening his heart" in letters to her, "& has an Idea they will be seen sometime, perhaps published – he is always exhorting *me* not to write Letters, nor put my Mind upon Paper, lest it should be seen in some future Time and known forsooth: vain Exhortation!" But this is strangely at odds with Johnson's repeated urgings to Thrale that she should write as often, as fully, and as frankly as she can. Also, at this point, Thrale had just recalled her own letters to Sir Philip Jennings Clerke, for fear that they were too "free & unrestrained" (*Thraliana*, 1:444–6). Taken together, Johnson's and Thrale's various explanations of letter-writing, and of the conventions which underpin it, span the two poles between which all epistolary communication may be thought to lie: on the one hand, the pure, unrestrained ideal of venting the mind on paper; on the other, its impure, designing mirror image.

Johnson considered letters as "fill[ing] up the vacuities of action by agreeable appearances" (*Works*, 5:44); therefore, "when a post comes empty, I am really disappointed" (*Letters*, 3:62). "The vacuity of life," Thrale noted, was his "favourite hypothesis" (*Thraliana*, 1:179), encompassing (in the words of the *Dictionary* definition of *vacuity*) a physical "Emptiness" and a psychological "State of being unfilled." He treated the latter idea in a delicately overstated, comically despondent way, in a letter about Frances Reynolds:

> I was last week at Renny's Conversatione, and Renny got her room pretty well filled, and there were Mrs. Ord, and Mrs. Horneck, and Mrs. Bunbury and other illustrious names, and much would poor Renny have given to have had Mrs. Thrale too, and Queeny, and Burney, but human happiness is never perfect, there is always une vuide affreuse, as Maintenon complained, there is some craving void left aking in the breast. Renny is going to Ramsgate, and thus the world drops away, and I am left in the sultry town, to see the sun in the Crab, and perhaps in the Lion, while You are paddling with the Nereids. (*Letters*, 3:277)

The mock-heroic tone and mood of this letter, with its play of sea nymphs against English watering holes, are akin to that of Thomas Gray's "Ode on the Death of a Favourite Cat"; both have a melancholy, faded, smiling charm. There is an amusing disparity between a mere everyday room, "pretty well filled," and the theatricality of "some craving void left aking in the breast" – but, on second view, it turns out to be no flagrant disparity at all. "Poor Renny" is treated sympathetically, and the cause of her agony is Thrale's absence, so that the point of the exaggerated language is partly to compliment the letter's recipient. The treatment of full and empty spaces is perfectly balanced between weariness and affection: "thus the world drops away." Johnson thinks kindly and sadly, but on the right side of self-pity, about the people he misses.

PROMISE AND PERFORMANCE

Although letters, like prayers, are attempts to gain a response, the very act of composing them may bring about a salutary change in the mind of the petitioner. As Redford puts it, letters "permit Johnson to enact – instead of merely prescribing – a transition from raw grief to poised acceptance" (*Letters*, 1:xi). Writing to Hill Boothby in 1755, he set about turning a "waste hour" to use, to "amuse" a portion of time which would otherwise count as useless and therefore count against him. Again, Johnson makes something of nothing in a letter. Like Renny's room, by the end his page is "pretty well

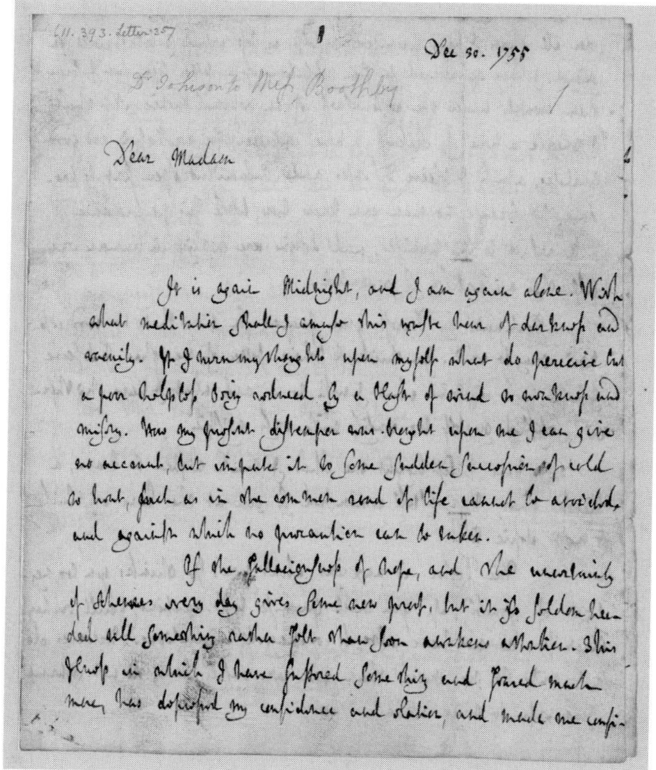
Dec 30. 1755

Dr Johnson to Mrs Boothby

Dear Madam

It is again Midnight, and I am again alone. With what meditation shall I amuse this waste hour of darkness and vacuity. If I turn my thoughts upon myself what do perceive but a poor helpless being reduced by a blast of wind to weakness and misery. How my present distemper was brought upon me I can give no account, but impute it to some sudden succession of cold to heat, such as in the common road of life cannot be avoided, and against which no precaution can be taken.

Of the fallaciousness of hope, and the uncertainty of schemes every day gives some new proof, but it is seldom heeded till something rather felt than seen awakens attention. This illness in which I have suffered something and feared much more has depressed my confidence and elation, and made me consi-

Figure 3 Samuel Johnson to Hill Boothby, December 30, 1755.

filled" and a duty has been fulfilled. Although he is able to give "no account" of his desperate condition to Boothby, and lamenting the discrepancy between human wishes and performances, Johnson writes to her in order to give the helpless, vagrant mind some employment. The repetitions and circlings around his own solitary despondency in the first paragraph yield to a passive, general form of considering himself part of fallible humanity in the second. Nothing comes repeatedly to be weighed against something, just as emptiness is weighed against fullness in the letter about poor Renny – only here, such weighing offers a "proof" of the writer's moral character:

Dear Madam:

It is again Midnight, and I am again alone. With what meditation shall I amuse this waste hour of darkness and vacuity. If I turn my thoughts upon myself what do [I] perceive but a poor helpless being reduced by a blast of wind to weakness and misery. How my present distemper was brought upon me I can give no account,

> but impute it to some sudden succession of cold to heat, such as in the common road of life cannot be avoided, and against which no precaution can be taken.
>
> Of the fallaciousness of hope, and the uncertainty of Schemes every day gives some new proof, but it is seldom heeded till something rather felt than seen awakens attention. This Ilness in which I have suffered some thing and feared much more, has depressed my confidence and elation, and made me consider all that I have promised myself as less certain to be attained or enjoyed. I have endeavoured to form resolutions of a better life, but I form them weakly under the consciousness of an external motive. Not that I conceive a time of Sickness a time improper for recollection and good purposes, which I believe Diseases and Calamities often sent to produce, but because no man can know how little his performance will conform to his promises, and designs are nothing in human eyes till they are realised by execution. (*Letters*, 1:117)

The phrasing here – "Diseases and Calamities often *sent* to produce"; "*designs* are nothing in human eyes" – seems to have in mind the occasion and form of a letter, a written design which is sent to produce something in its recipient, but which also accomplishes something unexpected in its author. Johnson asserted in *Rambler* 134 that "To act is far easier than to suffer" (*Works*, 4:347), and writing is an activity to which he doggedly sets himself, finding his way through an "Ilness in which I have suffered some thing and feared much more" partly in the mere act of temporal self-accounting with which a letter begins (Johnson was always huffy with Thrale for not dating her letters; see, for example, *Letters*, 3:244). This petition makes the happiness which it does not find: at the end, it turns the familiar theme of vacuity, and of promises weighed against performances, into courtliness and compliment.

For Johnson, as for the philosopher Ludwig Wittgenstein, "to imagine a language means to imagine a form of life."[1] So he ends by writing to Boothby: "You know Des Cartes's argument, 'I think therefore I am.' It is as good a consequence 'I write therefore I am alive.' I might give another 'I am alive therefore I love Miss Boothby,' but I hope that our friendship may be of far longer duration than life" (*Letters*, 1:118). A similar courtly flourish, married to a serious moral, concludes a letter to Thrale: "Against our meeting we will both make good resolutions, which on my side, I hope to keep, but such hopes are very deceitful. I would not willingly think the same of all hopes, and particularly should be loath to suspect of deceit my hope of being always, Dearest Madam, Your most humble Servant" (*Letters*, 3:364).

Writing to Thrale on another occasion, Johnson parodied the stock rhetoric of politicians while making good the discrepancy between promise and performance. The hollow rhetoric here conceals, even permits, a sincere effort to match intention with reality:

> When I miss a post I consider myself as deviating from the true rule of action. Seeing things in this light, I consider every letter as something in the line of duty, upon this foot I make my arrangement, and under whatever circumstances of difficulty, endeavour to carry them into execution, for having in some degree pledged myself for the performance I think the reputation both of my head and my heart engaged, and reprobate every thought of desisting from the undertaking ... He that can rattle those words well together may say all that political controversy generally produces. (*Letters*, 3:71–2)

Contained in this rattling joke are the Johnsonian moral and literary touchstones of arrangement, execution, and performance, terms that generate more than political controversy. The engagement of head and heart; the change from inertia to action brought about by a sense of duty; a turn to the addressee for a return of fondness and esteem; the formation of parallels and multiplication of examples – such epistolary acts, militating against suffering and solitude, are also a form of self-defense against Johnson's horror of endings. After all, most letters hope to generate another, rather than to have the last word.

THE IRREMEABLE STREAM

In what turned out to be his final letter to Hester Thrale – by now Mrs. Piozzi – Johnson drew a parallel between her intention to remove to Italy and the decision of Mary, Queen of Scots to take refuge in enemy territory:

> When Queen Mary took the resolution of sheltering herself in England, the Archbishop of St. Andrew's attempting to dissuade her, attended her on her journey and when they came to the irremeable Stream that separated the two kingdoms, walked by her side into the water, in the middle of which he seized her bridle, and with earnestness proportioned to her danger and his own affection, pressed her to return. The Queen went forward. – If the parallel reaches thus far; may it go no further. The tears stand in my eyes.
>
> I am going into Derbyshire, and hope to be followed by your good wishes, for I am with great affection, Your most humble servant,
>
> SAM. JOHNSON
>
> Any letters that come for me hither, will be sent me. (*Letters*, 4:343–4)

All the histories Johnson had read agree on the fact that, when Mary left Scotland, she took a fishing boat across the Solway Firth. Why, then, did he replace that boat with a rider? He was begging Hester Thrale to grant him one last wish, likening her to a doomed queen and himself to her sole true counselor. His striking choice of epithet for the stream is "irremeable," or "admitting of no return." It takes the word "irrevocable," which had appeared in different forms in his and Thrale's immediately preceding letters to one another, one stage further (*Letters*, 4:338 and n. 1). And it allows Johnson to countenance a world in which no redemption is possible. For *irremeable* is a poet's word, a classical badge, a ghost of a particular kind of past. John Dryden translates Virgil's Latin word *irremeabilis* that way, describing the river that permits no return (Johnson quotes the passage under *irremeable* in his *Dictionary*); Pope employed it, also in this sense, in his translation of *The Iliad*.[2]

Something in Johnson senses that, when Thrale crosses this stream, she is leaving him on the other side of the river of death. For that reason, *irremeable* chimes with the final couplet of his last English poem, a translation of Horace's *Diffugere nives*, completed in November 1784: "Nor can the might of Theseus rend / The chains of hell that hold his friend" (*Works*, 6:344). There is no consolation here, no way of making amends: "The irremeable waters of Styx … preclude for ever the return of hope."[3] One of the ways he begs for the impossible, a return to the past, is by repeating a letter he had composed seventeen years earlier. In 1767, he wrote to Thrale from Lichfield that

> I have felt in this place something like the shackles of destiny … I perhaps shall not be easily persuaded to pass again to the other side of Styx, to venture myself on the irremeable road. I long to see you and all those of whom the sight is included in seeing you. (*Letters*, 1:286)

So "the irremeable road" had long meant separation from Thrale. In his valedictory address to her, the tears stand in his eyes as he asks for her good wishes, and her letters, to follow him on the road to Derbyshire. Those letters, however, he burned.

NOTES

1 Ludwig Wittgenstein, *Philosophical Investigations*, trans. G. E. M. Anscombe, 2nd edn. (Oxford: Basil Blackwell, 1958), p. 8.

2 *The Iliad of Homer*, trans. Alexander Pope, ed. Steven Shankman (Harmondsworth: Penguin, 1996), 19:312.

3 François Fénelon, *The Adventures of Telemachus*, trans. William Henry Melmoth (London, 1785), p. 78.

PART II

Critical fortunes

CHAPTER 4

Editions

Adam Rounce

EDI'TION. *n.s.* [*editio*, Latin.]
2. Republication; generally with some revisal or correcting.

> The business of our redemption is to rub over the defaced copy of the creation, to reprint God's image upon the soul, and to set forth nature in a second and a fairer *edition*. *South.*

Editions of writers exert a great influence on their posthumous reputation, forming a canon of works, explicating their meanings by annotation (particularly where historical distance has made them obscure), and presenting the text as the author originally intended. When measured against these idealistic aims, editions of Samuel Johnson have tended to fall short until relatively recently, for reasons that are partly the result of the peculiar nature of his achievements, as well as the caprices of editing and printing in the decades following his death.

ANONYMITY

When the variety of Johnson's writings is considered, it is not hard to see why editions of him have been so affected with difficulties, both in forming a canon of works that can be attributed to him and in establishing an accurate text. While there are some works with Johnson's name on the title page, and others he later acknowledged as his own, in many other cases it is impossible to gauge the full extent of his involvement. Johnson lent his pen to anonymous contributions (and so-called "ghost writing") in the works of friends (such as prefaces, sermons, and lectures), collaborative works which had to be anonymous (accounts of parliamentary debates or other politically sensitive writing), and works of journalism where Johnson would have little reason to acknowledge his contribution, given that in selling such writings, he had also sold his name in them (see chapter 2, "Publication history").

To a modern audience, anonymity often suggests a need for secrecy; in Johnson's world, this was not the case, and it was entirely normal for such pieces as prefaces, book reviews, short biographical accounts, and essays either to be unsigned or to use some sort of pseudonym. The result is that, from Johnson's own time, there have been (and remain) items that are attributed to him because of the ideas or the style, but whose authorship is still disputed. While there is a broad consensus concerning writings known to be by Johnson, a complete canon remains elusive: the sheer amount of Johnson's miscellaneous writing suggests that he could not have remembered them all even if he had wanted to acknowledge them. On the other hand, there has rarely been a shortage of published editions of Johnson.

THE EARLY EDITIONS

The amount of Johnson's work that was reprinted, in one form or another, from the time of his death to the end of the nineteenth century, is vast: in the decades following 1784, various "Beauties" of Johnson appeared, anthologies containing his most well-known literary and moralistic writing, as well as collections known as *ana*, or table-talk, reprinting his most famous remarks and aphorisms. The periodical essays were also frequently reprinted, as were the *Lives of the Poets*, often split up and used to introduce the works of their subjects in poetic editions and anthologies. Editions of *Rasselas* are numerous in the nineteenth century, not least because of its role as a school and university textbook in England and America.

The first important and supposedly complete edition of Johnson, however, was that associated with his executor, Sir John Hawkins. Like many eighteenth-century publishing projects it was commissioned by a consortium of booksellers. Eleven volumes were published in 1787, with supplementary volumes taking it up to fifteen by 1789. Hawkins's edition is significant for many reasons, not least for being the textual basis for all complete editions of Johnson until the twentieth century.

The significance of this edition cannot be separated from its shortcomings, though, and these are related to the role of Hawkins, its editor. It is more accurate to describe Hawkins as supervising the edition in a somewhat distant sense. He certainly does not appear to have fulfilled the modern editor's role, which includes establishing as complete a canon as possible, choosing the most authoritative copy-text of a work to be printed (and rejecting those with problems, in terms of textual variants, punctuation, and spelling), checking the proof sheets to ensure their accuracy, and adding annotations. Hawkins's involvement is clearest in works such as the *Lives of the Poets*, where his hand can be seen in the footnotes and choice of text; more often, it is hardly seen at all, and the result is an edition that has substantial textual problems: Hawkins seems to have used the latest possible printed edition of a work, even where this was not corrected by the author, or where it was less accurate than an earlier version. This meant that he sometimes used corrupted textual sources, sometimes unintentionally added to these by unnoticed printing errors, and sometimes changed its texts (in terms of spelling and capitalization) in order to be consistent with the rest of the edition, at the cost of textual accuracy. The painstaking research of J. D. Fleeman proved that, for the majority of its texts, either Hawkins was an incredibly careless editor or he had only the most sporadic involvement with the edition.

One thing that Hawkins himself certainly contributed to the edition was a book-length *Life of Johnson*, which has always attracted controversy, given that Hawkins was a man not used to hiding his opinions (see chapter 1, "Life"). Nevertheless, it remains an important source for obscure areas of Johnson's life – Hawkins had known Johnson since 1738, twenty-five years before Boswell met him – and the many blanket dismissals of it are unfair (there is an excellent modern edition of it by O M Brack). Its unfavorable reception, however, persuaded booksellers to commission one of the critics most offended by Hawkins's effort, Arthur Murphy, to produce another collected edition. Murphy's twelve-volume *Works* (1792) adjusted and reordered the works included in it and added to the canon of Johnson's writings; its texts, though, remained inconsistent, in terms of accuracy, and when Murphy's edition was revised by Alexander Chalmers (in 1806, 1816, and 1823), there were still more additions and deletions of pieces included. This may have helped the evolving development of the canon, but no attention was paid to textual accuracy. The collected editions of Johnson's works were growing larger but not more accurate.

The result of this proliferation of editions was that subsequent editors and critics usually looked to Hawkins's edition of 1787, despite its many flaws. Moreover, the inaccuracies and inconsistencies of these texts were augmented by the number of times they had been reprinted. It is often assumed that the frequency of the appearance of a work in printed editions is likely to remove errors, because of the repeated checking of texts. With these early editions of Johnson, though, given the original problems of textual choices, the opposite is the case: the more a work was reprinted, the further its text was corrupted, as more and more errors entered in, whether of printing, proofreading, or the application of a house style of punctuation, spelling, and capitalization. Such flaws are not offset by the occasional correcting of past textual corruptions.

THE NINETEENTH CENTURY

The epitome of this process is an edition which was often cited as the most authoritative, the so-called "Oxford" edition of Johnson's works (11 vols., 1825). J. D. Fleeman summarized the problems of this Oxford edition when he noticed fifty-five unwarranted commas in its printing of the first chapter of *Rasselas* alone – and *Rasselas* hardly has long chapters. The volumes were part of the Oxford English Classics series, and although the purely commercial edition was in no way associated with the University Press, the title of the series gave it a spurious editorial authority. Its editor, Francis Pearson Walesby, took the canon of Johnson's works that had been arrived at in Chalmers's edition of 1823, but also copied the texts of these works, and augmented their errors, particularly by the addition of punctuation. This unreliable edition became for many years the standard collection of Johnson's writings.

Interest in Johnson's works was always combined with his appeal as a literary figure – a tremendous personality whose character had been captured in biographies, anecdotes, and reminiscences by Hawkins, Hester Lynch Piozzi and, above all, in James Boswell's *Life of Johnson*, which had quickly acquired the status of a classic in its own right, as a formative work in English literary biography. In 1831, John Wilson Croker brought out a new edition of Boswell's *Life*. Croker followed other contemporary biographies in inserting as many materials as possible. Therefore, whenever Boswell's own account allowed, he placed parts of the biographies and anecdotes of Piozzi, Hawkins, Murphy, and others within his text. He also reordered parts of Boswell's works, and relegated other parts to appendices. He added many footnotes, and these are full of identifications of figures not originally named, and other useful information, alongside much ephemera.

Unfortunately, Croker's notes are also full of mistakes, and Thomas Babington Macaulay, a personal and political foe of Croker, made the most of this in a notorious review in the *Edinburgh Review* (1831). Macaulay's compellingly readable demolition of the edition set in train a disastrous misreading of Johnson. Macaulay was a literary journalist of tremendous vigor, but this very quality resulted in superficial judgments and simplifications. In his swingeing attack on Croker, Macaulay backhandedly salutes Boswell as a buffoon who happened to write a work of genius. In fact, he argues, so great is the *Life of Johnson* that it reveals how commonplace and ultimately unnecessary are Johnson's own writings, the reading of which can be replaced by Boswell's immortal portrait: Johnson the writer is dull compared to the character of Boswell's pages, and therefore there is little point in looking at the former. The influence of this caricature of Johnson was profound, and would last well into the twentieth century – nor has its effect completely disappeared. For many readers, Samuel Johnson was Boswell's Johnson, and Johnson the writer was a subordinate and unimportant figure.

G.B. HILL TO THE PRESENT

Johnson continued to be read and his works reprinted throughout the nineteenth century, but the next significant editorial intervention would come from George Birkbeck Hill, a scholar dedicated to presenting and elucidating as much as possible about Johnson's milieu, through a series of editions published by Oxford University Press. His editorial labors began with his six-volume edition of Boswell (1887), with the *Life of Johnson* in four volumes, the *Journal of a Tour* in volume 5, and a vast index in volume 6. As well as editing *Rasselas*, Hill also published *Johnsonian Miscellanies* (1897) and (posthumously in 1905) the *Lives of the Poets*.

These editions are of their time, but also modern, in important ways: Hill's style of annotation, for example, was garrulous and digressive, and he rarely, if ever, stopped before making a comparison or suggesting an analogy. But the relative care taken over textual matters, and the importance given to Johnson's writing and thought, marked a welcome departure from the slapdash tradition embodied in the "Oxford Edition" of 1825 or the patronizing dismissiveness of Macaulay. Hill was aware of the intellectual value of Johnson in English literary history – the *Johnsonian Miscellanies*, for instance, collected various accounts of Johnson's life available to only the most diligent scholars, and the edition of the *Lives* for the first time gave Johnson's criticism the level of attention and erudition that it deserved. His edition of Boswell, later revised by L. F. Powell, remains the standard version in the twenty-first century. His editions are not flawless, of course, and parts of their late Victorian approach have aged badly. But the full critical apparatus and their publication by a major university press gave an appropriate stature to Johnson's writings.

In a similar way, R. W. Chapman's edition of Johnson's *Journey to the Western Islands of Scotland*, alongside Boswell's *Journal of a Tour to the Hebrides* (1924), although eventually superseded by J. D. Fleeman's edition (1985), offered new levels of attention to detail, particularly textual collation. Chapman, whose many labors included extensive bibliographical work on Johnson, played an advisory role in the inception of the important edition of Johnson that began to emerge in the 1950s. *The Yale Edition of the Works of Samuel Johnson* was a collective undertaking by Johnson scholars who wanted to redress the inadequacy of many of the writings of such a major figure being available only in such flawed earlier collections – if at all – and in so doing, to present the intellectual range of Johnson in all its richness and complexity.

From its first volume in 1958, the primary intention of the Yale edition was to establish and provide a correct and readable text of Johnson's writings. The concern with readability led the editors to modernize the text, out of fear that the reader of a modern (American-produced) edition might be alienated and confused by the retention of capitals for proper nouns, the use of italics, variant spellings, and obsolete styles of punctuation that might obscure meaning. The result – not to the tastes of those who would prefer an old-spelling edition – was a compromise, as it is in almost all editorial ventures: original punctuation, spelling, and other features could be retained where they were not confusing. There was a similarly utilitarian intent behind the Yale edition's approach to annotation: just as it did not attempt an exhaustive list of textual variants, so it did not try to annotate everything in Johnson's text; to do so would be impossible in some cases and impractical in most. The result is that the different volumes show different policies towards annotation: the political writings edited by Donald Greene (1977), for example, require much more context and explanation than most works; the periodical essays, by contrast (1963 and 1969), adopt a minimalist policy (perhaps too much so).

These problems are not easily solved. It might be considered how feasible it is to edit a work such as Johnson's edition of Shakespeare, given that all of its original eight volumes are too long to be reprinted, and that these volumes contained not only the plays but also the commentary of previous editors. The Yale compromise, to print sections of plays and commentators conversant with Johnson's annotations, may not please everyone, but a solution that would (and would allow an editor to fully annotate Johnson's own annotations) is far from obvious. As it finally nears completion, over half a century since its beginning, the Yale Johnson has accomplished its main aim of providing a text of Johnson's works, and critical introductions to them with (in many cases) very helpful annotation.

It can be said that the twenty-first century has seen the fulfilment of much that was needed in Johnsonian editions. As well as the imminent arrival of final volumes of the Yale Johnson, the posthumous publication of J. D. Fleeman's monumental *Bibliography of the Works of Samuel Johnson, Treating His Published Works from the Beginnings to 1984* (2000) has given scholarship an invaluable tool for understanding Johnson's writings. And Roger Lonsdale's four-volume edition of the *Lives of the Poets* (2006), appearing just over a century after Hill's version, has surpassed it in every way, providing an authoritative text, an introduction to the *Lives* which could serve as a monograph in itself, and annotation that in its fullness of explication, sensitivity to the nuances of Johnson's writing, and comprehensive explanation of Johnson's entire milieu has set a standard to which all future Johnsonian editions will have to aspire. Given the confusions surrounding Johnsonian editions for so long, it is a suitable point on which to end.

CHAPTER 5

Translations

John Stone

to TRANSLA'TE. *v.n.* [*translatus*, Lat.]
5. [*Translater*, old Fr.] To interpret in another language; to change into another language retaining the sense.

Nor word for word too faithfully *translate. Roscommon.*

Though Johnson has been translated into many languages – twenty-five at last count – his cross-linguistic afterlife attracted very little attention until the early twenty-first century. Among the many works of scholarship that link Johnson's name to the likes of the law, science, and history, there is as yet no *Samuel Johnson and the Continent*, *Samuel Johnson and Europe*, *Samuel Johnson and Translation* (though he was himself a translator), or *Samuel Johnson without English*. "The John Bull of Spiritual Europe," "a British superstition," Johnson seemed perversely ill-suited to re-creation in the medium of another language, to taking root in and being transformed by other cultures.[1] Accordingly, translations of his works have seldom been sought or studied by anglophone scholars. The study of Johnson in translation therefore retains the charm or thrill of the chance find – a single *Rambler* essay in the Marathi language, for instance, published in Mumbai in 1879 by Benjamin Shimshon Ashtamker – without the historiographical sophistication with which one might approach Shakespeare in German, Edgar Allan Poe in French, or Charles Dickens in Catalan.

Two observations on Johnson in translation recur in the scant but suggestive recent scholarship that touches on the question, and they seem likely to frame further inquiry for some time. The first is that Johnson's writings in translation were seldom preceded by his reputation; instead they circulated, often anonymously, unencumbered by Samuel Johnson the historical construct, and their agency was not tainted by the use of Johnson's name as shorthand for a politics, a poetics, or a national character. (In fact they continue to be mistaken for, and studied as, works native to the languages in which they appeared.) The second is that the advent of English studies as a globalized discipline has quickened the pace of translation, especially into such major languages as Spanish and Chinese. In the twenty-first century, more of Johnson is now, and will be, available to more readers than ever before.

DIFFICULTIES

In Boswell's *Life*, Johnson never obtains translations of his own work, promotes foreign-language editions, or corresponds with his translators, even though his friend the novelist Samuel Richardson did all of these. Rather, translations of his parliamentary reporting and his essays into French, German, Spanish, and Russian are reported to him, and his reactions are described or surmised. None of these translations was traced by J. D. Fleeman in his authoritative *Bibliography of the Works of Samuel Johnson*; their absence speaks to the difficulty of gauging just how much of Johnson's writing was translated in the long eighteenth century. To this day we do not know how many of Johnson's works have been translated, when, by whom, or into which languages.

Some of the difficulty comes from the nature of Johnson's oeuvre. With the exception of *Rasselas*, Johnson's best-known prose works were made up of short, discrete textual units – debates, essays, biographies, or criticism of individual plays – which might be translated on their own or, in the case of a few essays, in conjunction with their conclusions. To study *Rasselas* across languages is not easy; it entails tracing a few key words that may be expected to appear in the translated texts' titles. Translated, adjusted to the orthography of the target language or transliterated, combinations of the words *prince*, *Abyssinia*, *valley*, and *Rasselas* should yield results in national library catalogues, standard bibliographies, and (by outguessing the vagaries of optical character recognition) digital libraries. But to study the *Rambler* in translation properly is far more difficult: it entails tracing each of the 208 essays separately.

To complicate matters further, the immediate source text for a translated *Rambler* might be a reprint in a contemporary periodical, often without a number or title, or in an anthology such as Vicesimus Knox's *Elegant Extracts* (1784) under a title adapted, augmented, or wholly composed by the anthologizer. The immediate source text for a translated *Rambler* may itself be a translation, as French and, to a lesser extent, German and Italian served as "pivot languages," with further variance in title. A comprehensive survey of Johnson in translation would therefore require a team of polyglot Johnsonians reading their way through every miscellaneous publication appearing in every language for which cultural transfer from English is documented from the date of his first publication, and they would have to be familiar enough with both the Johnson canon and the target languages in their successive historical states to detect cross-linguistic borrowing. Such a comprehensive survey is beyond the scope of this chapter, but it is possible to look at a few representative translations of Johnson's works into Russian, Spanish, and French to illustrate the range of challenges that face students of Johnson's works in translation.

JOHNSON IN RUSSIAN

These problems are neatly illustrated with Russian examples, thanks chiefly to Yuri Levin. Fleeman lists just three Russian translations of *Rasselas*; Levin, in a survey of texts of English origin in eighteenth-century Russian periodicals and anthologies, lists ten translated *Ramblers*, one *Idler*, and "The Vision of Theodore, Hermit of Teneriffe."[2] Of the *Rambler* essays with Russian afterlives, six were Oriental tales or fables (nos. 38, 65, 120, 190, 204, and 205), two dream-visions (nos. 11 and 102), and one a character portrait, the story of Polyphilus, an inveterate dabbler (no. 19). Only *Rambler* 11, a meditation on anger, is purely discursive, as is *Idler* 68, on the history of translation in Europe. These figures are instructive: they tell us that it was chiefly as a writer of narrative that Johnson found an eighteenth-century Russian readership, as many of the fictive source texts were subsequently reprinted or retranslated, some of them as many as six times over. Retranslation was not, of course, a phenomenon peculiar to Russia: a *Rambler* essay might be translated from English into German and thence into French, where it is identified as a German text; into German and thence into English, identified as a German text; or into French and thence back into English, identified as a French one!

Among those to retranslate *Rambler* 65, "Obidah and the Hermit," into Russian was "a Youth Assiduously Devoted to Learning," whose work was printed in pamphlet form in 1786 and 1788. The former featured as a parallel text the immediate source for Johnson's tale, drawn from *Der Lehrmeister oder ein allgemeines System der Erziehung* (Leipzig, 1765–7), itself a German translation of *The Preceptor*. The text had been recommended by the studious youth's grandmother, Catherine the Great, at an uncertain date. It is possible, then, that news of Catherine's literary commission to her grandson Semyon Veliky lay behind the report that reached Johnson of a Russian *Rambler* in 1784 (Boswell, *Life*, 4:276–7). The appeal of Johnson's Oriental tales was also felt in more popular

Moscow periodicals later in the century, such as *Chtenie dlia vkusa, gasuma i chuvstvovanii* (1791–3), which printed a new translation of *Rambler* 38, of which yet another version appeared in *Ippokrena, ili utekhi liubosloviia* (1799–1801), for which the two-part "History of Seged" (*Rambler*s 204 and 205) was also translated. Levin notes that the *Rambler* and the *Adventurer* "acquired greater importance" as the century progressed, for "their scepticism and propagation of stoicism were in keeping with the sentiments of many Russian readers," and the numbers he offers bear this out, for though few texts by Johnson were translated, they were among those most often retranslated.[3]

JOHNSON IN SPANISH

If Johnson in Russia was known chiefly through the mediation of other languages, it is the lack of mediation – of a pivot language – that makes his fate in eighteenth-century Spain of particular interest. Until the 1790s Spain saw few translations of English texts, and fewer still directly from English-language sources. Translators based their work on French and, occasionally, Italian versions. To translate directly from English was the mark of either polyglot cosmopolitanism or Anglophilia; and Samuel Johnson may, quantifiably, by volume of words, be the author most extensively translated from English into Spanish in the eighteenth century.

Johnsonian in origin are the first direct English-to-Spanish translation of a periodical essay, that of *Idler* 102, which appeared unsigned in the Madrid weekly *El novelero de los estrados* in December 1764; the first such translation of a book-length English fiction, Inés Joyes y Blake's *El príncipe de Abisinia* (1798), for which *Rasselas* is the unacknowledged source text; and the first such translation of a series of English periodical essays, the thirteen unsigned *Rambler*s published in the biweekly *Correo de Valencia* in 1798 and 1799. Johnson's name would also be associated with the earliest translation of English Shakespeare criticism into Spanish: an extract from the preface to Shakespeare, included by German-born Johann Nikolas Böhl von Faber in his *Pasatiempo crítico*, a key text for the reception of German and English Romantic poetics in Spain.

Apart from their Johnsonian connection and status as landmarks, these translations are important to Spanish literary history. The concerns of *Idler* 102 – writers and literary biography, their reputations and experience of sociability as conditioned by their own participation in print culture, patrons, and coffee houses – are those of a writer addressing other writers, and the question of writers' status would seldom have been more topical in Spain than in 1764, when the regulatory framework of publishing had just been changed by royal decree, and intellectual property made transferable by inheritance. Written amidst the first flowering of the periodical press in eighteenth-century Spain, the translated *Idler* is locally inscribed by introductory matter and interpolations, becoming a reflection on the professionalization of *literatos*.

Joyes y Blake's translation of *Rasselas* is effectively an appeal for the better schooling of *literatas*, for her verbal portraits of the women characters, Nekayah and Pekuah, show them to be as linguistically and intellectually gifted as their male counterparts. In a sense, Joyes y Blake supplemented the famous conclusion "in which nothing is concluded" by having her only known original work, the proto-feminist tract "Apologia de las mugeres," bound together with her translation. The intended counterpoint between polemic and fiction makes Nekayah's choice in life – to found a college for learned women – all the more memorable when Joyes y Blake argues that women be allowed to undertake traditionally male studies. Gender was likewise at issue when *Rambler* 18 – whose persona is "a neutral being between the sexes" (*Works*, 3:98) weighing the claims of men and women – appeared in the *Correo de Valencia* months after Joyes y Blake's *Rasselas*.

JOHNSON IN FRENCH

The volume of translation into Russian and Spanish is dwarfed by the volume of translation into French, which was to educated Europeans of the eighteenth century the international language that English is today. Before Johnson had finished writing the *Rambler*, its assimilation by French-language print culture had already begun in the pages of Berlin's *Petit réservoir, contenant un varieté de faits historiques et critiques, de litterature, de morale et de poësies*, with *Rambler*s 15 and 18 appearing in 1751. Extracts from the *Rambler* or translations of whole essays may also be found in the *Journal britannique* in March 1751, in the Frankurt-based *Rambler ou Le Rodeur* in 1752, Copenhagen's *Traducteur* in 1754–6, and Jean-Jacques Rousseau and Friedrich Melchior Grimm's *Journal étranger* in 1754, among them the *Rambler* poached by Arthur Murphy and *Rambler* 4, treating fictions of contemporary middle-class life, on which a Spanish retranslation would be based in 1764. The following decades saw continuing translation and retranslation, particularly of the allegories and Oriental tales, as well as a *Morceaux choisis du Rambler* in 1785 and a complete set in two volumes, *Le Rodeur*, in 1786.

The *Morceaux choisis* mentions Johnson by name; *Le Rodeur* does not. It is not easy to judge whether these publications were capitalizing on Johnson's literary celebrity, magnified by his death in 1784. In the 1750s and 1760s Johnson's fame had been such that the editors of *Les Affiches de Lyons* were anxious to procure his works, while in the 1770s and 1780s two Swiss francophone journals included Johnson among the handful of English-language writers whose works were reviewed. And as a critic of Shakespeare, Johnson was sufficiently well known to be deployed against translators who accommodated national taste to the detriment of fidelity. Pierre le Tourneur, in affixing translated English Shakespeare criticism to the first volume of his *Shakespeare traduit de l'anglois, dédié au roi* (1776–82, a deliberate departure from the more transformative practice of Pierre-Antoine de la Place), took more from Johnson than from all other English Shakespeare critics combined. The same volume introduced French readers to the neologism "romantique," and the conjunction of Johnson, Shakespeare, and Romanticism would reoccur over forty years later in the works of Stendhal.

THE NINETEENTH CENTURY AND BEYOND

Howard Weinbrot has written eloquently of Johnson's historicization in nineteenth-century France, where his afterlife in English biography, and especially in Macaulay, came to tinge, or even to dye, responses to him. The phenomenon was not limited to France. What Weinbrot says of the French literary historian Hippolyte Taine holds for the similarly influential Spanish critic Marcelino Menéndez y Pelayo: their Johnson is a blunt, bad-tempered, narrow-minded zealot, as well as a poor stylist. The pace of Johnson translation would slow as a consequence, leaving *Rasselas* as the only text readily available to readers of other languages; and academic output on Johnson from Continental European Anglicists remains low in proportion to their work on other writers.

Simply put, Johnson was not part of everyone's English canon; English canons were local creations, existing at the confluence of the discipline of English and the publishing initiatives that rely on universities and high schools to foster demand. Like languages, they have both an internal and an external history: Japan, for instance, has had a rich tradition of Johnsonian scholarship and translation for over a century and boasts a large scholarly Johnson society. Interest may surge as knowledge of English and contact with English-speaking academe consolidate: thus Spain has seen eight Johnsonian publications and China two in the last decade. Peaks and troughs need historicizing, to be sure, but the need for dialogic engagement with the translations themselves, from whatever period, is far greater, for the original is to any translator what a score is to a pianist – a kind of backstory, understood differently with each performance.

NOTES

1 Thomas Carlyle, *Samuel Johnson* (London, 1853), p. 102; René Wellek, *A History of Modern Criticism, 1750–1950*, 8 vols. (New Haven, CT: Yale University Press, 1955–92), 1:84.
2 Y. D. Levin, *The Perception of English Literature in Russia*, trans. Catherine Philips (Nottingham: Astra Press, 1994), pp. 1–68.
3 Y. D. Levin, "English Literature in Eighteenth-Century Russia," *Modern Language Review* 89, no. 4 (1994), p. xxix.

CHAPTER 6

Critical reception to 1900

Katherine Turner

RESPO'NSE. *n.s.* [*responsum*, Lat.]
1. An answer.

> The oracles, which had before flourished, began to droop, and from giving *responses* in verse, descended to prose, and within a while were utterly silenced. *Hammond.*

Samuel Johnson, one of the earliest professional critics of literature, was writing at a time when literary criticism as a discipline was still in its infancy. The history of his early critical reception must therefore take account of a diverse range of published responses. Even once we move from the eighteenth century into the nineteenth, a period that witnessed the institutionalizing of English literature, it is important to register not only the high intellectual tradition of responses to Johnson, but also his significance within more popular cultural contexts. Still the most comprehensive list of early responses to Johnson, James L. Clifford and Donald J. Greene's indispensable *Samuel Johnson: A Survey and Bibliography of Critical Studies* (1970), admits in its introduction that it would be impossible to list "every discussion of Johnson."[1] Quite so: and yet critical work on the Romantic and Victorian periods in recent years has discovered unexpected new arenas of response to Johnson.

PUBLIC PROPERTY

"Long before his death on 13 December 1784, Samuel Johnson was public property," observe Robert E. Kelley and O M Brack, Jr., tapping into a rich vein of economic metaphor which often appears in discussions of Johnson's significance.[2] Beginning with the *Rambler* essays in 1750–2, Johnson's publications always generated discussion, and his private and social life soon became a topic of equal, if not surpassing, curiosity. James T. Boulton, compiler of the invaluable anthology of early responses,

Johnson: The Critical Heritage (1971), observes that Johnson "was constantly before the public: whether to acclaim or admonish, a succession of reviews, pamphlets, and books kept him there."[3] Helen Louise McGuffie's checklist of Johnson's appearances during his lifetime in British newspapers and magazines testifies abundantly to his celebrity status (and to his marketability for the publishing industry).[4] Johnson himself appears to have relished his controversial standing, doubtless aware that, for a man who made a living through writing, there was no such thing as bad publicity: "It is advantageous to an authour, that his book should be attacked as well as praised. Fame is a shuttlecock. If it be struck only at one end of the room, it will soon fall to the ground. To keep it up, it must be struck at both ends" (Boswell, *Life*, 5:400).

This was certainly the fate of the three books that established Johnson at the center of national literary life: the *Dictionary* (1755), *Rasselas* (1759), and the edition of Shakespeare (1765). Initial response to the *Dictionary* (including an anonymous notice by Adam Smith in the fledgling *Edinburgh Review*) was positive, but lexicographers soon found fault with Johnson's eccentric procedure and his faulty linguistic history. The authority of the *Dictionary* proved difficult to dislodge, however: as late as 1807, Noah Webster felt compelled to catalogue Johnson's shortcomings as a lexicographer in order to prove the necessity of his own projected dictionary for the American people. His opening remarks are couched in economic terms: "The great intellectual powers of Dr. Johnson, displayed in many of his works, but especially in his *Rambler* and his *Rasselas*, have raised his reputation to high distinction, and impressed upon all his opinions a stamp of *authority*, which gives them a currency among men, without an examination into their intrinsic value."[5] Echoing earlier commentators, Webster complains that Johnson's knowledge of early languages is deficient; that he includes many words which simply are not English, because they are either too "Latinate" or "vulgar and cant"; that his definitions are faulty and his chosen "illustrations" (quotations) often irrelevant; and that he therefore "tends very much to corrupt and pervert the language."[6] Not everyone, though, was impressed by Webster: Thomas Jefferson, for instance, not only failed to support Webster's own project, but also confessed privately to having used Johnson's *Dictionary* "as a Repertory to find favorite passages" from writers.[7] This is an early example of how the appeal of the *Dictionary* goes far beyond its actual use value as a source of accurate definitions.

As Webster's observations suggest, *Rasselas* received widespread respect for its moral value, but its stylistic heaviness was criticized – a duality which has continued to characterize responses to the tale. Owen

Ruffhead, for instance, derided it in the *Monthly Review* as "tumid and pompous."[8] By the time the Shakespeare edition appeared, Johnson had also begun to irritate people on personal and political grounds, particularly with his acceptance in 1762 of a pension from the king. Charles Churchill, the Whig satirist and debauched associate of the radical John Wilkes, included in his long satiric poem *The Ghost* an angry description of the critic "Pomposo," the "Vain idol of a *scribbling* crowd ... Who, cursing flatt'ry, is the tool / Of ev'ry fawning flatt'ring fool." He consolidated his attack a few months later, following news of the pension, by adding a section on "How he a slave to int'rest fell."[9] Reviewers of the Shakespeare edition were quick to pounce on Johnson's perceived unprofessionalism, complaining of his lack of editorial rigor and the absence of any really new textual scholarship. William Kenrick, a professional reviewer for the *Monthly Review* who was jealous of Johnson's reputation as the leading critic of the day, wrote a whole book attacking the edition, angrily describing Johnson's relation to Shakespeare as that of "a fungus attached to an oak," and including sarcastic remarks on "*places* and *pensions*."[10] Nevertheless, the preface was widely admired as a perceptive response to Shakespeare's genius as well as his shortcomings.

Johnson did himself no favors during the 1770s by publishing four outspoken political tracts, prompting numerous denunciations of his tyrannical Toryism: *The False Alarm* (1770), *Thoughts on the Late Transactions Respecting Falkland's Islands* (1771), *The Patriot* (1774), and *Taxation No Tyranny* (1775). The last of these, an attack on the revolt of the American colonists, aroused particular ire, and doubtless contributed to his problematic standing in America, though its abolitionist sentiments fostered admiration for Johnson in radical circles during the early nineteenth century. When *A Journey to the Western Islands of Scotland* appeared in 1775, the pleasure it afforded most English critics and readers was counterbalanced by the indignation of the Scottish press at Johnson's apparently derogatory observations on Scotland, which inspired several book-length ripostes lambasting the "contemptible ideas" of "the silly Doctor."[11] Mary Ann Hanway was one of the few women who joined the fray, weaving a critique of Johnson into her own *Journey to the Highlands of Scotland*.[12] After the initial flurry of nationalistic debate, the *Journey* rather disappeared from readers' Johnsonian horizons until George Birkbeck Hill published his pilgrimage narrative, *The Footsteps of Dr. Johnson*, in 1890.[13] But the contemptuous remarks Johnson had made in the *Journey* about James Macpherson's claims to have "discovered" the works of the ancient Scottish bard Ossian contributed to Johnson's lasting reputation as a

Scotophobe (see chapter 32, "Nationalism"). Not surprisingly, it was the controversial works and the *Journey* which inspired most of the satirical caricatures of Johnson that appeared during his own lifetime, including prints by Gillray and Bunbury.

The *Lives of the Poets* (1779–81) consolidated Johnson's standing as the preeminent critic of his day, and provoked a barrage of responses. While in general it was difficult to quarrel with the sheer bulk of his achievement in the *Lives*, eyebrows were raised at his sometimes eccentric inclusion of biographical detail. His hostile pronouncements on John Milton and Thomas Gray, moreover, prompted indignation well into the nineteenth century. Joseph Warton spoke for many in complaining of Johnson's "tasteless and groundless objections to the Lycidas of Milton, and to the Bard of Gray,"[14] and in suggesting that Johnson simply lacked the poetic sensibility to appreciate new developments in lyric poetry. In 1782 William Tindal published an anonymous book-length defense of Gray, while James Thomson Callender aired grievances about Johnson in general and the *Lives* in particular. His substantial pamphlet, *Deformities of Dr. Samuel Johnson*, provides "copious quotations from Dr. Johnson's ponderous abortions" to prove that "No writer … has discovered more contempt for other men's reputations, or more confidence in his own."[15]

The poet William Cowper's irritation with Johnson's remarks on Milton is often quoted – "he has no Ear for Poetical Numbers [meter]" – but in fact Cowper took the trouble to read all of the *Lives*, and pronounced himself "very much the Biographer's humble admirer."[16] Percival Stockdale, an irascible publisher, labored for years on his own *Lectures on the Truly Eminent English Poets*, which appeared in 1807, full of angry expostulation with Johnson's judgments, but did little to dislodge Johnson from his position of critical authority, and served mainly to renew public interest in the *Lives*. The posthumously published *Letters* of Johnson's acquaintance Anna Seward, testament to her longstanding "inability to stop arguing with Johnson," likewise revealed little more than their own "failure … to challenge his critical authority."[17] The *Lives*, for all the attacks they withstood, remained the standard template for literary biography throughout the nineteenth century.

THE POSTHUMOUS DOUBLE TRADITION

Johnson's death in December 1784 stimulated a rash of short biographies, generally structured around his publication career, though offering little critical discussion of the works themselves. Private information on

Johnson was not yet widely available: once it did emerge, however – in Boswell's *Life*, Hester Thrale Piozzi's *Anecdotes*, and Sir John Hawkins's *Life* – the stage was set for the gradual eclipse of Johnson's works by the increasingly potent myth of Johnson the man.

So, at least, the story goes in most accounts of Johnson's critical reception: critic Bertrand H. Bronson in 1951 identified a "double tradition" at work in the nineteenth century, by which the cult of Johnson's personality dominated popular perceptions, while his actual works became more and more the preserve of the learned.[18] Although subjected to more nuanced development by later scholars of Johnson's reputation, this view has still remained dominant. Equally pervasive has been the notion that writers of the Romantic period all reacted strongly against Johnson's critical tyranny, as part of a Freudian repudiation of their eighteenth-century forebears.

Not entirely logically, the Romantics' alleged criticisms of Johnson – that he did not have sufficient imagination to appreciate Shakespeare, that he overvalued John Dryden and Alexander Pope – became accepted as real shortcomings of Johnson, and also came to represent the mainstream Romantic response to Johnson. Philip Smallwood has recently illuminated the more complex realities of the Romantics' Johnson, showing how the processes of literary history-making elided the very real continuities between Johnson and several of the Romantics. So, although William Wordsworth did indirectly attack Johnson's own poetic diction as an example of the "adulterated phraseology" that his own work rejected, he also shared Johnson's commonsensical distaste for Gray's artificial diction.[19] Both Johnson and Wordsworth value a poetic language that reflects "the common intercourse of life" and "never becomes obsolete" (*Works*, 7:70); and Johnson's observations on Dryden and Pope include some trenchant criticisms of their overrefinement, which were to pave the way for the Romantics' reactions against their poetic grandfathers.

Percy Bysshe Shelley's indebtedness in the *Defence of Poetry* (1821) to Imlac's observations in *Rasselas* on the duty and character of a poet is one of the most remarkable instances of Romanticism's continuity with its Johnsonian past, and still has the power to surprise readers. Although Samuel Taylor Coleridge, Thomas de Quincey, and William Hazlitt all have a go at Johnson in their writings on Shakespeare ("he was neither a poet nor a judge of poetry," Hazlitt proclaims),[20] it has to be admitted that Johnson is not really at the center of their critical world, either as hero or villain. Similarly, while the Romantics did enthusiastically enshrine Milton as the archetypal poet, we should beware of suggesting that they did so primarily out of annoyance with Johnson. For Lord Byron, in fact, Johnson remained a source of bracing common sense and stoicism: his letters are peppered with admiring references to Johnson's poems and to the *Lives* ("which I think the type of perfection"), and with remarks like this one, in a letter to his publisher John Murray: "you are in the very uttermost decline and degradation of Literature … I wish that Johnson were alive again to crush them."[21]

Johnson's standing within the diverse cultures of the Romantic period was also more complex than has traditionally been acknowledged. James G. Basker has shown that women readers and abolitionist readers, both black and white, from the late eighteenth and the nineteenth centuries in both Britain and America, found in Johnson's works a humanitarian sensibility that was more complex and powerful than his too-often-quoted private observation on women preachers – "a woman's preaching is like a dog's walking on his hinder legs. It is not done well; but you are surprized to find it done at all" (Boswell, *Life*, 1:463) – might suggest.[22] Isobel Grundy has recently developed this argument in relation to the many women writers – including Mary Wollstonecraft, as well as lesser-known novelists, travel writers, and essayists – who found in Johnson's works (not simply his biography) a valuable source of quotation and allusion, and a touchstone for morality and reason. Grundy observes that, "during the revolutionary and Napoleonic years," just when – so the story goes – everybody was supposed to be reacting against Johnson, he was in fact "much read and respected by women, who often found him useful for their own writings." She establishes an important "continuity between a Johnsonian moral humanism and a Victorian feminist sensibility."[23]

THE VICTORIANS

Rather in the way that the Romantic attack on Johnson has been exaggerated, the extent to which his works were forgotten during the Victorian period has also been overemphasized. Thomas Babington Macaulay's notorious review of Croker's edition of Boswell's *Life* (1831) and Thomas Carlyle's lecture on Johnson, Jean-Jacques Rousseau, and Robert Burns ("The Hero as Man of Letters," 1840) contributed to the growing tendency to downplay Johnson's works and focus on his personal eccentricities – whether presenting him, as Carlyle does, as a prophet and moralist, "one of our great English souls"; or, *pace* Macaulay, as a more grotesque oddity, who "dressed like a scarecrow, and ate like a cormorant."[24] But many of the pronouncements made in "high" literary circles – such as

Macaulay's observation in the *Encyclopædia Britannica* in 1856 that "the popularity of his works … has greatly diminished," or James Hay's declaration in 1884 that "Johnson's works are now almost forgotten" – bear little relation to what was happening on the ground.[25] The continuing stream of editions of Johnson's works during the nineteenth century, and the thriving trade in secondhand books, ensured Johnson's continuing popularity with Victorian readers.

Among the Victorian literati we can find evidence of admiration for Johnson in John Ruskin, George Eliot, Robert and Elizabeth Barrett Browning, and Charlotte Brontë. There is even more evidence of the currency of his works among poorer readers, including Chartists and other working-class groups. The increased provision of public education and the need for well-educated civil servants in India contributed to the institutionalization of English literature, and Johnson's writings were especially congenial to such projects on both moral and stylistic grounds. His prominence in Victorian educational anthologies continued a long-standing tradition of excerpting the highlights from his works: *The Beauties of Johnson*, arranged alphabetically by theme, had appeared as early as 1781, was many times reprinted, and was used in "several of the most reputable schools, for both sexes, in the Kingdom."[26]

The preeminent Victorian critic, Matthew Arnold, was deeply convinced of the value of Johnson's *Lives of the Poets*. In the prefatory essay to his selected edition of *Six Chief Lives* (1878), he insists that "I know of no such first-rate piece of literature, for supplying in this way the wants of the literary student, existing at all in any other language; or existing in our own language for any period except the period which Johnson's six lives cover." He contends that they will offer "young people" a unique starting point from which "they might desire to ascend upwards to our anterior literature … or downwards to the literature of yesterday and of the present."[27] Arnold chose to produce this edition of *Lives* as a means of raising money to fund his retirement, which speaks volumes about their perceived marketability.

Late nineteenth-century Johnsonian studies are dominated by Leslie Stephen and George Birkbeck Hill. Stephen wrote about Johnson at various points in his career as a critic, and his growing appreciation of Johnson's value as the embodiment of critical integrity led him to reappraise the eighteenth century that he and his contemporaries had hitherto denigrated as corrupt, godless, and frivolous. As editor, he launched an influential series of biographies – clearly modeled on Johnson's *Lives* – called the *English Men of Letters*, the first of which was his own life of

Johnson (1878), as well as the monumental sixty-three-volume *Dictionary of National Biography*, for which Stephen himself wrote the entry on Johnson in 1892.

Hill began his biographical and editorial work on Johnson and Boswell in the 1870s. His initial labors privileged the life over the work – his six-volume edition of Boswell's *Life* appeared in 1887 – but he later edited Johnson's *Letters*, two volumes of *Johnsonian Miscellanies*, and the *Lives of the Poets* (see chapter 4, "Editions"). Exhausted by ill health and extensive footnoting, Hill died in 1903, but his work had done much to position Johnson's works, not merely his personal eccentricities, at the center of English literary history. Between them, Stephen and Hill had consolidated Johnson's own brand of literary biography and affective critical response to make it freshly useful for new generations of students, scholars, and common readers.

NOTES

1 James L. Clifford and Donald J. Greene, *Samuel Johnson: A Survey and Bibliography of Critical Studies* (Minneapolis: University of Minnesota Press, 1970), p. v.
2 Robert E. Kelley and O M Brack, Jr., *Samuel Johnson's Early Biographers* (Iowa City: University of Iowa Press, 1971), p. xi.
3 James T. Boulton, ed. *Johnson: The Critical Heritage* (London: Routledge & Kegan Paul, 1971), p. 1.
4 Helen Louise McGuffie, *Samuel Johnson in the British Press, 1749–1784: A Chronological Checklist* (New York and London: Garland, 1976).
5 Boulton, *Critical Heritage*, pp. 126–7.
6 Boulton, *Critical Heritage*, p. 131.
7 James G. Basker, *Samuel Johnson in the Mind of Thomas Jefferson with Thomas Jefferson's Letter to Herbert Croft, 30 October 1798* (privately printed for the Johnsonians, 1999), p. 8.
8 Boulton, *Critical Heritage*, p. 141.
9 Charles Churchill, *The Ghost*, 2.654–62 and 3.778, in *Poetical Works of Charles Churchill*, ed. D. Grant (Oxford: Clarendon Press, 1956), pp. 97 and 126.
10 William Kenrick, *A Review of Doctor Johnson's New Edition of Shakespeare, in Which the Ignorance, or Inattention of That Editor Is Exposed* (London, 1765), pp. v, 88.
11 A. G. Sinclair, *The Critic Philosopher; or, Truth Discovered* (London, 1789), pp. 86–8.
12 Mary Ann Hanway, *A Journey to the Highlands of Scotland: With Occasional Remarks on Dr. Johnson's Tour* (London, 1776).
13 George Birkbeck Hill, *The Footsteps of Dr. Johnson (Scotland)* (London, 1890).
14 Joseph Warton, *The Works of Alexander Pope*, 9 vols. (London, 1795), 1:73 n.

15 William Tindal, *Remarks on Dr. Johnson's Life, and Critical Observations on the Works of Gray* (London, 1782); James Thomson Callender, *Deformities of Dr. Samuel Johnson: Selected from His Works*, 2nd edn. (London, 1782), pp. 88, 12.

16 *The Letters and Prose Writings of William Cowper*, ed. James King and Charles Ryskamp, 5 vols. (Oxford: Clarendon Press, 1979–86), 1:307 (letter to William Unwin, October 31, 1779); 2:226 (letter to William Unwin, March 21, 1784).

17 Adam Rounce, "Toil and Envy: Unsuccessful Responses to Johnson's *Lives of the Poets*," in Greg Clingham and Philip Smallwood, eds., *Johnson after 300 Years* (Cambridge: Cambridge University Press, 2009), pp. 186–206, at p. 186.

18 B. H. Bronson, "The Double Tradition of Dr. Johnson," in *Johnson Agonistes and Other Essays* (Berkeley: University of California Press, 1965), pp. 156–76.

19 *The Prose Works of William Wordsworth*, ed. W. J. B Owen and Jane Worthington Smyser, 3 vols. (Oxford: Clarendon Press, 1974), 1:161.

20 William Hazlitt, preface to *Characters of Shakespear's Plays* (1817), in *Selected Writings of William Hazlitt*, ed. Duncan Wu, 9 vols. (London: Pickering & Chatto, 1998), 1:88.

21 *Byron's Letters and Journals*, ed. Leslie A. Marchand, 13 vols. (London: John Murray, 1973–94), 6:72, 7:175.

22 James G. Basker, "Dancing Dogs, Women Preachers and the Myth of Johnson's Misogyny," *The Age of Johnson*, 3 (1990), 63–90.

23 Isobel Grundy, "Early Women Reading Johnson," in Clingham and Smallwood, eds., *Johnson after 300 Years*, pp. 207–24, at pp. 207, 214.

24 Thomas Carlyle, "The Hero as Man of Letters: Johnson, Rousseau, Burns," in *The Works of Thomas Carlyle*, 30 vols. (London, 1897), 5:178; *The Complete Works of Thomas Babington Macaulay*, 10 vols. (Boston and New York: Houghton Mifflin, 1910), 10:68.

25 Macaulay, *Works*, 10:95; James Hay, *Johnson: His Characteristics and Aphorisms* (London, 1884), p. vi.

26 Boulton, *Critical Heritage*, p. 14.

27 *The Complete Prose Works of Matthew Arnold*, ed. R. H. Super, 11 vols. (Ann Arbor: Michigan University Press, 1960–77), 8:310–12.

CHAPTER 7

Critical reception since 1900

Greg Clingham

RECE'PTION. *n.s.* [*receptus*, Latin.]
7. Opinion generally admitted.

> Philosophers, who have quitted the popular doctrines of their countries, have fallen into as extravagant opinions, as even common *reception* countenanced. *Locke.*

Like Chaucer, Shakespeare, Milton, Wordsworth, Austen, and Dickens, Samuel Johnson has been accepted by the twentieth century as one of the great English writers. His life and writings have attracted enormous scholarly attention, yet they also appeal to students, professionals, and ordinary readers. Challenging and full of life, Johnson's writings continue to hold out the possibility of new discoveries for many different kinds of readers, even those who know him well.

Scholarly attention to Johnson in the twentieth century falls into four general categories:

1 great scholarly editions of Johnson's works by G. B. Hill, David Nicol Smith and E. L. McAdam, R. W. Chapman, J. D. Fleeman, Bruce Redford, and Roger Lonsdale, and *The Yale Edition of the Works of Samuel Johnson*;
2 impressive bibliographical works by J. D. Fleeman and others, which have established the large Johnson canon from his own time down to ours;
3 informative, inquiring biographies of Johnson by James L. Clifford, John Wain, Walter Jackson Bate, Thomas Kaminski, Robert DeMaria, Lawrence Lipking, and David Nokes, which have helped to structure the narrative of his intellectual and personal life; and
4 abundant and various critical interpretations which have increased our understanding of Johnson's works in themselves, in relation to his life and the lives of his friends and associates, and in relation to a comprehensive range of historical and literary records.

The intellectual richness of Johnson's writings is suggested by the many contexts in which they have been discussed: religion, morality, the problem of evil, hope, ideas of greatness, ideas of littleness, psychological theory, happiness, the crowd, law, science, medicine, politics, Jacobitism, journalism, Grub Street, book reviewing, history, intellectual history, literary history, property, slavery, the body, women, feminism, the history of scholarship, travel, the Celtic revival, Romance, lexicography, philology, Augustanism, neoclassical theory, literary criticism, literary and critical theory, biography, the essay, poetry, tragedy, the arts, landscape, authorship, print culture, engrammatology, philosophy, skeptical thinking, postcoloniality, and cosmopolitanism are just some of the approaches critics have taken in recent years. We have fine monographs on individual works or groups of Johnson's works, particularly the Shakespeare edition, the *Lives of the Poets*, *Rasselas* (now the most widely read single work by Johnson), and the *Dictionary* (which runs *Rasselas* a close second in popularity). And among the best works on Johnson are overarching accounts of his whole oeuvre, such as Walter Jackson Bate's *Achievement of Samuel Johnson* (1955), Paul Fussell's *Samuel Johnson and the Life of Writing* (1971), and Charles H. Hinnant's *Samuel Johnson: An Analysis* (1988).

T. S. ELIOT

In many ways, how we read Johnson today originates with T. S. Eliot and F. R. Leavis almost a hundred years ago. Readers in 1900 inherited a Johnson whose celebrity was rooted in the moral rectitude of his arguments, and the power and eccentricity of his personality. But Walter Raleigh's *Six Essays on Johnson* (1910) took Johnson's criticism seriously for the first time since Matthew Arnold, and Eliot and Leavis found his literary thinking and his poetry to be grist to their mill as they developed their own views.

In "Tradition and the Individual Talent" (1917), Eliot – followed by the New Critics – argued that great poetry was not necessarily expressive of a "great personality": "the more perfect the artist, the more completely separate in him will be the man who suffers and the mind which creates; the more perfectly will the mind digest and transmute the passions which are its material."[1] Eliot sought impersonality and technical virtuosity in literature, and found them, to some extent, in Johnson's poetry. Unlike most readers of Johnson since the Romantic era, but very much in keeping with eighteenth-century values (and with Wordsworth's preface to *Lyrical Ballads*), Eliot affirmed the continuity of good poetry and good prose; for

Eliot both Johnson's poetry and his prose reflected his profound thoughtfulness and powerful style. Eliot implicitly appeals to this unity of mind in Johnson when, in a much-quoted essay, "The Metaphysical Poets" (1921), he took Johnson's analysis of Metaphysical wit seriously, even though it was critical of a style in which, in Johnson's words, "the most heterogeneous ideas are yoked by violence together" (*Lives*, 1:200). While John Donne, Andrew Marvell, and other Metaphysical poets feature prominently in Eliot's own aesthetic, he nonetheless values Johnson's *resistance* to their writing, for Eliot saw Johnson as a skilled and profoundly knowledgeable reader of poetry who deserved careful consideration.

THE MID-CENTURY

It would be sixty years before Eliot's view – that Johnson could actually teach us something about literature – would resurface. The 1940s, 1950s, and 1960s saw the development of two generally related lines of inquiry constituting the growing field of Johnson studies, formulated in Bertrand Bronson's essay, "The Double Tradition of Dr. Johnson" (1951). One line of inquiry concerned the popular image of Johnson the eccentric man of letters, the bluff Tory, and boisterous conversationalist, celebrated in Boswell's *Life of Johnson*, and popularized by Macaulay's caricature of Johnson. Boswell's biography continued to be a main source of biographical information, though used with growing skepticism as to its own fictional nature, and in some ways surpassed by modern biographers, who draw on a broader archive and richer contextual materials.

The second line of inquiry identified by Bronson had to do with the consideration of Johnson's writings in their own terms and as part of literary history. This trend generated very wide critical attention to the whole range of Johnson's works, producing scholarship that helped to form Johnson's identity as a great English writer, including (among many other books and important articles) William K. Wimsatt's *Prose Style of Samuel Johnson* (1941) and *Philosophic Words* (1948), Jean Hagstrum's *Samuel Johnson's Literary Criticism* (1952), Walter Jackson Bate's *Achievement of Samuel Johnson* (1955), Edward Bloom's *Samuel Johnson in Grub Street* (1957), Donald Greene's *Politics of Samuel Johnson* (1960), Robert Voitle's *Samuel Johnson the Moralist* (1961), Maurice Quinlan's *Samuel Johnson: A Layman's Religion* (1964), Paul Alkon's *Samuel Johnson and Moral Discipline* (1967), and Chester Chapin's *Religious Thought of Samuel Johnson* (1968). This body of work established Johnson as a serious moral, religious, and political writer, an identity that has continued to be refined and developed since the 1980s, as we see, for example, in the contribution made to the understanding of Johnson's political thinking by Jonathan Clark, Howard Erskine-Hill, and other scholars arguing both for and against Johnson's putative Jacobitism and the nature of his party affiliation (see chapter 35, "Politics").

JOHNSON AS CRITIC

At the same time, however, while Eliot's essay on "Johnson as Critic and Poet" (1944) still adverted to his critical acumen, few saw anything other than commonplaces in Johnson's reading of the writers in the English canon, especially Shakespeare, the Metaphysical poets, and Milton. Influential critics – F. R. Leavis, Allen Tate, M. H. Abrams, Hagstrum, and Wimsatt – referred to Johnson's greatness as a critic while providing inadequate accounts of his particular judgments, his general critical propositions, or, with the exception of Wimsatt's view of Johnson's philosophical rationality, the creative use of his prose as a critical tool. Instead critics generally found evidence of Johnson's *inability* to read poetry well. Thus for Tate and Abrams, Johnson fails to understand the nature of metaphor when discussing Donne's poetry and four famous lines in Sir John Denham's *Cooper's Hill*:

> O could I flow like thee, and make thy stream
> My great example, as it is my theme!
> Though deep, yet clear; though gentle, yet not dull;
> Strong without rage, without o'er-flowing full.
>
> (*Lives*, 1:238–9)

For Leavis, Johnson's view of Shakespeare's plays as a "mingled drama," in which "nature" is the touchstone eliciting a moral response, reveals his "inability to appreciate the more profoundly creative uses of language … concreteness and metaphorical life."[2] For Hagstrum, Johnson held a simpleminded epistemology based on the work of John Locke, and thus produced abstract, neoclassical commonplaces when compared to the more sophisticated psychological and linguistic astuteness of Samuel Taylor Coleridge and modern critics. Many echoed these views of Johnson's limitations in reading literature, even though they failed to consider the dynamic function of Johnson's style and the form of his thought, his particular use of common eighteenth-century terminology, and a full range of literary contexts. They also took as a given the notion of the rational, formal, neoclassical nature of eighteenth-century thought, and thus failed to *read* Johnson critically: to give due weight to his particular judgments and insights about the experiential power of Shakespeare's drama, Milton's poetic sublimity, Abraham Cowley's fecundity, the imaginative pleasures of John Dryden's and Alexander Pope's translations, the surprising sensibility of Pope's elegies and satires, and the lively blank verse of James Thomson, Edward Young, and Mark Akenside, to mention only some topics on which Johnson writes critically and appreciatively (see chapter 27, "Literary criticism").

Between the 1940s and the 1970s scholars had difficulty escaping the idea that Johnson was so embedded in the culture of his own time and place that he could not see beyond the refined, artificial, and polite Augustan couplet popularized by Matthew Prior, Edmund Waller, and John Denham, and brought to perfection by the greater energy and satiric discursiveness of Dryden and Pope. But there were important exceptions to this trend, including Bate's *Achievement of Samuel Johnson* – supplemented in 1977 by his monumental biography, *Samuel Johnson* – and Fussell's *Samuel Johnson and the Life of Writing*. Both were sensitive to the social, psychological, moral, *and* literary aspects of Johnson's thought, especially as it was shaped by the creativity and ironic deliberation of his style. And the continuing relevance and acuteness of Johnson's literary criticism for our own day has been argued by Leo Damrosch's *Uses of Johnson's Criticism* (1976), G. F. Parker's *Johnson's Shakespeare* (1989), Greg Clingham's *Johnson, Writing and Memory* (2002), and Philip Smallwood's *Johnson's Critical Presence: Image, History, Judgment* (2004).

It is no accident that these books – in addition to others by Lawrence Lipking, Philip Davis, Catherine Parke, and Blanford Parker – appreciate the *inwardness* of Johnson's thought. Common among these very different scholars is the view that the quality of Johnson's thought, in its search for truth, is inseparable from the *manner* of his writing. It is as imaginative literature – rather than as a series of abstract ideas – that his thought is most effective and most fully engaged. The great praise that Johnson gives to Dryden's critical prose applies to Johnson himself: "the criticism of Dryden is the criticism of a poet … a gay and vigorous dissertation, where delight is mingled with instruction, and where the author proves his right to judgment by his power of performance" (*Lives*, 2:120).

THE 1980S AND AFTER

Since the 1980s we have immersed ourselves in Johnson's words and views, increasing our familiarity and appreciation, as we see in the success of the leading journal in the field, *The Age of Johnson: A Scholarly Annual* (first published in 1987), and the huge number of articles on every conceivable aspect of Johnson's writing registered in Jack Lynch's online bibliography of Johnsonian studies.[3] Johnson has simultaneously become for us a more contemporaneous thinker about language, literature, time, politics, identity, writing, meaning, class, gender, race, and slavery. We have acquired a fuller understanding of the interpretive contexts of his writing and of their range and caliber in a number of areas, as we see in Nicholas Hudson on Johnson's intellectual and social world, James Engell on Johnson's position in the history of criticism, Lynch on Johnson's knowledge of literary history, Weinbrot on the nature of Johnson's political thought, and DeMaria and Reddick on the remarkable linguistic and encyclopedic entity that is the *Dictionary of the English Language*. And we also now find Johnson to be increasingly consonant with contemporary priorities and theoretical interests. Isobel Grundy, Kathleen Kemmerer, Charles Haskell Hinnant, and Freya Johnston have identified Johnson's feminist perspectives and his textual relationship with women writers, James G. Basker has developed the deep emancipatory narrative in Johnson's life and writings, Greg Clingham and Philip Smallwood have elicited Johnson's historiographical thought about past and present, and Clement Hawes has argued for a cosmopolitan, anti-imperialistic consciousness in Johnson's writings.

JOHNSON AND THE THEORISTS

In looking back over a century of extraordinary technological and critical change it is remarkable that none of the major critical paradigm shifts have had much use for Johnson. This may be a product of the tyranny of academic orthodoxies, but it also reflects the difficulty in a postmodern culture, given to the sheer relativity of the sign, of appropriating a writer who combines skepticism with definitiveness, relativity with truth, and particularity with universals so seamlessly and authoritatively across such a variety of texts. None of the main New Critics had any positive use for Johnson in their poetic or critical pantheons. Neither has deconstruction, postmodernism, discourse analysis, or the new historicism acquired much purchase on Johnson. Stephen Greenblatt and Stanley Fish have had nothing to say about him, Jacques Derrida's eighteenth-century icon was not Johnson but Jean-Jacques Rousseau, and Harold Bloom's bland assertions about Johnson as poetic "agon" have no chance of capturing his complexities or appealing to modern readers.[4]

Notable exceptions to this indifference to Johnson among literary theorists, however, include Terry Eagleton's account of Johnson's importance in the development of the modern institution of literary criticism, and David Simpson's appreciation of Johnson's understanding of language and writing, making Johnson "the exemplary man of letters of the modern period" and perhaps even the "complete candidate for the title of the first postmodernist."[5] Striking too is Frank Kermode's discussion of Johnson's oft-misunderstood remarks on the horror of *King Lear* – a vision of tragedy that is felt as unnatural by Johnson – as an indication that he "is responding to tragedy more deeply than we, who profess to be more easily persuaded."[6]

The principle of thought in Johnson identified by Kermode here is perhaps Johnson's most valuable contribution to contemporary *theory*. The *resistance* of Johnson's critical formulation, in his comment on *King Lear*, to the death of Cordelia registers the "confrontation" of different values, that of tragedy and nature. Johnson's own writing is crucial in creating that confrontation, for it is in his *writing* that he registers and mediates the experiential *difference* that is the very subject of theoretical thinking. Yet this manner of thinking (and of writing) is for Johnson very much part of the "task of criticism," which is, he says in *Rambler* 92, to "establish principles" (*Works*, 4:122). As Christopher Ricks explains, Johnson "everywhere made clear that his refusal to elaborate and concatenate the needed concepts beyond a certain point (a point reached early) was not a refusal to continue to think, but a decision to think thereafter about the application of the principles and not to elaborate principles into theory."[7] In this application of principle to experience through writing lies Johnson's "vast honesty" (in Ricks's words), and it makes him one of the great English critics.

NOTES

1 T. S. Eliot, *Selected Essays* (London: Faber and Faber, 1972), p. 18.

2 F. R. Leavis, "Johnson and Augustanism," in *The Common Pursuit* (Harmondsworth: Penguin, 1952), pp. 97–115, at p. 110.

3 http://andromeda.rutgers.edu/~jlynch/Johnson/sjbib.html
4 Harold Bloom, *The Western Canon: The Books and School of the Ages* (New York: Harcourt, Brace, 1994).
5 Terry Eagleton, *The Function of Criticism: From the Spectator to Post-Structuralism* (London: Verso, 1984), chaps. 2 and 4, and David Simpson, *The Academic Postmodern and the Rule of Literature* (Chicago: University of Chicago Press, 1995), pp. 36–7.
6 Frank Kermode, *Renaissance Essays* (London: Collins, 1973), p. 171.
7 Christopher Ricks, "Literary Principles as against Theory," in *Essays in Appreciation* (Oxford: Clarendon Press, 1996), pp. 322–3.

CHAPTER 8

Representations

Robert Folkenflik

> PO'RTRAITURE. *n.s.* [*pourtraiture*, Fr. from *portray*] Picture; painted resemblance.
>
> By the image of my cause I see
> The *portraiture* of his. *Shakesp. Hamlet.*

The emphasis in this chapter is on representations of Johnson from his lifetime, as well as those from the years between his death and 1800. This terminus leaves out the Victorian paintings and engravings usually based upon scenes described in Boswell's *Life of Johnson*. Along with portraits I will consider caricatures and other satiric representations, as well as some statues, busts, and engravings.

EARLY PORTRAITS

Until he was almost forty Samuel Johnson was nearly anonymous: only four short publications had appeared with his name (see chapter 2, "Publication history"). It is therefore unsurprising that there are no paintings of Johnson before he achieved fame. Two images supposedly dating from Johnson's youth – the miniature said to have been worn by his wife in a bracelet and a moony young man leaning on a copy of *Irene* – are unlikely to be what they claim, and the so-called *Infant Johnson*, even if it should prove to be of him, is a later production of Sir Joshua Reynolds. The earliest verifiable visual representation of Johnson, in which he is also anonymous, appears in the allegorical frontispiece to the *Gentleman's Magazine* (1747) showing the editor, Edward Cave, and his assistants. Johnson, second of those behind the six-foot Cave, towers recognizably over the others (figure 4).

DIFFUSING FRIENDSHIP

Unlike Jonathan Swift, Johnson was a willing sitter, and criticized a friend's parents who refused to have their portraits painted: "Sir, among

Figure 4 Frontispiece to the *Gentleman's Magazine* (1747).

the anfractuosities of the human mind, I know not if it may not be one, that there is a superstitious reluctance to sit for a picture" (Boswell, *Life*, 4:4). (His *Dictionary* defines *anfractuousness* as "Fulness of windings and turnings.") *Idler* 45 displays Johnson's personal preference for portraits over historical paintings: "I should grieve to see Reynolds transfer to heroes and to goddesses, to empty splendor and to airy fiction, that art which is now employed in diffusing friendship, in reviving tenderness, in quickening the affections of the absent, and continuing the presence of the dead" (*Works*, 2:140).

Johnson had his own collection of portrait prints, and at the height of his fame there was a demand for engravings of him. A printed receipt requiring Charles Dilly to deliver thirty "heads of Dr. Johnson, large octavo" (1781) is tipped into an extra-illustrated volume of Croker's edition of Johnson's *Lives* in Harvard's Houghton Library. After Johnson's death, Boswell remarks "the extraordinary zeal of the artists to extend and perpetuate his image" (Boswell, *Life*, 4:421). Despite the cultural roles he

Figure 5 Sir Joshua Reynolds, *Dictionary Johnson* (1756–7).

saw portraiture playing and his own willingness to sit, Johnson was often satiric about the resulting images. He characterized three portraits of himself as "Blinking Sam," "Surly Sam," and "Johnson's Grimly Ghost."

SIR JOSHUA REYNOLDS

The foremost portraitist of Johnson was also the first, and became one of his closest friends: Joshua Reynolds, the most famous British painter of his day (see chapter 45, "Visual arts"). Reynolds's four portraits are the best-known images of Johnson. Listed in probable chronological order and including current owners, they are *Dictionary Johnson* (National Portrait Gallery, London), the Knole portrait (in private hands), *Blinking Sam* (Henry E. Huntington Galleries), and the Streatham portrait (Tate Britain). No British writer has been portrayed in a better series of paintings.

Dictionary Johnson (1756–7) is a distinctly different painting now from what it was between 1977 and 2009, thanks to the sensitive and informed

Figure 6 Sir Joshua Reynolds, *Samuel Johnson* (1769); the Knole portrait.

restoration at the National Portrait Gallery by Helen White of a painting vandalized with a hammer-blow in 2007 by what the National Portrait Gallery delicately calls a "member of the public." Johnson, sitting with a quill pen in his right hand and his cramped left hand upon a desk, is no longer cartoonish and pink, as he had appeared before the painting was restored (figure 5). One volume of Johnson's *Dictionary* now appears next to another book, as it does in the engraving of 1791. (It had been painted over by the previous restorer under the false impression that it was a later addition.) The extra pen in the inkpot on the desk is typical of a number of Reynolds's male portraits. Reynolds kept this painting of Johnson in his house until he gave it to Boswell at the time of the publication of the *Life* (1791), where an engraving of it serves as frontispiece. Reynolds's portrait captures Johnson accurately – "while talking or even musing as he sat in his chair," Boswell observed, Johnson "commonly held his head to one side towards his right shoulder" (Boswell, *Life*, 1:485) – but Reynolds has handled this detail wittily: in context, the head tilt becomes part of

Figure 7 Johnson copper halfpenny (1785).

a typical portrait of the inspired writer, such as we also see in portraits of Alexander Pope, William Blake, and others, a convention that probably derives from the writers of the Gospels taking dictation from above. The defect becomes a virtue.

The Knole portrait (1769, though it may have been begun earlier in the decade) represents Johnson in profile. The hair, like the rest of the portrait, is highly idealized (figure 6). The pose evokes the Renaissance version of a Roman orator or thinker. It is Reynolds's only portrait of him of which Johnson spoke with undisguised liking. Profiles were much more common on coins and medallions, probably the source in antiquity for this sort of representation, and Johnson himself appeared in profile in the year of his death on a copper halfpenny token used in Birmingham, 1784–90 (figure 7). In 1785 his profile appeared on a Wedgwood ceramic medallion designed by John Flaxman (figure 8), and the same year "Johnson's Head" became the shop sign for George Kearsley, publisher of a number of Johnsonian texts, though not written for him by Johnson. The sign was probably by or after Thomas Trotter, whose etching Kearsley used in 1782 as a frontispiece for his *Beauties of Johnson*, another version of which appears on the title page itself in the so-called "sixth edition." Trotter also etched a near-profile drawing "from the life" by J. Harding for Kearsley (1782). In 1782 Johnson was still alive and could give the lie to a false claim. Trotter had engraved the authorized frontispiece after Reynolds's Streatham portrait of the 1779 and 1781 prefaces to the *Lives of the Poets*. Of an image Trotter produced, perhaps for the *Lives*, Johnson said "Ah ha! – Sam Johnson! – I see thee! – and an ugly dog thou art!"[1]

In the Knole portrait – now, unfortunately, in dreadful shape – Johnson's hands are clenched in front of his chest as though he is "a peripatetic philosopher, almost physically wrenching reason into words."[2] When the painting appeared in 1770 at the Royal Academy, those in attendance saw Johnson, whom they might have seen in person at the Royal Academy

Figure 8 John Flaxman, *Samuel Johnson*, Wedgwood medallion (1785).

as well, stilled and pulled up into dignity. Nicholas Penny is right to stress that "the gestures here are surely intended as a dignified version of [Johnson's] 'gesticulations.'"[3] As with *Dictionary Johnson*, Reynolds turns a defect into an asset. But we can go a step farther: Sir Joshua's sister, Frances Reynolds, said, "as for his gestures with his hands … sometimes he would hold them up with some of his fingers bent, as if he had been seized with the cramp, and sometimes at his Breast in motion like those of a jockey on full speed" (*Miscellanies*, 2:274). The characteristic "cramp" is present from the first of Sir Joshua's portraits; in fact Reynolds never paints him with a straight hand. The analogy of the jockey is close to one classic description of a symptom of Tourette's syndrome, from which Johnson is now widely believed to have suffered: like playing piano. If we rotate both hands, we find Sir Joshua Reynolds has idealized not just Johnson's "gesticulations," but one of the characteristic symptoms of a Tourette's sufferer.

The Streatham portrait (1772 or 1778; figure 9) does not show "indigestion," as David Mannings suggests. Rather, Johnson's cramped hand

Figure 9 Sir Joshua Reynolds, *Samuel Johnson* (1772? 1778?); the Streatham portrait.

is subsumed in a format possibly related to such portraits by Sir Godfrey Kneller as that of Sir Richard Steele, who elegantly fingers several of his buttons. This is also not, *pace* Mannings, the portrait of "Blinking Sam" but, as Johnson himself later characterized the engraving, "Surly Sam," displaying something like the haughtiness Hester Thrale praised in a poem on this portrait: "To his Comrades contemptuous, we see him look down, / On their Wit & their Worth with a general Frown."[4] It may be the intellectual equivalent of the class attitude admired then but not now, condescension. Perhaps we can get closest to what is at stake by recalling that Reynolds said of Titian, "there is a sort of senatorial dignity about him," and praised the "nobleness" and "simplicity" of his portraits.[5] Certainly there is a gravitas about this portrait as well as the Knole.

The portrait known as *Blinking Sam* (figure 10), which represents Samuel Johnson in his familiar brown coat intensely and nearsightedly reading a pamphlet or unbound book bent back to front, is now out of private hands for the first time, and hangs at the Huntington (San Marino, California). Inevitably, the portrait elicits Boswell's well-known

Figure 10 Sir Joshua Reynolds, *Blinking Sam* (1775).

quotation of a claim about Johnson: "He knows how to read better than any one (said Mrs. Knowles); he gets at the substance of a book directly; he tears out the heart of it" (Boswell, *Life*, 3:285). But it also conveys the little known mock threat of Topham Beauclerk to his Irish friend Lord Charlemont: "Johnson shall spoil your books."[6] *Blinking Sam* is not the name Reynolds gave it, nor is it the name by which Johnson would want it to be known. He did not want it to be known at all. This is the portrait Hester Thrale Piozzi refers to in her *Anecdotes of Johnson*:

> When Sir Joshua Reynolds had painted his portrait looking into the slit of his pen, and holding it almost close to his eye, as was his general custom, he felt displeased, and told me "he would not be known by posterity for his *defects* only, let Sir Joshua do his worst." I said in reply, that Reynolds had no such difficulties about himself, and that he might observe the picture which hung up in the room where we were talking, represented Sir Joshua holding his ear in his hand to catch the sound. "He may paint himself as deaf if he chuses (replied Johnson), but I will not be *blinking Sam*." (*Miscellanies*, 1:313)

Johnson, whose second meaning for the verb *blink* in his *Dictionary* is "to see obscurely," may have remembered the line he quotes from the

Merchant of Venice to illustrate this definition: "What's here! the portrait of a *blinking* idiot." Hester Thrale mistook what he was doing when staring intently, but James Northcote, Reynolds's student and assistant at the time, assigns the date as 1775, corrects the activity, and gives another anecdote of Johnson's displeasure with the portrait in his *Life of Reynolds*. The portrait contains only Johnson and what he reads within an illusionistic oval. The light falls on his face and hands. Reynolds, who sometimes thought of his portraits as paired, may have had the idea of linking his self-portrait as a deaf man cupping his hand to his ear (which also lacks any background and focuses solely on the man portrayed) to the portrait of the nearsighted Johnson. Reynolds may owe something to the tradition (especially Dutch) of the representation of the senses in a series. Here the topic takes the witty form of representing sight (Johnson) and hearing (Reynolds) by their lack, not their presence.

OTHER PORTRAITISTS

In addition to the Reynolds portraits, Johnson was represented during his lifetime by an impressive range of artists, engravers, and sculptors: John Bacon, James Barry, Francesco Bartolozzi, John Flaxman, Joseph Nollekens, John Opie, James Roberts, Johan Zoffany, as well as Reynolds's sister Frances, among many others. Nollekens's wavy-haired bust (1777) is the best sculpture, though it was not admired by Johnson or his friends. Bacon's larger-than-life-size statue of him, nude but for a toga, irreverently known as "Johnson at the Baths" (1796; figure 11), is at St. Paul's Cathedral, London.

Late in life Johnson became friendly with Barry, who joined his new club, the Essex Head Club (of which Reynolds wanted no part). Barry's powerful oil sketch of Johnson at the National Portrait Gallery (1778–80) clearly shows the outline of the face of Elizabeth Montagu, whom he points out for emulation in the mural *The Distribution of Premiums in the Society of Arts*, for which his portrait was a study (figure 12). Opie's portrait (1783) was probably commissioned by John Harrison, who had James Heath engrave it for his edition of Johnson's *Dictionary* (1786). Opie, the largely self-taught "Cornish Wonder," was generally successful early in his career portraying the young and the old. A somber and moving portrait, his *Johnson* (figure 13) displays the simplicity and Rembrandtesque chiaroscuro for which Opie was acclaimed, though Johnson said this portrait was "not much admired" (*Letters*, 4:193). Only the pencil sketch from the life by James Roberts (1784), which portrays a simplified Johnson who

Figure 11 John Bacon, *Samuel Johnson* (1796). St. Paul's Cathedral, London.

does not look his age, is known to be later. Roberts's commission from Sarah ("Slim") Adams, the daughter of the Master of Pembroke College, Oxford, is now at Pembroke (figure 14). Roberts may also be behind one of the more mysterious portraits of Johnson, given to Haverford College in 1941 (figure 15). Long thought to be by Sir Joshua Reynolds, it has been rightly deattributed. The actual painter is most likely to be Frances Reynolds, and the portrait is very likely the one which Johnson mentions in a letter to Hester Thrale (*Letters*, 4:188).

The Haverford is an important portrait of Johnson which some have thought the finest image of him, undoubtedly because of its lack of idealization. Max Beerbohm, British caricaturist and author, wrote on a copy of A. Edward Newton's frontispiece to *A Magnificent Farce*:

> Where is this portrait? Not in America, I do hope – for I've never seen it, and should like to, inasmuch as it's far more convincing and *telling* than any of the others. This is the man that said those things. This is how he looked when he was saying them. This is intimately the dear man himself – not the legendary monster.[7]

Figure 12 James Barry, *Samuel Johnson* (1778–80).

Figure 13 John Opie, *Samuel Johnson* (1783).

Figure 14 James Roberts, *Samuel Johnson* (1784).

Although the Streatham portrait looks more like "the man that said those things," the Haverford – in its pathos, in its presentation of the old, sick, stooped, asthmatic man – may be the best likeness. The stooping, which is characteristic of Johnson, as we know from verbal portraits, is something that Reynolds does not convey in his representations, probably because it demeans despite its sympathy.

CARICATURE AND SATIRE

Johnson was not portrayed by friends and admirers alone. Caricaturists and satirists portrayed him in magazines, books, prints, and the press. Surprisingly, he sometimes received these representations with more equanimity than those that ostensibly celebrated him.

Figure 15 Frances Reynolds?, *Samuel Johnson* (1783?).

Figure 16 *The Hungry Mob of Scriblers and Etchers* (1762).

Figure 17 *The Irish Stubble Alias Bubble Goose* (1763).

Figure 18 Anonymous, *The Combat* (1763).

The caricatures fall into groups. The political ones revolve around a few issues. In those attacking the Earl of Bute, Prime Minister under George III, Johnson sometimes makes an appearance as pensioner: into this class fall *John a Boots's Asses* (1762), *The Hungry Mob of Scriblers and Etchers* (1762; figure 16), and *The Irish Stubble Alias Bubble Goose* (1763; figure 17), the last elaborately engraved and full of text. He was also among the artists satirized in *The Combat* (1763; figure 18) and *The Secret Councel of the Heads* (1768). These two concerned disagreements at the Society of Arts and the establishment of the Royal Academy. In the latter, Johnson – literally a talking head atop a "Dictionary of hard words" – says that he has supplied "as fine words as your plan would admit of." Others focus on his writings, though those related to Scotland respond more directly to Boswell's *Tour to the Hebrides* (1785). Thomas Trotter's stiff full-length engraving of a Brobdingnagian Johnson writ large upon the treeless landscape followed by a Lilliputian Boswell (1786; figure 19) is one of the enduring images of the trip. In *A Tom Tit Twittering on an Eagle's Back–side* (1786; figure 20), Boswell licks Johnson's breeches as they creep together up a hill. *A Tour to the Hebrides: Bossy Bounce Preparing for the Scotch Professors to Kiss* (1786; figure 21) is a variation on *A Tom Tit*'s crude theme. *Scotch Worship of an English Idol* (1786) presents a similar view of the bear-like Johnson. The best engravings to reflect on the trip are Thomas Rowlandson's series of twenty after the drawings of Samuel Collings, *The Picturesque Beauties of Boswell* (1786; figure 22), which only rarely attempt a likeness of Johnson.

Following the appearance of Johnson's *Lives of the Poets*, James Gillray, the most talented caricaturist other than Rowlandson to depict Johnson, engraved two successful satiric images: *Old Wisdom Blinking at the Stars* (1782; figure 23) and *Apollo and the Muses; Inflicting Penance on Dr. Pomposo, round Parnassus* (1783; figure 24). Both adapt Trotter engravings for the visage. In the former, the envious Johnson – in the shape of an owl with ass's ears (an iconography drawn from Pope's *Dunciad*) – stares ahead sullenly as library busts of Milton, Pope, and others shine above him. In the latter, his dunce's cap is inscribed with the names of those he was thought to defame in the *Lives*: Milton, Otway, Waller, Gray, Shenstone, Lyttelton (see chapter 6, "Critical reception to 1900"). The beauty of Apollo and the nine muses is played off against the ugly and ungainly Johnson, who admits to "defaming that genius I never could emulate," as Pegasus alights from the top of Parnassus. An anonymous satirical drawing of

Figure 19 Thomas Trotter, *Dr. Johnson in His Travelling Dress* (1786).

Figure 20 Anonymous, *A Tom Tit Twittering on an Eagle's Back–side* (1786).

Figure 21 Anonymous, *A Tour to the Hebrides: Bossy Bounce Preparing for the Scotch Professors to Kiss* (1786).

Figure 22 Thomas Rowlandson after Samuel Collings, "The Embrace," detail in *The Picturesque Beauties of Boswell* (1786).

Figure 23 James Gillray, *Old Wisdom Blinking at the Stars* (1782).

Figure 24 James Gillray, *Apollo and the Muses; Inflicting Penance on Dr. Pomposo, round Parnassus* (1783).

Figure 25 Charles Bestland?, *Dr. Johnson's Ghost*: "*Thou Art a Retailer of Phrases*" (1803).

uncertain date ushered in a supernatural theme: *The Ghost of the Poet Blackmore Appearing to Dr. Johnson* (1781 or after) shows a major figure in Pope's *Dunciad* returning not on a pale horse but an ass (Pope notes his liking of the term "bray") to haunt the man who added his biography to the *Lives*.

Caricaturists turned from Johnson's works to his life as major biographies were published following his death: his bust scowls down at Hester Piozzi, Boswell, and Sir John Hawkins in James Sayers's *Biographers* (1786); his ghost (modeled on Trotter) surprises Boswell in *Dr. Johnson's Ghost* (1803; figure 25); and his ghost upbraids Hester Piozzi in Sayers's mock *Frontispiece to the 2nd Edition of Dr J——n's Letters* (1788; figure 26).

When told that he was flogged round Parnassus in Gillray's print, Johnson responded, "Sir, I am very glad to hear this. I hope the day will never arrive when I shall neither be the object of calumny or ridicule, for then I shall

Figure 26 James Sayers, *Frontispiece to the 2nd Edition of Dr J____n's Letters* (1788).

be neglected and forgotten" (*Miscellanies*, 2:419–20). Whether represented as dignified or ridiculous, Johnson has never been ignored from his time to ours.

NOTES

1 Frances Burney, *Memoirs of Doctor Burney* (London, 1832), 2:180.

2 David Piper, *The Image of the Poet: British Poets and their Portraits* (Oxford: Clarendon Press, 1982), p. 93.

3 *Reynolds*, ed. Nicholas Penny (London: Royal Academy of Arts in association with Weidenfeld and Nicholson, 1986), p. 240.

4 Nadia Tscherny, "Reynolds's Streatham Portraits and the Art of Intimate Biography," *The Burlington Magazine*, 128 (1986), 4–11; David Mannings, *Sir Joshua Reynolds: A Complete Catalogue of His Paintings*, 2 vols. (New Haven, CT: Yale University Press, 2000), 1:282–3; James Boswell, *Boswell, Laird of Auchinleck, 1778–1782*, ed. Joseph W. Reed and Frederick A. Pottle (New York: McGraw-Hill, 1977), p. 369; *Thraliana*, 1:476.

5 Sir Joshua Reynolds, *Discourses on Art*, ed. Robert R. Wark (New Haven, CT: Yale University Press, 1975), pp. 138–9.

6 Beauclerk to Charlemont, in *Manuscripts and Correspondence of James, First Earl of Charlemont*, Historical Manuscripts Commission, Thirteenth Report, Appendix, Part VIII (London: Her Majesty's Stationery Office, 1894), 2:360.

7 Max Beerbohm, facsimile page on John Overholt's "Hyde Collection Catablog," http://blogs.law.harvard.edu/hydeblog/2006/09/25/not-the-legendary-monster.

CHAPTER 9

Reputation

Helen Deutsch

REPUTA'TION. *n.s.* [*reputation*, Fr. from *repute.*] Credit; honour; character of good.

Versoy, upon the lake of Geneva, has the *reputation* of being extremely poor and beggarly. *Addison.*

Let's begin with a paradox: in the monumental *Dictionary* that made his literary reputation in both senses of the word, the English author who gave his name to an age has little to say about *reputation* in its first neutral sense – "Credit" – and undermines his second definition – "honour" – with two ironic authorities he quotes to illustrate the word. Shakespeare's Iago, having just destroyed the virtuous Cassio's reputation, dismisses the concept entirely: "*Reputation* is an idle and most false imposition; oft got without merit, and lost without deserving: you have lost no *reputation* at all, unless you repute yourself such a loser." "Reputation" for "honest" Iago is only a social fiction. And the next quotation, Alexander Pope's epigram from *The Rape of the Lock* – "At ev'ry word a *reputation* dies" – shows the true power of reputation's "false imposition": when it comes to the frivolous, cutthroat universe of polite drawing rooms, where surface appearance is all, reputation is a matter of life and death.

But perhaps this contradiction should not surprise us too much. That grand word *lexicographer* after all, is defined in the *Dictionary* as "harmless drudge." Johnson concludes his preface to the completed volume with prideful despair:

In this work, when it shall be found that much is omitted, let it not be forgotten that much is likewise performed; and though no book was ever spared out of tenderness to the authour, and the world is little solicitous to know whence proceeded the faults of that which it condemns; yet it may gratify curiosity to inform it, that the *English Dictionary* was written with little assistance of the learned, and without any patronage of the great; not in the soft obscurities of retirement, or under the shelter of academick bowers, but amidst inconvenience and distraction, in sickness and in sorrow. It may repress the triumph of malignant criticism to observe, that if our language is not here fully displayed, I have only failed in an attempt which no human powers have hitherto completed ... I have protracted my work till most of those whom I wished to please have sunk into the grave, and success and miscarriage are empty sounds: I therefore dismiss it with frigid tranquillity, having little to fear or hope from censure or from praise. (*Works*, 18:111–13)

This declaration of resolutely English authorial independence – most famously enacted in Johnson's rejection of the Earl of Chesterfield's belated offer of patronage in the famous letter of February 1755 – is shadowed by what the reputation that accompanies such achievement effaces: an interior self that is haunted by self-reproach, suffering, loss, and isolation. (Johnson's wife Tetty died shortly before his labors ended. He never remarried.)

Enacting another paradox that preoccupied his imagination throughout his career, from the "volunteer Laureate" and subject of his first biography, Richard Savage, to the aspiring young Oxford scholar doomed to "Toil, Envy, Want, the Patron, and the Jail" in *The Vanity of Human Wishes* (line 160), to the catalogue of human misery chronicled in the *Lives of the Poets*, Johnson presents himself as both exceptional in his achievement and typical in his disappointment. This definer and proprietor of meaning, who assembled and displayed the best that the English language had produced in meaning's service, now considers censure and praise "empty sounds." No other English writer could balance such a magisterially dignified assessment of his work with such a pained recognition of its flaws and costs. No other author could solicit his reader so powerfully while maintaining his indifference to an audience.

THE CALIBAN OF ENGLISH LITERATURE

The *writer* of these distinctive sentences is better known today as a singular *character*, the quintessential Englishman whose pithy sayings were quoted by London cabbies – or so John Bailey boasted in his oft-reprinted book of 1913 on Johnson for England's Home University Library[1] – and now adorn souvenir mugs and T-shirts. In a tableau which has transfixed readers ever since, in a seminal review of John Wilson Croker's edition of Boswell's *Life of Johnson* (1831), Thomas Macaulay envisions Johnson as a childhood familiar composed of verbal tics and anecdotal detail culled from the pages of his biographers:

In the foreground is that strange figure which is as familiar to us as the figures of those among whom we have been brought up, the gigantic body, the huge massy face, seamed with the scars of disease, the brown coat, the black worsted stockings, the grey wig with the scorched foretop, the dirty hands, the nails bitten and pared to the quick. We see the eyes and mouth moving with convulsive twitches; we see the heavy form rolling; we hear it puffing; and then comes the "Why, sir!" and the "What then, sir?" and the "No, sir"; and the "You don't see your way through the question, sir!"

What a singular destiny has been that of this remarkable man! To be regarded in his own age as a classic, and in ours as a companion! To receive from his contemporaries that full homage which men of genius in general received only from posterity! To be more intimately known to posterity than other men are known to their contemporaries! That kind of fame which is commonly the most transient is, in his case, the most durable. The reputation of those writings, which he probably expected to be immortal, is every day fading; while those peculiarities of manner and that careless table-talk the memory of which, he probably thought, would die with him, are likely to be remembered as long as the English language is spoken in any quarter of the globe.[2]

In "The Double Tradition of Dr. Johnson" (1951), critic Bertrand Bronson spoke for many fellow scholars when he deplored the dominance of this "eidolon," or phantom, over the energetic substance of Johnson's writing. Yet even he is compelled to pay homage to this charismatic ghost:

But how can we sufficiently admire the vitality of this folk-image? It captures the imagination of generation after generation; it takes possession of some minds to such an extent that they spend years reading about Johnson and his circle, and even publish their own books on him, and all the while before them looms the same imago, unabashed and incorrigible. It is a humbling spectacle and a chastening one to the specialist. Each of us brings his burnt offering to the altar of truth, and the figure we invoke becomes momentarily visible, obscurely forming and reforming in the smoke above us, never the same. But the folk-image moves irresistibly onward, almost unaffected by our puny efforts to arrest or divert it:

> We do it wrong, being so majestical,
> To offer it the show of violence;
> For it is, as the air, invulnerable,
> And our vain blows malicious mockery.[3]

Substantive truth about Johnson is protean and ephemeral, Bronson regretfully asserts, and the appearance of three new biographies in 2009, the tercentenary of Johnson's birth, supports his point. But his popular image remains solidly itself, often quoted in newspapers around the globe, appearing as a character in a popular British comedy series, as a hero in a series of mystery novels, and in a whole subgenre of "dialogues of the dead" in which he chats with Socrates, Jonathan Swift, and a host of others.

This familiar Johnson is in motion: rebounding from the stone he kicked to refute George Berkeley's philosophy, fond of a race, an ocean swim, or a good roll down a hill. But standing bareheaded in the rain in Uttoxeter Market, in an act of silent penance for youthful disobedience (to which Nathaniel Hawthorne would pay homage over a century later), he is still enough to become his own monument. He is as heavy as the massive folio with which he is said to have assaulted the bookseller Thomas Osborne, and as solid as the English oak staff with which he measured the Scottish highlands (an emblem of the trees he found wanting). And yet he is also as light as the trifles of which he opined our existence was made. Early in their acquaintance, Johnson instructed Boswell to keep a journal; when the younger man worried about the plethora of "little incidents" in that record from which the *Life* would ultimately be formed, Johnson replied, "there is nothing, Sir, too little for so little a creature as man. It is by studying little things that we attain the great art of having as little misery and as much happiness as possible" (Boswell, *Life*, 1:433).

Johnson's ghost haunts us both as a kindly denizen of a national childhood and as a Caliban of English literature, who walked with the struggling gait of one in fetters, punctuating his pronouncements with unintelligible gestures, vocalizations, and rituals that twentieth-century doctors have diagnosed as Tourette's syndrome. He personifies both the pleasures of sociability – most happily evinced in the company of the famous Club that serves as a prototype for Johnsonian societies around the globe – and the terrors of religious melancholy that once impelled him to disrupt polite dinner conversation to insist on the horror of hell and eternal punishment. He inspires affection and he provides consolation: the prayer he wrote as he faced impending death alone has now become a hymn for Anglican congregations. His sociability and solitude mirror our own.

BOSWELL

This imago is largely the product of a legendary collaboration between Johnson himself and the most accomplished of his many biographers, James Boswell. The two men first met in 1763 in the bookshop of the actor Thomas Davies who, with an uncanny prescience, announced Johnson's approach by alluding, as Bronson would two centuries later, to the ghost of Hamlet's father: "Look, my Lord, it comes" (Boswell, *Life*, 1:391–2). In Philip Baruth's thriller, *The Brothers Boswell* (2009), Boswell's mad brother John, who has a truth of his own to tell about Johnson, jealously describes their relationship in terms that evoke this novel's debt to

Vladimir Nabokov's homage to Boswell's *Life*, *Pale Fire* (1962): "playing Plato to Johnson's Socrates," John observes of his brother, "he has found a way not merely to write a true romance but to live it as well."[4]

Boswell took his inspiration from Johnson's own love of anecdotes, and from his assertion in *Rambler* 60 that "no species of writing seems more worthy of cultivation" than biography, the art of which consists in choosing the personal detail that in the right hands is "more important than publick occurrences" (*Works*, 3:319, 321). An anecdote from the *Life* that has traveled through Anglo-American literature – from the notebooks of Samuel Beckett for his first unfinished play *Human Wishes* (begun 1936), to the poems of James Merrill, to Beryl Bainbridge's novel on Johnson's relationship with Hester Thrale, *According to Queeney* (2001) – exemplifies the partnership between biographer and subject, the inextricability of immortal reputation and individual mortality, and the importance of the most trivial of things:

> I won a small bet from Lady Diana Beauclerk, by asking [Johnson] as to one of his particularities, which her Ladyship laid I durst not do. It seems he had been frequently observed at the Club to put into his pocket the Seville oranges, after he had squeezed the juice of them into the drink which he made for himself. Beauclerk and Garrick talked of it to me, and seemed to think that he had a strange unwillingness to be discovered. We could not divine what he did with them; and this was the bold question to be put. I saw on his table the spoils of the preceding night, some fresh peels nicely scraped and cut into pieces. "O, Sir, (said I,) I now partly see what you do with the squeezed oranges which you put into your pocket at the Club." JOHNSON. "I have a great love for them." BOSWELL. "And pray, Sir, what do you do with them? You scrape them, it seems, very neatly, and what next?" JOHNSON. "Nay, Sir, you shall know their fate no further." BOSWELL. "Then the world must be left in the dark. It must be said (assuming a mock solemnity,) he scraped them, and let them dry, but what he did with them next, he never could be prevailed upon to tell." JOHNSON. "Nay, Sir, you should say it more emphatically: – he could not be prevailed upon, even by his dearest friends, to tell." (Boswell, *Life*, 2:330–1)

Johnson's ironic refusal to tell – "you shall know their fate no further" – reminds us of the indifference to reputation at the heart of his fame. While his character was constructed with Boswell's help, he insisted on keeping a part of himself undiscovered. In perhaps the most dramatic moment of Sir John Hawkins's biography of 1787, the dying Johnson, provoked by his surgeon's caution when scarifying his leg to relieve him of dropsy, cries out: "'Deeper, deeper; – I will abide the consequence: you are afraid of your reputation, but that is nothing to me.' – To those about him, he said, – 'You all pretend to love me, but you do not love me so well as I myself do'" (Hawkins, *Life*, p. 358). Such acts of refusal prompted Boswell and a host of other biographers to an endless search for truth in the biographical domain of what Johnson termed "domestick privacies" (*Works*, 2:158), and led the surgeons Johnson defied in his last days to perform an autopsy on his corpse. They made special note of his enlarged heart and preserved his lung, riddled with emphysema, in a collection of specimens from which it has never been recovered. Its image still adorns the pages of medical textbooks today.

THE ART OF THINKING

But Boswell learned how to read, write, and think from Johnson. He struggled to define in his journal the "high test of great writing" as "when what we read does so fill and expand our mind that the writer is admired by us instantaneously as being directly impressing us, as the soul of that writing, so that for a while we forget his personality, and, by a reflex operation, perceive that it is Mr. Johnson who is speaking to us."[5] As a reader, Boswell infuses the universal truth of "great writing" with his particular awareness of "Mr. Johnson"; as a biographer, he constructs a monument to Johnson's exemplification of general virtue out of anecdotal particulars. When thousands of such anecdotes culminate in Boswell's final "character" of Johnson – the summation of an individual personality that Johnson himself perfected in the *Lives of the Poets* – we see in Boswell's praise of his hero's distinctive "art of thinking" the magic by which an exceptional mind achieves immortality by putting itself to use. Johnson was superior to "other learned men," Boswell writes, because of a "certain continual power of seizing the useful substance of all that he knew, and exhibiting it in a clear and forcible manner; so that knowledge, which we often see to be no better than lumber in men of dull understanding, was, in him, true, evident, and actual wisdom" (Boswell, *Life*, 4:427–8). The ensuing centuries have proven that wisdom's use.

William Makepeace Thackeray's heroine Becky Sharpe might have thrown her schoolgirl's gift of the *Dictionary* out of her coach window when she embarked on her way to Vanity Fair, but the Victorian art critic John Ruskin was one of many writers who took Johnson with him on the journey – and the ranks include Frances Burney, Jane Austen, Samuel Beckett, and Harold Bloom, just to name a few. Inheriting his father's belief that "four little volumes of Johnson, the *Idler* and the *Rambler* … contain more substantial literary nourishment than could be, from any other author, packed into so portable compass," Ruskin learned from

Johnson "carefully to measure life, and distrust fortune." Leafing through the volume of the *Idler* at his side, this author of a self-confessed most un-Johnsonian "sanguine and metaphysical temperament," contemplating his own life and achievement, stumbles upon sentences from *Idler* 65 that suit his and our purposes:

> Let it be always remembered that life is short, that knowledge is endless, and that many doubts deserve not to be cleared. Let those whom nature and study have qualified to teach mankind, tell us what they have learned while they are yet able to tell it, and trust their reputation only to themselves.[6]

These are the same sentiments with which Johnson prefaced his *Dictionary* in all its magnificent imperfection. This diligent certainty about doubt, this trusting of his reputation only to himself, continues to inspire readers to believe not only in the familiar character of this particular author but in the power of literature which gave him life and afterlife.

NOTES

1 John Bailey, *Dr. Johnson and His Circle*, 2nd edn., with the assistance of L. F. Powell (1913; repr. London: Oxford University Press, 1945), pp. 10–11.
2 *The Complete Works of Thomas Babington Macaulay*, 10 vols. (Boston and New York: Houghton Mifflin, 1910), 1:741–2.
3 Bertrand H. Bronson, "The Double Tradition of Dr. Johnson," in *Johnson Agonistes and Other Essays* (Berkeley: University of California Press, 1965), p. 176.
4 Philip Baruth, *The Brothers Boswell* (New York: Soho Press, 2009), p. 18.
5 James Boswell, *Boswell: The Ominous Years, 1774–1776*, ed. Frederick A. Pottle and Charles Ryskamp (New York: McGraw-Hill, 1963), p. 80.
6 John Ruskin, *Praeterita and Dilecta* (New York: Alfred A. Knopf, 2005), pp. 198, 199.

PART III

Contexts

CHAPTER 10

America

Thomas M. Curley

CO'LONY. *n.s.* [*colonia*, Latin]
1. A body of people drawn from the mother-country to inhabit some distant place.

Osiris, or the Bacchus of the ancients, is reported to have civilized the Indians, planting *colonies* and building cities. *Arbuthnot on Coins.*

Samuel Johnson's lifetime circumscribed the most momentous political episode in eighteenth-century English history, the rise and fall of the British empire in North America. His notorious hostility towards America rested on a potent mixture of insular nationalism and cosmopolitan humanitarianism, which fueled his lifelong hatred of imperialism and racism. Few other major English authors wrote more, or more passionately, about America than he did.

HOME AND COLONIES

Home undoubtedly came first to Johnson, as it did to his countrymen. Colonists were a new and suspect category of citizenry unknown to ancient common law. In his *Dictionary*, a definition of *land* as "Nation; people" is a revealing conflation of soil and subjects, of locality and loyalty. This nativism had feudal origins in the unwritten British constitution for an agrarian society, where landholding meant subsistence and allegiance to the monarch as supreme owner of the island's real property. The homeland was a largely self-sufficient entity for survival and civilization, and had precedence over extra-territorial concerns of foreign trade and distant empire: "We have at home," Johnson wrote, "all that we can want, and … we need feel no great anxiety about the schemes of other nations for improving their arts, or extending their commerce" (*Works*, 10:125).

Many therefore argued against emigration to North America for weakening domestic strength and eroding English civilization. In this concern, Johnson shared with fellow subjects a preference for kingdom over colonies. But Johnson's nationalism had a unique infusion of cosmopolitanism (see chapter 32, "Nationalism"), in the form of a respect for universal human rights, which underlay his dislike of Americans and their terrible legacy of racial exploitation. Philosophically consistent in his nativism, he granted fundamental legal priority to natives anywhere on earth as the first occupants of the land. This conviction played into his fierce advocacy of the two principal victims of imperialism in America: the native tribes deprived of an ancestral homeland and the black slaves deprived of a home in both Africa and the New World. In his distinctive compassion for indigenous peoples, he ranks perhaps as the foremost champion of Native Americans among canonical authors in English literature.

NATIVE RIGHTS

Johnson's watershed statement about the gross violation of native rights appeared in his youthful "Debates in the Senate of *Magna Lilliputia*," in which he recast the British Parliament as a deliberative body in Jonathan Swift's Lilliput:

> The People of … *Lilliputian Europe* … are, above those of the other Parts of the Worlds, famous for Arms, Arts, and Navigation, and, in consequence of this Superiority, have made Conquests, and settled Colonies in very distant Regions, the Inhabitants of which they look upon as barbarous … and seem to think that they have a Right to treat them as Passion, Interest or Caprice shall direct, without much Regard to the Rules of Justice or Humanity; that they have carried this imaginary Sovereignty so far, that they have sometimes proceeded to Rapine, Bloodshed and Desolation.

He went on to note that the Lilliputian conquests in "Columbia (which is the *Lilliputian* for the Country that answers to our America), have very little contributed to the Power of these Nations, which have, to obtain them, broke thro' all the Ties of human Nature."[1]

The legal assumptions of this Swiftian satire deserve careful scrutiny. Johnson extols what has come to be called the "noble savage" in order to emphasize the worse barbarity of the supposed civilizers. Carving out an empire, whether by conquest or settlement, was essentially unlawful as a matter of might making right, in violation of the natural law vesting ownership in the original inhabitants (see chapter 21, "Empire"). European expansionism amounted to a wanton theft perpetrated against indigenous occupants by plundering their property without their consent or just cause. Johnson never forgot or forgave the robbery and rape of America.

THE SEVEN YEARS' WAR

At no stage in his career was his anti-imperialism more pronounced than during his short-lived editorship of the *Literary Magazine* in 1756, at the beginning of the Seven Years' War. The immediate cause of this global conflict was French encroachment on the northern and western borders of Britain's colonies (see chapter 46, "War"). Some contemporary maps reveal French territorial ambitions by distorting actual geographical possessions: "Le Canada" and "La Nouvelle France" made up almost the top half of North America, and "La Louisiane" in the bottom half, excluding "La Florida" and English settlements, extended westward, midway into modern Texas and upward along the Mississippi River. British America, by contrast, with an ever-expanding population of about two million white Protestants and roughly a quarter-million African slaves, covered only a narrow strip of Atlantic coastline, giving the false impression of being hemmed in to the north by a New France of a mere 75,000 or so Catholics, forced for their survival to establish better relations with natives than their more prosperous Anglo-American rivals ever cared to cultivate.

Under Prime Minister William Pitt, the diehard imperialist, the conduct of the Seven Years' War went badly at first, but by 1758 British fortunes were on the rise, and the conquest of Quebec in 1759 led to the Peace of Paris, formalizing the first British empire in 1763. The Seven Years' War proved the costliest contest in English history thus far – possibly £137 million a year – but also the most successful, yielding a vast increase of territory and winning almost unanimous support from the nation. France was forced to abandon Canada and most of its Caribbean, African, and Indian holdings, and for the first time the sun never set on the British empire.

Although the *Literary Magazine* came into being to further Pitt's expansionist agenda, Johnson turned this propagandistic purpose on its head by his overall condemnation of the Great War for Empire, and this apparently doomed his connection with the journal. The very first article in the *Literary Magazine*, "An Introduction to the Political State of Great-Britain," is as good a summing-up of early modern British history as can be found in recent scholarship. Three factors, Johnson wrote, accounted for his country's political situation: (1) the emergence of Protestantism; (2) the resultant trading rivalries first with Catholic Spain and then with Catholic France for control of the seas; and (3) the concurrent growth of empires "in America, which was become the great scene of European ambition … upon no very just principles of policy, only because every other state … concludes itself more powerful as its territories become larger" (*Works*, 10:130).

Compounding the British problem of vying with the French for North America was the hostility of "unhappy Indians," angry over their loss of ancestral lands "by no right of nature or of nations" (*Works*, 10:148). Simple self-interest should have convinced embattled British "usurpers" of native territory to be kinder towards indigenous people and "at least content themselves to rob without insulting them" (10:150). Already Johnson professed himself to be a confirmed mercantilist, upholding the priority of the homeland while affirming the common good of all constituents of the far-flung British empire: colonies "must keep a perpetual correspondence with the original country, to which they are subject, and on which they depend for protection in danger, and supplies in necessity" (10:141). Here in miniature is the major thesis of all his later anti-American pamphlets. His exposé of European warmongering abroad culminated in an admonishment for promoting statecraft that had no place for condoning the kind of awful atrocity done to Native Americans: "no people can be great who have ceased to be virtuous" (10:150). The sentiment was a fitting finale for his brief against American empire.

A RACE OF CONVICTS

Detestation of empire provoked in Johnson a blanket distaste for Anglo-Americans, whom he typecast in four unsavory ways. Colonists were, first and foremost, descendants of the hypocritical Christian usurpers of native lands, "a Race of Mortals whom I wish no other man wishes to resemble" (*Letters*, 1:269), for selfishly withholding Christian conversion from their victims. Second, they often came from the dregs of society, forced by crime or misfortune to abandon their homeland: "they are a race of convicts, and ought to be thankful for any thing we allow them, short of hanging" (Boswell, *Life*, 2:312). Third, they represented a backward people who forfeited civilization for a savage wilderness: "a man of any intellectual enjoyment will not easily go and immerse himself and posterity for ages in barbarism" (Boswell, *Life*, 5:78). Finally, they included a large group of extremist Dissenters and Whig firebrands, tending towards what he saw as a Satanic anarchy lethally dangerous to a well-ordered state.

Johnson of course crossed paths with Americans, even eminently rebellious ones. One of his most anthologized encounters in Boswell's *Life*, the hilarious meeting with John Wilkes in May 1776, also involved rubbing shoulders with Arthur Lee, a secret agent of the First Continental Congress seeking ties with France. More noteworthy was an almost certain connection between Benjamin Franklin and Johnson, who publicized the American's electrical discoveries in the *Literary Magazine* and then, on May 1, 1760, attended with Franklin a small gathering dedicated to founding African American schools. The American Revolution soured the relationship: Johnson's *Taxation No Tyranny* took a covert swipe at Franklin, who, in turn, bristled at its call for blacks and Native Americans to rise up against their rebel oppressors. Far more satisfying was the moralist's friendship in London with his near-namesake William Samuel Johnson of Connecticut, another founder of the United States and its Constitution.

A WIDENING GULF

Johnson's abhorrence of empire in the later 1750s put him out of step with growing public enthusiasm for the Seven Years' War and the immense territorial gains newly brought under British dominion. But the huge rewards of the war soon created the huge burden of administering far-flung holdings with more efficient centralization and taxation than had ever before been imposed on the Thirteen Colonies. Tightening loose reins of government and levying new taxes to offset a mammoth national debt for military campaigns put the king and Parliament on a collision course with their subjects on the other side of the Atlantic. Longstanding indifference about Anglo-American ways and aspirations resulted in poor policy-making by a home government understandably sure of its right to seek some financial return for protecting its subjects abroad. But obstacles increasingly stood in the way of resolving conflicting political interests. When an Atlantic crossing took about a month in good sailing weather, distance bred differentiation, disagreement, and disintegration of the old bonds of ethnic kinship.

A gulf was widening, and even though a majority of Americans may have been loyalists, a new nation was already probably in embryo. A colonial inferiority complex and commercial self-interest fed resentment of the Sugar Act of 1764, the Stamp Act of 1765, the Townshend Acts of 1767, the Tea Act of 1773, as well as the Coercive Acts of 1774 and the Restraining Act of 1775 (punishing insurrectionist Massachusetts after the Boston Tea Party of 1773).

POLITICAL WRITING

Despite the ominous drift in political affairs, the period between the Seven Years' War and the American Revolution encouraged popular self-satisfaction over Britain's new superpower status in Europe. The conflict with the colonies made clear the competing ideas about the nature of authority and liberty, the complex meaning of patriotism, and the people's role in governmental process. On the battlefield and in political assemblies, these ideas would precipitate not only nation-building in America but also eventual parliamentary reform in England, entailing considerable soul-searching about the future cast of British empire after the rise of the United States.

Colonists had deprived original occupants of their land with criminal injustice and now contemplated compounding the theft by taking away America from Britain, the successor to ownership of the land by right of prescription. Johnson had in the past sided with the exploited non-Europeans rather than with their Anglo-American exploiters. Now he vigorously championed his country under threat from upstart persecutors of natives and slaves. To grant such ungrateful subjects independence was to lose Britain's prolonged and costly investment in their well-being during and after the Seven Years' War. As a consequence, he portrayed himself as faithful devotee of the great mother country for engendering peace and progress among her obedient children who constituted organic extensions of herself. In contrast to Jefferson's Declaration of Independence, *Taxation No Tyranny* was Johnson's declaration of needful political authority for the good order and prosperity of the state.

Abhorrence of racism accounted for Johnson's memorable criticism of the hypocrisy of American colonists who cried for freedom and yet kept slaves: "How is it that we hear the loudest yelps for liberty among the drivers of negroes?" (*Works*, 10:454). It also motivated his inflammatory suggestion for instituting a free state of liberated loyal slaves and his "wild proposal" – never to be forgiven by Benjamin Franklin – for arming Native Americans "now and then to plunder a plantation" (10:451) in retaliation for ancient injuries.

In standing up for the mother country against the American rebels, did Johnson contradict his vigorous anti-imperialism? Not really. There was a career-long philosophical consistency and a general legal soundness behind the thinking of *Taxation No Tyranny*. Far better, according to the drift of its argument, had imperialism never corrupted the New World or the Old World. But since history could not be reversed, nor the wrongs of European usurpation effaced, England had at least a tarnished prescriptive title to British America and might as well keep what it had come to own by virtue of its long possession and expensive protection of the place.

Running through a pamphlet supportive of the status quo was a contrary anti-imperialist leitmotif indicative of subliminal ambivalence about defending an empire worth preserving, and yet rooted in an ugly legacy of European encroachment abroad. Hints of his habitual nativism, antiracism, and anticolonialism are discernible. A passing censure of Columbus occasioned a devastating condemnation of the whole early modern era of geographical discovery and expansionism "hitherto disastrous to mankind" (*Works*, 10:421). The primary manifestation of his nativism was his assigning less than first-class citizenship to Anglo-Americans because of their physical separation from homeland, despite his firm belief in their qualifying as bona fide British subjects who were by no means a conquered alien people, but had settled the continent, carrying with them an allegiance, by inherited birthright, to the mother country.

THE WAR OF AMERICAN INDEPENDENCE

Coming from the most famous living author in the English-speaking world at a time of looming crisis, *Taxation No Tyranny* excited more attention – mainly of a negative nature because of its unabashed authoritarianism – than any of his other political writings. In addition to three more printings, a lightly revised edition soon appeared as part of Johnson's *Political Tracts* in April 1776. Its aim was not the impossible task of persuading Americans to end insurrection, but to make a strong case for the hard-line ministerial policy adopted by Lord North, who commissioned this brilliant and legally well-reasoned Johnsonian propaganda. In time the public generally came to support the government's stand, once the skirmish between British troops and colonial irregulars at Concord and Lexington on April 19, 1775, commenced armed conflict.

The Battle of Bunker Hill near Boston on June 17, 1775, dashed British hopes of a quick victory. When the colonials eventually retreated from the field, nearly half of the British regulars lay dead or wounded in this opening round of the American Revolution. Johnson had the magnanimity to praise the patriots' courage for waging a prolonged war that would spell disaster for his country in the long run. "If we make war by parties and detachments," he warned, "dislodge them from one place, and exclude them from another, we shall, by a local, gradual, and ineffectual war, teach them our own knowledge, harden their obstinacy, and strengthen their confidence, and at last come to fight on equal terms of skill and bravery, without equal numbers" (*Letters*, 2:259). And this was almost precisely what happened. His countrymen at first felt buoyed by successes in Canada and then around New York against Washington's fleeing army, but the British General John Burgoyne's momentous loss at Saratoga in 1777 brought France in 1778, Spain in 1779, and Holland in 1780 into the war on the patriots' side. This led to General Charles Cornwallis's decisive surrender at Yorktown in October of 1781, when red-coat pipers made their final defiant march on United States soil to the forlorn tune of "The World Turned Upside Down." Although the British actually experimented with black emancipation and Indian uprisings projected in *Taxation No Tyranny* against colonials, the odds for smothering rebellion by force, as Johnson predicted correctly, were abysmally small from the start. Any triumph required subduing a faraway continent with overextended supply lines in the midst of guerilla terrorists, colonial sympathizers, and mobile patriot armies difficult to catch, contain, and conquer on their home turf.

The mismanagement and misfortunes of the American war left Johnson with a growing impression of Britain's enfeeblement abroad, made all the worse at home by the spectacle of successive tottering ministries serving a thoroughly dismayed king: Lord North fell from power in 1782, and William Petty, the second Earl of Shelburne, brokered major concessions to keep Ireland in the fold before offering the victorious United States exceedingly generous terms in the hope of future economic cooperation. Coming exactly two decades after the similarly named treaty made Britain a world power in 1763, the Peace of Paris of 1783 officially recognized the new country created by Jefferson's Declaration of Independence in 1776. The end of the Revolution, the signal political upheaval of the Age of Johnson, was widely considered a national humiliation in Britain. Johnson went to his grave unrepentant about opposing American independence and European imperialism, even though he recoiled at the thought of his weakened homeland at the end of his illustrious career, "when we have all the world for our enemies, when the King and parliament have lost even the titular dominion of America, and the real power of Government every where else" (*Letters*, 4:277).

NOTE

1 "Debates in the Senate of *Magna Lilliputia*," *Gentleman's Magazine*, 8 (June 1738), 286.

CHAPTER 11

Anglicanism

Melvyn New

CHRI'STIAN. *n.s.* [*Christianus*, Lat.] A professor of the religion of Christ.

> We *christians* have certainly the best and the holiest, the wisest and most reasonable religion in the world. *Tillotson.*

Much that we might want to know about religion in the eighteenth century is suggested by Johnson's seven-word definition of *Christian* and the choice of his illustrative quotation from the late seventeenth-century Archbishop of Canterbury (the highest authority in the Anglican Church), John Tillotson. Before we look at eighteenth-century Anglicanism more closely, however, it may be helpful to envision a moment to come in the twenty-first century when Jews, Muslims, and Christians all decide they have had their fill of bloody efforts to overwhelm those who do not believe as they do and, laying down their arms, create a brave new world in which we can hold to our own faiths without wanting to punish those who think differently. Perhaps, since we are generating visions, we might even see a world in which religious differences are fully tolerated within every community. Some will mutter on the sidelines that such faith is nominal and lukewarm – some will even label it heretical. Since such mutterers want to lead us back to a renewal of warfare (we might today label this as terrorism and antiterrorism), they will have to be forcefully discouraged, and the power of all countries will have to be solidly engaged in disarming religious conviction (literally and figuratively), finally bringing to all religions the virtues of peace and goodwill. The paradox of our vision, the need to pacify people by brute power, does not escape us.

RELIGIOUS CENTRISM

Christianity is a religion built on mysteries and paradoxes, but the one that most concerned the eighteenth century has been fundamental to the faith since its Gospel beginnings: insisting on the Truth of God is in direct conflict with the message of peace professed by Jesus. Even without the New Testament injunction to spread the Word, the very nature of knowing the Truth seems to entail, as Jonathan Swift astutely argued in the most brilliant of all eighteenth-century satires, *A Tale of a Tub* (1704), the desire to impart it to others – in a friendly way if possible, forcibly if necessary.

That had clearly been the history of the West, at any rate. Martin Luther challenged the Roman Catholic Church in 1517, inaugurating the Protestant Reformation; Rome responded with the Counter-Reformation and the Roman Inquisition. In the decades to come, both sides would fight for supremacy. The quarrels were made all the more complicated by the tendency of Protestantism to split into factions, with Jean Calvin of Geneva promoting a theology to rival Luther's, leading to the rise of Presbyterianism. In post-Reformation England, the official Church of England found itself between the Roman Catholics on one hand and the radical Calvinists known as Puritans on the other. By the end of the seventeenth century, after 250 years of religious wars, England – perhaps all of Europe – was thoroughly exhausted by the bloodletting.

The climax of religious conflict for the English had been the beheading of Charles I in 1649, and the Puritan reign of Oliver Cromwell – the only time in England's long history when the country was without a monarch (hence the "Interregnum," or "between the kings"). With the return in 1660 of both Charles II as king and Anglicanism as the state religion (hence the "Restoration"), the English nation declared itself firmly committed to a Christianity that had begun to define itself as the middle way between religious extremes, a moderate course between the Catholicism of Rome and the Calvinism of Geneva. In 1688, with the ouster of Charles's brother and successor, James II (whose Catholicism made him unacceptable to Parliament), and the invitation to the Protestant William and Mary to sit on the English throne, the religion of moderation had its greatest triumph. The event has come down in history as the "Glorious Revolution" – glorious because it was uniquely bloodless.

One of the most astute theological voices helping to define this mode of Anglican belief was that of Archbishop Tillotson, who led the clergy and their congregations into the eighteenth century with the basic message that the Church of England – the Anglican communion – was more inclusive than exclusive, an ever-expanding and moderating centrist religion. Tillotson hoped that, over time, the less extreme Roman Catholics and Dissenters (non-Anglican Protestants) would adopt his way of thinking, but, from this point on, the established Church would no longer persecute those who wanted to exercise their faith in other congregations and by other means. And having established its authority over the clergy by ousting one king and establishing another, the state withdrew more or less into an era of benign neglect of the fortunes of Anglicanism.

THE EVANGELICAL MANDATE

To modern ears, this may sound like a good idea – a "Christian" idea of tolerance and goodwill – but the century discovered it was a devastating path for Christian belief. On the one hand, if toleration is based on the notion that one system of belief is no better than another, the promise of salvation through a particular organization of worship is significantly watered down, if not altogether canceled. If a Catholic priest or a Presbyterian pastor could then argue that *his* system was the only true "religion of Christ," to invoke Johnson's simple but telling definition, why would we want to practice a religion that refused to make a similar claim, and thus endanger our own salvation? On the other hand, if we are convinced, as the quotation from Tillotson asserts, that ours is "the best and the holiest, the wisest and most reasonable religion in the world," we have already joined with that priest and that pastor in maintaining our faith's superior claims over every other religion "in the world." Not only would we want to belong to the communion that worships "correctly," but we would want our faith to be invested in a Church that was not second best. Tillotson was not speaking of Christianity in general; his appeal to reasonableness – evoking the unreasonableness of Catholics and Dissenters – would have fallen on knowing ears in the eighteenth century. The archbishop of the Anglican communion was stating, even while promulgating his brilliantly conceived religion of moderation, the absolute superiority of his own Church as the true religion of Christ.

To Tillotson's quite natural belief that his own religion was the one true faith, we must add the fundamental command of the New Testament: dutiful Christians should spread the Word and convert the unbeliever. Europe was actually still conducting crusades in the Middle East in the eighteenth century; closer to home, it was considered theologically uncharitable and unchristian to condemn the unbeliever to damnation. To be a good Christian means working to convert the world – and, more practically, our wrongheaded neighbors – to our own beliefs. They are, after all, "the best and the holiest, the wisest and most reasonable," and the religion of Christ mandates sharing this certainty. This is the paradox that now confronted the eighteenth century, first manifested with the Glorious Revolution and culminating in that immensely paradoxical assertion one hundred years later, in the American Bill of Rights (1789), that the state, despite having a vested interest in the welfare of its citizens, cannot privilege one religion over another. To be "free" now meant having the freedom to condemn yourself to eternal damnation by practicing the wrong religion – the state, even those leaders who knew the proper road to salvation, could not impose "right religion" on benighted citizens. Political power, the only power left in the state, controlled one's earthly existence, but how one would spend eternity was not its business.

THE GOOD HEART

To be sure, deists and "freethinkers" of widely varying degrees (a minute minority, however one defines those who opted out of organized Christian communions) could argue that, as long as one believed in any sort of God and the promptings of a good heart, salvation would be assured. We inherited this argument from the eighteenth century and it underlies the religion of many today, both in and out of denominational systems. The problem is that the argument destroys most, if not all, of what validated Christian belief for 1,700 years. The evangelical mandate is canceled, since the Word has now become simply words among words. Salvation is no longer particular to modes of ritual, sacrament, and communion, and one performs in church without any assurance at all that one is moving closer to God by one's practices – a much more acceptable service may well be taking place in a neighboring church.

Above all, trusting in one's "good heart" indicates a fundamental disbelief in the Fall in the Garden of Eden: a long tradition of Christian thought held that the heart was corrupted and rendered sinful by Adam's disobedience. Moreover, if the first Adam did not sin, the "second Adam," Jesus Christ, had no reason to die on the Cross; redemption from sin necessitates a belief that the human heart is in a state of sin and separated from God until thus redeemed. The philosopher John Locke pointed this out as the first premise of his *Reasonableness of Christianity* (1695): without the Fall in the Garden, Christ would have no reason to come into the world, much less to be crucified; hence Christianity, the "religion of Christ [crucified]," would have no justification. Salvation, under this new dispensation, would be equally available to Jews and Muslims – if, in fact, anyone needed to be "saved," since we are now able to judge for ourselves the extent of our own virtues and vices. Our neighbor might be a sinner, but we are quite certain that our own foibles are explicable and excusable, given our "good-hearted" desire to do the right thing. One might well argue, as Edmund Burke would do at the end of the century, that the French Revolution was the natural outcome of such thinking. ("Sensibility" and "sentimentalism" are the names given to this school of "moral" thought.) Religion would have no place in the perfect new state of liberty, fraternity, and equality: a little more than a century after killing one another over the finest theological points the armies of God could muster, religion was found to be superfluous to mankind.

JOHNSON'S PRAGMATIC PIETY

For an alert and sensitive eighteenth-century believer like Samuel Johnson – and Johnson was a committed Anglican Christian, though he sympathized with both Catholics and Dissenters (represented at mid-century by a revivalist movement within Anglicanism, the Methodism of John Wesley and George Whitefield) – this was the essential paradox that marked his faith. It manifests itself most dramatically, I believe, in the intricate accommodation between piety and pragmatism that seems to be the defining characteristic of his thought. The accommodation might also serve to define the century as a whole, which was never an "Age of Reason" – a modern, ill-fitting label – but also never an "Age of Faith," a label that sits far more comfortably on any one of the seventeen centuries preceding the eighteenth. The rise of individual rights on the one hand, and Western capitalism and imperialism on the other, have long been considered the conflicted legacy of the century to modern times.

Behind this "paradox," I would suggest, is the century's distinctive blend of pragmatism and piety. Pragmatic piety taught Johnson and his age to live within a commercial society by invoking notions of God's providential care for those who worked hard, exercised thrift, and provided charity to the less fortunate, while prudently ignoring the impossible commercial advice to give up *all* material things in order to follow Christ. Similarly, a pious pragmatism taught imperialists that the goodness of its religion of peace justified its extension among the heathens, especially if one proselytized with a bit less violence than the Catholic imperialists of France and Spain. The war at mid-century (known as the French and Indian War in America, and the Seven Years' War in Europe) was one of many engagements during the century reflecting this conflict, although religion was now negligible as the direct cause of warfare. It was replaced by the struggle for territory and markets. Still, the "Manifest

Destiny" that drove Americans westward in the nineteenth century was a direct descendant of the faith in a providential Anglican Christianity that enabled eighteenth-century England to become the most far-flung and powerful mercantile power the world had ever known.

PARADOXES

It would be a huge mistake to suggest that pragmatism in any way watered down the Christian belief of that vast majority of British subjects who continued to believe in its pieties. The essence of Christianity is in its paradoxes. One might suggest that the decisive spiritual talent of Christian believers is indeed the ability to hold two conflicting ideas in their heads at the same time: that Christ is both human and divine; that God is omnipotent and omniscient, but that we nonetheless have free will; that the crucified man can rise from the dead; that God decided to save Europe while leaving the rest of the world in spiritual darkness.

The Christian mind is trained to absorb these inherent contradictions and complexities in a system of thought that has always attempted – never quite successfully, but always magnificently – to merge this world and the beyond-this-world, as if the two could ultimately be rendered coherent to a logician (or pragmatist). What is perhaps different from the past in the eighteenth century, however, is the increased toleration that now accompanied faith. When one is no longer ready to kill others to support the righteousness of one's spiritual system, when one begins to accept the possibility that individual citizens have the right as well as the duty to define their own path towards salvation, and especially when one retains a belief that individuals are ill-equipped to do so without the providential hand of God and the sacrifice of his Son on the Cross, then a pious pragmatic Christianity emerges, arguing that, although we cannot force others to agree with us (except by oral persuasion), it would certainly be in everyone's best interests to adopt "the best and the holiest, the wisest and most reasonable religion in the world."

Historians have long recognized that the result of this moderate religion was that the eighteenth century became ever more secular in its outlook. Often missing in their formulation of "secularization," though, is an awareness that, for most in the eighteenth century, it was the desire to become "more Christian" that produced this secularity. Anglicans intended only to strengthen their faith when, for example, they argued that the equality of souls formed the basis of equal rights for men *and* women – thus undercutting the authority of the patriarchal society the

Church had abetted almost consistently since the epistles of Paul. Again, the abolitionist movement was headed not by secular thinkers but by Christians who argued that native societies had the same right to life, liberty, and the pursuit of happiness as their own – but who thus relativized the religion and culture they wanted to believe was the "best" in the world (see chapter 41, "Slavery and abolition"). And when Anglicans suggested that it was best not to kill one another over differences of religious opinion, could they have predicted that the resultant loss of religious fervor would evolve over the century into tired indifference? Looking backward at centuries of religious warfare, their foresight fell victim to the law of unintended consequences.

WORD AND WORLD

Thirteen days before his death, Johnson composed the following prayer to recite before he took what proved to be his final communion (receiving the sacrament of the Lord's Supper):

> Almighty and most merciful Father, I am now, as to human eyes it seems, about to commemorate for the last time, the death of thy Son Jesus Christ, our Saviour and Redeemer. Grant, O Lord, that my whole hope and confidence may be in his merits and thy mercy; forgive and accept my late conversion, enforce and accept my imperfect repentance; make this commemoration [of] him available to the confirmation of my Faith, the establishment of my hope, and the enlargement of my Charity, and make the Death of thy Son Jesus Christ effectual to my redemption. Have mercy upon me and pardon the multitude of my offences. Bless my friends, have mercy upon all men. Support me by the Grace of thy Holy Spirit in the days of weakness, and at the hour of death, and receive me, at my death, to everlasting happiness; for the sake of Jesus Christ. Amen. (*Works*, 1:417)

The prayer is steeped in the traditional language of the Book of Common Prayer of the Anglican communion, yet is also a highly individualized utterance of one man. As with the many similar prayers Johnson wrote out for himself, it is a particularly humble statement of inadequacy and sinfulness, as befits a fallen Adam, but it comes from the pen of a particularly profound and moral human being. Above all, it moves from this world to the next world in a rhythm that fully acknowledges the existence of both as equal realities to the man in prayer: the mention of "human eyes" in the opening, which must always be qualified with "it seems," is a particularly typical gesture of the pragmatic mind, but also of the firm believer in original sin. On the other hand, the piety of his faith in the redemption of his own sins through the death on the Cross, the hope of "everlasting happiness," the reality of his concrete belief in heaven and hell – these are the most unpragmatic assertions possible. Yet, given the time and the situation, we cannot doubt Johnson's full commitment to these highly spiritualized abstractions.

The most beautiful aspect of the prayer to me, however, is its interlocking of the world ("Bless my friends") and the Word ("have mercy upon all men"). Here, in miniature, is all that one need say about religion in eighteenth-century Britain. For the vast majority, Christianity remained a prevalent universal truth, a divine mercy made available and necessary to all human beings because of an original fall from grace. At the same time, Christianity was a private providential dispensation operating within the smallest circles of one's own existence, a God to whom one could recommend one's family and friends as well as oneself and mankind.

Johnson never did formulate a theology of pragmatic piety or pious pragmatism, but if one could be written, it would have been written in the eighteenth century and written by him. That he failed to do so opens yet another paradox: human beings could no longer unify factuality with the Christian faith by which they lived. The result, oddly enough, was an intensified search for more facts (the scientific revolution that began in the eighteenth century and continues today), on the one hand, and for a living faith, on the other, that manifested itself in Romanticism and aestheticism in the nineteenth century, and, horribly, as the positivist ideologies and fundamentalisms of the twentieth. One can hope that the rough beast slouching to Bethlehem in the twenty-first century might look again to the irenic religion that Tillotson, Johnson, and their contemporaries had envisioned – a religion, though the "best" in the world, yet entailing sufficient doubtfulness to render unjustifiable the murdering of others in order to promulgate it. But let Johnson have the last word on the century's pragmatic and pious religion: "No rational man can die without uneasy apprehension" (Boswell, *Life*, 3:294).

CHAPTER 12

Anthropology

Jonathan Lamb

ANTHROPO′LOGY. *n.s.* [from ἄνθρωπος, man, and λέγω, to discourse.] The doctrine of anatomy; the doctrine of the form and structure of the body of man.

ESSENTIALISTS AND ENVIRONMENTALISTS

Insofar as it could be said to exist then as a system of knowledge, anthropology in the eighteenth century was a branch of natural history. Natural history fell into two broad divisions. There were those who believed in the reality of species, and there were those who believed that species were merely faint calibrations in an endless process of speciation. Joseph Banks, the English naturalist who accompanied Captain James Cook on his first voyage to the South Pacific, followed the botanist Carolus Linnaeus in believing that a species was forever. He refused to admit the possibility of its extinction: somewhere all plants and creatures had a place, and they would keep it.

The French naturalist, the Comte de Buffon, on the other hand, considered the forms of nature to be changing all the time, owing to factors such as soil, climate, transplantation, and geology. In terms of the myth of the four ages, Banks believed in a golden age, when everything had a settlement and a fixed character, and natural history was conceived as a map rather than a sequence; while, for his part, Buffon believed in an iron age, when time was on the march and everything was in motion, when differences in development were visible indicators of passage, like the divisions on the dial of a clock.

Of course this broad division between "essentialists" (who believed in an unchanging essence) and "environmentalists" (who believed the environment brought about fundamental changes) was permeable. No one was more active in the transplantation of species than Banks, most notoriously in his plan to grow breadfruit trees native to Tahiti in the West Indies as cheap food for slaves, an initiative that erupted in the famous mutiny on the *Bounty* and, in the end, proved a feeble alternative to existing sources of nutrition. As for the environmentalists, they could never be sure when time started, and whether the history of species spelled improvement or degeneration. Time had a disconcerting habit of running backwards as well as forwards, creating doubts that colored the later theories of evolution developed by Charles Darwin and Alfred Russel Wallace.

HUMAN POPULATIONS

In trying to account for the diversity of human populations, the same broad divisions survived, and the same doubts and contradictions. In the sphere of ethnology, those who believed in "polygenesis" – namely, that inhabitants of different regions were separately created and therefore originally distinct, and would always bear the same character – echoed essentialists such as Banks on the immutability of species. Thus Henry Home, Lord Kames, a powerful advocate of polygenesis, argued that chance has nothing to do with differences in what he called "national character":

> Where the greatest part of a nation is of one character, education and example may extend it over the whole; but the character of that greater part can have no foundation but nature. What resource then have we for explaining the opposite manners of the islanders [of the South Seas], but that they are of different races?[1]

The environmentalist position among early students of human development, on the other hand, was founded on "monogenesis," according to which a single human species had acquired wide variations as the familiar factors of soil, climate, and geology operated on it. Now, though, the transformation was affected by many other supplemental causes, such as material culture, technology, travel, systems of law, education, government, property, relations between the sexes, and exchange. One of the most eminent of the monogenesists was the cantankerous Johann Reinhold Forster, the official natural historian on Cook's second voyage to the South Seas (1772–5), who used the laboratory of the Pacific to make the first serious attempts at comparative ethnology. Correctly hypothesizing that the Polynesian islands – stretching from Aotearoa (New Zealand) in the west to Rapanui (Easter Island) in the east – had been colonized in a general migration eastwards from Malaysia by a people of the same original culture and language, he had an unrivaled view of how variations in environment resulted in changes not only in politics and wealth,

Figure 27 A late eighteenth-century engraving of four Tahitian natives.

but also physique, complexion, and temperament. "Nay," he wrote, "they often produce a material difference in the color, habits, and forms of the human species."[2] In terms of the Polynesian diaspora, the inhabitants of the Society Islands (Tahiti and its neighboring islands) came out on top, in Forster's opinion, with a climate so pleasant, vegetation so lush, and seas so bountiful that there emerged not only an opulent chiefly system of government and property rights for everyone, but also distinctive coloring, muscle tone, and stature. Near to the bottom came the inhabitants of Dusky Bay, in the south of New Zealand's South Island, who were poor, violent, and ill-conditioned – but not so utterly wretched as the non-Polynesians of Tierra del Fuego, a benighted people who represented the bottom of Forster's scale.

THE GREAT MAP OF MANKIND

When Edmund Burke said that navigators such as Cook had unrolled the great map of mankind, he was using a cartographical metaphor to make sense of the kind of anthropology Forster was writing. Here a history of the human world was spread out, proceeding from primitive beginnings to its flourishing amidst commerce and civility, and yet entirely detached from European influence. For the first time, the early sequences of what was known as "conjectural" or "stadial" history – the history of humanity as it passed through stages – were available for experimental study. Travel through space amounted to travel through time: the different eras of social development were accessible by ship. The curious observer could travel back and forth between them, discriminating as minutely as he pleased.

It was soon clear to Forster, however, that it was not quite so simple, because the map of humanity in the Pacific did not reveal an advancing set of coordinates between lines of latitude and stages of development, which is what he first hypothesized. Clearly some nations had done well, and others poorly; and even within one nation, such as the Tahitians, a privileged class (the *arioi*) had thrived, while those beneath (who, Forster suspected, were the remains of a vanquished population) were visibly less wealthy and physically smaller and darker. The regular four-part pattern of development charted by stadialists such as John Millar in his *Observations concerning the Distinction of Ranks in Society* (1771) – which traced human progress from hunting and gathering to pastoral nomadism, thence to agriculture, and finally to *doux commerce* – was contradicted not only by examples of primitivism that were clearly derived, not original, but also by degeneration occurring in places of great natural amenity, often alongside manifest proof of its opposite.

PRIMITIVES

In Europe there were a number of efforts made to smooth out these contradictions, either by praising the nobility of "savagery" or by insisting on the value of "politeness." Rousseau's influential *Discourse on the Origin and Basis of Inequality among Men* (1754) was an attempt to harness the best examples of so-called savage culture to a prehistorical primitive innocence that begins to spoil as soon as social formations take place, and is ruined utterly by the institution of private property. Politeness was supported by the bulk of stadial thinkers, who interpreted the growing extent of trade, knowledge, and productive techniques as the welcome destiny of humankind and the justification of empire. Johnson often undertook to be the spokesman for this view, as when he saw Omai, the native Raiatean brought to London from Cook's second voyage, silhouetted against a window in conversation with Lord Mulgrave: "they sat with their backs to the light fronting me," he said, "so that I could not see distinctly; and there was so little of the savage in Omai, that I was afraid to speak to either, lest

I should mistake one for the other" (Boswell, *Life*, 3:8). All things are possible, he concluded, if savagery is exposed to civility.

The most subtle handling of this debate was Denis Diderot's, and the most prophetic, Jonathan Swift's. Armed by his contributions to Guillaume Thomas Raynal's *Histoire des deux Indes* (translated as *A History of the East and West Indies*, 1783) and with the advantage of recent accounts of visits to Tahiti, Diderot wrote his *Supplement au voyage de Bougainville* (1772), in which he pretended to ventriloquize the speech of a heroic primitive dwelling in what had, until the arrival of Europeans, been a terrestrial paradise. Hymning the joys of an uninhibited and innocent sexuality in a land where men and women went naked without shame and bread grew on trees, Orou holds up to ridicule the scruples of Bougainville's chaplain, who cries out, "My order! My order!" when beautiful young women expect his company in bed. Located in "the ocean of fantasy," this dialogue merges into another that reveals how necessary to the formality and repression of sexual relations in France is the dream of an uninhibited other place. Diderot seems to be saying that we use the remotest places of the earth to discover what society needs to find – not as an alternative, but as a supplement.

For his part, Swift turns to a utopia of horses in the South Seas as his litmus test for the contradictions that were to surface in Forster's anthropology. The Yahoos of the fourth part of *Gulliver's Travels* (1726) present an enigma: it is not certain whether they are the degenerate offspring of European castaways or autochthonous (indigenous) monsters. Gulliver is never sure how to process and express this – whether to explain that he has had a sight of perfect human figures in all their native nastiness, hence his horror and disgust, or to suppose that he is shocked by descendants of someone exactly like himself, now rendered ugly by privation and acquired ignorance. Are beast-like humans the originals from which we spring? Are they the repulsive and degenerate outcome of bad chances and miserable accidents? Gulliver is touring the same difficulties as Forster, but without any Rousseauvian ideas about primitive innocence or any theory of development that might serve to obscure the resemblances between Yahoos and modern exemplars of civility.

WHAT CAN SAVAGES TELL?

Samuel Johnson approached anthropology from a position of willful or disguised ignorance. Of the information brought home from the South Seas he was generally contemptuous. He thought the younger Forster's

Voyage Round the World (1777) was tedious, and John Hawkesworth's redaction of Cook's not much better: "Hawkesworth can tell only what the voyagers have told him; and they have found very little, only one new animal, I think" (Boswell, *Life*, 2:247).

That new nations with unique sexual customs had been discovered in places hitherto not known to exist seems not to have impressed him at all. A summary of his views of the anthropological importance of the South Seas is to be found in an exchange with Boswell, who was filled with a romantic desire to live in Tahiti or New Zealand for three years in order to understand the customs and beliefs of people living in a state of nature. Johnson demanded of him,

> What could you learn, Sir? What can savages tell, but what they themselves have seen? Of the past, or the invisible, they can tell nothing. The inhabitants of Otaheite and New-Zealand are not in a state of pure nature; for it is plain they broke off from some other people. Had they grown out of the ground, you might have judged of a state of pure nature. Fanciful people may talk of a mythology being amongst them; but it must be invention. They have once had religion, which has been gradually debased. And what account of their religion can you suppose to be learnt from savages? Only consider, Sir, our own state: our religion is in a book; we have an order of men whose duty it is to teach it … yet ask the first ten gross men you meet, and hear what they can tell of their religion. (Boswell, *Life*, 3:49–50)

On one level this is a denial of every principle of anthropological research: native informants are ignorant; a savage life is only the sum of what can be collected from an imperfect memory; mythology is a fiction invented either by the savages themselves or by those who wish to render them interesting; there is no truly primitive state of savagery to be observed. What scoundrels such as Rousseau dignify with the name of a "state of nature" is really always corrupt, for nobody grows out of the ground – and even if they did, their lack of pity, curiosity, and letters would mean that what we mistook for innocence would really be imbecility or cunning.

At the same time, Johnson's repudiation of fieldwork reveals a canny but largely submerged estimate of what is at stake in the discussions generated by the elder Forster and Kames. For example, everyone agreed that savagery is always a relative estimate of progress or degeneration; when Forster discovered what he took to be the degree-zero of prehistoric life in the inhabitants of Tierra del Fuego, he was at length inclined to believe that humans so poor, so dull, and so unlovely somehow must have been reduced to this condition. Clearly Johnson had read enough of the voyages to know that no one believed in an autochthonous origin of any

Polynesian nation in the South Seas, that these were migratory cultures that had risen or fallen according to the amenity of the landfall or, in the case of the Rapanuians, their own profuseness. What Johnson wishes to impress upon the naive Boswell is that the history of that rising and falling is purely conjectural, and that conjecture is worth nothing: "What strange narrowness of mind now is that, to think things we have not known, are better than the things which we have known" (Boswell, *Life*, 2:147).

A SYSTEM OF ANTIQUATED LIFE

Johnson set off with Boswell for the Highlands of Scotland in 1773, the year Hawkesworth published his *Account of the Voyages* and a year after Cook set sail on his second voyage through the Pacific. This was the closest Johnson came to doing fieldwork on his own account, and what he meant to collect were facts. If he might be said to be testing a theory, it was his own version of stadial development, according to which civil society had reached its apex in the rich material and intellectual culture of metropolitan London. In his *Journey to the Western Islands of Scotland* (1775) he aimed to measure the distance separating the primitive stage of development of the region (hovering somewhere between pastoralism and subsistence farming) from the standards of politeness that he and his companion represented. Here are his alpha and omega: old traditions and antiquated manners on the one side, and a nation emerging into modernity and civility on the other. Of his host at Anoch he reported that his life was "merely pastoral," his wealth consisting entirely of "one hundred sheep, as many goats, twelve milk-cows, and twenty-eight beeves [beef cows] ready for the drover" (*Works*, 9:37). He explains how such a mountainous fastness defends "the original, at least the oldest race of inhabitants" (9:43); and so it is with a sort of comical vainglory he takes his first step towards Loch Ness and into the past: "We were now to bid farewell to the luxury of travelling, and to enter a country upon which no wheel has ever rolled" (9:29). Nevertheless he detects many signs of progress in the circulation of money and the reach of the law, concluding, with apparent approval, "There was perhaps never any change of national manners so quick, so great, and so general, as that which has operated in the Highlands, by the last conquest, and the subsequent laws" (9:57). There is only one way for the Highlands to go, and that is rapidly into the present.

Such stadial certainty is undercut, however, by melancholy reflections: "We came thither too late to see what we expected, a people of peculiar appearance, and a system of antiquated life" (*Works*, 9:57). When he does behold antiquated manners he is for the most part impatient with them, especially if they require him to go to bed on straw, to travel without wheels, and to listen to a pack of lies from people who will tell the curious traveler anything they think he wants to know. It is then that he catches a strong flavor of clan life and its "muddy mixture of pride and ignorance" (*Works*, 9:89). At the same time, he reports the general discontent among Highlanders of all classes owing to the rise of rents, the plague of emigration, and the laws against wearing the plaid and the carrying of arms. He recurs to the same theme that Cook was to rehearse when on his return he saw Tahiti blasted by venereal disease, and predicted in the South Seas the same miseries of disease and depopulation for the indigenous people that had been endured for so many centuries in the Americas. In a solemn moment Johnson assesses the damage to what was once a cultural focus with a lot of heat in it: "The clans retain little now of their original character, their ferocity of temper is softened, their military ardor is extinguished, their dignity of independence is depressed, their contempt of government subdued, and their reverence for their chiefs abated" (*Works*, 9:57). What is he describing but the degeneration that is the result of modernization, the retrogradation that accompanies progress? If he came too late to witness antiquated life, he came too early to see unequivocal signs of progress.

There are a number of symptoms of Johnson's failure to find the right time for his history. What objectively he identifies as the intellectual poverty of a nation that has no historians (*Works*, 9:50), or the intellectual retrogradation of the Highland traveler who "knows less as he hears more" (9:51), is finally thoroughly internalized as his own inability to process facts that seem to belong to different eras, confounding his ability to distinguish between true knowledge and fiction. Opulence, for example, is alive and well in the Highlands, and all the more surprising for its sudden appearance amidst scenes of natural barrenness. The house of McLeod at Raasay was "such a seat of hospitality, amidst the winds and waters, [as filled] the imagination with a delightful contrariety of images ... without is the rough ocean and the rocky land, the beating billows and the howling storm: within is plenty and elegance, beauty and gaiety, the song and the dance" (9:66).

Johnson compared the effect on the mind to the fictions of Gothic romance: "Whatever is imaged in the wildest tale, if giants, dragons, and enchantments be expected, would be felt by him, who, wandering in the mountains without a guide, or upon the sea without a pilot, should be carried amidst his terror and uncertainty, to the hospitality and elegance of Raasay or Dunvegan" (*Works*, 9:77). Despite his perpetual reminders to the reader of the ignorance of bards and genealogists in the Highlands, it is in these Gothic havens that Johnson learned the tales of the McLeods and the traditions of the Macleans and had no difficulty in believing them as family history. Although he warns us not to fill the vacuum of information with the pseudo-primitivism of Ossian (see chapter 32, "Nationalism"), he spends pages discussing evidence of the extrasensory perception known as "second sight," described as "a mode of seeing, superadded to that which Nature generally bestows" (*Works*, 9:108). Of this faculty, which might have been suspected of being the most romantic of all, Johnson says, "The local frequency of a power, which is nowhere totally unknown … [instructs us that] where we are unable to decide by antecedent reason, we must be content to yield to the force of testimony" (*Works*, 9:107). No anthropologist could be more judicious or less partial; no conjectural historian could be more ready to admit that things we have not known are more interesting than those we have.

NOTES

1 Henry Home, Lord Kames, *Sketches of the History of Man*, 4 vols. (London, 1778), 1:39–40.

2 J. R. Forster, *Observations Made during a Voyage Round the World*, ed. Nicholas Thomas, Harriet Guest, and Michael Dettelbach (Honolulu: University of Hawai'i Press, 1996), p. 152.

CHAPTER 13

Authorship

Dustin Griffin

> A'UTHOR. *n.s.* [*auctor*, Lat.]
> 4. A writer in general.
>
> Yet their own *authors* faithfully affirm,
> That the land Salike lies in Germany. *Shakesp. Henry V.*

To understand both Johnson's career as an author and his writings about authorship, it can help to situate him in the context of mid-eighteenth-century authorship: who were authors in Johnson's day? What changes were under way in the conditions and forms of authorship, from the days of Johnson's first publication in 1735 to his posthumously published piece in 1785? What kinds of literary work were available to them? How were authors regarded by their contemporaries?

A REPUBLIC OF LETTERS

It is commonly suggested that over the course of Johnson's lifetime authorship was transformed – partly by Johnson's own example – from ill-paid drudgery, ignominious dependence on a patron, or gentlemanly amateurism to a highly respected and well-remunerated "profession." Literary historians in recent years focusing on the growth of print culture in the eighteenth century, on the development of a literary marketplace, on the Copyright Act of 1709 and the end of perpetual copyright in 1774, and on the "birth of the modern author" have supported this picture of progress by authors towards "independence." But these terms have been underdefined, and their loose use distorts the world in which authors worked. The Copyright Act, for example, was regarded in its own day as a "booksellers' bill": it protected not an author, who commonly sold his rights, but the bookseller who bought them. The end of perpetual copyright had virtually no effect on new writing. It would be more accurate to say that change was slow and uneven, that authorship took many forms, that some older cultural practices persisted, including patronage and what has been called "scribal culture" (writing but choosing not to print), and that in the closing years of the eighteenth century most authors who sought to print still struggled not only to succeed but also to gain respect.

Who were authors? When Johnson began writing, authorship – once a relatively privileged domain largely restricted to men of education and gentlemanly status – had become open to almost anybody. Or so traditionalists like Alexander Pope complained. His *Dunciad Variorum* (1729), a great poem about bad writers, was prompted, he declares satirically, by the deplorable fact that paper had become so cheap and printers so numerous "that a deluge of authors cover'd the land."[1] Most of them, Pope claimed, had no qualifications – no talent, no command of the classical or native literary tradition, no taste – and were only published because publishers (then mostly called "booksellers") had no taste either, and cared only to produce cheap goods that they thought might sell to an expanding reading audience that could not tell the difference between true wit and trash.

It is true that, in the course of Johnson's writing life, many of his fellow authors were obscure and anonymous, producing copy for booksellers and printers, or for political paymasters who needed a sharply worded pamphlet in defense of the ministry, or a timely piece of character assassination. They worked in Grub Street – as Johnson defines it in the *Dictionary*, "Originally the name of a street in Moorfields in London, much inhabited by writers of small histories, dictionaries, and temporary poems; whence any mean production is called *grubstreet.*" Many authors were women, especially from the "middling orders." But many other writers came from the traditional authorial class: university-educated gentlemen, or clergymen seeking to get their sermons published. A number of writers regarded themselves as "gentleman authors," emphasizing that they were writing for fame, not money. This group included some of the best writers among Johnson's contemporaries: Thomas Gray, David Hume, Edward Gibbon, Edmund Burke, and James Boswell. Oliver Goldsmith aspired to this status, though he never quite made it. Some authors were members of the landed gentry or even aristocracy – Henry St. John, Viscount Bolingbroke; Lady Mary Wortley Montagu; Philip Stanhope, fourth Earl of Chesterfield; Henry Home, Lord Kames; James Burnett, Lord Monboddo; George, Lord Lyttelton – but there were far fewer titled writers of note than in John Dryden's or even Pope's day: Pope's nemesis, the influential satirist John Lord Hervey, died in 1740.

Demographically various, writers in this period are sometimes said to have belonged to a "republic of letters," in which social rank counted for nothing and literary merit for everything. But the "republic of letters" had always been an idealization of real relations among writers, and in practice, as some eighteenth-century observers noted, it could be more like an anarchy than a republic. Authors, perhaps more in London than in Edinburgh, could be fiercely critical of their fellow authors: the novelist and editor of the *Critical Review*, Tobias Smollett, sneered at the writers for the rival *Monthly Review* as "wretched Hirelings, without Talent, Candour, Spirit, or Circumspection ... obscure Hackney Writers, accidentally enlisted in the service of an undistinguishing Bookseller." But such sneers, like the fulsome praise of the republic of letters, ought to be read with a grain of salt: Smollett had a financial interest in discrediting writers for the rival publication.

THE CONDITIONS OF AUTHORSHIP

How many authors were there in Johnson's day? Far more than those mentioned in the typical literary history, which focuses on a few particularly eminent writers who worked in what we now think of as the "literary" genres of poetry, drama, prose fiction, and perhaps periodical essays. But much of the "literature" of the day took the form of history, political economy, travel writing, natural philosophy (what we would call "science"), sermons, and even medicine. When those forms are included, and when we look beyond the highly selective list of writers in a typical anthology of eighteenth-century writing, the number of writers working in London was perhaps, as Johnson suggested, "several thousands" (*Works*, 5:10), including a significant number of women novelists and playwrights. It has been reliably estimated that the number of women authors was increasing at mid-century by 50 percent per decade (see chapter 47, "Women writers").

Conditions of authorship were already changing when Johnson began to think of himself as a writer, beginning with the genres in which an author might work. Most genres – the various kinds of poetry, tragedy and comedy, sermon, philosophical treatise, periodical essay, prose fictional romance – were already well-established literary forms. Newer forms, such as the novel, the Oriental tale, and the essay in literary criticism, had widened the range of available choices. An aspiring writer might well set out for London, the literary capital, with an unpublished play in his pocket, as Johnson did in 1737. Or he might begin more cautiously by sending an anonymous contribution to the new *Gentleman's Magazine*, founded in 1731, or to another of the thirty or so periodicals being published in 1760, and about eighty by 1800 (see chapter 25, "Journalism"). In time he – or, less commonly, she – might become a regular contributor and even a subeditor. Two other new publications offered other opportunities: the *Monthly Review*, which began publishing in 1749, and the *Critical Review*, which began in 1756, promised to provide reviews of all new books of note, and signed up reviewers to produce the copy. (Smollett's reviewers at the *Critical* included an ordained clergyman and Fellow of the Royal Society, a physician, and a professor of Greek at Cambridge.)

COMMISSIONS

Enterprising booksellers, who saw a market for abridgments of long treatises, popular treatments of such topics as "The Natural History of the Earth," translations of modern writings from Continental Europe, and anthologies and compilations of all kinds, commissioned writers, at very modest wages, to supply them. Johnson perhaps had such writers in mind when he referred to "the drudges of the pen, the manufacturers of literature, who have set up for authors, either with or without a regular initiation, and like other artificers, have no other care than to deliver their tale of wares at the stated time" (*Works*, 5:10). Such writers for booksellers were typically paid so much per printed sheet, and for most of them the earnings were barely enough to pay the rent. But booksellers sometimes initiated much more ambitious and rewarding projects: Johnson's *Lives of the Poets*, for which he was paid a handsome lump sum, were commissioned by a group of booksellers for a new edition of "the English Poets."

Another form of commissioned work in Johnson's day was political writing on behalf of a party, a faction, or even the governmental ministry, which by the first quarter of the eighteenth century had recognized that hired writers could help defend government policy, shape public opinion, and ultimately put pressure on Members of Parliament. Such writing, often ad hominem and virulent in tone, was usually published anonymously, and was not surprisingly regarded (by those on the other side of a political divide) as well-paid prostitution of the pen. Still, it attracted a number of talented pens, including those of Henry Fielding, Edmund Burke, and Johnson himself.

A BUYER'S MARKET

More commonly an author in Johnson's day would approach a bookseller with a piece of finished work. It was a buyer's market, and booksellers would pay no more than they thought they had to. (Historians of book publishing currently debate whether booksellers were also animated by idealistic motives.) The amount of "copy money" varied considerably, depending on the reputation of the writer and the estimated market for the work (see chapter 15, "Book trade"). A few success stories have attracted a disproportionate part of scholars' attention. Less known is the fate of most writers, especially novelists, who were paid as little as £1 for all rights. If you were a dramatist, the challenge would be to persuade one of the two or three theater managers in London to produce your play, which would earn you the receipts of every third performance. If your play were accepted, you might (at mid-century) hope to get £150–200, including payment for subsequent publication of the play text (see chapter 43, "Theatre"). One scholar has concluded that, until the 1780s, virtually nobody could earn a living just by writing plays.[2]

An author in Johnson's day might also choose to take on some of the financial risk of publishing, agreeing, for example, to reimburse any losses, in exchange for a share of the profits; or selling the rights to a single edition only (in hopes of selling rights to a second edition later). A small percentage of books were still being published "by subscription," whereby a writer tried to round up commitments to buy the book (when eventually published) from friends, colleagues, and would-be patrons. In some instances, such books included printed lists of the subscribers. An author who wanted badly enough to get into print could pay the costs of printing and distribution, in which case the title page might say that the book had been "printed for the author." As a form of vanity publishing, it had little status in the book trade; authors were not often willing to expose themselves in this way, and booksellers were not inclined to push sales of the books. But some successful and respected works were in fact published "for the author," including Boswell's *Life of Johnson*.

AUTHORS BY PROFESSION

Very few authors made a living from their writing. Those who lived in some comfort usually did not depend on their writing to support them. Some, like Johnson, had government pensions. Some received other forms of support from sinecures or even annuities from a private patron, even though the patronage system was in decline in Johnson's day. (Some writers little known today, such as Johnson's friends Thomas Birch and William Oldys, received considerable patronage into the 1750s.)

To refer to those who received payment for their writing as "professional writers" is misleading. The contemporary term was "author by

Figure 28 Thomas Rowlandson (?), *Bookseller & Author.*

profession," which carried the sense of publicly hanging out a shingle, and perhaps some irony, since writing was so unprofitable and so little like the learned professions (the Church, the Law, medicine, and teaching, each of which required university education). As Johnson's friend Sir John Hawkins observed, writing was a profession "that leads to no preferment … and confers no greater a reward than a supply of natural wants" (Hawkins, *Life*, p. 98). Many writers were in fact members of other professions (especially the Church and the Law), and depended on their earnings from them to produce the leisure and independence they needed for their writing. (Women writers did not have such opportunities.) As for their "independence," historian Richard B. Sher notes that many writers who had secured appointments as judges, professors, or churchmen only succeeded in doing so because they had the support of powerful and influential patrons who recommended or appointed them. The patronage system did not disappear during the period; it persisted to the end of the century, and also took forms (particularly employment-based patronage) that we still do not sufficiently recognize.

Finally, it should be noted that not all writers in Johnson's day sought the publicity of print. Some still shared the old prejudice that publishing one's work for all to see, and taking money for it, was beneath one's dignity – especially for a woman. And although ambitious writers mostly aspired to print, it was not the case that all writers who avoided print were dismissed as lightweight amateurs. Elements of the old "scribal culture" of the late seventeenth century persisted not only into Pope's time but even to the end of the eighteenth century: Frances Burney struggled to resolve the contradiction she sensed between the "woman writer" and the "proper lady," and held back some of her writing from print. The young Jane Austen wrote in the 1790s for a private circle of family and close friends.

SOCIAL CIRCUMSTANCES

If the material conditions of authors varied, so too did their social circumstances, and they probably did not improve over Johnson's lifetime. Conventional images of the life of an "author" that have endured from Johnson's own day to ours, picturing them in the cold impoverishment of a barely furnished garret (attic), gathered with fellow writers in a tavern or coffee house, or engaging in high-minded correspondence with other members of the pan-European "republic of letters," are reasonably accurate. This was the era of some famous literary "clubs," including Johnson's own "Ivy Lane Club" and "Literary Club," whose members met regularly for drink, dinner, and vigorous conversation (see chapter 16, "Clubs"). Several booksellers, including Thomas Davies, welcomed authors at their places of business, and others, including the Dilly brothers, invited them to sumptuous dinners. Some writers gathered at meetings of the newly proliferating learned societies. But most of the life of a writer, then as now, was solitary, and most authors would not have attained sufficient eminence to receive invitations to a club or bookseller's table. As Gibbon (who enjoyed eminence and financial security) put it, a gentleman author "possessed of leisure and competency may be encouraged by the assurance of an honorable reward: but wretched is the writer, and wretched will be the work, where daily diligence is stimulated by daily hunger."[3] The life of a writer in Edinburgh (Britain's second literary city) was perhaps more sociable than in London, where, as David Hume complained, "the little Company, there, that is worth conversing with, are cold & unsociable or are warmd only by Faction and Cabal."[4]

In recent years historians of the book and of bookselling have begun to build a base of factual knowledge about the financial and social circumstances of writers. This helps to substantiate, and in some cases to qualify, what we have long known about authorship in the eighteenth century from contemporary representations. When they describe the life of writing, Gibbon and his contemporaries commonly use binary pairs of terms that they inherited from earlier generations of commentators going back at least to Dryden's day in the late seventeenth century – the leisurely man of letters *vs.* the wretched scribbler, the well-compensated author *vs.* the exploited and underpaid hack, the author who attains reputation and dignity *vs.* the one who lives and dies in bitter obscurity, the proudly independent figure who wins the admiration of the public *vs.* the flatterer dependent on a patron or the servile dependent on a bookseller. The persistence of such tropes suggests that broad conceptions of authorship did not change much from 1700 to 1800.

EIGHTEENTH-CENTURY INNOVATIONS

But some new ways of thinking about authorship did arise in the century, or at least became more prominent. Among them is the idea that the author is not just one who skillfully represents received truths about nature and human nature, but also a creator of some "original composition" – *originality* is one of the buzzwords of late eighteenth-century literary culture. One of Johnson's definitions of *author* is "The first writer of any thing; distinct from the *translator* or *compiler*," emphasizing the author's independence from what has come before. And although many books still appeared anonymously, the author was increasingly one whose name appeared on a title page and who was thus regarded as a particular individual. Title pages also note that a book has been written "by the author of ...," implying that a good "author" is someone who has produced a distinctive body of work.

The author is also increasingly regarded as a biographical subject, whose writing life may be traced from beginning to end, someone with a personal history that may (or may not) match the image projected by his writings. Hence the sharp increase, during the period, of discussions of an author's life and works, considered together or separately. Some of the best writing in the period deals with the working lives of authors, from James Ralph's *Case of Authors by Profession* (1758) to Goldsmith's *Citizen of the World* essays (1762) and Johnson's own *Lives of the Poets*. Finally, as there emerged the idea that, in Johnson's words, "The chief glory of every people arises from its authours" (*Works*, 18:109), the practice arose of proposing lists of the "best" writers and of forming and debating a "canon" of the standard or "classic" English authors, from Chaucer, Spenser, Shakespeare, and Milton down to more recent classics such as Dryden, Addison, Swift, and Pope.

NOTES

1 Alexander Pope, *The Twickenham Edition of the Poems of Alexander Pope*, ed. John Butt *et al.*, 11 vols. in 12 (New Haven, CT: Yale University Press, 1939–69), 5:49.
2 Robert Hume and Judith Milhous, "Playwrights' Remuneration in Eighteenth-Century London," *Harvard Library Bulletin*, n.s. 10 (Fall 1999), 1–90, at p. 53.
3 *The Autobiographies of Edward Gibbon*, ed. J. Murray (London, 1896), p. 347.
4 *The Letters of David Hume*, ed. J. Y. T Greig, 2 vols. (Oxford: Clarendon Press, 1932), 1:272.

CHAPTER 14

Biography

H. J. Jackson

BIO'GRAPHY. *n.s.* [βίος and γράφω.]

> In writing the lives of men, which is called *biography*, some authors place every thing in the precise order of time when it occurred. *Watts's Logick.*

Of the various realms of learning enriched by Johnson and the various good reasons that we have for valuing him, his contributions to biography rank at or near the top of the scale. Himself the author of the most influential literary biographies and the most respected commentary on biography ever written in English, he was also the subject of the uncontested (though perennially controversial) leader among British biographies. But the superlatives that we use to describe Johnson's place in the history of biography should not blind us to the contexts that produced his essays on biography in the *Rambler* and the *Idler* in the 1750s, his *Lives of the Poets* (1779–81), and Boswell's *Life* (1791). These are great works, but they are not incomparable, and it is no diminution of their greatness to see how they arose out of, and fed into, the popular literature of their time. Johnson could no more have written his essays without having had plenty of examples to think about than Aristotle could have composed his *Poetics* without a dramatic tradition to draw on. Nor would Johnson and Boswell have struggled as they did with their biographical works, or their publishers have put up with their repeated failures to meet deadlines, if they had not been confident about finding an appreciative audience.

BACKGROUNDS

The deep history of biography, or accounts of the lives of individuals, stretches back as far as we can see. The first subjects were holy men, their lives held up as models of goodness and they themselves as objects of reverence: this is the tradition that is described as "hagiographical," now usually with implicit disparagement, though the term ought to be neutral and the type is still prevalent. The hagiographic treatment was soon extended from prophets, saints (women found an opportunity here), and churchmen to secular figures – great rulers and statesmen, military leaders, and others – whose lives affected the welfare of nations. The second-century Greek biographer Plutarch set the standard in his *Lives of the Emperors* and *Parallel Lives*. High achievers in other fields were added gradually, philosophers being among the first of them, thanks to the efforts of Diogenes Laertius in the first century – and "philosopher" came to be an elastic term that could include scholars and thinkers more generally. Although Boswell begins the *Life of Johnson* by praising Johnson's achievements in biography, the real justification was his status as the learned "philosopher" who had produced the *Rambler* and the *Dictionary* (Boswell, *Life*, 1:25). Writers were paid tribute in biographical prefaces to their collected works from early on, but the tribute was applied sparingly, and mainly to poets. (Johnson's *Lives of the Poets* were originally commissioned as a series of such prefaces, intended to be dispersed among the volumes of a large edition.) Biographies reflect the values of the societies for which they are produced as well as the state of the genre at a given moment, and the range of possibility was by our lights relatively restricted in the eighteenth century.

Restricted, that is, but for the shadow tradition of notoriety. If it was possible to be exceptionally good and to be celebrated on that account, it was also possible to be exceptionally bad in one way or another. A lucrative market for lives of tyrants, outlaws, courtesans, and criminals emerged towards the end of the seventeenth century and gained ground steadily throughout the eighteenth, as we can tell by the still tangible success of their fictional counterparts, the *Roxana*s and *Moll Flanders*es and *Jonathan Wild*s which represent barely the tip of the iceberg of the literature of scandal. These popular narratives could be excused, even promoted, for their cautionary value, especially if they took the form of a deathbed repentance or gallows confession, and illustrated the dangers of a life of vice. But they also aroused suspicion as an illicit, voyeuristic pleasure and a bad precedent. Johnson's circle, for instance, debated the widespread belief that *The Beggar's Opera*, with its glamorous highwayman hero, seduced young men into a life of crime (Boswell, *Life*, 2:367). Its real-life equivalents, *A Complete History of the Lives and Robberies of the Most Notorious Highwaymen* (1714) and *A General History of the Pyrates* (1724), went through many editions – the *Pyrates* reprinted, by one count, eighteen times before 1800. Throughout the century biography and autobiography were undifferentiated; there was no separate word for the latter, so the poet and actor Colley Cibber's amusing and commercially successful *Life* of 1740, for instance, was simply described on the title page as "written by himself."

MARKETS

The market for gallows literature and lives of scandal was fostered by new media, the newspapers and magazines that proliferated in the eighteenth century and were always on the lookout for fresh material – or warmed-over old material, come to that. Johnson got his start as a biographer in just such a setting, writing short, anonymous, potboiler biographies for the *Gentleman's Magazine* from 1738 onward (see chapter 25, "Journalism"). But with his first extended biographical work, even though it was published anonymously, he nailed his colors to the mast and set out to distinguish responsible biography from its less scrupulous rivals. The life of his friend Richard Savage might have been presented almost as a fairytale: it was the story of an illegitimate son rejected by his aristocratic family, rising by his own merits to become the protégé of the queen, being convicted but then pardoned of murder, and dying in a debtors' prison. But in *An Account of the Life of Mr Richard Savage, Son of the Earl Rivers* (1744), Johnson played down the lurid details to give a nuanced, compassionate, tragicomical account of a complex and conflicted man. His subject is not Savage the supposed murderer but Savage the man of rare intellectual gifts that did not bring him contentment – a sad addition to the many volumes already in print that "enumerate the miseries of the learned, and relate their unhappy lives, and untimely deaths" (*Lives*, 3:120).

Because it was so popular, biography was a very competitive kind of writing, as the careers of Johnson and Boswell indicate. Johnson had a notice printed in the *Gentleman's Magazine* right after Savage died, declaring his credentials as a confidant of Savage's and warning off less qualified would-be biographers who might be tempted, he said, to "supply from Invention the want of Intelligence, and … publish only a Novel filled with romantic Adventures, and imaginary Amours" (*Lives*, 3:382). Boswell used a similar tactic when he announced his forthcoming biography in 1785 in an advertisement at the end of the *Journal of a Tour to the Hebrides*, but his rivals ignored him; since it was another six years before his work appeared, he was able both to incorporate materials from the earlier biographies and to attack or disparage them in print. On the whole, competition in the marketplace was a good thing for biography, since it fostered innovation and improvement, led to a diversification of different kinds of biography, and gradually freed biography as a genre from the possessive grip of history.

BETWEEN HISTORY AND FICTION

For all its distinction, Johnson's *Life of Savage* is fundamentally flawed. Modern research has demonstrated that it is more than likely that Johnson's subject was not, after all, the son of the Earl Rivers, but was either deluded or an impostor. Johnson's biography makes no allowance for this possibility. In lesser ways too, his work has been accused of inaccuracy. It nevertheless exhibits the qualities that Johnson admired in biographical writing, as he articulated them in later essays. It combines the firsthand evidence of someone who had been on close terms with his subject with other sources. It does not conceal faults. It makes pertinent use of detail and anecdote. It focuses on the inner rather than the outer life, since external circumstances vary but thoughts and feelings are widely shared, and we can learn from the experiences and reactions of others. "The prince feels the same pain when an invader seizes a province," Johnson wrote, "as the farmer when a thief drives away his cow" (*Works*, 3:263); "We are all prompted by the same motives, all deceived by the same fallacies, all animated by hope, obstructed by danger, entangled by desire, and seduced by pleasure" (*Works*, 2:320). The case that Johnson made for biography as the best kind of narrative writing, "that which is most eagerly read, and most easily applied to the purposes of life" (*Works*, 2:261), rests on its position halfway between history and fiction: it tells stories about manners and behavior in private life (such as history did not usually offer) that are believed to be true (as is not the case with fiction).

By the time he published *The Life of Savage* in 1744, when he was in his mid-thirties, Johnson had already consumed more than his share of bad biographies that erred on the side either of history (too many pointless facts) or of fiction (invented plots). Most of these were ephemeral, the work of hack writers like himself aiming to satisfy public curiosity about the recently dead. Alexander Pope's enemy Edmund Curll, for example, was a bookseller infamous for rushing out "lives" padded out with documents such as the will and whatever other unpublished manuscripts he could get his hands on – hence John Arbuthnot's quip that Curll had "added a new terror to death."

Two things need to be emphasized: the ubiquity of life stories in the culture of the time, and the comparative rarity of substantial, freestanding biographies. Even *The Life of Savage*, an octavo pamphlet of 180

AN
ACCOUNT
OF THE
LIFE
OF
Mr *Richard Savage,*
Son of the Earl RIVERS.

LONDON:
Printed for J. ROBERTS in *Warwick-Lane.*
M.DCC.XLIV.

Figure 29 Samuel Johnson, *An Account of the Life of Mr. Richard Savage.*

pages when it first appeared, was long for its day, when the norm was quickie articles in newspapers and magazines, or pamphlets or funeral sermons in a slightly longer-lasting format. Most of these were what we call junk reading, meant to be read and cast aside. The odd one might go into a second edition, but for the majority, their prospects of survival depended on being anthologized and thus forming part of a set.

BIOGRAPHICAL COLLECTIONS

The best chance for all but the starriest characters was to be carried by others of their kind: hence collections like the *Lives of All the Chancellors*, *Lives of the British Admirals*, *Memoirs of Several Ladies of Great Britain*, and so on. Anthologies were legion, the serious and sensational ends of the spectrum being best represented by the imposing, scholarly *Biographia Britannica* of 1747–66 (which Johnson made use of in the *Lives of the Poets*) and the *Newgate Calendar; or, Malefactors' Bloody Register*, based on a monthly record of executed criminals, which first appeared in five volumes in 1773. Only the second of these includes an entry (not by Johnson) for Richard Savage.

The Life of Savage was by this standard remarkably successful, with or without Johnson's name on it. Before he recycled it himself in the *Lives of the Poets*, it had gone through five editions on its own or with a couple of Johnson's shorter lives tacked on; had been adopted as a prefatory biography in editions of Savage's *Works*, which were themselves regularly reprinted; and had been pirated or plagiarized in some prominent places, notably William Ayre's *Memoirs of Pope* (1745) and the *Lives of the Poets of Great Britain and Ireland* (1753), credited to Theophilus Cibber, though actually ghostwritten by Robert Shiels. The collections were naturally, as is the custom with reference books, vulnerable to pillaging by other collections lower down in the publishing food chain, so Shiels's abridgment can be found reprinted without acknowledgment either to him or to Johnson in a two-volume schoolbook of 1777, the long title of which reveals commonplace notions about biography in the period: it is *The Beauties of Biography ... Extracted ... for the Instruction of Youth of Both Sexes, and Calculated to Inspire Them with a Love of Virtue, and Create a Spirit of Emulation Absolutely Necessary to Those Who Would Wish to Arrive at Any Degree of Superiority in Their Different Professions, or Amusements.* Johnson would surely have had mixed feelings if he had found his *Life of Savage* in this context, and not only because of the motley company he kept, which included (surprisingly) the sixteenth-century Italian writer Niccolò Machiavelli and the debauched Earl of Rochester. "Love of Virtue" has to be a good thing, but "Spirit of Emulation" and the desire to achieve superiority in a profession would seem to miss the point with characters like these. While Johnson certainly thought that biographies could and should be instructive, he did not have in mind direct professional training but something more profound.

INTERESTING AND USEFUL

Rambler 60 argues that biography strengthens human sympathies by exercising the imagination. It outlines a theory about the psychology of reading which also constitutes a program for the writer of biography. Both writer and reader, Johnson says, ideally put themselves in the place of the other person, "so that we feel, while the deception lasts, whatever motions would be excited by the same good or evil happening to ourselves" (*Works*, 3:319). A concomitant of this approach is the challenge that he casually offers to the genre as a whole, one so radical that I believe it has yet to be taken up by any writer, publisher, or reader – the idea that, in the right hands, *any* life could be made interesting and useful. In fact the life of people other than heroes and emperors may be most illuminating of all, since, as Johnson writes, "It is not easy for the most artful writer to give us an interest in happiness or misery, which we think ourselves never likely to feel … Histories of the downfal of kingdoms, and revolutions of empires, are read with great tranquillity" (*Works*, 3:319).

Johnson spent more than four decades as a practicing writer (only incidentally a biographer) aiming to reach a broad-based public, and gradually making a name for himself. As he worked, conditions changed and biography evolved, steadily gaining respectability. Boswell – consumed, as he frankly admitted, by literary ambition – proudly put his name to his first book, *An Account of Corsica, the Journal of a Tour to that Island; and Memoirs of Pascal Paoli* (1768), which highlighted his encounters with a military hero. For Boswell the subject had to be an exceptional person, and the biographer's natural attitude was not, as Johnson would have it, fellow feeling but awe. The scale of the work reflected the importance of the subject; the biography was to be a permanent monument. So Boswell's biography of Johnson, when it finally appeared, aimed to rout the opposition by its exhaustiveness. If the *Life of Johnson*, a work stuffed with documents and encyclopedic in scope, strikes us today almost as an archive rather than a book, it may be because its models were not Johnson's own tightly controlled biographies but some of the other kinds that his and Boswell's contemporaries enjoyed – the gossipy, the anecdotal, the epistolary, the documentary, and so on. The ingredients had been ready to hand, though the combination was *sui generis*. In different ways, working within the confines of eighteenth-century convention, Johnson and Boswell lifted biography out of the ruts of the exemplary and the cautionary.

CHAPTER 15

Book trade

Michael F. Suarez, S.J.

> BOOK. *n.s.* [*boc*, Sax. supposed from *boc*, a beech; because they wrote on beechen boards, as *liber* in Latin, from the rind of a tree.]
> 1. A volume in which we read or write.
>
> See a *book* of prayer in his hand;
> True ornaments to know a holy man. *Shakesp. Richard III.*

Most of Samuel Johnson's major undertakings – *A Dictionary of the English Language*, *The Plays of William Shakespeare*, and *The Lives of the Most Eminent English Poets* – were commissioned by booksellers. As the son of a bookseller, a professional author, and a keen observer of the book trade, Johnson understood the business of books far better than most of his contemporaries. Accordingly, no student of Johnson should neglect this highly important aspect of his life and times.

PRICES

Books were expensive. For most of the eighteenth century, the price of a pamphlet ranged, depending on its length, between six and eighteen pence (1*s.* 6*d.*) (see chapter 31, "Money"). Early in the eighteenth century, most newspapers cost 1½*d.* (the halfpenny paying for the stamp duty), although the *Spectator* sold for 2*d.* By the 1770s, a thrice-weekly London newspaper such as the *St. James Chronicle* was 3*d.* per number. A single play, which was almost always less than a hundred pages, commonly cost 1*s.* 6*d.* Novels and collected essays were generally issued at 2*s.* 6*d.* per volume "sewn" in paper wrappers, without a proper binding, and 3*s.* in a generic trade binding; *Clarissa* (1747–8) and *Humphry Clinker* (1771), for example, were priced in this way.

To understand just how much books cost, consider that an unskilled laborer earned only around £15 or £20 a year, and that a year's rent in London in 1771 was £1 8*s.* 2*d.* A typical two-volume novel, selling at 5*s.*,

Figure 30 Sutton Nicholls, *The Compleat Auctioner*, *c.* 1700, depicting a bookseller.

seems very expensive – nearly a fifth of a laborer's annual rent. The popularity of literary fiction, then, came not from those at the bottom of the social scale; only those who earned substantially more could think about buying new books.

FORMATS AND BINDINGS

The size of books changed considerably during the eighteenth century. Folios – the largest books, in which the large printed sheet of paper is folded just once to make two leaves (or four pages) – had been the proper dress of "serious literature" until the early 1740s, but afterwards they came to be used primarily for large works of reference or texts featuring important engraved illustrations. The *Biographia Britannica* (1747–66), for example, Johnson's *Dictionary*, and the publisher John Boydell's *Collection of Prints … Illustrating the Dramatic Works of Shakespeare* (1803) were all printed as folios. But folios increasingly became associated with imposing and extensive works. When Boswell suggested to Edmond Malone in 1790 that his biography of Johnson should be printed in folio, his friend replied that he "might as well throw it into the Thames, for a folio would not now be read."[1]

Quartos – roughly half the size of a folio, since each sheet is folded to give four leaves (or eight pages) – became the most common format for substantial literary works other than novels, though quartos that proved popular were often reprinted in less expensive octavo editions – in which each sheet is folded to give eight leaves (or sixteen pages) – to boost sales. Duodecimos – in which each sheet is folded to give twelve leaves (or twenty-four pages) – became increasingly common for a wide range of publications, as booksellers sought to exploit the demand for more economical books.

Novels were usually small octavos or duodecimos. The duodecimo was highly economical, and thus the favored format for the novel. Because the smaller page was suited to smaller type, a duodecimo might have almost as many words per page as a large octavo, allowing the bookseller to reduce his paper costs considerably because the duodecimo yielded half again as many pages per sheet. Large octavos typically cost 5*s.* per volume, sometimes 6*s.* or more if they were quite long. Quartos were still more expensive: Boswell's *Life of Johnson* (1791) was originally published in two quarto volumes for two guineas (£2 2*s.*); even the far less expensive second edition in three ample octavos cost 8*s.* per volume, a total of £1 4*s.*, more than a workman's annual heating bill. Because the price of print was consistently high, there was a lively collateral trade in used books, scribally published works, cheap piracies, and even counterfeit books.

Until the 1820s, most books were not offered for sale uniformly bound. A book could be bought in a plain and inexpensive generic "trade binding" of undecorated brown calf or sheep leather, or it could be purchased entirely unbound "in sheets," "sewed," or bound but uncut and undecorated "in boards." It would then be taken to a binder who worked independently of the bookseller to be custom-bound in conformity with the owner's particular tastes. "Edition binding," the uniform binding and covering of an entire edition according to the specifications of the bookseller, made its first appearance in England on a grand scale in the 1760s, when the highly entrepreneurial printer and children's bookseller John Newbery of London sold thousands of books for the juvenile market ready-bound in standardized inexpensive covers that were one-quarter leather (the spine) and three-quarters plain paper boards (the sides).

PUBLISHERS

Before a book was available for sale, the publisher had to invest a great deal of money in its production: buying paper – which accounted for some 50 percent of a book's cost – and paying typesetters ("compositors") and pressmen. Of course, not all the copies were sold at once, and the edition might not begin to make a profit for a year or two after it was printed. Meanwhile, other manuscripts that the bookseller might like to publish would come along, and he might wish to print new editions of slow-but-steady selling books, each time initiating the same process of heavy investment with delayed profits, thereby straining his financial resources. If one or more of the books did not sell, debts could accumulate.

The great majority of editions were made in quantities ranging from 500 to 1,500 copies. Between 1738 and 1785, for example, more than 90 percent of the books printed in William Strahan's large and successful London printing house were produced in edition sizes of fewer than 2,000 copies. Editions running to fewer than 500 copies generally had a higher unit cost, but press runs over 2,000 rarely reduced the production cost of each book enough to justify the longer production time, increased financial risk, and the tying up of additional capital in paper and pressmen's wages that they required. A press run of 500–750 copies may be considered typical, with 500 being most common. Although small, inexpensive books with a large audience – almanacs, catechisms, and primers – were often produced in large edition sizes, it was rarely in the bookseller's financial interest to invest in a large press run for literary works.

Booksellers often joined forces and divided a copy into shares: one bookseller might invest in two-fifths of a copy, for example, while three others might pay for a one-fifth share each. Income was proportionate to risk, which was distributed; each bookseller could invest in many different titles, diversifying his business. Moreover, the book was more likely to succeed in the market because several booksellers were actively promoting its sale in a variety of London locations. Shares in profitable copies were bought and sold by publishers, sometimes in increments as small as one sixty-fourth. These "share-books" were emblematic of the way in which the eighteenth-century book trade was a mixture of financial cooperation and competition among its members. The last three decades of the century, however, witnessed a gradual shift from shareholding arrangements to independently operating publishers with large capital resources and a growing division between wholesale and retail bookselling.

Another form of financing with implications for distribution was the serial publication of books in "parts." Serial publication, in which books were usually sold one sheet (from four to twenty-four pages, depending on the format) at a time, most commonly in weekly installments, had distinct advantages for both purchaser and publisher. The customer was able to buy on a kind of "installment plan" a work he typically could not afford to purchase outright; the bookseller reached a broader market, received income while incurring production costs, could adjust the size of each print run in keeping with recent sales, and could charge more per sheet than he would have when selling an ordinary book.

AUTHORS

Authors who could not get booksellers to publish their work – or who wished to exercise greater control over marketing, expenditures, and revenues – often resorted to private subscription to finance printing costs (see chapter 13, "Authorship"). Subscribers, whose names were listed in the front of the work, typically paid half the book's price in advance, half upon delivery of the volume. The practice was particularly popular from roughly 1710 to 1745. Subscription solved many of the problems associated with the financing, distribution, and even advertising of books; Alexander Pope had used this expedient to become very rich from the sales of his translations. But subscription grew less fashionable as it came to be regarded as an imposition on the public. Johnson revealed some of the dangers of subscription in his edition of Shakespeare: when a bookseller asked him for his list of subscribers, Johnson replied, "I have two very cogent reasons for not printing any list of subscribers; – one, that I have lost all the names, – the other, that I have spent all the money" (Boswell, *Life*, 4:111).

The bookseller's business, explained *The London Tradesman* (1747), is "to purchase original copies from authors, to employ printers to print them, and publish and sell them on their own account … but, their chief riches and profit is in the property of valuable copies." Owning "copies" – holding the right to reproduce works – was, when those works proved to be steady sellers over many years, the key to many a bookseller's long-term financial success. For more immediate profits, most booksellers also sold quills, ink, stationery, pounce, blotting paper, etc.; many dealt in patent medicines and other goods as well.

The "Act for the Encouragement of Learning," the world's first copyright law, which came into effect in 1710, gave non-renewable protection against piracy to current copy holders for twenty-one years. The owner of a new copy was entitled to legal redress against infringement for fourteen years, with fourteen more if the author were still alive at the end of the first period. Copies had to be entered in the Stationers' Register for proof of ownership. Henry Fielding's remark in *The Author's Farce* (1730) that "*Grub-Street* harbours as many Pirates as ever *Algiers* did" almost certainly occasioned a laugh from the audience, but the pirating of works by London and provincial booksellers was a persistent problem. Moreover, because the act did not extend to Ireland, Dublin conducted a lively trade in unauthorized reprints of London publications; these so-called "moral piracies" were not illegal unless they were offered for sale in England, Scotland, or Wales.

Even after a copyright had expired under the 1710 Act, however, mainstream members of the book trade continued to behave as if copyright were perpetual by respecting it as the "owner's" property and, where appropriate, even buying and selling shares in the copy. The Edinburgh bookseller Alexander Donaldson mounted a legal challenge to the idea of perpetual copyright by publishing and selling in London reprints of works that the London booksellers believed they still owned by virtue of common law, even though the copyrights had expired and the works were now in the public domain. In *Donaldson v. Becket* (1774), one of the most important legal decisions in the history of intellectual property, the Lords ruled that copyright was not perpetual. Although many long-established booksellers continued to buy and sell old copies, the book trade gradually adapted to the new ruling.

Booksellers ordinarily purchased copy from authors for a fixed sum. When appraising the worth of a writer's manuscript, the bookseller considered both the likely demand for the text and the number of printed pages it would make, which largely determined its retail price. "A sheet is a sheet with the booksellers," we read in Henry Fielding's *Amelia* (1752); "and whether it be in prose or verse, they make no difference." Authors typically sold their books to booksellers for approximately 2*s.* 5*d.* per printed sheet (i.e., four pages in folio, eight in quarto, sixteen in octavo, or twenty-four in duodecimo) in the middle decades of the eighteenth century. Booksellers manipulated the length of the works they sold – by abridging or augmenting the original text, choosing a format (e.g., quarto versus octavo), selecting a type size, and determining layout – in order to make the book cheaper or more expensive according to the market they were targeting.

Booksellers were routinely accused of exploiting writers, most of whom found it difficult to earn a living solely by writing. In *The Author* (1763), poet Charles Churchill describes writers as the "slaves of booksellers." Robert Burns similarly wrote (in "To Robert Graham of Fintry") of "Vampyre booksellers" who "drain" poor authors for their own selfish gain. But the book trade was a risky business: for every bookseller who grew rich there were many who went bankrupt, and many more still who earned a decent living, but whose prosperity was hardly noteworthy.

As many Grub Street tales attest, authorship was most often a not particularly remunerative profession. Alexander Pope was paid £15 for his *Essay on Criticism* (1711) and £7 for *The Rape of the Lock* (1714). Samuel Johnson, who called the bookseller Robert Dodsley "my patron," received from him ten guineas (£10 10*s*.) for *London* and fifteen guineas for *The Vanity of Human Wishes*. Even when lengthy, new poems typically earned less than popular prose. Edward Young's *Night Thoughts* (1742–5), a poem some 10,000 lines long, brought him 220 guineas, while Goldsmith received twenty guineas (£21) for *The Traveller* (1764), a poem of fewer than 450 lines. Needing money while working on the *Dictionary* (1755), Johnson undertook the task of writing the *Rambler* (1750–2) twice each week, for which he was paid two guineas per essay. He made nearly £426 directly from his writing, and probably at least £100 more from the sale of part or all of the copyright.

Payments to fiction writers varied considerably: Swift received £200 for *Gulliver's Travels* (1726), while Fielding was paid £700 for *Tom Jones* (1749). *Rasselas* (1759) earned Johnson £100, which was less than he had hoped for; Frances Burney, whose novel *Evelina* (1778) appeared anonymously, received only £30 from her publisher. Most novelists were paid far less. Nonfiction works, especially in multiple volumes, could be highly lucrative. Gibbon commanded two thirds of the profits for his *Decline and Fall of the Roman Empire* (6 vols., 1776–88), amassing about £6,000 – a substantial fortune, enough to support a middle-class family for a lifetime. Less sensationally, the first edition of *The Wealth of Nations* (1776) earned £500 for Adam Smith. In light of such figures, it seems scandalous that Johnson received just 300 guineas (£315) for the *Lives of the Poets*, though that was half again as much as the 200 guineas (£210) he had requested. Edmond Malone speculated that Johnson could have set his price at 1,000 or even 1,500 guineas.

READERS

Authors' compensation rose faster than inflation as the century progressed, not least because the reading public was expanding, and, with it, the market for books. The efflorescence of circulating libraries and reading clubs throughout England, and a concomitant rise in literacy, especially among women, increased the demand for books. (Begun around 1740, there were some 390 circulating libraries in England by 1800, most run by booksellers.) The tremendous popularity of the novel did much to promote the growth of literature as an important form of popular entertainment. In the first decade of the eighteenth century, only about five separate volumes of prose fiction were published each year, but in the 1750s more than forty fictional works, including reprints, were issued annually. By 1800, that number had risen to more than 150.

How did potential customers know what was available for sale? Booksellers made "sticking titles" by printing several hundred extra title pages, which were then posted as advertisements. These title pages – which often had long descriptive titles, and included the name and location of the bookseller – were stuck on walls and on the wooden "show-boards" and "rubric posts" set out in front of booksellers' shops. Booksellers also advertised to a very promising market by listing a select inventory of their wares, often with prices, on the final pages of the books they published. Edward Cave's highly successful monthly, the *Gentleman's Magazine*, founded in 1731, featured a useful list comprising many of the books published in the preceding month. Other periodicals followed suit, most notably the *London Magazine* (1732–85). Between 1773 and 1823, William Bent published a series of catalogues not unlike *Books in Print* today. These lists provide valuable information for historians, and reveal which kinds of books attracted the greatest attention at the time. Although students of English are understandably most interested in the fiction, poetry, and drama we have come to call "literature," the largest publishing category in England throughout the century was actually theology and ecclesiastical affairs.

Advertisements in London and provincial newspapers became the most important means of reaching the reading public. By the end of the 1720s, almost every sizeable provincial town had its own local weekly newspaper. Stamp duty returns indicate that in 1750 total sales of all newspapers in England amounted to some 7.3 million copies, rising to more than 16 million in 1790. The mutual growth of the periodical press and of the book trade was a synergistic phenomenon. The advent of book reviews had a strong and largely salutary effect on the book trade. The *Monthly Review* (1749–1845), brainchild of the bookseller Ralph Griffiths, became the most important source of book reviews in the eighteenth century. The *Monthly*'s main competitor was the *Critical Review* (1756–90), co-founded by Tobias Smollett; it too featured regular book reviews (see chapter 25, "Journalism").

THE PROVINCIAL TRADE

For most of the eighteenth century, the provincial trade, which came into existence only after the lapse of the Licensing Laws in 1695, was primarily a distribution network for books published in London. The income of most printers outside the metropolis came from jobbing printing and newspaper work, rather than from books. Similarly, most provincial booksellers earned the majority of their living through the sale of stationery and other goods. Nevertheless, the distribution networks and the infrastructures for the dissemination of information established by local newspaper proprietors and booksellers were vital for the success of the book trade in the provinces. Long before he came to London and began to work for Edward Cave, Johnson was witness to the slow growth of the provincial trade. Perhaps it was in Michael Johnson's Lichfield bookshop that the hungry teenager, whether satisfying his appetite by looking for apples, reading Petrarch, or taking in the ways of his father's trade, received his most important education.

NOTE

1 James Boswell, *Boswell: The Great Biographer 1789–95*, ed. Marlies K. Danzinger and Frank Brady (New Haven, CT: Yale University Press, 1989), pp. 32–3.

CHAPTER 16

Clubs

Peter Clark

CLUB. *n.s.* [*clwppa*, Welsh; *kluppel*, Dutch.]
4. An assembly of good fellows, meeting under certain conditions.

What right has any man to meet in factious *clubs* to vilify the government? *Dryden's Medal. Dedication.*

Samuel Johnson was a fractious, combative, gloomy member of a number of London clubs – the Ivy Lane Club, later on the Club (which he co-founded with Sir Joshua Reynolds), and, shortly before his death, the Essex Head Club. But there was nothing exceptional in this. Members of the educated, professional, and bourgeois classes in the Georgian capital regularly belonged to several clubs and societies. The physician turned clergyman and pioneer archaeologist William Stukeley, for example, was a member of the Royal Society, the Society of Antiquaries, the Egyptian Society, and London Masonic lodges, as well as helping to set up associations in the provincial town of Stamford where he lived for part of his life. By the 1730s one London writer remarked, "what numbers of these sociable assemblies are subsisting in this metropolis. In the country not a town … is without its club."[1]

ORIGINS

When and why did clubs and societies start? What kinds of activities did they engage in? How were they organized? And what benefits did members enjoy?

Though an earlier type of voluntary association, the religious confraternity, had flourished in the late Middle Ages, modern-style, essentially secular clubs and societies developed in the sixteenth century, both in England and on the Continent. The first real takeoff occurred in England during the English Revolution of the 1640s and 1650s. Benefiting from looser government controls and greater freedom of the press, a flurry of new political, scientific, social, musical, and other societies appeared on the scene, principally in London.

Even after the Restoration of Charles II in 1660 and the return of press censorship, the associational genie was difficult to put back into the bottle, and the number of associations continued to grow. After the Glorious Revolution of 1688 there was a powerful upsurge of associational activity, helped by political liberalization and the end of press censorship in 1695. Though London remained the noisy beehive of clubs and societies, with several thousand in the capital, others spread steadily across England and later to Ireland, Scotland, the American colonies, and India. In early eighteenth-century England associations appeared not just in bigger provincial capitals such as Norwich and Bristol, but in country towns such as Maidstone, Gloucester, and Johnson's native Lichfield, which had societies from the 1680s. During the Georgian era the English-speaking world may have had 25,000 voluntary associations.

TYPES OF ASSOCIATION

It was not just numbers that were important but the growing variety of different types of association. While Germany and France had around a dozen different types of society, Britain may have had about 130. Among the most important categories were alumni associations (for school and university), artistic societies (like the Royal Academy of Arts), book clubs, benefit clubs, debating societies, gambling clubs, horticultural societies, literary clubs, Masonic and pseudo-Masonic orders, medical clubs, music societies, neighborhood clubs, philanthropic societies, political associations, professional societies, regional and ethnic associations, sports clubs, and scientific and learned societies.

Undoubtedly, the most successful of all the voluntary associations of this period were Masonic lodges. Modern Freemasonry (as distinct from the earlier masonic craft guilds) began in London in 1717, when four local lodges, probably founded not long before, set up a federal organization headed by Grand Lodge. Within a generation Masonic lodges had spread like wildfire across the British Isles, to the British colonies, and also to a growing number of European countries. Towards the end of the eighteenth century, England had about five hundred lodges (most belonging to the original Modern order, but others to the Ancients, a breakaway order set up in the 1750s), with important clusters not just in London but in provincial cities and smaller towns. Smaller numbers flourished in both Scotland and Ireland. A survey of Masonic lodges in Europe in 1778 catalogued about 120 each in France and Germany, nearly fifty in the Netherlands, and smaller contingents in other European countries. Early ones often had English connections, having been set up by British traders or visitors, but a growing proportion of European lodges had their own national rites and practices.

Why did so many societies of such diverse types flower in eighteenth-century Britain? Two reasons have already been adduced. First, the reordering of the British political system after 1688, with the emergence of parliamentary governance and decentralization of political power to local landowners, meant not only increased political liberty but also reduced state intervention in many sectors of national administration – leaving all kinds of political, philanthropic, medical, and other societies to fill the governmental vacuum. Second, the general freedom of the press from the 1690s led to a major expansion of the media. Newspapers multiplied: by the 1780s, readers could choose from over a dozen London newspapers and fifty or so published by provincial newsmen. But so did magazines like the *Spectator*, the *Gentleman's Magazine*, or the later *Sporting Magazine* (see chapter 25, "Journalism"). Newspapers as well as magazines supplied the vital helium of publicity – advertisements, reports, commentaries – about societies, which were critical in helping them to recruit new members and giving them public recognition.

MEMBERSHIP

Club membership could be expensive, so another essential factor propelling the proliferation of voluntary associations was the improvement in living standards for the better-off classes in the eighteenth century – landowners, professional men, traders, shopkeepers, and skilled artisans – who were the principal groups joining clubs in our period. In contrast to France and the Low Countries, where living standards moved sluggishly during this period, the picture for England was one of general advances at least until the last decades of the eighteenth century.

The vast majority of clubs were urban. This reflected the dynamism and affluence of English towns and, to a growing extent, their Scottish counterparts in the period. London became the largest European metropolis during the eighteenth century, its population rising from 600,000 at its start to nearly a million by its close – buoyed up by its expansive global trade, by its role as the capital of the most powerful European state, by the influx of prosperous landowners attending Parliament and spending the season there, and by the growth of manufacturing and service trades.

At the same time British towns in general, both large and smaller centers, prospered. During the eighteenth century over two thirds of all European urban growth occurred in England, creating a large market for associational and other leisure activity.

Fueling urban population growth were high levels of migration to town. A million people may have migrated to London in the two centuries before 1750, and in 1700 around 9,000 new migrants poured into the capital each year. Here newly arrived landowners were joined by lawyers, medical men, authors and other professional groups, traders and skilled workers, wealthy widows, laborers, and poorer folk, including many young people as well as female servants (male servants largely disappeared). Those men who could afford it joined clubs and societies as a way of gaining a foothold in their new communities, making economic and other contacts, and passing time. Immigrants appeared prominently in the membership lists of all kinds of association; some societies, like the Freemasons and benefit clubs, had special procedures to help their integration.

GENDER

As we have already indicated, British societies were almost exclusively masculine bodies. Why? Women constituted the majority of the population in numerous towns in this period, and better-off women increasingly penetrated fashionable cultural and leisure life in Georgian Britain – attending the theater, going to concerts, patronizing fashionable shops, and being prominent at assemblies and routs, pleasure gardens, and the like. At home, too, a feminization of the household occurred with women taking a growing role in the furbishment of the home, in the organization of sociable activity there, and in the management of household affairs – aided by the growing number of female servants. It is arguable that men patronized societies as a refuge, as a segregated space, against this feminine invasion of public and private space. Few societies explicitly excluded women from membership: only the Freemasons did that openly in their rules. But still it is clear that the general bias was against the admission of women.

Not that women necessarily wanted to join. There are several good reasons why women may have found it unattractive to become members of clubs and societies. One was their inferior legal status: married women were dependent on their husbands. This meant that they might have to ask their husbands' permission to join a society and pay the fees. Even if a husband agreed, his spouse would not be able to hold club office and so serve as a full member. Those female clubs which did operate, mostly benefit societies, always had male officers.

Another reason, no less important, for the relative absence of women from club membership was that the great majority of societies gathered in public houses – inns, taverns, and alehouses. Publicans were leading promoters and sponsors of clubs, part of their expanding entrepreneurial role in the British economy and society at this time. They provided rooms, credit, and advertising for associations. But if clubs found an often congenial home in drinking premises, this relationship was particularly problematic for women. Traditionally, respectable women were excluded from public drinking houses except in the company of husbands or boyfriends, or on specific ritual occasions.

A final reason why women would not have felt at home in many clubs and societies was because an important part of the proceedings involved traditional male fellowship: heavy drinking, swearing, dirty songs, sexual banter, and party tricks and other forms of male bonding nowadays associated with rugby clubs. When women did attend club events – for instance, as guests on feast nights – members were warned to avoid such antics in order not to offend the ladies present.

ORGANIZATION

Johnson was rather vague in his *Dictionary* definition of the club as "An assembly of good fellows, meeting under certain conditions" – understandably so, since clubs and societies came in many different shapes and sizes. Some, particularly social and drinking clubs, tended to be small and informal, with only a handful of rules; others, like the Society of Arts or Society of Antiquaries, might have several hundred members and elaborate rules. Small clubs often had only one or two officers; bigger organizations might boast a raft of officials and bureaucratic structures. During the eighteenth century there was a trend towards more oligarchic, formal, public subscription associations rather like modern associations; this was especially the case with the great wave of philanthropic associations established from the 1780s.

In the same fashion, membership dues could vary between the high charges of elite societies like that fashionable archery club, the Kentish Bowmen – twelve guineas for admission plus annual charges of over five guineas a year – to the two-guinea admission of middle-class societies of a typical Masonic lodge, and the three- or four-shilling admission fees of a tradesmen's benefit or box club, with further costs of a few pennies a week (see chapter 31, "Money"). Again, associations varied greatly when they met: a few, mainly neighborhood drinking clubs, assembled every evening, but others gathered once a week, once a month, or at every conceivable periodic interval. Leading London societies clustered most of their main meetings during the fashionable winter season, when many of their genteel members were up from the countryside and staying in town.

At the same time, almost all clubs and societies were united by a common venue, by shared procedures, and by broadly similar social activities. First, as we have noted, the meeting place was almost invariably a public drinking house – only a tiny minority of major societies like the Royal Society, Society of Arts, or the Grand Lodge of the Modern order of Freemasons had their own private premises before 1800. Normally, societies, whether smart political or learned societies or artisan box clubs, gathered in a back room of a tavern, inn, or alehouse, sometimes with their own special furnishings kept there. Second, associations almost always had a set of rules – more or less formal – and these regulated admission requirements (usually entrance fees, nomination by existing members, sometimes balloting, and initiation rituals), finances, election of officers, penalties for misbehavior, and so on. Finally, though societies, as we know, often had a diversity of interests and activities, the typical meeting program included a business meeting, drinking, conversation and discussion, and often a song at the end. There might also be more public events – an annual feast to which visitors, including spouses, might be invited, sometimes preceded by a procession through the streets (benefit clubs and Masonic lodges regularly processed in this way with music and banners), attendance at the funeral of a deceased member, gifts to charities, and so forth.

FUNCTIONS

What benefits did members receive in return for their club subscription? Conviviality, entertainment, even fun were evidently important. Alexander Hamilton declared of the Tuesday Club at Annapolis, "we meet, converse, laugh, talk, smoke, drink, differ, argue, philosophize, harangue, pun, sing, dance and fiddle together." A Dorset social club boasted it had "for a fundamental principle [to] eat drink and be merry."[2] Heavy drinking was de rigueur. At the Zodiac Club in Cambridge, the eight or nine members usually put away four bottles of wine apiece. Drunkenness leading to disputes and disorder was commonplace. Still, for many newcomers to town, as well as established residents with time on their hands, the club provided a relaxed place to gather in male company away from women. Sir John Hawkins wrote of the Ivy Lane Club how Johnson "would pass those hours in a free and unrestrained interchange of sentiments [with fellow members], which otherwise had been spent at home in painful reflection" (Hawkins, *Life*, p. 134).

Societies, however, had other important social and economic functions. They offered solidarity, advice, and help for fellow members, not least the many young men who joined them. One writer observed of Freemasonry that membership is "no small Advantage to a Man who would rise in the World."[3] The same could be said of many other societies. Those looking for employment might find a job or a business deal through a fellow member. Mutual aid was particularly significant. When a member suffered bad health or economic hardship, club comrades would often rally around to give money or assistance. The charitable funds of Masonic lodges were particularly extensive (the Modern Grand Lodge of Masons gave out £300 a year in relief in the 1770s, and local lodges smaller amounts) and were a powerful recruiting attraction for the order.

Less tangibly, but still important in an urban world experiencing accelerating social upheaval, membership of societies offered status and credibility. Members who had passed through the admission procedures to a respectable club acquired by default some measure of respectable status, important for doing business. Societies were places to hear the latest news – political, economic, or social – again valuable in an increasingly fast-moving information society. Not least, the contacts made at societies helped members to form new social networks across the urban community and between urban centers – vital as old elites and networks began to fragment.

CIVIL SOCIETY AND "MODERNIZATION"

To conclude, it might be useful to ask: What did this explosion of clubs and societies mean for the Georgian world of Samuel Johnson? As we have already suggested, clubs and societies may have been important for integrating migrants and young people into urban communities and for promoting social networking within and between communities. It has been suggested that at the end of the eighteenth century they contributed to the formation of a new middle-class identity in British towns. As we have noted, they may have also contributed to the greater definition of gender boundaries in leisure and cultural activities. In the 1970s the

German philosopher and sociologist Jürgen Habermas argued that clubs, along with other new social institutions of the eighteenth century, played an influential role in the creation of a new-style "public sphere" of bourgeois public discourse and debate. More recently, political scientists have argued the case for identifying associations with the evolution of civil society and modernization. Certainly there is some evidence that societies – through their democratic processes, through their internal debate, through giving members experience of polite social interaction, elections, finance and decision-making – offered some basic form of political training or education, though it is arguable that other institutions such as parish vestries did the same. Associations also, as we have seen, helped to generate new notions and realities of trust, so essential in modern business as well as political life.

At the same time, clubs and societies were as much the beneficiaries as the engines of modernizing forces, their growth stimulated by urbanization, and by political and press liberalization after the Glorious Revolution. In some ways, clubs and societies have to be seen as backward-looking institutions. Though socially integrative in some contexts, they could also be highly divisive institutions. They excluded more than they admitted – among the former, women, the lower classes (the bulk of the urban population), and most of the resident rural population. Too often, as nowadays, they competed fiercely with one another for visibility, members, and finance. At the same time, they incorporated traditional practices of hierarchic patronage and masculine conviviality. Yet for all their complexity, their variety of activity and organization, their mix of modernity and traditionalism, clubs and societies were a critical part of the social, political, and cultural universe of Georgian Britain.

NOTES

1 Peter Clark, *British Clubs and Societies, 1580–1800: The Origins of an Associational World* (Oxford: Oxford University Press, 2000), pp. 1–2.

2 Clark, *British Clubs*, pp. 491, 225, 226.

3 "A Gentleman in the Country" (pseud.), *The Free-Masons Accusation and Defence: In Six Genuine Letters: Between a Gentleman in the Country, and His Son a Student in the Temple* (London, 1726), p. 23.

CHAPTER 17

Conversation

Pat Rogers

CONVERSA'TION. *n.s.* [*conversatio*, Latin.]
1. Familiar discourse; chat; easy talk: opposed to a formal conference.

What I mentioned some time ago in *conversation*, was not a new thought, just then started by accident or occasion. *Swift.*

It may not greatly surprise us that Johnson became famous in his own time for extraordinary conversational powers. His formidable reputation as a talker still survives, even among people who have read scarcely a word that he wrote. But to his contemporaries it must have seemed a strange and paradoxical thing. In the West the eighteenth century placed a greater emphasis than any age before or since on the art of conversation. Johnson flouted many of the rules, and yet he was widely recognized as an outstanding exponent of the game. To see what lay behind this contradiction, we need to look a little into the theory and practice of what the *Dictionary* calls "familiar discourse."

BACKGROUNDS

The body of ideas that went into this activity came to full expression in the Renaissance. As that label suggests, however, the humanist scholars of the period found much of their raw material in the classical world. Thus, to take a single influential case out of hundreds, Cicero had written in the first book of his late moral treatise *De Officiis* ("On Obligations") about the requirements for good conversation in familiar situations: he also distinguished between its needs and the qualities demanded of an orator in courts and senates. In the sixteenth century the topic became a central feature of courtesy literature, notably in Baldassare Castiglione's *Courtier* (1528), a work translated into English more than once during Johnson's lifetime.

The most influential single manual was probably Stefano Guazzo's *La Civil conversazione* (1574), which appeared as *The Art of Conversation* in

1738. We might note two things here. First, the original Italian title stresses the link with the key notion of "civility," which refers to an elevated level of politeness embracing moral and even political virtue as well as mere social convention. Second, the work was translated from a French version, and France remained the most important conduit of ideas for Britons who wished to shine as talkers in an informal setting. It was in Paris that the salon achieved its summit of influence under the aegis of figures such as the Marquise de Rambouillet, Madame de Lafayette, and Julie de Lespinasse. London achieved nothing similar until the Bluestocking assemblies of Elizabeth Montagu (see chapter 47, "Women writers"). Nor was Johnson's Club truly comparable: it gave less attention to philosophy, science, and contemporary literature, and permitted some rough masculine exchanges. Its members included the eloquent but not always courtly Edmund Burke, the silent Edward Gibbon, the surly Sir John Hawkins, and the indiscreet gossip James Boswell.

THE RULES OF CONVERSATION

In England one of the best known, if exceedingly brief, treatments came with an essay by Francis Bacon, "Of Discourse," published in 1625: "*Discretion* of *Speech*, is more than *Eloquence*; And to speak agreeably to him, with whom we deale, is more then to speake in good Words, or in good Order."[1] Coming nearer to Johnson's day, we could take Henry Fielding's "Essay on Conversation," written around 1741, as a representative statement of current views. Although Fielding claims (as Cicero had almost two millennia earlier) that the rules of conversation remain to be set out, his discussion follows orthodox lines. He begins by defining the key term as "that reciprocal interchange of ideas by which truth is examined, things are, in a manner, turned round and sifted, and all our knowledge communicated to each other."[2] Further, "As this good-breeding is the art of pleasing, it will be first necessary with the utmost caution to avoid hurting or giving any offence to those with whom we converse"[3] – yet inoffensiveness is not enough. Fielding says little about the content of private speech, except to warn against taboo subjects – it is vital to avoid "discoursing on the mysteries of a particular profession, to which all the rest of the company, except one or two, are utter strangers." Lawyers, he adds, "are generally guilty of this fault."[4] Equally to be shunned, as previous commentators always stressed, were indecency, irreverence, and slander. Slightly more individual advice comes with Fielding's condemnation of the "temper which constitutes the supercilious eye, the reserved look, the distant bowe, the scornful leer, the affected astonishment, the loud whisper, ending in a laugh directed full in the teeth of another."[5] Here we might recall not just the vulgarians who populate the novels of Frances Burney, but also the initial behavior of Jane Austen's Darcy to the Bennet family. What, then, is permissible? Most obviously, light banter that hurts no one present: "The raillery which is consistent with good-breeding is a gentle animadversion on some foible; which, while it raises a laugh in the rest of the company, doth not put the person rallied out of countenance, or expose him to shame and contempt."[6]

ELOQUENCE AND ELOCUTION

Johnson, of course, would have been familiar with the attitudes expressed by Fielding and others, living as he did in an era which highly prized the art of eloquence. He wrote a few brief pieces on the subject in places such as the *Rambler*, but no fully elaborated discussion. At this time young people were brought up to exercise the skills of composition rather than to analyze them in the work of others: parliamentary oratory was still regarded as one of the highest modes of discourse, and the budding politician devoted his energies to the periods of Cicero more often than to the calculations of economists. Adults devoted long hours to mastering "elocution," which was not then (as it later became) a subject for lisping young misses. Thomas Sheridan, father of the dramatist, and a man well known to Johnson, moved from the profession of actor to that of teacher of elocution (Boswell attended his lectures in Edinburgh). The role of such a figure embraced those of speech therapist, dialogue coach, theatrical director, and specialist on accents, but the closest modern analogy is perhaps the public-speaking consultant who teaches aspiring public figures how to present their views on television.

Allied to this activity was the ambition to codify the speech and gestures of stage actors: the dynamic theatrical presence of David Garrick had inspired this quest, and Garrick himself took an interest in the attempt to establish a kind of oral authority. Johnson respected the talents of the great comic impersonator Samuel Foote, and the most popular mode of popular education in the 1760s, 1770s, and 1780s was the so-called "Lecture on Heads," in which George Alexander Stevens and a host of imitators anatomized social types in a monologue replete with classical allusions and moral caricatures. People were bred into a culture that put immense importance on these matters, seeing the mastery of oral communication as something central to civilized living. We are told by Sir John Hawkins that, when Johnson interviewed an elderly peer in 1778 as part of his preparations for the *Life of Pope*, the first thing he wanted to know was, "What kind of a man was Mr. Pope in his conversation?" (*Miscellanies*, 2:4).

A VERY TALKING MAN

We need to recall, too, that in this period conversation was regarded as a serious cognitive activity, rather than a mere social acquisition. Johnson believed that it was incumbent on people to *use* their knowledge instead of hoarding it to themselves. According to Hester Piozzi,

> As he was a very talking man himself, [he] had an idea that nothing promoted happiness so much as conversation. A friend's erudition was commended one day as equally deep and strong – "He will not talk Sir (was the reply), so his learning does no good, and his wit, if he has it, gives us no pleasure." (*Miscellanies*, 1:289)

She also observed that Johnson "always made a great difference in his esteem between talents and erudition: and when he saw a person eminent for literature, though wholly unconversible, it fretted him" (*Miscellanies*, 1:280–1). (The *Dictionary* defines *conversable* as "Qualified for conversation; fit for company; well adapted to the reciprocal communication of thoughts; communicative.")

Others report Johnson's determination to do himself full justice in conversation. Thus, Thomas Tyers states that "he always talked as if he was talking upon oath" (*Miscellanies*, 2:365). His general habits in society can be gauged from this passage by Boswell:

> Sir Joshua Reynolds once asked him by what means he had attained his extraordinary accuracy and flow of language. He told him, that he had early laid it down as a fixed rule to do his best on every occasion, and in every company: to impart whatever he knew in the most forcible language he could put it in: and that by constant practice, and never suffering any careless expression to escape him, or attempting to deliver his thoughts without arranging them in the clearest manner, it became habitual to him. (Boswell, *Life*, 1:204)

An important distinction lay between trivial chatting and the serious exchange of ideas: "I asked him if there was good conversation, he answered, 'No, Sir: we had *talk* enough, but no *conversation*: there was nothing *discussed*'" (Boswell, *Life*, 4:186). Perhaps the most striking testimony comes in the words of an awestruck listener at Ullinish on Skye in September 1773, when Johnson discoursed on a variety of topics including tanning and dairy products: "It is musick to hear this man speak" (Boswell, *Life*, 5:246).

Long before the volumes of Johnsoniana or the posthumous biographies transmitted his famous bons mots, he had been recognized as supremely good at one of the activities most generally admired in the Hanoverian world. Abundant evidence survives to show that Johnson's contemporaries thought his distinction as writer and as speaker proceeded from the same source. Perhaps the best example is supplied by a comment of the novelist Frances Burney, stating that Johnson "had a facility so complete, that to speak or write produced immediately the same clear and sagacious effect. His pen was as luminous as his tongue and his tongue was as correct as his pen." She also recalled "how much the same thing it was to hear or to read him."[7] Similarly Hester Piozzi observed that the *Rambler* essays expressed his ideas "in a style so natural to him, and so like his common mode of conversing" (*Miscellanies*, 1:348). One acquaintance noted that everything Johnson said was "correct as second edition." Thomas Tyers agreed that his conversation "was thought to be equal to his correct writings" (*Miscellanies*, 2:401, 366). His auditors often wished for a written transcript of his conversation: thus, when Boswell deplored the inability of his record to do justice to the "forcible and brilliant" expression of words pouring forth, a bystander whispered to him, "O that his words were written in a book" (Boswell, *Life*, 3:39). Equally, Sir Joshua Reynolds instanced Johnson as the rare case of a writer who was equally impressive in his conversational powers, thought by some to be superior in this regard (*Miscellanies*, 2:220).

We are told that Johnson would pick up a topic in social converse and "utter upon it a number of the *Rambler*" (*Miscellanies*, 2:391). He had taken immense trouble to equip himself; he had undertaken a private regime that would enable him to think in an orderly way and to find suitable expressions to render his ideas; and this applied equally to written and oral communication. Boswell wrote late in life to a friend that Johnson had taught him "to cross-question in common life." A lady who met him only once on a coach from London to Oxford was immediately struck by his powers: "How he does talk! Every sentence is an essay" (Boswell, *Life*, 4:284). The accounts of the way Johnson spoke, then, give a fair sense of his characteristic manner. We can see his almost forensic zeal for precision; his typical swoop from particular cases into generalized principles; his wish to deflate cant and humbug; his aim to unmask sophistry and paradox, and to reassert time-honored wisdom; his relish of fun and his disdain for solemn pedantry. Almost any extended passage in Boswell or Burney will illustrate these characteristics; many of them come through in the dialogues that Reynolds wrote in imitation of his manner.

Plainly Johnson would have failed some of the traditional tests. He could be boorish, ill-tempered, bumptious, just plain rude. As he admitted to Boswell, he "often talked for victory" – a serious breach of conversational decorum. He sometimes went too far, "so much was he accustomed to consider conversation as a contest, and such was his notion of Burke as an opponent." At times aggression took over, and he "tossed and gored several persons" (Boswell, *Life*, 2:238, 450, 66). At the same time, knowing the rules, he would reprove Boswell for perceived lapses: once he broke out in irritation, "Sir, you have but two topicks, yourself and me. I am sick of both. A man … should not talk of himself, nor much of any particular person" (Boswell, *Life*, 3:57) – standard advice. Similarly the Irish clergyman Dr. Campbell heard him say, "Boswells conversation consists entirely in asking questions, & it is extremely offensive."[8] Moreover, Johnson had another handicap to overcome, if he wished to achieve the graces in social deportment recommended by his would-be patron Lord Chesterfield: "He spoke in the Lincolnshire [actually Staffordshire] dialect. His articulations became worse, by some dental losses."[9] Add to this impediment his notorious oddities in body language with many disconcerting tics, and it seems a miracle that he could have shone so brightly in a competitive activity promoted by a brilliantly accomplished society. His success makes it clear that the art of conversation could embrace a wider display of intellectual power than the manuals had dictated.

NOTES

1 Francis Bacon, *The Essayes or Counsels, Civill and Morall*, ed. Michael Kiernan (Cambridge, MA: Harvard University Press, 1985), p. 105.

2 *Miscellanies, by Henry Fielding Esq.*, 3 vols. (London, 1743), 1:117–78, at p. 119.

3 *Miscellanies*, 1:127.

4 *Miscellanies*, 1:162–3.

5 *Miscellanies*, 1:129.

6 *Miscellanies*, 1:174.

7 *Diaries and Letters of Madame d'Arblay*, ed. Charlotte Barrett, 7 vols. (London, 1842), 1:120.

8 *Dr. Campbell's Diary of a Visit to England in 1775*, ed. James L. Clifford (Cambridge: Cambridge University Press, 1947), p. 79.

9 Thomas Tyers, "A Biographical Sketch of Dr. Samuel Johnson" (1785), in *The Early Biographies of Samuel Johnson*, ed. O M Brack, Jr., and Robert E. Kelly (Iowa City: University of Iowa Press, 1974), pp. 85–6.

CHAPTER 18

Dictionaries

Lynda Mugglestone

DI'CTIONARY. *n.s.* [*dictionarium*, Latin.] A book containing the words of any language in alphabetical order, with explanations of their meaning; a lexicon; a vocabulary; a word-book.

An army, or a parliament, is a collection of men; a *dictionary*, or nomenclature, is a collection of words. *Watts*.

By the eighteenth century the monolingual English dictionary, alphabetically organized and equipped with some form of definition for the words which it contained, was, as the lexicographer Benjamin Martin confirms, already a familiar work of reference:

> It is customary among all People to make an orderly *Arrangement* of all the *Letters* used in their *Language*, which we call by the Greek name *Alphabet*; as also of all the Words and Terms which compose the same: And such a *Collection* or *Catalogue* of Words is by Us called a *Dictionary*.[1]

As Johnson commented, this was in many ways to be an "age of dictionaries" (*Letters*, 1:79), characterized by both abundance and diversity. Small dictionaries "fit for the pocket" vied with larger multivolume works for a share of the public's attention. Dictionaries were written for school and home, for incidental reference or systematic self-improvement, and offered information on a variety of heads. When Johnson began composing his own dictionary in 1746, Nathan Bailey's *Universal Etymological English Dictionary* already contained 42,000 word entries. A new edition of Bailey appeared in 1755, containing some 65,000 words and actively competing with Johnson's *Dictionary of the English Language*, which had been published in April of that year.

EARLIER ENGLISH DICTIONARIES

While Johnson is popularly described as the "father of the dictionary," the reality was therefore rather different. The monolingual English dictionary can be traced to 1604, with the publication of Robert Cawdrey's *Table Alphabeticall*, aimed at "unskilful readers" and containing roughly 2,500 "hard, usual words" such as *bankerupt* and *rapacitie*. Nevertheless, as Johnson argued in his *Plan of a Dictionary of the English Language* (1747), "a very miscellaneous idea" had so far seemed to characterize English lexicography (*Works*, 18:30). The image of the dictionary as a remedy for educational deficits of particular kinds – able in particular to democratize the kind of polysyllabic and Latinate vocabulary which marked the classically educated "gentleman" – remained popular. The *Glossographia Anglicana Nova: Interpreting Such Hard Words of Whatever Language, as Are at Present Used in the English Tongue* (1707) therefore stressed its utility to those who could find themselves "not able to read a good Historian, or any Polite English Writer without an Interpreter." Thomas Dyche and William Pardon likewise stressed the value of their own *New General English Dictionary* (1735) for the "Improvement of such as are Unacquainted with the Learned Languages." "Hard words" had pride of place in most early English dictionaries, and familiar words and meanings were often neglected.

That dictionaries might be directed to wider ends was, however, also becoming apparent. Lexicographers such as John Kersey criticized the erudite emphasis of some earlier dictionaries; these, he argued, could be discouraging for "a plain Countryman looking for a common *English* word."[2] Dictionaries, as he argued, ought to include "the genuine and pure Words of the *English Tongue*" – not just a "monstrous Heap of difficult and abstruse Terms, obsolete and forced Words, taken from *Foreign* Languages."[3] Kersey's own work aimed to provide a "brief, but Emphatical and Clear Explication of all sorts of difficult Words," together with common words and the potentially unfamiliar forms that readers might also encounter in domains such as medicine or science, gardening or divinity.

Nathan Bailey also made significant advances in this respect. For Bailey, the ideal dictionary was to be a "Store-House," which provided information about the "Generality of Words" – including ordinary words such as *case* or *cat* (the latter defined simply as "a Creature well known"). Works such as these move towards the notion of the modern general dictionary, a trend equally evident in Johnson's *Dictionary*, in which entries such as *demulcent* ("softening; mollifying") and *mouse* coexist, even if the definition of the latter – "the smallest of all beasts; a little animal haunting cornfields and houses, destroyed by cats" – also serves to reflect Johnson's status as a "poet doomed at last to wake a lexicographer" (*Works*, 18:100).

PRINCIPLES OF INCLUSION

Other aspects of eighteenth-century lexicography nevertheless remained highly distinctive. The 1727 edition of Bailey's *Dictionary* included "The Theogony, Theology, and Mythology of the Egyptians, Greeks, Romans," as well as "Auguries" and "Hieroglyphicks"; his *Dictionarium Britannicum* (1730) comported a "mathematical part" and a "Botanical part," each with separate and specialist authors. Benjamin Martin included extensive mathematical and scientific information in his *Lingua Britannica Reformata* (1749), aiming to "explain all Words and Terms in *Astronomy, Geography, Optics, Hydrostatics, Acoustics* ... According to the Latest Discoveries and Improvements in this part of Literature."[4] As here, the range and detail of many works could incline towards the encyclopedic ("The whole compass of learning," as Martin's definition of *encyclopædia* states), as well as being, as in his corresponding definition of *dictionary*, "a book containing a collection of the words of a language, and explaining them."

What exactly should be included within a dictionary remained a matter of considerable variation, a fact which underpins at least some of Johnson's critical assessment of the "miscellaneous idea" which previous English lexicography could reveal. As John Bevis contended in his *Pocket Dictionary* (1753), dictionaries seemed "capable of continual improvement, by correcting what may be found amiss in former ones, retrenching what is no longer useful, or adding whatever may conduce to render them more perfect and compleat."[5]

While notions of "utility" and "perfection" (as well as completeness) could, in practice, be subject to a range of individual interpretations, the resulting lack of consensus presented Johnson with a productively wide range of precedents for his own work which, like the "modes of expression" he discussed in his preface, he could likewise choose whether to "reject or receive" (*Works*, 18:74). The nature of the vocabulary to be included was clearly of prime significance. Should a dictionary include primarily modern words – as Martin argued, "A Dictionary is a Collection of *All the Words in Use* in any Language"[6] – or should it favor a broader historical range, reaching back to earlier phases of the language? The case was advanced on each side, with Martin censuring the "Redundancy of useless and obsolete Words" and Bailey including an abundant collection of obsolete and modern alike. Johnson's *Dictionary*, illustrated largely by writers from before the Restoration in 1660, often looks at language retrospectively, exemplifying "best" usage via the past rather than the present, and including a range of obsolete forms such as *to tud*, used by Edmund

Spenser to mean "to make red," or *agnize*, used by Shakespeare in *Othello* to mean "to acknowledge" or "avow." Change in progress within contemporary English, as in his entry for *precarious* – "No word is more unskilfully used than this with its derivatives" – could be treated with distrust.

ETYMOLOGY AND DERIVATION

The treatment of time, history, and language could be divisive in other ways. Dyche and Pardon had – in Bevis's terms – deliberately "retrenched" in their *New General Dictionary* by excluding "Etymology and Derivation" because of "their Uselessness to those Persons that these Sort of Books are most helpful to."[7] Instead, in the assumed interests of greater utility, they added "the Market-Towns in England and Wales ... a General Description of the Places ... Market-days, Government, Manufactures," and "Number of representatives sent to Parliament" in their third edition of 1740. Information about etymology or the derivation of words had, in fact, been a feature of Bailey's work since the 1720s (it first appeared in Blount's *Glossographia* in 1656); Bailey had also provided historical authority for particular usages, as in *cark* ("care"), which he supported by a reference to Edmund Spenser. In Martin's critical engagement with the nature of English lexicography, etymology is moreover presented as "absolutely necessary to a *due Understanding and Emphatical* Expression of many or most of our principal Words." As he added, "how extremely deficient ... must that Dictionary be which has no Etymology at all!"[8]

Johnson's sense of the past and the importance of historical origin (what he describes as "legitimate derivation") meant that etymology – rather than market days – was rightly selected as a central component in his own dictionary, even if etymological accuracy could be hampered by the limitations of what James Murray (editor of the *Oxford English Dictionary*) would later characterize as the essentially "pre-scientific philology" of this period. While etymology could occasionally go awry, as in Johnson's comments on *tatterdemalion* ("a ragged fellow"), given as deriving from "*tatter* and *I know not what*," Johnson's treatment of etymology, used systematically through the dictionary, nevertheless represented a significant advance.

PRINCIPLE AND PRACTICE

Detailed comparison of different dictionaries can be very illuminating for understanding the wider contexts – of both lexicographical principle and practice – in which Johnson's work came into being. As the various entries below confirm, the same word could receive significantly different treatment.

An innovation in Dyche and Pardon, for example, was the provision of grammatical information. While they identify *abolish* as a verb, there is no such information in Kersey, Bailey, or Martin (though it would be adopted by Johnson). In contrast, their respective dictionaries all engage with etymology to various degrees, whereas Dyche and Pardon had omitted it. Bailey, Dyche and Pardon, and Martin also indicate the position of main stress within the word (a feature omitted in Kersey, and first introduced by Bailey in 1727):

> To Abolish, (*L.*) to Destroy or to Deface utterly, to Reduce to nothing, to Repeal. (Kersey, 1708)
>
> To ABO'LISH [*abolir,* F. of *abolere,* L.]. to deface, to destroy utterly, to reduce to nothing, to repeal. (Bailey, 1727)
>
> ABO'LISH. (V.) to put away, repel, destroy, or utterly erase, so that no remains of a thing may be seen. (Dyche and Pardon, 1735)
>
> To ABO''LISH (of *aboleo,* lat. Of *ab* from, and *oleo* to smell). 1 to take away even the smell of a thing. 2 to destroy or consume. 3 to disannul, or make void. 4 to rase out, or deface. (Martin, 1749)

None of these dictionaries indicates pronunciation. Vowel quantity would first be indicated in James Buchanan's *New English Dictionary* (1757), while diacritical marks intended to indicate individual sounds would appear in later dictionaries such as William Kenrick's *New English Dictionary* (1773) or Thomas Sheridan's *General Dictionary of the English Language* (1780). Even in the substantially revised fourth edition of his *Dictionary* (1773), Johnson maintained continuities with Martin and Bailey in this respect, giving merely the position of the main stress in words of more than one syllable. For Johnson, the utility of the dictionary in regulating the spoken word was questionable. As he observed in 1772, Sheridan's proposed dictionary "may do very well … you cannot always carry it about with you: and, when you want the word, you have not the Dictionary" (Boswell, *Life*, 2:161).

As the entries above also illustrate, the most significant innovation was in fact introduced by Martin, with the inclusion of numbered sense-divisions rather than a more fluid sense structure (evident in Kersey and Bailey) in which it remains formally unspecified whether the various interpretations illustrate different aspects of the same sense, or different senses entirely. Martin – in this and other matters – viewed eighteenth-century lexicography as ripe for transformation. Texts indicating merely the

"Meaning of a Word *in the gross*" were, in his opinion, "notoriously deficient" (p. viii). Instead, "the chiefest Care of every Writer of Dictionaries" rested in the "Critical and accurate Enumeration and Distinction of the Several Significations of each respective Word" (p. vii), a practice evident in the four senses he specifies for *abolish*; his entry for the verb *turn* would have twenty-five sense-divisions. Johnson had, however, stated his own intent to "sort the several senses of each word" two years earlier (*Works*, 18:47), and his engagement with the "exuberance of signification" in English (*Works*, 18:92) would be both more rigorous and more extensive. *Turn* in Johnson had forty-five senses; *put* had sixty-six.

THE BEST WRITERS

Most senses in Johnson were supported, moreover, not only by careful definition but also – in a further innovation in English lexicography – by quotations exemplifying the relevant shade of meaning in writers such as Pope and Milton, Addison and Dryden. Eight citations illustrated *abolish*; over 110,000 would be included in the first edition.

Lexicographical appeals to the authority of the "best writers" can, of course, be found in earlier texts. Blount's *Glossographia* (1656) includes occasional references to actual usage, and the title page of the *Glossographia Anglicana* specifies its use of "the best Modern Authors" – including "Sir *Isaac Newton* … Mr. Evelyn, Mr. Dryden." Bailey, as we have seen, likewise supported occasional entries by references to writers such as Geoffrey Chaucer or Spenser. Evidence of usage – and empirical investigation – was not, however, a strong point of early lexicography. Instead, previous dictionaries often served as a resource from which dictionary-makers appropriated material with various degrees of independence. On one hand, this explains the prevalence of "ghost-words," words never really used but included in dictionaries by mistake, such as *abacot* – in reality, a mistranscription of *bycoket* ("a Cap of State, made like a double Crown, worn anciently by the Kings *of England*") – which appeared on the opening page of many dictionaries, including Bailey's (though not Martin's or Johnson's). Johnson's *Dictionary* is not entirely free of ghost-words: *foupe*, often copied into later dictionaries, is a mistranscription of the long *s* in *soup*. The problem was minimized, however, by Johnson's practice of supporting word entries as far as possible by quotations deriving from his own extensive reading and research. Words for which the only evidence was in previous dictionaries are labeled accordingly, attributed not to important writers but to "*Dict.*" or "*D.*" Illustrative evidence hence served to substantiate meaning and usage in ways which clearly distinguished Johnson's work as being of a different order of lexicography in eighteenth-century England.

FIXING THE LANGUAGE

The most critical debates about lexicographical practice, and the role of the dictionary, however, occurred in European rather than merely national contexts. Both the Accademia della Crusca (established in Florence in 1582) and the Académie Française (inaugurated in 1635) offered influential precedents for the dictionary as an image of standard and standardized usage. As one of the original statutes of the Académie Française affirmed, it aimed to provide definitive rules for linguistic usage, securing both purity and eloquence. The first edition of the *Dictionnaire de l'Académie françoise* appeared in 1694, and the second in 1718; a third was published in 1740. All were characterized by a normative thrust by which language was not merely to be recorded, but actively purified or corrected.

The absence of a similar body, with a similar remit, in Britain was for some a cause of anxiety. Specific proposals for the regulation of English (and the establishment of a national academy) had earlier been issued by writers such as Jonathan Swift and Daniel Defoe, for whom lexical innovation was a topic of particular concern. That "our Language is less Refined than those of *Italy*, *Spain*, or *France*" was given as axiomatic by Swift, and he urged its "Reformation" by the introduction of "some Method … for *ascertaining* and *fixing* our Language for ever, after such Alterations are made in it as shall be thought requisite."[9]

That the English dictionary should participate in this reformist agenda also featured in contemporary discussions. Thomas Wilson, for example, specifically advanced lexicography as a means "to fix what is right … streighten what is crooked, and make [English] easy to be learnt and remembred." While "such Undertakings in other Countries have had the Countenance and Assistance of the greatest Men," English, he complained, lacked a "good *Dictionary* to bring it into *Method*." Instead, in a powerful image of national neglect (and patriotic shame), "our best Words lie scattered in dark Corners, and are not easy to be found by the Youth or others that want them."[10]

Johnson's *Dictionary* would, in various ways, deliberately engage with issues of this kind. His reading of Swift's *Proposal* is reflected in evidence included in his entry for *standard* ("The English tongue, if refined to a certain standard, perhaps might be fixed for ever"). His *Plan of an*

English Dictionary, drafted in 1746 and published the following year, likewise makes explicit reference to precedents established by the Académie Française, and affirms the desirability of stasis and the role of a dictionary in ascertaining linguistic purity.

While Johnson's *Dictionary* remains prescriptive in parts – declaring how words *should* be used, rather than simply recording how they *have* been used – Johnson would ultimately contest the viability of these ideas. Echoing earlier writers such as Blount, he stressed the naturalness and inevitability of change so that, even while a dictionary is "hastening to publication, some words are budding, and some falling away" (*Works*, 18:110). Notions that a dictionary might successfully "embalm" language were, moreover, "derided"; as Johnson pointedly remarked, the "vigilance and activity" of academies "have hitherto been vain." Even the forty *immortels* of the Académie Française could not provide an "elixir" which maintained words and meaning in a particular form (*Works*, 18:104).

Experience rather than aspiration here led Johnson to understand time, change, and usage in ways that can seem remote from public desires for a dictionary that would fix and control language. Language, as Johnson had early noted, "is the work of man, of a being from whom permanence and stability cannot be derived" (*Works*, 18:44); his *Dictionary* was written "in the hope of giving longevity to that which its own nature forbids to be immortal" (*Works*, 18:109). As in other aspects of life, the vanity of human wishes was here both understandable and impossible to realize. As Johnson recognized, fixing language was like trying to "lash the wind"; both are "the undertakings of pride, unwilling to measure its desires by its strength" (*Works*, 18:105).

NOTES

1 Benjamin Martin, *Bibliotheca Technologica* (London, 1737), p. 133.
2 John Kersey, *A New English Dictionary* (London, 1702).
3 John Kersey, *A New Classical English Dictionary* (London, 1707), p. vi.
4 Benjamin Martin, *Lingua Britannica Reformata; or, A New English Dictionary* (London, 1749).
5 John Bevis, *Pocket Dictionary; or, Complete English Expositor* (London, 1753), p. 3.
6 Martin, *Lingua Britannica Reformata*, p. iv.
7 Thomas Dyche and William Pardon, *A New General English Dictionary; Peculiarly Calculated for the Use and Improvement of Such as Are Unacquainted with the Learned Languages* (London, 1735), sig. A2^{r}.

8 Martin, *Lingua Britannica Reformata*, pp. iv, v.
9 Jonathan Swift, *A Proposal for Correcting, Improving and Ascertaining the English Tongue* (London, 1712), pp. 9, 31.
10 Thomas Wilson, *The Many Advantages of a Good Language to Any Nation* (London, 1724), pp. 5, 6, 24.

CHAPTER 19

Domestic life

Jaclyn Geller

FA'MILY. *n.s.* [*familia*, Latin; *famille*, French.]
1. Those who live in the same house; household.

> The night made little impression on myself; but I cannot answer for my whole *family*; for my wife prevailed on me to take somewhat. *Swift.*

Johnson's *Dictionary* defines *family* as "those who live in the same house," without reference to kinship or marriage. It is telling that, in the early eighteenth century, no word existed to denote just the biological relatives within a household: servants, guests, students, patrons, governesses, tutors, apprentices, and unrelated children could fall within the category of family. Most of the terms for kinship had multiple meanings: a noun as apparently simple as *father* had multiple denotations that bled into each other. It could refer to the Deity, to the nation's monarch, to a natal parent, to an adoptive or stepfather, to a father-in-law, or to a deceased male ancestor. Or it could mean a seminal individual or an august male friend. Other terms – *mother*, *brother*, *sister* – were similarly multivalent. To understand family life in the eighteenth century, we have to abandon many of our modern preconceptions about what a family is and try to examine the past without prejudice.

VARIETIES OF THE FAMILY

Social historians disagree on the particulars, but most concur that the early modern family was an institution in transition. In one popular account, the eighteenth century witnessed the birth of the insular married couple: throughout the era the custom of arranged, honor-based unions gave way to a more companionate model. Others suggest the transition from pragmatic to affective marriage took place in or before the late Middle Ages, and others still that such a change never took place: the nuclear family, they argue, with a married couple that was both *emotionally* and *instrumentally* bonded, was a long-standing feature of British life.

Whenever it arose, this "nuclear family" coexisted with a "household family," one headed by a householder, usually male, and populated by related and non-related dependents. Flexibly open, this household family did not depend on conjugal bonds, but rather on shared residence and deferral to the authority of a single figure. And both of these domestic units coexisted with the "lineage family," made up of one's ancestry and the recorded pairings of relatives and social superiors. Redolent of notions of honor attached to name, the lineage family gave individuals a sense of historical continuity and their place within the social hierarchy.

MARRIAGE

Whether it was an honor-based alliance aimed at generating male heirs, a romantic coupling, or some combination of the two, eighteenth-century wedlock was financially circumscribed with customs and laws that contemporary readers often find coldly utilitarian. It was impossible to miss the pecuniary character of wedlock. Parish costs were advertised in churches: marriage fees were placed on prayer books during the nuptial. (A marriage license could cost between ten and twenty shillings; see chapter 31, "Money.")

Among the upper classes, the custom of arranged marriages persisted throughout the century, with parents and lawyers playing a central role and employers and patrons making introductions and offering advice. Marriage remained an essential means of transferring property. Because only female chastity guaranteed the biological certainty of male heirs, premarital "bundling" – sexual interplay that was supposed to fall just short of intercourse – was common. Marriage contracts involved a portion brought by the bride and typically paid to her father-in-law to be, and a settlement to provide for her upkeep in the event that she was widowed. Money, land, and matrimony were inseparable.

The emotional realities of conjugal life must have varied greatly from household to household. Even in the most sexist cultures there are women who stand on equal footing with, or even dominate, the men in their lives. And even as wedlock became increasingly bureaucratic and prescriptive, a range of sexually nonconforming behaviors existed. But as a system, eighteenth-century matrimony was biased in favor of the male. It was also permanent: until 1857, divorce in England was unavailable to all but the wealthy. And marriage-oriented courtship was characterized by unabashed pragmatism and self-interest. Family life could have a formal quality. The practice of wedded couples addressing each other by their first names was controversial, and overt deference to parental authority was still the rule. For much of the century children called their fathers "Sir," and sons removed their hats in the presence of both parents.

THE MARRIED WOMAN

Once married, a woman eschewed her legal status as a *feme sole* for that of a *feme covert*: she lost the ability to sue or enter into legal contracts independently. She forfeited to her husband control of her assets, including the money and property she had brought into the relationship. An English wife could be ejected from her husband's home – a house he might have purchased with her settlement. Technically her sexual and reproductive systems were not her own but his, and sex outside of marriage – "criminal conversation" – was a crime for which husbands could sue for damages.

A paradox faced by many eighteenth-century writers was the fact that marriage incapacitated a woman legally, yet it was often her sole path to respectability. This was especially true in the second part of the century, when, in accordance with Hardwicke's Marriage Act of 1753, weddings required a church ceremony, entry in a parish register, the reading of public banns, and the participation only of parties who were of age (or had parental consent). Streamlining marriage and rendering it ceremonially public, this law invalidated cohabitation, verbal contracts of partnership, and other informal arrangements that had long been common. A woman who had sex outside of wedlock as delineated by the state was now basically a prostitute; her natal children were bastards with no claim to financial support.

RESISTANCE TO MARRIAGE

Matrimonial mores were not accepted with universal complacency. Alongside the officially sanctioned marriages, a clandestine wedding trade flourished throughout the first part of the century, practiced by unbeneficed clergyman and ministers who hoped to augment their salaries. The business in clandestine services was alleged to provide £100 per year to the cleric presiding at Peak Forest Chapel in Derbyshire. More notoriously, the Fleet district of London, a neighborhood exempt from ecclesiastical jurisdiction, was a destination for craftsmen, day laborers, servants, apprentices, sailors, tradespeople, and a modicum of genteel and professional types, who sought ceremonies without the requisite banns or licenses. In the year 1700, 2,251 ceremonies – approximately one third of all London marriages – were performed in the Fleet. And many observers of the eighteenth-century British marriage market found the institution itself prejudiced, crass, and mercenary. At the turn of the century the feminist philosopher and pamphleteer Mary Astell depicted courtship as a pecuniary bidding game: "For pray, what do Men propose to themselves in Marriage? What qualifications do they look for in a Spouse? What will she bring is the first enquiry? How many acres? Or how much ready Coin?"[1]

FRIENDSHIP

Marriage struck many as mercenary and unfairly biased. Friendship, by contrast, could seem comparatively pure. As an alliance it must have appeared informal, equal, freely chosen, and separate from the mitigating pressures of class achievement.

A striking feature of eighteenth-century British life is the depth of emotion displayed between friends. An absorbing concern with friendship characterizes this period, crossing the boundaries of gender, class, and region. Rather than providing a backdrop for the pursuit of amorous relationships, friends were vital – sometimes volatile – allies. Eighteenth-century men and women took this commitment seriously and invested it with much of the passion that twenty-first-century readers associate exclusively with love affairs.

What was the source of this exalted view of friendship? It may have resulted from the common practice of leaving home in early adolescence. Young people who relocated to receive education, professional training, or employment, or who, for practical or personal reasons, boarded with distant relatives or neighbors, may have found psychological support among peers. For writers, the sense of friendship as sacrosanct was fueled by classical sources; authors of antiquity exert a strong influence on eighteenth-century literary practitioners, and Cicero's *On Friendship* was widely known. Marked by the notion of disinterested virtue, classical friendship includes the martial ideal in which men fight side by side in battle.

SOCIAL SPACES AND PRIVACY

Urbanization, with its proliferation of public meeting places, provided a space for men to socialize. There were more than 2,000 coffee houses in London by the turn of century, offering a zone of male companionship outside the home. It was in these spaces that segregated male clubs formed, providing a framework in which to drink, converse, and forge political and intellectual affiliations (see chapter 16, "Clubs").

Pervading the eighteenth century was a lack of privacy. Private experience, distinguished from public experience, was an important topic in eighteenth-century discourse, as when Johnson defined the adjective *domestick* as "not relating to things publick." But true privacy was very hard to find. The lack of personal space crossed boundaries of marital status, class, and region. Among the upper strata a period of post-wedding travel was customary but, unlike the modern honeymoon, it was not private. It typically included a retinue of relatives, siblings, and servants. In urban centers, when industrialization was under way, it was common for couples to take in older relatives as lodgers, providing room and board in exchange for childcare. Rural laborers tended to share cramped living quarters, occupying cottages of one to five shared rooms.

The standard terraced house, built in London after the Great Fire of 1666 destroyed much of the city, included a basement, a kitchen, a cellar, and quarters for servants. The grander homes would have a parlor on the ground floor as well as a dining room, drawing room, and "office" (lavatory). The second floor would have (shared) bedrooms and perhaps a closet, offering a modicum of discreet space to the man or woman of the house. Narrow, with two or three rooms to a floor, these structures were intended to lodge a man and woman, their biological children, and two to four servants. Occupants often included apprentices and lodgers, who were taken in to supplement household income. Renters taking over once-grand homes that had been abandoned or had fallen into disrepair might share a room or a bed with others. Even in the better inns, travelers would share rooms, and sometimes beds, with strangers.

The lack of privacy continued outside the home. Disappearing entirely from view was difficult, and readers of the period's fiction often note the protagonists' lack of anonymity. Whether it is a village, an extended household, or a disparate but intertwined group of individuals, an intrusive community always tends to monitor the behavior of each person. In a stylized way, these plots probably reflect social reality. The marital tie was considered not a private bond but a public relationship in which the community had a stake, and to which it could apply pressure in the enforcement of gender roles and obligations. Especially in rural areas, husbands whose wives were perceived as sexually loose or domineering were mocked publicly. In a custom known as the Skimmington, the pair (or stand-ins, or figures in effigy representing the accused couple) was paraded on horseback by a crowd that jeered, blew horns, and beat on pots and pans.

SERVANTS

On small farms, servants were an integral part of the household, sharing meals, work, and pastimes with their employers. Jane Austen's *Sense and Sensibility* demonstrates the extent to which servants were an ever-present feature of eighteenth-century life, even for the genteelly impoverished. Austen's plot centers on the disenfranchised female wing of the Dashwood family. Cut out of the family patriarch's will, Mrs. Dashwood and her three daughters leave the estate that had been their home and rent a small cottage, where they struggle to make ends meet. Disadvantaged on the marriage market, reduced to a state of grinding subsistence – even these women have servants.

Servants were spectators of all aspects of a household – perhaps a reason they often figure prominently in literary plots. They witnessed their employers' most personal activities. In his ironic *Directions to Servants* (1745), Jonathan Swift advises:

> When your Master and Lady are talking in their Bed-chamber, and you have some Suspicion that you and your Fellow-servants are concerned in what they say, listen at the Door for the publick Good of all the Servants; and join all to take proper Measures for preventing any Innovations that may hurt the Community.[2]

Aside from cleaning and food preparation servants emptied chamber pots, either into a vault in the basement of a home or into an exterior cesspit. Males generally used these pots in view of each other, in public areas of the home such as the dining room.

JOHNSON'S DOMESTIC LIFE

Married for a short time, a widower for most of his adult life, Johnson had an extended network whose members provided different kinds of companionship. His household included, at various points, a wife, servants, apprentices, and lodgers.

By all accounts his grief at the death of his wife Elizabeth ("Tetty") in 1752 was real. But for the ensuing thirty-two years the loss did not render him a fragmentary half-self in the eyes of his contemporaries. Rather than awaiting social completion in the next marriage, the widower Johnson developed a network of interconnected relationships that were homosocial, heterosocial, transgenerational, interracial, intellectual, and domestic. It is telling that, when Johnson wrote a work of fiction, he eschewed the common plots of courtship and marriage that dominated the contemporary novel. His *Rasselas* deals with two men and two women, a traveling community of intellectual seekers, none of whom pursues wedlock or even mentions it as a goal. After Tetty's death, Johnson surrounded himself with artists, like the painter Joshua Reynolds; players in national politics, like the Whig Parliamentarian and political philosopher Edmund Burke; and authors, like the dramatist and poet Oliver Goldsmith. He developed friendships with female Bluestockings, like Elizabeth Carter, the translator who contributed two essays to his *Rambler* (see chapter 47, "Women writers"). He mentored younger intellectuals like the lawyer and biographer James Boswell and the novelist Frances Burney.

Johnson's house was always full. He shared three successive London homes with a number of domestic companions. He maintained a close relationship with his servant, Francis Barber, whose education he financed, who named both his sons after Johnson, and who was Johnson's main legatee. An important friend was the poet Anna Williams, who boarded with him from 1752 to her death in 1783, overseeing aspects of the household. From 1762 until his demise in 1782, the would-be physician Robert Levet, who administered to Johnson's health, was a full-time lodger. And for approximately fifteen years Johnson was himself an integral part of the household of Henry and Hester Thrale. He maintained his own room in their Streatham home and attended to the education of their four daughters.

THE STATE OF COMMON LIFE

Eighteenth-century England produced a prodigious advice literature that promoted ideals of hospitality, household management, amorous relations, servitude, and friendship. But there is always a chasm between cherished standards – what a society prescribes and how it describes itself – and the ways in which people live. This gap can be made out in every period of which there is a recorded history. In Johnson's day it was commonly said, for instance, that women were capricious and mentally inferior. The official view seems to have been that females were overgrown children in need of male protection.

Yet, as we have seen, luminaries like Johnson were connected to women who were clearly intelligent, and in some cases truly learned.

Such relationships could not have flourished had eighteenth-century men and women fully internalized the notion of female inferiority. The study of domestic life is worthwhile, in part, because it helps to complicate our view of the past, taking us beneath the surfaces presented by cultural arbiters. Johnson himself acknowledged the significance of that which goes unrecorded in his *Journey to the Western Islands of Scotland*:

> But it must be remembered, that life consists not of a series of illustrious actions, or elegant enjoyments; the greater part of our time passes in compliance with necessities, in the performance of daily duties, in the removal of small inconveniences, in the procurement of petty pleasures; and we are well or ill at ease as the main stream of life glides on smoothly, or is ruffled by small obstacles and frequent interruptions. The true state of every nation is the state of common life. (*Works*, 9:22)

NOTES

1 Mary Astell, *Reflections upon Marriage*, in *Astell: Political Writings*, ed. Patricia Springbourg (Cambridge: Cambridge University Press, 1996), p. 38.

2 Jonathan Swift, *Directions to Servants*, in *The Prose Works of Jonathan Swift*, ed. Herbert Davis, 14 vols. (Oxford: Blackwell, 1939–68), 13:43.

CHAPTER 20

Education

Catherine Dille

> EDUCA'TION. *n.s.* [from *educate.*] Formation of manners in youth; the manner of breeding youth; nurture.
>
> *Education* and instruction are the means, the one by use, the other by precept, to make our natural faculty of reason both the better and the sooner to judge rightly between truth and error, good and evil. *Hooker, b.* i. *s.* 6.

It is seldom recalled that Johnson pursued his vocation as a writer against the background of repeated attempts to become a teacher. Before arriving in London in 1737 he worked as an usher or assistant schoolmaster in Market Bosworth Grammar School, acted briefly as private tutor in the family of Thomas Whitby, opened a boarding school at Edial near Lichfield, and applied unsuccessfully for at least four teaching posts. From his work as a classroom educator, Johnson brought to his writing career an engagement with the debates of the period regarding pedagogical methods, curricula, and the process of learning generally. His periodical essays often address the moral and social instruction of youth, and Catherine Neal Parke has examined "*Rasselas* as a parable about how teaching and learning are central to human relationships."[1] A tour of Scotland enabled him to compare the provision of schooling in two countries, while the theme of education serves as one of the unifying motifs of his biographical writings.

PHILOSOPHICAL FASCINATION

Conceptions of childhood were evolving in the eighteenth century in response to changing social conditions and new ideas of how knowledge was acquired. The belief that the infant was inherently sinful, expressed forcefully by St. Augustine, was increasingly giving way to a developmental model of childhood, founded on John Locke's theory that children were potentially rational beings as yet uninformed by experience. This view gained ascendancy in the first decades of the century, and proved especially influential with middle-class parents increasingly involved in their children's education. In the latter half of the century, Jean-Jacques Rousseau, in his widely read *Emile* (1762), proposed that the naturally moral child should be liberated from the routines of traditional learning and educated in the natural world – a philosophy that had minimal impact on mainstream English education in the period, owing to its focus on private education and later association with French radicalism.

The contemporary notion of education embraced the instruction of youth in its broadest sense to include moral and religious instruction, social training, and formal schooling. Education became a source of philosophical and cultural fascination, and a steady stream of books and pamphlets was published on the subject. Booksellers capitalized on the popular interest in education by publishing works directed at children, such as John Newbery's highly popular *History of Little Goody Two-Shoes* (1765) or Robert Dodsley's *Preceptor* (1748), an anthology of school subjects to which Johnson contributed a preface and an allegory on education, "The Vision of Theodore, the Hermit of Teneriffe." The growth of commercial circulating libraries and the expansion of newspapers and periodicals attest to the spread of reading among the British public. An estimated 60 percent of men could read by the 1750s, nearly double the figure from the previous century, with a corresponding rate among women of 35–40 percent.

Formal schooling in early modern Britain encompassed an unprecedented variety of institutions of all standards and at every stage of learning, from dame schools and petty schools at the elementary level to charity schools and grammar schools, Dissenting academies, and the universities. Scotland had a form of universal schooling, and state-organized systems were emerging on the Continent, but the voluntary institutions of England and Wales have traditionally been characterized as in a state of decline in the eighteenth century, as evidenced by inflexible curricula, uneven standards of teaching, and devalued endowments. Later assessments, though, suggest a more complex picture of the evolving nature of schools as they adapted to altered economic and cultural circumstances.

EARLY EDUCATION

Responsibility for children's early education generally fell to women: mothers in the domestic sphere and schoolmistresses outside of the home. The dame school was the province of a widow or spinster who taught local children the alphabet and reading for a few pennies per week in her front parlor. This was the only schooling many children received. While the schoolmistress was sometimes satirized for her lack of learning, Johnson fondly recalled his first teacher, Ann Oliver, whose school he attended until age six or seven, when he moved to the local day school of Thomas Browne, a cobbler turned schoolmaster. Small private schools, variously known as petty, ABC, or parish schools, furthered the instructional beginnings of the dame school and prepared students for grammar school. Here boys and girls learned reading, writing, and basic arithmetic. Teachers were poorly paid, and for many it was not their first or sole occupation.

Rudimentary education for impoverished boys, and less often girls, was provided by charity schools, such as those founded by the Society for Promoting Christian Knowledge (1699). Often funded through subscriptions, charity schools were popular beneficiaries of middle-class philanthropy. While emphasizing religious instruction, charity schools and workhouses also taught basic literacy and arithmetic (replaced by sewing or spinning for girls) and often placed pupils in apprenticeships or domestic service. But the contentious question of what to teach the poor was complicated by class-based anxieties: opponents of such schools objected that they threatened the social order by educating the poor beyond their station. Johnson, who mistrusted attempts to limit anyone's educational opportunities, observed in his review of Soame Jenyns's *Free Inquiry into the Nature and Origin of Evil* (1757) that "Those who communicate literature to the son of a poor man, consider him as one not born to poverty, but to the necessity of deriving a better fortune from himself" (*Works*, 17:410). Sermons preached annually to promote charity schools urged the early inculcation of piety in poor children to preserve them from a life of vice, while the secular argument held that the educated poor would find employment more easily and keep off the poor rates. Some boys of lower status went on to grammar school, but for the most part this was the province of the middle classes.

GRAMMAR SCHOOLS

The endowed grammar school, the traditional mainstay of secondary education, experienced variable fortunes in the period: some ancient grammar schools became elementary schools by abandoning a classical curriculum, while others were rejuvenated as fee-paying schools or refounded as charity schools. A great number simply disappeared. Whereas there were an estimated 1,320 grammar schools in England and Wales in the seventeenth century, Nicholas Carlisle described only 475 in his survey published in 1818. The foundational statutes of many schools specified that Latin and Greek were the subjects to be taught and that education should be free for local residents. In practice, though, many endowments were no longer adequate after inflation, and schoolmasters took fee-paying boarders into their homes while neglecting local pupils.

Boys began school at age eight or nine and remained for seven or eight years. (Girls were almost unheard of in English grammar schools, although in Scotland they were sometimes admitted.) School hours were long, and corporal punishment was a common and accepted means of controlling classes averaging thirty to forty pupils, but sometimes reaching one hundred in the largest schools. Seven "great schools" rose to prominence in the period – Charterhouse, Eton, Harrow, Rugby, Shrewsbury, Westminster, and Winchester – to become the institutions of choice. Elite families sent their sons to these so-called "public schools" to establish connections that would serve them in later life. Some affluent parents, sensible of the public schools' reputation for bullying and brutality, educated their sons at home with private tutors, although the rough environment of the schools was also thought to foster a "manly" character in boys.

The primary business of grammar schools was the instruction of Latin and some Greek. Latin was the language of learning, and the immersion of boys in classical literature served as an initiation into their cultural heritage. The standard primer was based on William Lily's *Short Introduction of Grammar* (*c.* 1550), which boys memorized before construing and reading classical texts and, in the upper forms, making Latin compositions. Increasingly, though, the regimen of Latin and Greek came under questioning. A principal objection was that long years spent learning classical languages that would soon be forgotten might be better invested in learning practical subjects. Some schools, however, found means to expand their curricula by altering their statutes or using freelance tutors to teach such subjects as modern languages and mathematics.

Whereas teaching in a grammar school usually required a university degree, the masters of small private venture schools were less restricted. These smaller, often short-lived institutions filled the gap left by the declining number of grammar schools. The private academy that Johnson opened in late 1735 lasted a little over a year and attracted only a handful of students. The school's failure was attributed to what was assumed to be Johnson's temperamental unsuitability to teaching, but the proximity of the well-respected Lichfield Grammar School was also a possible factor.

Johnson's syllabus mainly followed the orthodox classical model of education with the innovation of contemporary editions of classical school texts intended to facilitate translation. Other private schools, and in particular those founded to educate students dissenting from the established religion, introduced practical subjects often in lieu of classical studies.

UNIVERSITIES

Much of the criticism of education in the period was directed at the English universities, Oxford and Cambridge, both founded in the Middle Ages. Johnson, who entered Pembroke College, Oxford, in 1728, but was forced to leave just over a year later without a degree, praised the university's "opportunities of books and learned men" and the "excellent rules of discipline in every college." To Boswell's objection that "the rules and indeed the whole system is very ill observed," Johnson responded that this was "nothing against the institution. The members of an university may, for a season, be unmindful of their duty. I am arguing for the excellency of the institution."[2] For many, such excellence resided in the university's role as a bastion of stability in a changing world, while reformers and critics cited dissipated students, idle tutors, and a general air of misrule.

Both universities were governed by antiquated regulations that were not reformed until the nineteenth century. Written examinations began at Cambridge in the 1740s, but at Oxford the farcical exercise of oral examinations, based on standardized exchanges of pre-set questions and answers, continued until the end of the century. There were, however, positive developments; Cambridge, influenced by Isaac Newton, had embraced science and mathematics, and new lectures in natural philosophy were introduced at Oxford. Johnson's friend Thomas Warton helped raise the profile of Greek literature with his lectures at Oxford in the 1750s and 1760s, and Johnson himself assisted clandestinely with the second series of Vinerian Lectures on the common law, originally given by William Blackstone.

ALTERNATIVES TO OXFORD AND CAMBRIDGE

As one of the primary functions of the English universities was to educate Anglican clergymen, the requirement that students take an oath of allegiance to the Church of England excluded Dissenters, Roman Catholics, and other non-Anglicans. As alternatives to Cambridge and Oxford, non-Anglican students often attended the Continental universities, particularly Leyden for medical studies, or those in Scotland. Johnson visited the Scottish universities when he toured that country in 1773, but he concluded that, although learning was relatively widespread in Scotland, the standard of scholarship in its schools and colleges was not as high as their reputation suggested. He was, however, impressed with Thomas Braidwood's school for deaf children in Edinburgh, where he examined the pupils, later describing Braidwood's method of instruction in his *Journey to the Western Islands of Scotland*.

Not everyone excluded from Oxford and Cambridge was forced to study abroad. Dissenters – Protestants who did not belong to the Church of England – established their own schools beginning in the late 1600s in response to legislation excluding them from the universities. Sons of prosperous trades families, both Anglican and Dissenting, received in these academies an education that was seen as a practical alternative to the English universities. The curriculum at the Warrington Academy, to take one prominent example, where the natural philosopher Joseph Priestley lectured, included theology, mathematics, natural science, geography, history, commerce, chemistry, anatomy, French, writing, drawing, bookkeeping, and surveying, in addition to the more traditional Latin and Greek. As in the English universities, the standard length of study was three years, with an additional year for students of theology; compared with Oxford or Cambridge, the academies had longer terms and more rigorous examinations. English rather than Latin was typically the language of instruction, and the academies have been credited with pioneering the study of English composition. Although the curricular innovations of the academies have been praised as being among the few eighteenth-century advancements in education, it has also been suggested that grammar schools may have resisted change longer because of the modern curriculum's anti-establishment associations.

A GENTLEMANLY EDUCATION

Beyond the learning to be gained in the schools and colleges, young men also required lessons in socialization to complete a gentlemanly education. Johnson's periodical essays feature men deficient in this important dimension of education, such as Verecundulus, the shy and tongue-tied scholar of *Rambler* 157. Travel was one means of gaining the polish associated with status and quality, and wealthy heirs were consequently sent on the Grand Tour of European capitals in search of social grace and knowledge of the fine arts. Conversation in polite company was another aspect of social training, and female society in particular was viewed as a refining influence conducive to the cultivation of good manners.

FEMALE EDUCATION

For their part, daughters of middle-class and elite families received sufficient education to equip them to be amiable partners and capable mothers, but scholarly attainments were seldom encouraged. In Johnson's *Rasselas*, though, the princess Nekayah envisions founding a college of learned women: a proposal reminiscent of Mary Astell's late seventeenth-century scheme for a female academy, but one that remained in the realm of fiction in the eighteenth century. Johnson, who numbered among his friends women authors, poets, translators, and artists, placed great value on female education and believed that learning enriched women's lives (see chapter 47, "Women writers"). Most women, however, did not have leisure to pursue scholarly studies; far more usual were the circumstances of middle-class daughters who were instructed in household management and religion by their mothers and perhaps gained a little more "female learning" from tutors or in boarding schools.

Private girls' boarding schools or ladies' academies began to flourish in the early decades of the eighteenth century; here girls gained some general learning and were taught the "accomplishments" – including dancing, music, singing, and drawing – that would confer social distinction and improve their chances in the marriage market. Such schools were typically run by enterprising women, often widows and impoverished gentlewomen, for around a dozen girls of all ages. They ranged from the expensive to schools affordable for trades families. Without challenging the male domain of Latin and Greek, girls learned writing, French and other modern languages, some arithmetic, and a little geography or "globes." Towards the close of the century, the polite education of the ladies' academy was sometimes criticized as frivolous, and teachers of girls, including Johnson's friend Hannah More, called for a more intellectually rigorous education to prepare women for their "profession" as wives and mothers.

BEYOND THE SCHOOLROOM

Opportunities for education in eighteenth-century Britain extended beyond the schoolroom into society at large: coffee houses and philosophical societies served as forums for debate, lectures on natural science were offered to the public in metropolitan centers, and the popular press continued expanding to serve an increasingly literate nation. Autodidacts emerged from the trades class to take a role in the Industrial Revolution, and women in unprecedented numbers entered the literary profession. Johnson welcomed this general increase in learning, which he associated with a civilized national culture. Commenting in 1783 on the progress of education during his lifetime, he noted, "there is now a great deal more learning in the world than there was formerly; for it is universally diffused" (Boswell, *Life*, 4:217). Founded on the extension of education to a wider populace and facilitated by the proliferation of print, this "universal diffusion of learning" was a significant factor in shaping Britain's thriving public culture at the turn of the nineteenth century.

NOTES

1 Catherine Neal Parke, *Samuel Johnson and Biographical Thinking* (Columbia: University of Missouri Press, 1991), p. 7.
2 *Boswell in Search of a Wife: 1766–1769*, ed. Frank Brady and Frederick Pottle (London: Heinemann, 1957), p. 163.

CHAPTER 21

Empire

Sharon Harrow

> E'MPIRE. *n.s.* [*empire*, French; *imperium*, Latin.]
> 2. The region over which dominion is extended.
>
> A nation extended over vast tracts of land, and numbers of people, arrives in time at the ancient name of kingdom, or modern of *empire*. *Temple*.

During Samuel Johnson's life England became a global colonial power. Just three years after Johnson arrived in London with his former pupil, David Garrick, James Thomson wrote his famous nationalistic poem "Rule Britannia" (1740). It was a patriotic poem *extraordinaire*, set to music and performed in celebration of George II. The refrain is a perversely ironic rhyme:

> Blest isle! with matchless beauty crown'd
> And manly hearts to guard the fair.
> Rule, Britannia, rule the waves:
> *Britons* never will be slaves!

The lines boast of Britain's navy, a prowling force that had, in 1739, embroiled them in the War of Jenkins's Ear, a campaign over rights to the exclusive sea tentacles of the slave trade.

By 1759, at the height of England's first Great War for Empire, the Seven Years War (1756–63), both Johnson and Garrick had achieved fame in their respective fields. In that year each published a work that reflected the nation's imperial ambitions. Echoing Thomson's nationalistic call, and even borrowing his rhymes, Garrick wrote a patriotic sea song, "Heart of Oak," which was still sung by Horatio Lord Nelson's sailors at the battle of Trafalgar in 1805. The song celebrated the imperial victories of 1759: "To honor we call you, as free men, not slaves / For who are so free as the sons of the waves." The focus on naval puissance and on slaves is fitting: foreign policy between the Treaty of Utrecht (1713) and the War of Jenkins's Ear (1739) pursued trading rights, trading routes, and profits from the slave trade. Garrick's words were accurate: Englishmen were not slaves. But slaves were their bread and butter – or, more precisely, slaves were their sugar and spice (see chapter 41, "Slavery and abolition"). Britain had become an imperial power.

COMMERCE AND DOMINION

The Treaty of Utrecht and the War of Jenkins's Ear had secured Britain's slave trade in Spanish America; the Seven Years War brought English gains in North America, India, the Caribbean, and West Africa (see chapter 46, "War"). Great Britain emerged as the European power with the largest slave-trading network. At the same time Britain's East India Company battled the French (and, to a lesser extent, the Portuguese) over trading privileges in Hyderabad and the Carnatic region.

In India, the line between licit and illicit trade – that is, between exchange and plunder – became increasingly thin. The history of Anglo-Indian relations is a story of transformation from colonial enterprise to imperial domination. As England's commercial interests grew, the East India Company (a private company endorsed by Parliament) negotiated with compliant nabobs to expand outlying trading posts into a vast corporate enterprise that was ultimately underwritten by institutions of empire, including educational, political, and administrative institutions. Trade with India – in tea, silks, indigo, salt, opium, and other goods – was a major source of revenue for England. And with vast amounts of money came vast amounts of corruption, especially in the 1770s, when war with America diverted attention from India and allowed corruption to grow unchecked. The East India Company effectively replaced nabobs who refused to roll over with nabobs who would serve as pliable subalterns.

An emblem of colonial corruption was Warren Hastings, governor-general of Bengal from 1773 to 1785. He was accused of abusing his authority and impeached in the House of Commons; Edmund Burke led the prosecution. His indictment of Hastings reveals the rot that resulted from Parliament's authorization of the East India Company to function as a government rather than as a mere corporation. "To increase [India's] commerce without increasing its honour and reputation," Burke asserted, "would have been … a bad bargain for the Country."[1] The honor about which Garrick wrote in "Heart of Oak" was conspicuously absent under the East India Company's rule.

POWER, KNOWLEDGE, AND EMPIRE

Johnson's work of 1759, *Rasselas*, shows another side of the imperial project. The business of empire was everywhere bound up with the impulse to catalogue and categorize that which had been observed at first hand. One major theme of *Rasselas* – that we come to understand the world through experience – was a primary philosophical doctrine of Enlightenment thought; empiricism dominated eighteenth-century British philosophy (see chapter 33, "Philosophy"). A philosophical and moral fable written largely in the mode of the Oriental tale and the travel narrative, *Rasselas* is set in Abyssinia (Ethiopia) and Egypt. Imlac comments on England's global domination:

> From Persia … I travelled through Syria, and for three years resided in Palestine, where I conversed with great numbers of the northern and western nations of Europe; the nations are now in possession of all power and all knowledge; whose armies are irresistible, and whose fleets command the remotest parts of the globe. (*Works*, 16:46)

Imlac's connection between power and knowledge reveals the intellectual and philosophical underpinnings of empire. Since the beginning of the century, colonial corporations such as the East India Company and the Royal Africa Society capitalized on and helped to popularize proto- and pseudoscientific documents that justified the imperial project.

The sinister marriage of empiricism to bureaucracy made the English effective colonizers. Corporations produced travel narratives, natural histories, maps, and drawings of Africa, the West Indies, North America, and India. Such cataloguing provided empirical data to support what some have called the Great Chain of Being, in which all of creation is arranged in a vast hierarchy. In *Spectator* 519, Joseph Addison anthropomorphized the world, claiming that "every part of Matter is peopled."[2] Having catalogued the beings in the world, he then proceeded to rank them. In Addison's view, man occupies the middle state between God and worms:

> In this system of Being, there is no Creature so wonderful in its Nature, and which so much deserves our particular Attention, as Man, who fills up the middle Space between the Animal and Intellectual Nature, the visible and invisible World, and is that Link in the Chain of Beings which has been often termed the *nexus utriusque mundi* [the joining of two worlds]. So that he, who in one Respect is associated with Angels and Arch-Angels, may look upon a Being of infinite Perfection as his Father, and the highest Order of Spirits as his Brethren, may in another Respect say to *Corruption, thou art my Father, and to the Worm, thou art my Mother and my Sister*. (*Spectator*, 4:349)

Hierarchy permeated the system, and sexism was inherent to this world view. Angels were gendered male, whereas worms, earthly beings, were gendered female. Alexander Pope's *Essay on Man* similarly naturalizes hierarchy. He asks, "What can we reason, but from what we know?" Pope reserves such reasoning for the English and for members of European temperate zones: "Lo! The poor Indian, whose untutored mind / Sees God in clouds, or hears him in the wind."[3] Even as he goes on to sentimentalize the freeing of a slave, he writes his philosophical poem in hierarchical condescension towards non-Europeans. Hierarchies based on evolving concepts of racial and sexual difference and on geography served the ideology of empire well, for they naturalized and legitimized economic domination. That Johnson sets *Rasselas*, a tale peopled with wise and reasonable characters, in Africa speaks to his anti-imperialist views.

RACE AND EMPIRE

Unlike Johnson, but like Pope, many writers of natural histories, travel narratives, plays, and novels ascribed moral and industrial characteristics to people on the basis of geography. Writers often depicted the world as divided into temperate and torrid zones. People who resided in temperate zones were said to exhibit the civilized qualities – industry, moderation, Christianity – whereas people of the torrid zones were said to embody the dirty underbelly of the Enlightenment: they were lazy, lascivious, and heathen. Ideas about what we now call race – though the word did not pick up that meaning until late in the eighteenth century – were in flux throughout the period, as thinkers tried to account for human diversity (see chapter 12, "Anthropology"). Were different kinds of human beings different species? Were their differences fundamental or merely skin-deep? Writers of the later eighteenth century developed an ideology of difference.

In his *History of Jamaica* (1774), slaver, planter, and colonial administrator Edward Long detailed plantation life, trade, geography, and politics, and colorfully described the people of that island. His characterization of Africans and of Afro-Caribbeans reflected a common belief that morality linked sexuality and racial purity to property. To recall that property was the ticket to political voice, and that the majority of crimes in the eighteenth century were crimes against property, is to recall that property safeguarded the economic and social status quo – property equaled power. Long viewed women as the gatekeepers for, and producers of, legitimate heirs through whom property could pass. He saw racial miscegenation as an assault on English property, and therefore on white liberty: "A promiscuous intercourse and an uncertain parentage, if they were universal, would soon dissolve the frame of the constitution."[4] His most infamous pronouncement on the differences among groups of people is the flagitious statement about "Hottentot" (African) women: "I do not think an oran-outang husband would be any dishonour to an Hottentot female; for what are these Hottentots? – they are, say the most credible writers, a people certainly very stupid, and very brutal. In many respects they are more like beasts than men" (1:364).

The increasing obsession with categories of difference is perhaps best exemplified by Moreau de Saint Mery's strict cataloguing of 128 parts of a person, documented in his *Description de la partie française de l'Isle Saint-Domingue*, written while Moreau was living in Philadelphia in the 1790s. Moreau was a French Creole from Martinique who was trained in the law. His catalogue of race codified people based upon 128 different blood and color combinations, from whole white (128 parts white = *blanc*) to whole black (128 parts black = *nègre*), with various categories of mixed blood, or *sang-mêlée*, between them. Penned in Philadelphia, the "cradle of liberty," Moreau's analysis recalls American Revolutionary jurisprudence, which notoriously afforded three-fifths of personhood to African slaves in the United States Constitution. Increasingly, eighteenth-century bodies of law came to depend upon the racialized body of the resident. Moreau's document is a perfect instance of what I call "empirial" (empiricist + imperial) writing: it is obsessive, pseudoscientific, and imperial in intent. Such documents served as the philosophical and legal foundation of plantation slavery, and trade with and colonization of India and the Pacific region. Put more broadly, empirial ideology underwrote the state-sponsored piracy, or privateering, that enabled England's growing empire.

NATURALIZING RACE

The move towards seeing race in terms of physiology supported the racial hierarchy of nineteenth-century scientific racism and, before that, of Enlightenment and empirial thought. As the philosopher Richard Popkin has established, theories about human nature and mental ability in relation to racist discourse were intricately tied to "an economic need to justify African slavery and the rape of America." Popkin begins a landmark article with David Hume's famous footnote in "Of National Characters"

(1748): "I am apt to suspect the negroes and in general all other species of men (for there are four or five different kinds) to be naturally inferior to the whites. There never was a civilized nation of any other complexion than white, nor even any individual eminent either in action or speculation."[5] Hume's passage anticipates the kind of racism exemplified in two texts often quoted as characteristic of the shift in late eighteenth-century racial ideology, Thomas Jefferson's *Notes on the State of Virginia* (1782) and Long's *History of Jamaica*. Taken together, the attitudes of Hume, Jefferson, and Long typify a conception of race that was beginning to view difference in terms of fixed physical traits that corresponded to moral character and mental ability – a discursive shift that some critics have associated with the British abolitionist debates and literary depictions of non-Europeans.

IRELAND

The discourse of race is illustrated even within Europe: it can be seen in English attitudes towards the nation's nearest, and most troublesome, colony, Ireland. English and Irish Protestants deprecated Irish Catholics. Irish philosopher and Anglican bishop George Berkeley famously denigrated Irish Catholics by using the same terms as were used to dehumanize people of African descent: "these proud People are more destitute than *Savages*, and more abject than *Negroes*. The *Negroes* in our Plantations have a saying, *If Negro was not Negro, Irishmen would be Negro.*"[6] Like Jonathan Swift's Yahoos, Berkeley's Irish Catholics are "savages," atavistic ancestors of Enlightened, Protestant Englishmen.

Like many contemporaries who wrote on the colonial questions, Berkeley had economic ties to empire. He had a plantation in North America, and he founded religious institutions in Bermuda. Though Ireland could be called a colony of England, Berkeley could view himself as one of the Irish elite because the colonization of Ireland was predicated on religious difference, a difference that was tied directly to land ownership and political rule. Penal laws and the Protestant Ascendancy debarred Catholics from political and civic life, and it squelched Irish literary development. The theme of linguistic imperialism has been a dominant one in Irish literature since the eighteenth century. Harsh trade restrictions excluded Ireland from the commercial advantages of trade with India and the Americas. Ireland's few exports included linen and humans; indentured servants were a profitable source of labor. Many Irish emigrated to

Australia after Captain James Cook brought it into England's line of sight during the 1770s, just as England suffered the loss of the American colonies. England's colonial relationship with the Pacific would not expand until the nineteenth century, though narratives of Cook's voyages fired the imagination of English readers. In 1773, John Hawkesworth was paid the enormous sum of £6,000 for his published account of Cook's voyages; it was one of the most widely sold texts of its day.

THE BUSINESS OF EMPIRE

The marriage between the politics and literature of empire was an exceedingly profitable one. As subject and theme, empire appeared in literature and art in an array of genres. "The Toilette," plate 4 of William Hogarth's *Marriage à la Mode*, for instance, depicts the dissipated Countess's African page sitting in a corner while unpacking curios. Objectified like the objects before him, he is a human decoration dressed and plumed in the style of the Orient. Modish entertainments reflected the fashion for Oriental masquerade. Architecture followed suit. In 1762, Sir William Chambers built a fifty-meter faux-Chinese pagoda in Kew Gardens. Eliza Haywood's political satire *The Aventures of Eovaai* (1741) was written as an Oriental tale. By 1771, the character Miss Melford in Tobias Smollett's *Humphry Clinker* goes to London and is dazzled by performances of the *Tales of the Arabian Nights*.

Sometimes the connections between literary exoticism and the business of empire is clearer still. William Beckford's popular novel *Vathek* (1786) was first published as an "Arabian Tale." Beckford's family had amassed enormous riches in the West Indian sugar plantations; his wealth allowed him to pursue the travel and leisure that produced his novelistic fancies. Beckford was not alone in this regard: many planters and politicians turned to account the business of empire. Richard Cumberland, for instance, secretary to the Board of Trade and Plantations, wrote a popular sentimental comedy, *The West Indian*, in 1771. The central character is a West Indian sugar planter whose wild manner must be domesticated in London. The plot reflects widespread and racialized concern that Creole planters would menace England's economy. Cumberland was a schoolfellow of Warren Hastings, governor-general of Bengal. In his memoirs, Cumberland writes that, before he turned his hand to drama, he penned a poem in heroic verse about India. The writer of Cook's account, Hawkesworth, also published an Oriental tale, *Almoran and Hamet*, in 1761, two years after Johnson's *Rasselas*.

Johnson had no patience for most imperial developments. He distrusted the bellicose nationalism that appeared in many patriotic declarations of English superiority: he famously dismissed "patriotism" as "the last refuge of the scoundrel" (Boswell, *Life*, 2:348). And he particularly despised slavery, at a time when England's economy was becoming ever more dependent on profits from the slave trade. While "Britons never will be slaves," as Thomson's poem declared, Britons' notion of liberty did not preclude the enslavement of others. Johnson derided this contradiction when he wrote "How is it that we hear the loudest yelps for liberty among the drivers of negroes?" (*Works*, 10:454).

And Johnson was not alone in his growing concern that such pernicious capitalism would dry-rot the "heart of oak." Oliver Goldsmith, an Anglican Irishman and member of Johnson's Literary Club, depicted the ills of colonialism in his poem "The Deserted Village" (1770). The poem agonizes over enclosure, overpopulation, and urbanization, but the great villains are the luxuries of empire. According to the poem, "Trade's unfeeling train" enriched the urban wealthy at the expense of innocent, communal, and moral country folk. Colonial trade invites dangerous encounters with "torrid tracts" of land deleteriously described as "those poisonous fields with rank luxuriance crowned." Luxury is the poison of colonial wealth that can transform a kingdom into "a bloated mass of rank unwieldy woe." England, Goldsmith worries, must take heed, lest "Trade's proud empire [hasten] to swift decay."[7] Goldsmith was wrong. In 1770, empire was nowhere near its twilight. England was, in fact, well on its way to strengthening its global supremacy, so that by the early nineteenth century, the sun never set on the British empire.

NOTES

1 *The Writings and Speeches of Edmund Burke*, ed. Paul Langford, 9 vols. in 10 (Oxford: Clarendon Press, 1981–2000), 6:34.

2 Joseph Addison and Sir Richard Steele, *The Spectator*, ed. Donald F. Bond, 5 vols. (Oxford: Clarendon Press, 1965), 4:346.

3 Alexander Pope, *An Essay on Man*, in *The Twickenham Edition of the Poems of Alexander Pope*, ed. John Butt *et al.*, 11 vols. in 12 (New Haven, CT: Yale University Press, 1939–69), vol. 3.1, epistle 1, lines 18, 99–100.

4 Edward Long, *The History of Jamaica; or, General Survey of the Antient and Modern State of That Island*, 3 vols. (London, 1774), 2:325.

5 Richard Popkin, "The Philosophical Basis of Eighteenth-Century Racism," *Studies in Eighteenth-Century Culture* 3 (1973), 245–62, at p. 254.

6 George Berkeley, *A Word to the Wise; or, An Exhortation to the Roman Catholic Clergy of Ireland* (Dublin, 1749), p. 8.
7 Oliver Goldsmith, "The Deserted Village," in *Collected Works*, ed. Arthur Friedman, 5 vols. (Oxford: Clarendon Press, 1966), 4:287–304, lines 63, 343, 351, 392, 427.

CHAPTER 22

Essays

Paul Tankard

E'SSAY. *n.s.* [from the verb. The accent is used on either syllable.]
2. A loose sally of the mind; an irregular indigested piece; not a regular and orderly composition.

My *essays*, of all my other works, have been most current. *Bac.*

One problem with Samuel Johnson's reputation as a writer, rather than as a character in literature, is a problem of genre. He contributed to a dozen genres, including drama, poetry, biography, criticism, lexicography, homiletics, scholarly editing, bibliography, travel writing, and fiction; to which we could add – to account for the rest of the contents of his collected works – translations, political and controversial literature, and letters. If one had to limit Johnson's most characteristic work to a single form, though, it would be the troublesome but delightful genre of the essay. Johnson wrote or contributed to three series of essays: 203 of the 208 essays in the *Rambler* (1750–2), ninety-two of the 104 essays in the *Idler* (1758–60), and twenty-eight of the 140 essays in John Hawkesworth's series the *Adventurer* (1753–4). These 323 essays amount to more than 400,000 words of original prose.

Furthermore, most of the rest of his work is in the linguistic register of the essay, nonfictional prose. As critic Gérard Genette points out, nonfictional prose embraces all sorts of purely functional writing, and this troubles the essay's status as a literary form: there are few major writers whose work is predominantly in this essentially minor form. Whenever we engage with Johnson, though, we are engaging with an essayistic intelligence. His biographies and major prefaces are long essays; his critical notes and *Dictionary* definitions are précis of essays; his poems are essays in verse; his *Parliamentary Debates* and *Rasselas* are vehicles for essayistic reflections.

THE GENRE

The essay is a marginal and imprecise genre: it might be narrative or discursive, expository or descriptive. If it includes a narrative component, the narrative might be fiction or nonfiction. Essays can be formal or familiar. They can be of any length, from that of a lyric poem to that of a longish short story – or longer. Individual essays and essayists certainly find readers, but this flexibility makes it difficult for the essay, as a genre, to find a general audience, or even a niche within the academy.

For much of the time since Johnson's day, we have been accustomed to a hard sense of literary genre. Poems, plays, novels – these are "literature." Anything else must be assessed on a case-by-case basis. Under the influence of postmodernism and the new media this may be breaking down, but the essay has long been an unfashionable form. The consolidation of the novel as the preeminent popular literary genre in the nineteenth century took something from the readership of the periodical essay, and essays have become either more exclusively critical, on the one hand – the kind of work found in the monthly reviews – or more familiar, character-driven, autobiographical, and belletristic.

The boom in the familiar essay in the early twentieth century led to the form being regarded, particularly after the Second World War, as essentially nostalgic and trivial. A very astute scholar of Johnson (and an essayist himself), Paul Fussell, observes that "what literature is at any historical moment depends wholly on conventions which appear and depart," and that (in 1971) literature was expected to occur only as "autobiographical fiction, confessional lyric, and Absurd play."[1] Essays, while continuing to be written, have been either regarded as trivial – or, in the words of Graham Good, "seen somehow as adjuncts to 'major' genres or ideas, not as works in themselves."[2] Everyone in the academy writes essays, but students of literature study only those essays that are secondary sources for the study of other texts.

JOHNSON AS ESSAYIST

When Johnson was awarded his first honorary degree, a Master of Arts from Oxford, there was no doubt what it was for. He was not yet a lexicographer, a Shakespearean editor, or a literary critic: he was an essayist. The letter proposing him for the award, in order that the letters A.M. (the Latin form of the English M.A.) might grace his name on the title page of his *Dictionary*, says Johnson has "very eminently distinguished himself by the publication of a series of Essays, excellently calculated to form the manners of the people, and in which the cause of religion and morality is every where maintained by the strongest power of argument and language" (Boswell, *Life*, 1:280). That "series of Essays" was the *Rambler*.

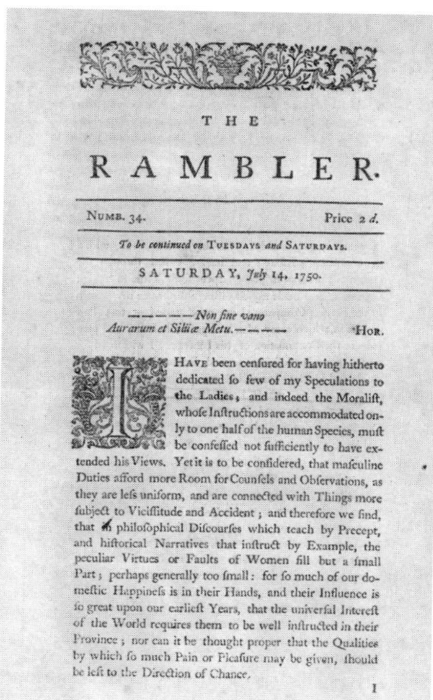

THE

RAMBLER.

NUMB. 34. Price 2 *d.*

To be continued on TUESDAYS *and* SATURDAYS.

SATURDAY, *July* 14, 1750.

——— *Non fine vano*
Aurarum et Siliiæ Metu. ——— HOR.

I HAVE been cenfured for having hitherto dedicated fo few of my Speculations to the Ladies, and indeed the Moralift, whofe Inftructions are accommodated only to one half of the human Species, muft be confeffed not fufficiently to have extended his Views. Yet it is to be confidered, that mafculine Duties afford more Room for Counfels and Obfervations, as they are lefs uniform, and are connected with Things more fubject to Viciffitude and Accident; and therefore we find, that in philofophical Difcourfes which teach by Precept, and hiftorical Narratives that inftruct by Example, the peculiar Virtues or Faults of Women fill but a fmall Part; perhaps generally too fmall: for fo much of our domeftic Happinefs is in their Hands, and their Influence is fo great upon our earlieft Years, that the univerfal Intereft of the World requires them to be well inftructed in their Province; nor can it be thought proper that the Qualities by which fo much Pain or Pleafure may be given, fhould be left to the Direction of Chance.

I

Figure 31 Samuel Johnson, *Rambler* 34, July 14, 1750.

The term *series* alerts us to the fact that Johnson's essays were not first published as collections, in bound volumes, as we usually now experience them; instead they appeared periodically.

A periodical essay series may be published in either of two ways: either as a column in a newspaper or magazine (like Johnson's *Idler*, published in a weekly newspaper, *The Universal Chronicle*), or as a single-essay periodical (like the *Rambler*). This latter form is less familiar today. Starting on Tuesday, March 20, 1750, and continuing for the next two years, each numbered issue of the *Rambler* would appear on Tuesdays and Saturdays as a six-page folio pamphlet, priced twopence (see chapter 31, "Money"). By the time the series concluded on Saturday, March 14, 1752, the first two volumes of a four-volume collected edition had already been published. Latter-day readers, who have generally encountered the essays in collections, need to be reminded of the original publishing circumstances. The individual essays were not originally given titles; they remain, even when collected, distinguished only by their issue numbers and dates.

Although Johnson's essays belong to the tradition established by Michel de Montaigne and Francis Bacon in the sixteenth and seventeenth centuries, they also depart from that tradition in strategic ways. Montaigne invented both the form of the essay and its name. His *Essais* (1580) – the French *essai* means "trial" or "attempt" – consists of 107 pieces of varying length, addressing a variety of topics, in a speculative, subjective, and anecdotal manner. The first English essays, adopting Montaigne's label, were *The Essayes or Counsels, Civill and Morall* of Sir Francis Bacon. In their first edition (1597), Bacon's *Essayes* were more like a series of topically organized aphorisms, which in later editions (1612, 1625) were expanded in length and in number to become the series of connected paragraphs that we expect. For all the differences between the styles of Montaigne and Bacon, their essays are similar to each other's, and different from Johnson's, in that they were originally published in books, as collections, and that each of their essays is a focused and unified meditation on a given topic: "Of Truth," "Of Revenge," "Of Boldness," "Of Travel" (Bacon); "Of the Education of Children," "Of Cannibals," "Of Idleness," "Of Presumption" (Montaigne). The unity of a particular essay in a periodical series is found not so much in the topic as in the *occasion* of reading.

MR. RAMBLER

A third important point of difference between Johnson's essays and those of his distinguished predecessors is that, whereas Bacon's and Montaigne's essays were published under the names of their authors, Johnson's were anonymous – or at least, the author was said to be simply "Mr. Rambler." They are not, of course, anonymous now, and they did not remain genuinely anonymous for long – within weeks of the *Rambler* first appearing, one could discover who the author was, if one knew whom to ask – but the tendency of commentators has been to understate the importance of the anonymity of the *Rambler*, seeing it as a mere convention. Anonymity was common in the eighteenth century, and in the field of journalism it endured into the late twentieth century. But anonymity, with the non-book format and the circumstance of periodical publication, is a defining characteristic of the subgenre with which Johnson's essays were readily aligned: the tradition that begins with the work of Joseph Addison and Sir Richard Steele, who established the form four decades earlier in the *Tatler* (1709–11) and *Spectator* (1711–12). In their essay series they invented the periodical rather than topical method of organization, the use of a disguised conductor, together with a slight narrative frame that nevertheless enabled them to engage with current society and events.

Most eighteenth-century periodical essays have titles that evoke a disguised figure, with a clear character and social position, who edits or "conducts" the paper. The paper called the *Rambler* is conducted by a man who calls himself "the Rambler." For its first readers, this title would have been reminiscent of the *Spectator* and other early essay series such as the *Tatler*, the *Guardian*, *Examiner*, *Moderator*, *Plain Dealer*, *Whisperer*. Some titles of those belonging to the (post-*Rambler*) "second flowering" of the periodical essay – often found in magazines – are the *Connoisseur*, *Entertainer*, *Remembrancer*, *Lounger*, and *Adventurer*. There were literally dozens of such series.

The name Johnson chose for his first series stresses the conductor's reliability as a reporter. He is reliable because he has viewed society extensively, but also because he is slightly distanced from society; he is independent and impartial. Also, by frankly admitting in his name his temper and prejudices, Mr. Rambler guarantees his trustworthiness and the openness of his personal character. Johnson told his friend Sir Joshua Reynolds that the *Rambler* was the first name that occurred to him when the necessity of naming the new journal could be put off no longer. Boswell commented that this title "certainly is not suited to a series of grave and moral discourses" (Boswell, *Life*, 1:202). But "grave and moral" is a most incomplete account of the *Rambler*, though it is true that the title has interesting and perhaps misleading implications.

The term *rambling* was used in Johnson's day, as in ours, to describe wandering from place to place, and wandering in thought or speech. Johnson's *Dictionary* defines *to ramble* as "To rove loosely and irregularly." Looseness and irregularity may refer simply to undertaking a journey, either physical or mental, without a clear aim or set route. But Johnson gives an etymology from the Dutch, "to rove loosely in lust," which is confirmed by the *Oxford English Dictionary*: "probably adopted from Middle Dutch *rammelen* (of cats, rabbits, etc.) be excited by sexual desire and wander about, frequentative form of *rammen* copulate with, cover." Whether it is "rambling" geographically, mentally, or morally, this group of words appears to have always had a connotation of sexual license, of roving in search of carnal encounters. In *Spectator* 203, Addison inveighs against "the infamous Race of Propagators," which he describes as "a loose Tribe of Men … that *ramble* into all the Corners of this great City, in order to seduce such unfortunate Females as fall into their Walks."[3] It is hard to imagine that Johnson would have been unaware of the suggestion that surrounded (and continues to surround) "rambling" and its cognates.

SOCIAL COMMENTARY

Predating the realistic novel, the periodical essay series is often seen by literary historians as a precursor to that now most dominant of literary genres (see chapter 23, "Fiction"). In the *Spectator* in particular, the writers exploit London's coffee house milieu as a setting for the meetings of a cast of characters, the proceedings of whose informal club the papers report (see chapter 16, "Clubs"). This apparently new combination of fictitious characters and a realistic environment enabled the writers to comment on society and its customs without having to resort to the didactic analysis and moral language of the sociologist or preacher, which would inevitably limit the appeal of the text to the scholarly and pious. Johnson, in his *Life of Addison*, gives a discerning assessment of that writer's pioneering work in one of his own chosen genres:

> Before the Tatler and Spectator, if the writers for the theatre are excepted [Johnson here means Shakespeare], England had no masters of common life. No writers had yet undertaken to reform either the savageness of neglect, or the impertinence of civility; to shew when to speak, or to be silent; how to refuse, or how to comply. We had many books to teach us our more important duties, and to settle opinions in philosophy or politicks; but an *Arbiter elegantiarum*, a judge of propriety, was yet wanting, who should survey the track of daily conversation, and free it from thorns and prickles, which teaze the passer, though they do not wound him.
>
> For this purpose nothing is so proper as the frequent publication of short papers, which we read not as study but amusement. If the subject be slight, the treatise likewise is short. The busy may find time, and the idle may find patience. (*Lives*, 3:7)

In his own periodical essays, Johnson clearly aims to adopt or renew the Addison–Steele model, but he does not avail himself of all their conventions – at least, he did not exploit them to the same extent. Like them, and unlike Bacon or Montaigne, he uses narrative, by scattering fables and allegories and character portraits throughout the series. The portrait papers, such as Squire Bluster (*Rambler* 142) and Dick Minim (*Idler*s 60 and 61), are among the most lively. The number of portrait-based papers increases in the later, shorter, and lighter *Idler* papers.

Each essay series has a fictional frame, but in Johnson's version it is very flimsy: there is no club, nor recurring characters, and his conductors, Mr.

Rambler and the Idler, are considerably less elaborate constructions than those of Steele and Addison. Of Mr. Rambler, for instance, the reader learns very little: he is a scholar, he seems to have no family, and in *Rambler* 59 (*Works*, 3:315) he is said to be in his early seventies (thirty years older than Johnson). He has had much experience as an observer of society; as he says in *Rambler* 10, "a diurnal writer ought to view the world" (*Works*, 3:52). The most vivid image of him comes from an entirely unreliable source: a letter to the Rambler from a fop, Florentulus, who imagines "the Rambler snuffing his candle, rubbing his spectacles, stirring his fire, locking out interruption, that he may enjoy a new calamity without disturbance" (*Works*, 4:215). Johnson makes it clear to his readers that they should recognize the conductor figure as a playful construct, part of the fiction.

LETTERS TO THE EDITOR

The device of the supposed letter to the editor, which Johnson uses in sixty-five of the 208 *Rambler* papers and thirty-two of the 104 *Idler*s, is another convention adopted from Addison and Steele. It varies the voice and point of view of the periodical and brings to his essays yet further elements of narrative and of fiction. Seven of these in the *Rambler* include the only contributions to that series which Johnson actually accepted from other writers.

In the supposed letters Johnson himself wrote, the illusion is unconvincing. Johnson seldom bothers to vary his diction much in the letters, and they are so often obvious and amusing caricatures that his actual readers are compelled to realize that these are not genuine correspondents but a literary device, a joke at the expense of an actually nonexistent class of readers, to whose sensitivities and prejudices Johnson pretends he must pander. Readers are invited by Johnson to enjoy, and yet to see through, both the fictitious conductor and the fictitious correspondents to understand that these devices are a concession to those who will not take to his serious purposes unless they are amused as well.

MORAL DISCOURSES

Boswell's description of the *Rambler* essays as "grave and moral discourses" and the commendation of them as maintaining "the cause of religion and morality" must therefore be seriously qualified. It is true that Johnson began the project only after composing a solemn prayer, and that in his post hoc statement of his aims for the work, in the final paper, he writes, first, that "I have laboured to refine our language to grammatical purity," but, second, that "It has been my principal design to inculcate wisdom and piety" (*Works*, 5:318–19). Still, these overdetermined occasional statements do not account for his actual biweekly engagement with the demands of composition or for his sense of the subtle operations of literary form.

The form of the essay, and in particular the periodical essay, is deployed by Johnson to deflect readerly resistance to moral writing. Morality may be Johnson's subject matter, but "moral writing" is not of itself a literary genre. Following the Addison–Steele model, Johnson devotes a considerable number of *Rambler*s to literary subjects: twenty-two on specific authors, texts, and genres, a further twenty on the life of writing, and many more that use writers as examples. By writing about the problems of writing, Johnson implicitly invites the reader to empathize with the problems of the writer who is most immediately present to them, that is, himself. The fictitious contributors of letters are presented as part of the problems faced by writers.

Bellaria, a very young lady, writes frankly to Mr. Rambler in no. 191,

> My aunt has just brought me a bundle of your papers for my amusement. She says, you are a philosopher, and will teach me to moderate my desires, and look upon the world with indifference. But, dear sir, I do not wish, nor intend to moderate my desires, nor can I think it proper to look upon the world with indifference, till the world looks with indifference upon me. (*Works*, 5:234)

The actual readers are amused by this image of the *Rambler*'s other readers, and with Mr. Rambler shake their heads at Bellaria's naiveté and flippancy. There are many other papers of which giving advice is not the object but the subject; it is hard to find an essay by Johnson in which the reader is actually advised "to moderate my desires, and look upon the world with indifference." In no. 40, we are told that the "chief rule to be observed in the exercise of this dangerous office [of giving advice], is to preserve it pure from all mixture of interest or vanity" (*Works*, 3:220). Later, the Rambler reflects,

> If we consider the manner in which those who assume the office of directing the conduct of others execute their undertakings, it will not be very wonderful that their labours, however zealous or affectionate, are frequently useless. For what is the advice commonly given? A few general maxims, inforced with vehemence and inculcated with importunity, but failing for want of particular reference, and immediate application. (*Works*, 4:94)

We realize with gratitude that such "general maxims" are not the stock-in-trade of the Rambler – he is not vehement – and through his many characters and correspondents he provides a great deal of "particular reference." By thus engaging his readers in a discussion about giving advice, Johnson invites them to be critically aware of (and not unsympathetic towards) the traditional moralist, and arranges that their suspicions will be deflected towards this decoy.

Although some commentators have treated the essay as an artless form, defined only by what it lacks (it is not fiction, not verse, not narrative), and Johnson's choice of it as accidental and arbitrary, we can see that Johnson is at all times alive to its tensions and opportunities. He is perhaps the most knowing writer to submit himself to its discipline.

NOTES

1 Paul Fussell, *Samuel Johnson and the Life of Writing* (New York: Harcourt, Brace, Jovanovich, 1971), pp. 38–9.

2 Graham Good, *The Observing Self: Rediscovering the Essay* (London: Routledge, 1988), p. vii.

3 Joseph Addison and Sir Richard Steele, *The Spectator*, ed. Donald F. Bond, 5 vols. (Oxford: Clarendon Press, 1965), 2:297, 295 (emphasis added).

CHAPTER 23

Fiction

John Richetti

> NO'VEL. *n.s.* [*nouvelle*, French.]
> 1. A small tale, generally of love.
>
> Nothing of a foreign nature; like the trifling *novels* which Ariosto inserted in his poems. *Dryden*.

Although he never wrote what modern readers would recognize as a novel, Samuel Johnson produced several kinds of fiction and articulated, both in his critical writings and in his conversations, influential views about the nature of fiction as new styles and approaches to narrative began to manifest themselves in the mid-eighteenth century. Examining his criticism of the novel against his own fictional practice lets us see more clearly some of the major developments in the eighteenth-century English novel.

THE HAZARDS OF REALISM

Johnson's most important critical statement on the new realistic novel appears in *Rambler* 4, for March 31, 1750: "The works of fiction with which the present generation seems more particularly delighted," he writes, "are such as exhibit life in its true state ... influenced by passions and qualities which are really to be found in conversing with mankind."

On the one hand, *Rambler* 4 outlines the requirements of these works of fiction, which eschew the staples of "heroic romance" such as knights, giants, and ladies in distress in order to depict "life in its true state." Writers of this fiction, Johnson argues, require not only book learning but "that experience which can never be attained by solitary diligence, but must arise from general converse, and accurate observation of the living world" (*Works*, 3:19–20). That would seem to be an unqualified endorsement of this new kind of fiction, as well as testimony to the general sense in the middle of the century that the novel as we now conceive of it was a genuinely new realistic direction in prose narrative. By 1750 English readers had been offered most of the works we now associate with the emergence of the modern novel in England: Daniel Defoe's *Robinson Crusoe* (1719), *Moll Flanders* (1722), and *Roxana* (1722); Henry Fielding's *Joseph Andrews* (1742) and *Tom Jones* (1749); Tobias Smollett's *Roderick Random* (1748); and Samuel Richardson's *Pamela* (1740) and *Clarissa* (1747–8).

On the other hand, Johnson worried about the moral dangers that he felt were built into this new kind of fiction. He recognized in these novels a powerful mode of representing reality, their potential to teach by "example" so that fiction can "take possession of the memory by a kind of violence, and produce effects almost without the intervention of the will" (*Works*, 3:22). Add to the almost irresistible power they can exert Johnson's recognition of the new appeal of the novel beyond an educated elite to its primary and dangerously impressionable audience – such books are "written chiefly to the young, the ignorant, and the idle, to whom they serve as lectures of conduct, and introductions into life" (*Works*, 3:21) – and much of his essay highlights the potential moral hazards of the new novel (a recurring concern, by the way, among moralists throughout the century). And yet, in literary criticism from his later years, Johnson is consistently on the side of the natural in literature – what would now be called realism – often ridiculing what seem to him ludicrous fictions and poetic conventions (such as those found in pastoral poetry). He praises Shakespeare in his preface to his edition of the dramatic works, for example, as the poet of nature: "his drama is the mirrour of life." Shakespeare, says Johnson, "has no heroes; his scenes are occupied only by men, who act and speak as the reader thinks that he should himself have spoken or acted on the same occasion" (*Works*, 7:64–5).

MOST PROPER FOR IMITATION

The contradiction between Johnson's admiration for realism in literature and his fear of its ambiguous moral effects is worked out in the *Rambler* essay by his insistence that, although "the greatest excellency of art" is to "imitate nature," authors must decide which parts of nature are "most proper for imitation" (*Works*, 3:22). Some aspects of nature should not be depicted, Johnson argues, and he may well have had in mind Richardson's seductively attractive villain, Lovelace, in his *Clarissa*, or Fielding's virtuous but impulsive and promiscuous hero, Tom Jones. Johnson warned of the erosion of moral clarity when a writer, "for the sake of following nature," mingles good and bad qualities in a character, leads us to identify with them, and potentially causes us to "lose the abhorrence of their faults." Vice, he concludes, needs to be shown, but it should always "disgust; nor should the graces of gaiety, or the dignity of courage, be so united with it as to reconcile it to the mind" (*Works*, 3:24).

Later in his life, Johnson was a staunch defender of the novels of his friend, Samuel Richardson, but was deeply critical and even dismissive of the novels of Henry Fielding. As he remarked to Boswell in 1768, Richardson's novels created what he called "characters of nature," whereas Fielding's were "characters of manners" (Boswell, *Life*, 2:48). He said further that the differences between the two could also be illustrated by comparing "a man who knew how a watch was made, and a man who could tell the hour by looking on the dial-plate" (Boswell, *Life*, 2:49). Although the somewhat intolerant moralist in Johnson disliked Fielding for what he saw as the loose morality his novels encouraged and for his depiction of what he called "low" life, his preference for Richardson is part of his attraction for a type of naturalism, for what he referred to as Richardson's "knowledge of the heart." In a conversation that Boswell records in the *Life of Johnson* from April 1772, Johnson responds when a friend protests that Richardson's novels are "tedious" that one cannot read him "for the story." Rather, "you must read him for the sentiment, and consider the story as giving occasion to the sentiment" (Boswell, *Life*, 2:175). Johnson, that is to say, finds Richardson's novels powerfully engaging; their readers become deeply involved in the emotional lives of the characters. For Johnson, we may say, narrative representations of the real have to be linked to an emotional effect and to moral knowledge ("the heart") that transcends the particular realities of time and place.

Fielding's novels, especially his first two, *Joseph Andrews* and *Tom Jones*, are therefore realistic in a sense that Johnson's essentially moral approach to narrative would not tolerate. Fielding's characters, in Johnson's dismissive phrase, are "characters of manners" because his novels offer a historically accurate picture of life as his readers would have known it. *Tom Jones*, especially, is a comprehensive, satiric survey of a wide range of characters, institutions, and experience in mid-eighteenth-century England. He offers comic and satiric evocations of social groups such as the rural gentry and the peasantry. His novels are populated by members of the clergy and other professions such as lawyers, merchants, innkeepers, and soldiers. He depicts life in the country and the city among the servant classes, the upper bourgeoisie, and the aristocracy. Richardson, on the other hand, is more narrowly focused in *Pamela* and *Clarissa* on intense, but in the end simplified or melodramatic, conflicts among characters from opposing and strictly defined social classes: the servant girl Pamela Andrews versus her rich would-be seducer, Mr. B, a member of the landed gentry; the daughter of the upper bourgeoisie, Clarissa Harlowe, as she resists her unscrupulous aristocratic suitor, Robert Lovelace, as well as the importunities of her ambitious and heartless family that she marry a rich and repulsive man she cannot love. In place of the sociohistorical sweep Fielding offers, Richardson's novels delve deeply into the psychosocial realities of his characters.

THE ORIENTAL TALE

In his only extended (although still relatively short) fiction, *Rasselas* (1759), Johnson is not at all naturalistic, and Richardsonian innovations – intensely specific insights into human behavior as manifested by characters who possess a distinct individuality – are nowhere in sight. Nor, for that matter, does *Rasselas* attempt the broad socialhistorical representations Fielding offered readers.

At first glance, *Rasselas* belongs to a minor narrative genre that was quite popular in the early eighteenth century, the Oriental tale, which could take many forms, from Europeanized versions of the *Arabian Nights* (in English, translated from the French version of Antoine Galland, 1704–17), to pseudo-Oriental satires promoting Enlightenment values such as *The Persian Letters* (1721) by the Baron de Montesquieu, to Oriental tales taking up a few pages such as Johnson himself produced in the *Rambler*, following the example of previous periodical essayists such as Joseph Addison in the *Spectator*. *Rambler*s 204 and 205 (February 29 and March 13, 1752), for example, tell the story of Seged, absolute monarch of Ethiopia, who in the twenty-seventh year of his reign decides to devote ten days to full respite from the cares of office and retires to an island "to exclude all trouble from my abode and remove from my thoughts whatever may confuse the harmony of the concert, or abate the sweetness of the banquet." But of course such perfect retreat from the normal course of life turns out to be impossible, with each day bringing disappointments, frustrations, and fresh sorrows, including on the tenth morning the death of his daughter. So Johnson ends by saying that Seged has "bequeathed to future generations" the lesson "that no man may hereafter presume to say, 'This day shall be a day of happiness'" (*Works*, 5:296–300).

This tale predicts the pattern of *The History of Rasselas, Prince of Abissinia*, written in 1759, whose original title was to be "The Choice of Life." Along with other members of the royal family of Abyssinia, Rasselas, the fourth son of the emperor, is confined in the Happy Valley "till the order of succession should call him to the throne" (*Works*, 16:8).

But Rasselas finds life in this secluded luxury to be insipid and boring; he longs to escape to see the outside world and to "make the choice of life." With help from the poet and philosopher, Imlac, a fellow inhabitant of the Happy Valley who has lived in the outside world, the prince does escape, but the ultimate failure of his quest is a foregone conclusion from the resonant opening passage:

> Ye who listen with credulity to the whispers of fancy, and persue with eagerness the phantoms of hope; who expect that age will perform the promises of youth, and the deficiencies of the present day will be supplied by the morrow, attend to the history of Rasselas prince of Abissinia. (*Works*, 16:7)

This opening paragraph contains two distinguishing features that separate Johnson's narrative from the emerging novel that he wrote about so perceptively in *Rambler* 4: an elaborately balanced rhetorical style, and a pessimistic and ironic universalism whereby the characters will turn out to be subordinate to the ideas that they explore.

STYLE AND UNIVERSALISM

Even by the standards of mid-century England, Johnson's writing style was exceptionally formal, characterized by balanced constructions, periodic sentences, and generalized, sonorous diction. In *Rasselas*, all of Johnson's characters are themselves Johnsonian, exceedingly formal in their manner of speaking, and the book resembles a series of philosophical dialogues. As hostile readers complained at the time, they all sound the same. The result is a refusal of the effort most realistic novels make to imitate or to approximate actual and local speech, to move towards a certain particular reality, to ground individual destiny in specific historical and social circumstances. Defoe's narrators, for the best example, are richly individualized, and Defoe's approach in books such as *Moll Flanders*, *Colonel Jack*, and *Captain Singleton* (1720) is to mimic lower-class speech, to let characters speak for the most part in their own particular argot. Jack, for example, in the first parts of his story is a street urchin and petty thief who winds up as an indentured servant in Virginia; Bob Singleton is an orphan who drifts through service to various masters until he rises to become a pirate captain; and Moll Flanders is born in Newgate Prison and eventually, after many marital mishaps, takes up picking pockets and shoplifting to survive but ends up rich and happy with one of her husbands in Virginia.

In *Rasselas*, by contrast, Johnson sets out to illustrate the general truths of human psychology, as Rasselas and his sister, Nekayah, seek to explore the world they have never seen before in order to choose their way of life. In a sense theirs is a purely intellectual and moral, rather than an experiential, quest. The world they travel through, moreover, is never explored in its historical and geographical specificity, as Johnson sets up situations in which universal rather than specific or particularized truth is exemplified. His protagonists are also privileged spectators rather than the harried participants in difficult realities that the eighteenth-century realistic novel depicts so vividly. To the extent that his titular hero sets out to discover a new world and to expand his horizons and develop his character and personality, Johnson's tale resembles to some extent in its plot many eighteenth-century novels. Like Defoe's Robinson Crusoe, for one example, Rasselas is eager for adventure and personal expansion, although unlike Crusoe he is not out for wealth but for knowledge. But, unlike Crusoe and the male heroes of other eighteenth-century novels, the knowledge he does acquire is deliberately moral and conceived in general terms. Fielding's Tom Jones and Joseph Andrews and Smollett's Roderick Random or Matthew Bramble (the hero of *The Expedition of Humphry Clinker*, 1771) are immersed in the actualities of eighteenth-century British social life (and Random travels to Europe and to South America before his story is over), whereas Rasselas and his friends wander through a thinly evoked northern Africa, where they encounter nameless type characters, such as a Stoic philosopher who impresses Rasselas with his solution to the tragedies of existence. Convinced that he has found the man who will show him how to make his choice of life, he tells Imlac, "this man shall be my future guide: I will learn his doctrines, and imitate his life." To which Imlac replies, "Be not too hasty … to trust, or to admire, the teachers of morality: they discourse like angels, but they live like men" (*Works*, 16:74). And, indeed, when Rasselas returns to see the sage he finds him mourning the death of his daughter, violating the Stoic ideal, the mastery of the passions and indifference to calamity, that had so impressed the prince. Ingenuously, Rasselas repeats the sage's precepts: "Has wisdom no strength to arm the heart against calamity? Consider that external things are naturally variable, but truth and reason are always the same" (*Works*, 16:75). The philosopher answers that truth and reason now serve only to tell him that his daughter will not be restored, and Rasselas departs "convinced of the emptiness of rhetorical sound, and the inefficacy of polished periods and studied sentences" (*Works*, 16:76).

This conclusion is deeply ironic, since *Rasselas* is itself composed of "polished periods and studied sentences." And yet Johnson's philosophical tale is designed to show by its very eloquence how experience trumps theory, how the moral and psychological realities of human nature will always compromise personal autonomy and the "choice of life" that Rasselas thinks he will be able to make. On the one hand, Johnson's destructive ironies about the inevitable failure of human striving link *Rasselas* to much of the new fiction of the eighteenth century, where individuals discover the limitations of individual desire in the face of larger and determining social and economic forces. But, on the other hand, *Rasselas* is conceived in universalizing terms, and the negative lessons the characters learn apply to human nature and experience at their most generalized and not to particularized eighteenth-century English life such as the new novel aspires to explore.

ACTION *VS.* CONTEMPLATION

At length, Rasselas and his sister, Nekayah, decide to divide the work of investigating the world, he to "try what is to be found in the splendour of courts," she to "range the shades of humbler life" (*Works*, 16:89). Such deliberate and self-conscious exploration and intellectual purpose are a far cry from what happens in most eighteenth-century fiction, and they dramatize the distance between Johnson's philosophical and satiric tale and the realistic novel. Characters in various kinds of eighteenth-century novels acquire knowledge, of course, but incidentally, through their immersion in experience, which is often painful or even deadly (as in the case of Richardson's Clarissa). Rasselas and Nekayah, on the other hand, bring back reports from their observation of public and private life rather than their participation, and in subsequent chapters discuss the relative advantages of those spheres but always in the most generalized way. Nekayah's report on private life turns on the "evils [that] infest private life" (*Works*, 16:98), and she unsparingly describes not just the general failure of marriage as she has observed it, but the equally dismal lives that single people lead: "Marriage has many pains, but celibacy has no pleasures" (*Works*, 16:99). What these two survey and analyze – the pains of private life, especially family life – is nothing less than the main subject matter of many eighteenth-century novels, which deal with courtship and the resulting conflicts between parents and children about appropriate marriage partners. But they do not experience this state of affairs; rather, they observe and debate.

To be sure, all this intellectualizing is in the end a source of mild ridicule, as when Rasselas declares that his sister's "dismal history of private life" has almost discouraged him from his quest. Imlac then observes that, "while you are making the choice of life, you neglect to live." So even in the increasingly static dialogues that make up *Rasselas*, Johnson inserts an observation that undercuts the intellectualizing and returns the reader, after a fashion, to particular movement as Imlac persuades the prince and his sister to visit the Pyramids. Even there, though, his reasons are pedagogical: "To judge rightly of the present we must oppose it to the past; for all judgment is comparative, and of the future nothing can be known" (*Works*, 16:110–12). As true as this may be, it is foreign to the new novel of the mid-eighteenth century, for the realistic novel in its various forms is focused not on contemplation of the past but on vigorous and purposeful action in the present, as individuals seek fulfilment (or riches or power), and move hopefully through the present to a better future.

Rasselas is interesting precisely for its refusal of the energies and purposes of the new realistic novel. The last chapter is titled "The Conclusion, in Which Nothing is Concluded," as Rasselas and the others resolve to return to Abyssinia (although perhaps not to the Happy Valley). Neither happy nor tragic, Johnson's ending negates the closures that the new novel grants readers.

CHAPTER 24

History

Robert DeMaria, Jr.

HI'STORY. *n.s.* [ἱστορία; *historia*, Latin; *histoire*, French.]
1. A narration of events and facts delivered with dignity.

Justly Cæsar scorns the poet's lays;
It is to *history* he trusts for praise. *Pope.*

History was one of the most popular genres of literature in the eighteenth century. Publishing statistics make the case: the *English Short Title Catalogue* lists over 22,000 items with that subject. Limiting the search to works with the word "history" in the title, history as the subject, and published within Johnson's lifetime, still yields more than 3,000 items. To give another and somewhat more careful measure of the importance of history books in England at this time, historian Richard B. Sher finds that, of the 360 books of the Scottish Enlightenment first published in Britain, sixty-eight were on the subject of history, more than on any other subject.[1] The range of these works is enormous: from schoolbooks to learned, antiquarian tomes; from histories of small towns and groups of people to histories of the world. The genre is also elastic, stretching easily into the particulars of biography on the one hand and into the generalities of universal history on the other.

In addition, of course, history writing from earlier periods was still available to eighteenth-century readers. Greek and Roman historians such as Suetonius, Tacitus, Livy, Herodotus, and Thucydides continued to be published often, and the earlier British historians were also conspicuous on the shelves of eighteenth-century readers: Sir Walter Ralegh's *History of the World* (1614), Francis Bacon's *History of the Raigne of King Henry VII* (1622), Gilbert Burnet's *History of the Reformation in England* (1679–81), and the Earl of Clarendon's posthumously published *History of the Rebellion and Civil Wars* (1702), for example, were still widely read at mid-century. Some of these works prefigure innovations in historical writing usually ascribed to the eighteenth century. Nevertheless, some trends in the evolution of historical writing are properly assigned to Johnson's lifetime, and these may be described in terms of subjects, methods, scope, and style.

CONJECTURE, FABLE, AND UNCERTAINTY

Broadly speaking, history during Johnson's lifetime came to focus more often on the modern world, less often on the classical world, and much less often on the speculative world of mankind before the extant written histories existed. For example, William Robertson, who had more best-sellers in Britain than any Scottish Enlightenment author except Tobias Smollet, begins his *Historical Disquisition concerning Ancient India* with the following statement:

> Whoever attempts to trace the operations of men in remote times, and to mark the various steps of their progress in any line of exertion, will soon have the mortification to find that the period of authentic history is extremely limited. It is little more than three thousand years since the books of Moses, the most ancient and only genuine record of what passed in the early ages of the world, were composed … If we push our inquiries concerning any point beyond the æra where written history commences, we enter upon the region of conjecture, of fable, and of uncertainty. Upon that ground I will neither venture myself, nor endeavour to conduct my readers.[2]

Robertson begins his *History of America* and his *History of Scotland* with similar statements, and his Scottish predecessor as best-selling historian, David Hume, was of the same opinion. Early in his *History of England*, Hume writes:

> We shall not attempt to trace any higher the origin of those princes and nations. It is evident what fruitless labour it must be to search, in those barbarous and illiterate ages, for the annals of a people, when their first leaders, known in any true history, were believed by them to be the fourth in descent from a fabulous deity, or from a man, exalted by ignorance into that character. The dark industry of antiquaries, led by imaginary analogies of names, or by uncertain traditions, would in vain attempt to pierce into that deep obscurity, which covers the remote history of those nations.[3]

Less than a hundred years earlier, though he acknowledged that the "remote history" of England was unknown, John Milton nevertheless began his *History of Britain* (1670) with fables such as the myth of Brutus, grandson of Aeneas, crossing the channel and beginning the race of Englishmen. This myth had been enshrined by Geoffrey of Monmouth, whose *History of Britain*, first composed in the twelfth century, was still being reprinted in the eighteenth.

ANTIQUARIES

The early antiquaries whom Hume and Robertson reviled used myth, folk traditions, and fanciful etymologies to construct their histories, but their own historiographical tradition was not stagnant. Milton credited "antiquaries" with exploding myths, and the latter-day Society of Antiquaries, founded in 1707 and given its royal charter in 1751, worked hard to establish higher standards for evidence than their humanistic predecessors, supplementing written accounts with examination of coins, ruins, graveyards, and muniments. Although Alexander Pope dismissively said antiquaries "th'inscription value, but the rust adore,"[4] they contributed importantly to the new trends in historical writing.

It was not only that the antiquarians wrote learned books with compilations in them; they also encouraged the establishment of archives and libraries where more modern historians could do their research. The British antiquaries, moreover, focused exclusively on Britain and helped shift the center of historical investigation from the classical to the modern world. Thomas Birch, for example, a friend of Samuel Johnson, director of the Society of Antiquaries, and secretary of the Royal Society, as well as an original trustee of the British Library, had an important influence on all kinds of history writing in the eighteenth century, although his own, mainly biographical, works are so overwhelmed with footnotes and compilations of documents that they are difficult to read.

PHILOSOPHY TEACHING BY EXAMPLE

Hume and Robertson took the demand for written evidence and the contempt of traditional knowledge farther than the antiquarians: they were skeptical about getting at the truth of historical events, but their most significant complaint about the antiquarians was that they could not put historical information together in a meaningful way. For the great historians of the eighteenth century, giving facts meaning meant finding out how they were causally connected, and it meant appreciating what the course of events signified in terms of social progress. This latter meaning of history in the eighteenth century is often exemplified with a famous quotation from Lord Bolingbroke, "History is philosophy teaching by example."[5] This statement sounds as if it might belong to the humanistic historiography of the Renaissance, which aimed to be a mirror for magistrates teaching ethical lessons, except for the loaded word *philosophy*. That word carries associations with the *philosophes* of the French Enlightenment, including

Voltaire, whose *History of Charles XII* (1731) was frequently printed in Britain at mid-century. The philosophical historian is more skeptical about historical fact than the Renaissance ethicist; he is inclined to locate historical causation in larger social movements, rather than in the deeds of individuals; and he is inclined to focus on customs, laws, mores, commerce, manners, and social life in general to a greater extent than Renaissance historians, whose narratives are mostly about the actions of the court – their education, their diplomacy, their wars, and their religion.

SOCIAL AND SENTIMENTAL HISTORY

The shift of historical attention from movements of the court to the manners of society took place gradually, and history on the older model persisted well into the time that the newer kind of history was being written. The shift is brilliantly described in Mark Salber Phillips's landmark work *Society and Sentiment*. There are many aspects to the shift, but Phillips puts the greatest emphasis on the new historical attention to manners and the inherence of this attention with the shift of sensibility in the latter half of the century that increased the importance of sentiment and sentimentality. He points out that "Hume could not sustain the humanist's conviction of the (ideal) congruence of private and public character," and he cites Hume's telling wish to please both Mr. and Mrs. Mure: "The first quality of an historian is to be true and impartial … the next is to be interesting." In sum, Phillips writes, "manners was immediately recognizable as the brief signature of the new concern with the social that set the interests of this period apart from those of its classical and Renaissance predecessors."[6] Because of this emphasis, history veered towards biography, and especially biography in the mode of the Greek writer Plutarch, with its emphasis on character. James Boswell saw himself as a modern Plutarch, and Thomas Carlyle, as Phillips points out, described Boswell's *Life of Johnson* as the true history of the eighteenth century.

This movement to the social and the sentimental is seen in Hume's *History* in the kind of attention he pays to the fine points of character, as when he laments the lack of information for an adequate historical treatment of King Alfred:

> Fortune alone, by throwing him into that barbarous age, deprived him of historians worthy to transmit his fame to posterity; and we wish to see him delineated in more lively colours, and with more particular strokes, that we may at least perceive some of those small specks and blemishes, from which, as a man, it is impossible he could be entirely exempted.[7]

Hume also displays his sentimental leanings when he describes the departure of Catherine of Aragon from Henry VIII's court: "Having spoken these words, she rose, and making the king a low reverence, she departed from the court, and never would again appear in it" (3:181). More sentimental still is Hume's description of Charles I in his last days: "Holding him [the young Duke of Gloucester] on his knee, he said, 'Now they will cut off thy father's head.' At these words, the child looked very steadfastly upon him. 'Mark! child, what I say: They will cut off my head! and perhaps make thee a king'" (5:539).

WHIGGISH HISTORY

Implicitly denigrating Hume's sentimentality and his politics, Catharine Macaulay, though she quoted Hume's *History* in her own, does not give Charles a moment to excite the least bit of pity in her audience. Though admitting that, in the three days between his sentence and execution, he "united the magnanimity of heroism and the patience of martyrdom," she concludes her section on his death:

> Compassion is the constant attendant of liberal minds; and the commiseration of Charles's singular and unfortunate fate, but for the interests of truth and the violence of his partizans, would have inclined all such to have thrown the mantle of oblivion over the dark parts of his character, and only to have remembered that he bore his sufferings in a manner which would have done honor to the best cause. From such indulgence the ill-fated Charles is necessarily excluded: History is called upon to scrutinize with exactness his principles, conduct, and character; since, from the false colorings which by designing men have been thrown on these, and the rancor with which his opponents have been falsely aspersed, have been deduced consequences destructive to the security and welfare of man, and highly injurious to the reputation of patriot citizens.[8]

Catharine Macaulay's *History of England* is so politically tendentious that it is almost a Whig screed (see chapter 35, "Politics"), but some of her Whiggish tenets were accepted across the political spectrum. As Ernst Breisach maintains, there is agreement in eighteenth-century historiography on the importance and inevitability of progress, the idea at the center of what has been called "Whiggish history." For eighteenth-century historians, Breisach says, "the emancipation of rationality from error and superstition" is the destiny of mankind and the universal distribution of reason is its unifying thread.[9] Robertson describes the feudal world in his prolegomena to *Charles V* as barbarous and dark. Enlightenment, he writes, comes only with the growth of personal freedom and personal knowledge:

Charlemagne in France, and Alfred the great in England, endeavoured to dispel this darkness [the Dark Ages], and gave their subjects a short glimpse of light and knowledge. But the ignorance of the age was too powerful for their efforts and institutions. The darkness returned, and settled over Europe more thick and heavy than before.[10]

Although his politics are complex, Hume's historical writing means to reveal the enlightenment of constitutional, limited monarchy: "An acquaintance with the ancient periods of their government is chiefly *useful* by instructing them to cherish their present constitution, from a comparison or contrast with the condition of those distant times."[11] This view is clear in Hume's critical treatment of Queen Elizabeth:

The party among us, who have distinguished themselves by their adhering to liberty and a popular government, have long indulged their prejudices against the succeeding race of princes, by bestowing unbounded panegyrics on the virtue and wisdom of Elizabeth. They have even been so extremely ignorant of the transactions of this reign, as to extol her for a quality, which, of all others, she was the least possessed of; a tender regard for the constitution, and a concern for the liberties and privileges of her people.[12]

Praise of the constitution is bound up in Hume's and Robertson's rhetoric with their denigration of the superstition and darkness under which men labored before the Glorious Revolution of 1688–9, the end of the Stuart reign, and the climax of Hume's *History*.

THE HISTORIAN AS SKEPTIC

The greatest historical work of the eighteenth or perhaps any other century does not transcend politics, but by undertaking such a vast design, and by infusing skepticism into such a grand rhetorical style, Edward Gibbon made his genre of history more art than polemic. In his magnum opus, *The Decline and Fall of the Roman Empire* (1776–89), Gibbon contributes to his fellow eighteenth-century historians' effort to displace Rome from its position at the center of historical attention, and he builds on the growing interest in the "Orient" exhibited earlier in the century. Gibbon entirely discards the old tendencies to recur to myth or to focus exclusively on the deeds of great men; like Hume, Gibbon locates historical causes in general human nature; and he acknowledged Hume as his master in style and interpretation. Gibbon's style, however, excels Hume's and propels his history into a new generic realm.

When Gibbon describes individuals or their actions, he often elevates them to abstract principles or general ideas. He writes, for example, "The vain and ambitious mind of Julian might aspire to restore the ancient glory of the temple of Jerusalem."[13] It is not enough for him to say, "Julian aspired to restore …" The more abstract entity, the *mind* of Julian, has this aspiration, and since "mind" is abstract, compared to the proper noun "Julian," its characteristics – vanity and ambition – become almost substitutes for it. The result is a line that has nearly the grandeur and abstraction of Johnson's *Vanity of Human Wishes*, where "Hope and Fear, Desire and Hate, / O'erspread with snares the clouded Maze of Fate." While noting particular manners and Plutarchan characters, Gibbon describes broader human features in a philosophical manner.

As an aspect of its philosophical manner, Gibbon's style creates a degree of irony throughout the narrative: he often describes actions in terms of their subjects' motives and places in terms of contemporary perceptions, while implying a point of view that is distinct from and skeptical of them. Speaking, for example, about the use of the "True Cross" on which Christ was crucified as an inexhaustible source of relics sold by the early Church, Gibbon writes, "as this gainful branch of commerce must soon have been annihilated, it was found convenient to suppose, that the marvellous wood possessed a secret power of vegetation; and that its substance, though continually diminished still remained entire and unimpaired" (*Decline and Fall*, 2:481). The word *marvellous*, of course, is ironic in Gibbon's narrative, but it might have been used unironically, we are led to suppose, by the Bishop of Jerusalem, the beneficiary of the emoluments garnered by distributing mass-produced pieces of the True Cross.

Like the great satirists of the age, Gibbon lets us know more about what he rejects than what he embraces. Hume, in contrast, despite his own subtlety, seems direct in making British history a paean to the constitution, and Robertson seems reductive in discussing "eastern despotism"[14] or the ridiculous "political and permanent effects of the spirit of chivalry" (3:64). In shifting Rome to the side without admitting any miraculous reasons for its displacement by Christianity, Gibbon opened up the space for historical work to focus on the realities of daily life and universal, common human nature. In this way, he may be said to have extended the work of eighteenth-century poets and novelists to the realms of learned historical writing.

NOTES

1 Richard B. Sher, *The Enlightenment and the Book: Scottish Authors and Their Publishers in Eighteenth-Century Britain, Ireland, and America* (Chicago: University of Chicago Press, 2006), p. 700.

2 William Robertson, *The Works of William Robertson*, 8 vols. (Oxford, 1825), 8:129.

3 David Hume, *The History of England from the Invasion of Julius Caesar to the Revolution in 1688*, 6 vols. (Indianapolis: Liberty Fund, 1983), 1:17.

4 Alexander Pope, "To Mr. Addison, Occasioned by His Dialogues on Medals," line 36, in *The Twickenham Edition of the Poems of Alexander Pope*, ed. John Butt *et al.*, 11 vols. in 12 (New Haven, CT: Yale University Press, 1939–69), 5:216.

5 *Lord Bolingbroke: Historical Writings*, ed. Isaac Kramnick (Chicago: University of Chicago Press, 1992), p. xxiii.

6 Mark Salber Phillips, *Society and Sentiment: Genres of Historical Writing in Britain, 1740–1820* (Princeton, NJ: Princeton University Press, 2000), pp. 69, 60, 147. The present essay is pervasively indebted to Phillips.

7 Hume, *History*, 1:75.

8 Catharine Macaulay, *The History of England from the Accession of James I to the Elevation of the House of Hanover*, new edn., 8 vols. (London, 1771), 4:418–19.

9 Ernst Breisach, *Historiography: Ancient, Medieval, and Modern*, 3rd edn. (Chicago: University of Chicago Press, 1997), pp. 206–10.

10 Robertson, *Works*, 3:17–18.

11 Hume, *History*, 2:525.

12 Hume, *History*, 4:354.

13 *The History of the Decline and Fall of the Roman Empire*, ed. J. B. Bury, 7 vols. (1909; repr. New York: AMS Press, 1974), 2:482.

14 Robertson, *Works*, 3:169.

CHAPTER 25

Journalism

Lee Morrissey

> NEWS. *n.s.* without the singular. [from *new*, *nouvelles*, Fr.]
> 2. Papers which give an account of the transactions of the present times.
>
> Their papers, filled with a different party spirit, divide the people into different sentiments, who generally consider rather the principles than the truth of the *news*-writer. *Addis.*

In 1709, the year in which Samuel Johnson was born, London saw its first daily evening newspaper, the *Evening Post*, and Richard Steele began writing the *Tatler*. In these two periodicals from the same year, we have two different forms or genres – the newspaper and the literary essay. Although Johnson was born in Staffordshire, far from London, he would of course move to London and write for periodicals, and these two publications highlight one particularly important aspect of the impact of print on Johnson, while also pointing to tensions that animate Johnson's contributions to journalism.

By the early eighteenth century, periodicals such as the *Evening Post* had begun to compile a variety of different stories in the same publication, paving the way for the format that would become so prevalent in the nineteenth and twentieth centuries: newspapers providing daily updates on current events, across a wide range of fields, creating in the process, among other things, a narrative played out on what has come to be called the twenty-four-hour news cycle. On the other hand, with publications such as the *Tatler*, the eighteenth century began to see the development of the single-essay literary periodical. Typically published a couple of times a week, these journals might sustain a topic or a theme across a few issues. Usually, though, each prose essay offered anecdotal observations; what was sustained across them, instead of the narrative of the news, was the character created by the typically anonymous author of the journals' reflections.

It has become a commonplace among Johnson's readers that with the passage of the centuries we have received two Samuel Johnsons, the character and the writer. This state of affairs is accepted with resignation at best, in part because it appears that the personality is more familiar than the author, although the accuracy of that personality is always a matter for debate among those who read Johnson's writings. The situation is no clearer when considering Johnson's journalism, in which there are also several different Samuel Johnsons. There is, for example, the Samuel Johnson who reported on Parliament in the *Gentleman's Magazine* at a time when such reporting was still illegal; there is the Samuel Johnson who published literary journals such as the *Rambler* and the *Idler*, series of stand-alone essays often on topics relating to literary criticism; and there is the Samuel Johnson who founded the *Literary Magazine; or, Universal Magazine* (1756), which compiled articles and essays on a wide range of subjects. Part of the trouble we have with these different sides of Johnson has to do with changes in the look and function of journalism since the eighteenth century. But each of these aspects of Johnson also has a place within the history of journalism, before, during, and after the eighteenth century.

SIXTEENTH- AND SEVENTEENTH-CENTURY BACKGROUNDS

By the end of the sixteenth century, print – the mechanical reproduction of text using moveable type – had been in use in England for over a century. But print was still relatively expensive and relatively tightly controlled when the prospect of war with Spain (an international conflict that helped to create an interest in news) appeared in the second half of the 1580s. At the time, news – reporting on current events – was conveyed by letters, newsletters, and handwritten documents sent privately from a trusted correspondent to interested subscribers. In addition to these letters, which would have had a very small circulation, there were theatrical representations of recent events. Christopher Marlowe's play, *Massacre at Paris* (1593), for example, describes the St. Bartholomew's Day Massacre of twenty years earlier, while simultaneously referring implicitly to current tensions between Catholics and Protestants.

By the 1620s, London saw England's first periodicals devoted to current events. But it was still illegal at that point to print domestic news about England in England. What was published, therefore, to what purpose, and with what accuracy became such an intriguing question that Ben Jonson would write a play, *News from the New World Discovered in the Moon* (1621), whose title thematizes not so much current events as the sale of the papers that claimed to represent them.

In 1641, the Star Chamber that had censored publications was abolished by Parliament; in 1642, Parliament closed the theaters. This combination represents an important turning point in the development of English journalism. Print was now less regulated than it had been, and the possibility of representing current events on stage would not be available until the theaters reopened with the Restoration of the Stuart monarchy in 1660. The period therefore experienced a dramatic increase in the publication of pamphlets devoted to current events. Generations of scholarship have not dislodged Johnson's judgment that "this mode of conveying cheap and easy knowledge began among us in the Civil War," i.e., the 1640s (*Lives*, 3:7). These news pamphlets were sometimes published regularly (i.e., periodically), and, more important, also clarified that there was a paying market for published news. But the pamphlets of the 1640s differed from what would later become newspapers in several important ways, the most noticeable being that pamphlets usually focused on a single topic (although the fact that they also tended to be polemical and wildly inaccurate is also salient). Unlike the earlier newsletters, which were handwritten and private with a small readership able to afford them, news pamphlets were printed (and thus both cheaper and public), and had a wide circulation and a diverse readership.

THE NEWSPAPER

The material conditions for what would later become the newspaper had started to coalesce in the 1640s. By the 1650s, various organizations saw periodical publication as a means of addressing and organizing public opinion: the republican government via Marchamont Nedham's *Mercurius Politicus*, the Restoration government via the *London Gazette*, and natural philosophers (scientists) via the *Philosophical Transactions* of the Royal Society. In this process, which took decades, the pamphlets of the 1640s were replaced by newspapers with a regular publication cycle and a variety of different stories combined in the same issue.

According to one count, seventeen new newspapers appeared in the three years between 1679 and 1682.[1] By the first decade of the eighteenth century, London had daily newspapers printing morning and evening editions. While this was happening in periodical publications, the last third of the seventeenth century saw the emergence of occasional, albeit not periodical, literary criticism. In part because of the reopening of the theaters in 1660, criticism, often dramatic criticism, came to be published in prefaces, dedications, epistles, and related materials that accompanied

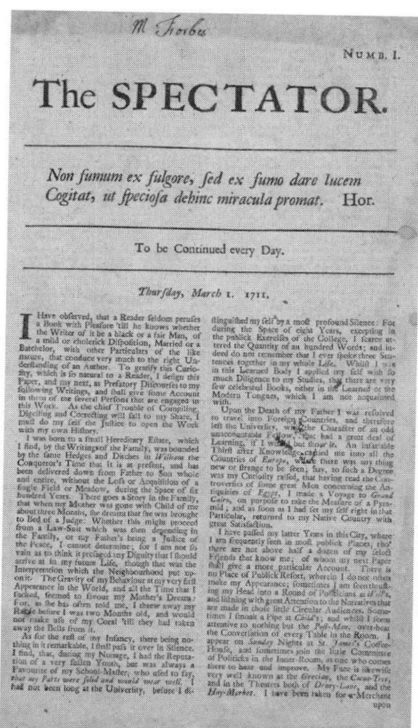

M Forbes

NUMB. I.

The SPECTATOR.

Non fumum ex fulgore, ſed ex fumo dare lucem
Cogitat, ut ſpecioſa dehinc miracula promat. Hor.

To be Continued every Day.

Thurſday, March 1. 1711.

I Have obſerved, that a Reader ſeldom peruſes a Book with Pleaſure 'till he knows whether the Writer of it be a black or a fair Man, of a mild or cholerick Diſpoſition, Married or a Batchelor, with other Particulars of the like nature, that conduce very much to the right Underſtanding of an Author. To gratify this Curioſity, which is ſo natural to a Reader, I deſign this Paper, and my next, as Prefatory Diſcourſes to my following Writings, and ſhall give ſome Account in them of the ſeveral Perſons that are engaged in this Work. As the chief Trouble of Compiling, Digeſting and Correcting will fall to my Share, I muſt do my ſelf the Juſtice to open the Work with my own Hiſtory.

I was born to a ſmall Hereditary Eſtate, which I find, by the Writings of the Family, was bounded by the ſame Hedges and Ditches in *William* the Conqueror's Time that it is at preſent, and has been delivered down from Father to Son whole and entire, without the Loſs or Acquiſition of a ſingle Field or Meadow, during the Space of ſix hundred Years. There goes a Story in the Family, that when my Mother was gone with Child of me about three Months, ſhe dreamt that ſhe was brought to Bed of a Judge: Whether this might proceed from a Law-Suit which was then depending in the Family, or my Father's being a Juſtice of the Peace, I cannot determine; for I am not ſo vain as to think it preſaged any Dignity that I ſhould arrive at in my future Life, though that was the Interpretation which the Neighbourhood put upon it. The Gravity of my Behaviour at my very firſt Appearance in the World, and all the Time that I ſucked, ſeemed to favour my Mother's Dream: For, as ſhe has often told me, I threw away my Rattle before I was two Months old, and would not make uſe of my Coral 'till they had taken away the Bells from it.

As for the reſt of my Infancy, there being nothing in it remarkable, I ſhall paſs it over in Silence. I find, that, during my Nonage, I had the Reputation of a very ſullen Youth, but was always a Favourite of my School-Maſter, who uſed to ſay, *that my Parts were ſolid and would wear well.* I had not been long at the Univerſity, before I diſtinguiſhed my ſelf by a moſt profound Silence: For during the Space of eight Years, excepting in the publick Exerciſes of the College, I ſcarce uttered the Quantity of an hundred Words; and indeed do not remember that I ever ſpoke three Sentences together in my whole Life. Whilſt I was in this Learned Body I applied my ſelf with ſo much Diligence to my Studies, that there are very few celebrated Books, either in the Learned or the Modern Tongues, which I am not acquainted with.

Upon the Death of my Father I was reſolved to travel into Foreign Countries, and therefore left the Univerſity, with the Character of an odd unaccountable Fellow, that had a great deal of Learning, if I would but ſhow it. An inſatiable Thirſt after Knowledge carried me into all the Countries of *Europe*, where there was any thing new or ſtrange to be ſeen; nay, to ſuch a Degree was my Curioſity raiſed, that having read the Controverſies of ſome great Men concerning the Antiquities of *Egypt*, I made a Voyage to *Grand Cairo*, on purpoſe to take the Meaſure of a Pyramid; and as ſoon as I had ſet my ſelf right in that Particular, returned to my Native Country with great Satisfaction.

I have paſſed my latter Years in this City, where I am frequently ſeen in moſt publick Places, tho' there are not above half a dozen of my ſelect Friends that know me; of whom my next Paper ſhall give a more particular Account. There is no Place of Publick Reſort, wherein I do not often make my Appearance; ſometimes I am ſeen thruſting my Head into a Round of Politicians at *Will's*, and liſtning with great Attention to the Narratives that are made in thoſe little Circular Audiences. Sometimes I ſmoak a Pipe at *Child's*; and whilſt I ſeem attentive to nothing but the *Poſt-Man*, over-hear the Converſation of every Table in the Room. I appear on *Sunday* Nights at St. *James's* Coffee-Houſe, and ſometimes join the little Committee of Politicks in the Inner-Room, as one who comes there to hear and improve. My Face is likewiſe very well known at the *Grecian*, the *Cocoa-Tree*, and in the Theaters both of *Drury-Lane*, and the *Hay-Market*. I have been taken for a Merchant upon

Figure 32 Joseph Addison and Richard Steele, *The Spectator*, no. 1.

publications – "every form except periodicals," as one literary historian puts it.[2] At the turn of the eighteenth century, these two developments – periodical publication and the rise of criticism – would come together in a new prose form, the periodical literary essay.

THE PERIODICAL ESSAY

Alongside the newspapers were the periodical essays, an eighteenth-century phenomenon (see chapter 22, "Essays"). Richard Steele created the *Tatler*, published three times a week from 1709 to 1711. In 1711, Steele and his *Tatler* collaborator Joseph Addison would go on to create the *Spectator*, which ran from March 1711 to December 1712. After ending the *Spectator*, Steele then went on to found another journal, the *Guardian*. In other words, across a remarkable four-year period, Richard Steele and Joseph Addison produced three different journals, stocking each with single, usually stand-alone essays.

Cumulatively, these periodicals brought to a wider readership the discussions of what would later be called "aesthetics" that had previously circulated only among the prefaces, dedications, and occasional monographs available to a much narrower clientele. Addison's reading of Milton – one of the earliest extended meditations on the poet and his masterpiece, *Paradise Lost* – was an important part of a larger shift that recuperated Milton's reputation from his defense of regicide and his work in Cromwell's republican government. A series of essays on what Addison called "the pleasures of the imagination" implicitly offered a popular, prose version of literary critical principles for a new readership, a combination of decorum, pleasure, ease, and class distinctions that has come to be associated with the Augustan era in English literature.

Other major authors from the early eighteenth century also wrote periodical essays at this time. Daniel Defoe single-handedly produced the *Review* from February 1704 to June 1713; Jonathan Swift collaborated with other authors who were producing periodicals, and relied on the periodical in his *Drapier's Letters* (1724–5). The authors involved in prose periodicals at the beginning of the eighteenth century testify to larger changes in literary production at the time, towards periodicity and prose, and also to a different understanding of journalism than would prevail in the nineteenth and twentieth centuries.

THE MAGAZINE

It was during these early decades of the eighteenth century, as the periodical and the periodical critical essay had begun to attract some of the period's best writers, that the young Samuel Johnson was becoming an avid reader. So it is perhaps not surprising that in his twenties Johnson would contact Edward Cave, founder of the *Gentleman's Magazine*, and propose to write for the periodical.

Started in 1731, the *Gentleman's Magazine* combined the newspaper model, a variety of different articles on different topics, with the periodical literary essay, placing a premium on the style in which the various pieces were written. Edward Cave called this combination a "magazine," after the older use of the word to describe a storehouse or armory, and created thereby the first publication to be called a magazine. The title of the *Gentleman's Magazine* thus has a double implication, indicating the variety of materials within stored for future reading on the one hand, while also hinting at the explosive nature of that *materiel* on the other.

The *Gentleman's Magazine* did manage one quite dramatic innovation – reporting on domestic news, especially news from Parliament, even though Parliament continued to exert its privilege by prohibiting outsiders from publishing parliamentary deliberations. The *Gentleman's Magazine* pulled this off by redescribing parliamentary debates through reference to Lilliput, the fictional land from *Gulliver's Travels*: debates in the British Parliament were transformed into "Debates in the Senate of *Magna Lilliputia*." This ingenious approach combined the newspaper and the literary essay, using literary techniques such as allegory and allusion to reveal the inner workings of Parliament. The author of these crafty pieces was none other than Samuel Johnson. His ability to find a way around the parliamentary prohibition, and an allusive, allegorical, literary way at that, speaks to the same animating tension or doubleness in Johnson's career as a journalist. At this point in his career, the literary and the investigative come together with periodicity and publicity to make a new kind of journalism possible.

After the *Gentleman's Magazine* showed the way forward for this new combination of articles called a magazine, the genre became a particularly influential format. By 1738, the *Gentleman's Magazine* was prefaced by a letter "To the Reader" claiming that "the success of the *Gentleman's Magazine* has given rise to almost twenty imitations of it," citing the *Weekly Magazine*, the *Gentleman's Magazine and Oracle*, the *Universal Magazine*, the *General Magazine*, the *Oxford Magazine*, the *Distillers Magazine*, the *Country Magazine*, the *Manchester Magazine*, the *Leeds Magazine*, the *Dublin Magazine*, and the *Lady's Magazine*. In the 1740s, Eliza Haywood wrote the *Female Spectator*, part of what one recent historian has called "the feminization of the periodical."[3] The same decade saw the beginning of the *Monthly Review* (1749). During the 1750s, the *Covent Garden Journal* (1752) was begun, as was the *World* (1753–6), the *Critical Review* (1756), and the *Universal Chronicle* (1758).

JOHNSON'S JOURNALISM

Throughout his career Johnson continued to contribute to journals. He wrote for the *Universal Chronicle*, and in 1756 he founded, edited, and wrote for the first several months of the *Literary Magazine; or, Universal Review*. Given the increasing importance of magazines, it is surprising that Johnson's prose writing would take the turn that it did in the 1750s. During this decade Johnson wrote three separate journals – the *Rambler* (1750–2), the *Adventurer* (1753), and the *Idler* essays included in the

Universal Chronicle (1758–60). With them, he turned back to the model of the single, stand-alone literary critical prose essay associated with Addison and Steele's publications four decades earlier.

Johnson's essays of the 1750s may have shared with other mid-eighteenth-century journals a self-consciously charitable concern for readers, but Johnson was not about to carve the mess of learning into particularly manageable portions for his readers. In the *Rambler*, Johnson referred to what he ambivalently called the "common reader" (*Works*, 3:20), a handy phrase that has taken on a life of its own since Johnson's coining it (becoming, among other things, the title of Virginia Woolf's collection of essays). James G. Basker offers a suggestive formulation for the impact of Johnson's phrase: "the common reader entered the history of criticism though periodical literature," meaning both that this idea of a common reader was created by Johnson and also that Johnson brought criticism to a new range of readers, in keeping with the popularizing project of mid-century periodicals.[4] Several of these essays are still among Johnson's most famous works of literary criticism: *Rambler* 4 on the novel, *Rambler* 60 on biography, and *Idlers* 60 and 61 on how to become a critic.

THE PUBLIC SPHERE

This question of the periodical's responsibility to educate the reader points to one of the largest claims made for the journalism of this period, even for the literary-critical periodical essay: what philosopher and sociologist Jürgen Habermas called "The structural transformation of the public sphere."[5] The "public sphere" is Habermas's influential name for the space that he claims eighteenth-century critics and periodicals such as Addison and Steele and the *Guardian* and the *Spectator* created, a space in which policy issues could be debated by an informed, literate citizenry: in short, the Enlightenment ideal. Occasionally Johnson shared in this optimistic sense of eighteenth-century publicity. In his "Observations on the Present State of Affairs" (1756), for example, Johnson contends, "The time is now come when every Englishman expects to be informed of the national affairs, and in which he has a right to have that expectation gratified" (*Works*, 10:185). In other words, by the middle of the eighteenth century, the common reader had a right to expect access to the news of national affairs, news that was illegal a century ago, in a country that banned reporting on Parliament just a few decades before Johnson's "Observations".

As influential and as attractive as this public sphere is, though, there has been debate over whether it ever existed in the ideal form Habermas suggests, and also whether it might have happened earlier in England than Habermas's Enlightenment model suggests. Johnson's experience in the eighteenth century did not leave him sanguine about the effects of a periodical press in the public sphere. In 1770, for example, Johnson published *The False Alarm*, responding to the controversy over the radical politician John Wilkes – itself a controversy tied to the development of the periodical press, as indicated by Wilkes's supporters being known after issue 45 of the *North Briton* criticized the king. To Johnson, the idea that Wilkes might be released from the prison in which he was serving time for libeling the king and, with some level of popular approval, retake his seat in Parliament showed that "this nation, with all its renown for speculation and for learning, has yet made little proficiency in civil wisdom" (*Works*, 10:318).

READING PRACTICES

For all the surprising shifts in or confusing doubleness to Johnson's career as a journalist – from describing closed meetings of Parliament to writing literary essays – we are in a better position today than we have been for more than a century to see journalism running through his career. Journalism and the lengthy daily newspaper or weekly or monthly magazine long went hand in hand; until recent developments in online publishing, the idea that journalism might consist of single, stand-alone essays published a couple of times a week would have seemed quite foreign. Between Johnson's time and the early twenty-first century, the single-essay periodical looked like a very strange form from an earlier and less developed period in the history of journalism. Today, though, blogs that feature a single essay regularly delivered bring us back to something closer to the literary periodical of Johnson's day.

Today's discussions of the fate of reading also have their precedents in the eighteenth century in general and the career of Samuel Johnson in particular. Boswell, for example, claimed that Johnson was capable of "seizing on what was valuable in a book without submitting to the labor of perusing it from beginning to end" (Boswell, *Life*, 1:71). There was a time when this might have been called "skimming," but that verb refers to the surface of a page; today we might call it "surfing," to reflect the sustaining of changes in readers' positions across the digital spaces. For one Johnson scholar, this kind of "mere reading" has been seen before, in the eighteenth century, and as a consequence of "the growth of the periodical press."[6] It is perhaps the most complicated aspect of Johnson's double legacy that the period's most famous reader and most influential literary prose essayist was also part of a process that may have contributed to such a change in reading patterns. But that implication of Johnson's work only adds to its urgency for readers today, as digital technologies similarly alter both reading practices and how journalism is conducted and understood.

NOTES

1 Ian Atherton, "'The Itch Grown a Disease': Manuscript Transmission of News in the Seventeenth Century," in *News, Newspapers, and Society in Early Modern Britain*, ed. Joad Raymond (London: Frank Cass, 1999), pp. 39–65, at p. 55.

2 James G. Basker, "Criticism and the Rise of Periodical Literature," in *The Cambridge History of Literary Criticism*, vol. 4, *The Eighteenth Century*, ed. H. B. Nisbet and Claude Rawson (New York and Cambridge: Cambridge University Press, 2008), pp. 316–32, at p. 320.

3 Iona Italia, *The Rise of Literary Journalism in the Eighteenth Century: Anxious Employment* (New York: Routledge, 2005), p. 6.

4 Basker, "Criticism," p. 323.

5 Jürgen Habermas, *The Structural Transformation of the Public Sphere: An Inquiry into a Category of Bourgeois Society*. trans. Thomas Burger and Frederick Lawrence (Cambridge, MA: MIT Press, 1989).

6 Robert DeMaria, Jr., *Samuel Johnson and the Life of Reading* (Baltimore, MD: Johns Hopkins University Press, 1997), p. 14.

CHAPTER 26

Law

J. T. Scanlan

LAW. *n.s.* [*laga*, Saxon; *loi*, French; *lawgh*, Erse.]
2. A decree, edict, statute, or custom, publickly established as a rule of justice.

He hath resisted *law*,
And therefore *law* shall scorn him further trial
Than the severity of publick power. *Shakes. Coriolanus.*

An internet advertisement for the *Johnsonian News Letter* characterizes its readers as follows: "Among subscribers to the *JNL* are teachers, scholars, librarians, book collectors, publishers, lawyers, and Johnsonian enthusiasts of every stripe." *Lawyers?* That's the unexpected category, and to those first looking into the vast scholarship on Johnson's many interests, law may seem peripheral. But the internet ad hints at a revealing fact: Johnson was involved with law, in one way or another, from the beginning to the end of his career.

JOHNSON'S LIFE IN THE LAW

From his teenage years in Lichfield to his final years in London, Johnson maintained an active interest in law. He knew many lawyers well, and he lived where they lived, close to the Inns of Court. As one of the most intriguing readers of the eighteenth century, Johnson knew well a wide range of legal materials. He was so adept at legal reasoning – for a non-lawyer – that he could offer decent (if sometimes limited) advice to lawyers. Johnson's own works, of course, from *London* (1738) to the *Lives of the Poets* (1779–81), are saturated with legal issues and legal characters. His *Dictionary* (1755) is especially subtle in handling legal terms and concepts. His long-standing interest in law may help explain why his argumentative writing and bracing conversation have become permanent contributions to the history of English literature.

Legal realities also created troubles and worries for Johnson, as they do for most people. In March 1756, only eleven months after completing his *Dictionary*, he was threatened with a stay in the abominable confines of a London debtors' prison. In October 1769, he gave evidence in defense of his friend, Giuseppe Baretti, who had stabbed a man and been charged with murder. And in early June of 1780, he lived through the Gordon Riots, which brought violence, destruction of property, and general lawlessness to within blocks of his house. Some rioters singled out for attack the houses of prominent legal figures. The house of Sir John Fielding, for example, a magistrate who lived in Bow Street (not far from Covent Garden), was attacked, as was the house of Lord Chief Justice Mansfield, who lived in fashionable Bloomsbury Square. Other legal buildings were torched, including Newgate Prison. In a letter to Hester Thrale on June 9, 1780, Johnson writes, "you might see the glare of conflagration fill the sky from many parts. The sight was dreadful. Some people were threatned, Mr. Strahan … advised me to take care of my self. Such a time of terrour you have been happy in not seeing" (*Letters*, 3:268–9).

To be sure, a handful of scholars have examined closely various aspects of Johnson's legal activities, as the section on further reading indicates. But given the complexity of Johnson's associations with law, many dimensions of his legal thinking remain relatively unexplored. Johnson seems to be a special case, too: he had no formal legal training or legal education, and his thoughts on law tend not to resemble those of other writers. Although Johnson criticized various aspects of eighteenth-century legal activity, he did not condemn law and lawyers with the virulence that is so easy to find in the works of other writers. "You are a lawyer," Johnson said in his later years to Oliver Edwards, an old friend from Pembroke College, Oxford. "Lawyers know life practically. A bookish man should always have them to converse with. They have what he wants" (Boswell, *Life*, 3:306).

Johnson's knowledge of legal matters was occasional rather than systematic, and any study of Johnson and his legal contexts must consider carefully the importance of this fact. His associations with particular legal figures often prompted a comment on law or initiated an attempt at legal research and writing. Without the professional advantages of barristers from the four Inns of Court, where young men received their training in the law – Lincoln's Inn, Gray's Inn, the Middle Temple, and the Inner Temple – Johnson was more or less on his own when reading and writing legal materials. Consequently, his associations with lawyers, along with the books he consulted, constitute his true legal contexts. How

Johnson responded to these legal figures provides an outline of Johnson's intellectual legal contexts. These legal contexts also indicate that the legal actuality of eighteenth-century England was strikingly different from the increasingly global and highly specialized contemporary legal scene of our own day – especially the American part of it. We should be on our guard against allowing the present to shape too much of our understanding of the past.

THE LAW IN EIGHTEENTH-CENTURY ENGLAND

The broader legal environment of London was strikingly different from our own. In the middle of the eighteenth century, law perhaps gained a new place in literary understanding in England because of a gradual change in intellectual outlook. As John Richetti has perceived, "The hunger for actuality and [the] belief that the actual is a separable category are features of Enlightenment thought … [and] were aggressively articulated in the mid-eighteenth century."[1] Inevitably, legal matters, along with other actualities of daily life, became leading subjects for writers of virtually all kinds. But while the number and complexity of legal issues in literary works may have expanded in the eighteenth century – think of the shelves of novels on marriage, property, and theft – the actual London legal world remained relatively small. This is especially important to keep in mind. Eighteenth-century legal London "was not a boom area for barristers," writes David Lemmings. "The four inns called [to the bar] fewer than 4,000 men over the years 1701 to 1800, or an average of nearly forty each year."[2] *Forty!*

Compare that number to the number of law students who typically graduate in a single year from the 200 or so accredited American law schools: 40,000. And these graduates enter a complex, highly stratified American legal culture often said to be dominated by law firms that employ more than 750 lawyers. Large firms typically handle the legal problems of large businesses, of course, but every large corporation worth its name has not only a general counsel or chief legal officer but a legal department of roughly 100 lawyers. Government lawyers, small firm lawyers, the American judiciary, not-for-profit advocates: there are so many different opportunities for lawyers that for many American undergraduates, the decision to go to law school has become, in the words of one law professor, a "default" choice.[3] The sheer difference in scale between today's vast, complex American legal scene and the much smaller, and more informal, London legal scene of the eighteenth century should warn researchers against using the present as a guide to understanding Johnson's legal contexts.

Bear in mind as well that, while legal education in the eighteenth century was becoming more "modern" because of the increasing influence of printed materials, young lawyers did not undergo anything remotely akin to the carefully conceived, systematic course of study one finds in the law school of today's American universities. The four Inns of Court in London, rather than the universities, were the centers of legal education, and those preparing to be called to the bar were more or less on their own in choosing their reading. Inevitably, such reading was ad hoc – completely unlike the "case method" first introduced by Christopher Columbus Langdell at Harvard Law School in the late nineteenth century. In general, lawyers of eighteenth-century London learned how to practice law by working with practicing lawyers, and by watching them. Even when Sir William Blackstone began lecturing on the English common law at All Souls College, Oxford, in the late 1750s, he was not doing it for tyro lawyers, as he plainly states in the opening of the written revision of those lectures, the *Commentaries on the Laws of England* (1765–9).

Furthermore, although American law developed out of English law, America became a quite different place from England early in its history, especially in the first decades of the early Republic. The concept of judicial review of legislative action, for example, a hallmark of the American legal system, was challenged by Sir William Blackstone. Blackstone felt such a move would give too much power to the judiciary. And there are other differences. Probably the best source for a solid introduction to how the English legal system has evolved over time is J. H. Baker's *An Introduction to English Legal History* (not least because of its superb lists of "Further Reading"). When one sets this book alongside, say, Gordon Wood's *Empire of Liberty: A History of the Early Republic, 1789–1815*, one sees clearly meaningful differences between English and American legal practice.

As Wood explains, the emerging democratic forces shaping the fledgling United States in the decades after the Constitution was ratified – the ideas and aspirations of such "middling sorts" as artisans and businessmen – gradually won the day, a situation markedly different in England at this time. In *Dartmouth College v. Woodward* (1819), for example, the ruling of the United States Supreme Court in favor of Dartmouth College strengthened the hand of corporations and entrepreneurs (in ways that Chief Justice Marshall and his colleagues could not have imagined).[4] Such innovative and pragmatic thinking from American justices lends support to Lawrence

Friedman's belief that in America, "the law in action reflect[s] the general culture."[5] To this day, many Americans (though surely not all) celebrate this explanation of legal change. In a recent essay lauding the achievements of Supreme Court Justice Thurgood Marshall – a major figure in the history of race relations in the United States from the 1950s through the 1980s – Deborah L. Rhode approvingly quotes what Justice Marshall once said to a law clerk who asked him for his "judicial philosophy." "You do what you think is right," said Marshall, "and let the law catch up."[6]

Both American and English law are rooted in the common law, which is based on tradition rather than a written code or a collection of statutes. But the English system perhaps puts more stock in tradition, as English life does generally. According to the always lively legal historian A. W. Brian Simpson,

> law is essentially a tradition … Some features of the law derive from the very distant past indeed … In English law, for example, the terms which are in use for talking about property rights in land are medieval; most of them would be perfectly intelligible to a fifteenth-century lawyer. So lawyers when they are being technical do not talk of *landowners*, but of *tenants in fee simple absolute in possession*, of *fees tail* and even more mysterious entities such as *possibilities of reverter*. There is even a poem about them:
>
> Fee simple, and the shifting fees,
> And all the fees in tail,
> Are nothing when compared to thee,
> Thou best of fees, female.[7]

All this suggests, again, that using one's own knowledge of modern American law can be extremely misleading when reconstructing the cast of Johnson's legal mind.

At the very least, Johnson and most English lawyers he knew did not view law as an instrument of social change. When Boswell, with seeming high-mindedness, wonders whether he can support a case that he knows to be bad, Johnson defends the system: "Sir, you do not know it to be good or bad until the judge determines it" (Boswell, *Life*, 2:47). Johnson thought of law as a field of disinterested research and combative, constructive disagreement, at least during those moments when he was actively engaged in legal thinking. Learning and argument: although Johnson never graduated from university, he nevertheless led a buried life as a scholar, according to biographer Robert DeMaria. And a scholarly orientation to legal materials, in ways that we have yet to understand fully, seems to animate his legal thinking.

JOHNSON AMONG THE LAWYERS

One of Johnson's earliest mentors was Gilbert Walmesley, a somewhat flashy barrister whom Johnson met when he was a teenager in the sleepy Midlands town of Lichfield. Walmesley, a much older man who worked as registrar for the Ecclesiastical Court in Lichfield, made a deep and lasting impression on Johnson. Walmesley honed Johnson's interest in legal argument, but without presenting himself as a narrow-minded grind. Many years later, Johnson recalled with warm appreciation Walmesley's "amplitude of learning" and "copiousness of communication" (*Lives*, 2:179). Younger men with legal backgrounds also influenced Johnson. Boswell, of course, was a lawyer. Edmund Burke, too, who studied law in London at the Middle Temple after he left Trinity College in Dublin, earned a degree of respect from Johnson that few men could rival, and not only because of his immense learning. "That fellow calls forth all my powers," Johnson stated (Boswell, *Life*, 2:450), perhaps recognizing that high among Burke's achievements was his skill in adversarial, constructive argument. As Burke himself writes in *Reflections on the Revolution in France*, "He that wrestles with us strengthens our nerves, and sharpens our skill. Our antagonist is our helper."[8]

Another younger man whose activities greatly directed Johnson's legal thought was Sir Robert Chambers, a man more than twenty-five years Johnson's junior. As Thomas Curley has shown, Chambers collaborated with Johnson in preparing his *Course of Lectures on the English Law, 1767–1773*.[9] Notably, Johnson helped Chambers on matters of international law – an interest of Johnson's easy to miss if one emphasizes excessively Johnson's Englishness.

Johnson knew many other legal figures, young and old. As even brief biographical research into the backgrounds of such men would make plain, the lawyers Johnson knew differed from one another significantly. Nevertheless, Walmesley, Burke, and Chambers are, as influences on Johnson's legal thinking, telling. All three worked outside of the day-to-day practice of law, and all three were broadly learned. Their mental and professional lives were not defined by mechanical or plodding research. All three perhaps helped encourage Johnson to believe that legal activities were not only stimulating but noble.

The presence of such legal figures in Johnson's life lined up well with Johnson's amateur inclination towards broad legal reasoning, and this orientation perhaps led Johnson to challenge the drift of things in eighteenth-century legal circles. In conversation, Johnson praised the older legal thinkers, who were known for their broad learning, and contrasted them against contemporary lawyers searching for precedents. In his own writing, he relied on older, established legal authorities – often professors – as opposed to everyday practitioners and attorneys. In his *Dictionary*, he depended heavily on *The Interpreter* (1607), an early seventeenth-century legal dictionary written by John Cowell, a professor of civil law at the University of Cambridge. Johnson notably lavishes special praise on Sir Francis Bacon, Hugo Grotius, Samuel Pufendorf, and Jean-Jacques Burlamaqui – all significant legal theorists who wrote on large topics and had capacious minds. Barristers, Johnson said to Boswell, "had more law long ago than they have now" (Boswell, *Life*, 2:158). And Johnson may have been right: as Sir William Holdsworth, David Lemmings, J. H. Baker, and others have written, practitioners at all levels of law in the eighteenth century had to wrestle with an exponential expansion in written legal records. The quality of law reporting improved, too, especially after 1750. Understandably, these developments in legal print culture urged lawyers to spend more and more time poring over the details of earlier cases. Furthermore, as John Langbein has shown, between roughly 1730 and 1780, the "prototype of the fully lawyerized trial" emerged, expanding lawyers' role.[10] Lawyers did not focus as much as they once did on investigating principles – Johnson's strength.

Although Johnson's legal activities often arose from quite specific matters – the help he provided Boswell on specific cases is one example – we can say, I think, that the ad hoc legal contexts that shaped Johnson's approach to the law encouraged him to remain both general and broadly conservative in outlook. Johnson wanted to retain the old, and he feared that during his own time the widely learned legal thinker would lose out to the crudely pragmatic legal functionary. It is no surprise that, when working on the legal terms for the *Dictionary*, Johnson turned to Cowell's *Interpreter* rather than to influential editions of Giles Jacob's legal dictionaries. Better to go with a learned scholar than with the author of *Every Man His Own Lawyer* (1740).

LEGAL SOURCES AND INTERDISCIPLINARY STUDY

There is no such thing as a single scholarly orientation. Scholars are conditioned by the evidentiary codes and folkways of their different fields, and although Johnson remained one of the last great generalists in English literature, he obviously had to work with legal sources written for specialized legal audiences. How did Johnson handle these sources? Did he handle them differently from the ways he handled his sources when working as a lexicographer, an editor, an essayist, or a biographer? We don't really know. We don't know because few if any scholars have addressed in a comprehensive way Johnson's legal reading and research. Such invaluable monographs as Donald Greene's *Samuel Johnson's Library: An Annotated Guide* (1975) and Robert DeMaria, Jr.'s *Samuel Johnson and the Life of Reading* (1997) helped teach us what Johnson read and what general assumptions he brought to his reading. But until we compare Johnson's legal reading to the legal reading of others in the middle of the eighteenth century, we will be hard pressed to reconstruct the character of Johnson's legal mind.

Studying Johnson and the law comes with special challenges. Scholars casually speak of the centrality of "interdisciplinary" approaches to their work, but mastering a discipline other than one's own is extraordinarily demanding – and perhaps contrary to our instincts. As Howard Gardner has emphasized in "The Synthesizing Mind," "how much more of a burden to master a number of perspectives and then piece them together in a useful amalgam! Adding to this difficulty is the fact that individual cognition is remarkably domain-specific: as a species, we are predisposed to learn skills in certain contexts."[11] And yet, if we are to comprehend Johnson's intellectual life, comparative, synthesizing thought seems the true desideratum. "We may be absolutely certain," writes Boswell of Johnson, "that his reading was very extensive. Dr. Adam Smith … once observed to me that 'Johnson knew more books than any man alive'" (Boswell, *Life*, 1:71). Although illuminating afresh Johnson's legal thinking will be hard work, his own example as a reader and thinker at least inspires us for the task.

NOTES

1 John Richetti, introduction to *The Cambridge Companion to the Eighteenth-Century Novel*, ed. John Richetti (Cambridge: Cambridge University Press, 1996), pp. 2–3.

2 David Lemmings, *Professors of the Law: Barristers and English Legal Culture in the Eighteenth Century* (New York and Oxford: Oxford University Press, 2000), p. 62.

3 Professor Stephen M. McJohn, Suffolk University Law School, in conversation with J. T. Scanlan, spring 2008.

4 Gordon Wood, *Empire of Liberty: A History of the Early Republic, 1789–1815* (New York: Oxford University Press, 2009), pp. 465–6.

5 Lawrence M. Friedman, *Law in America: A Short History* (New York: Modern Library, 2002), p. 53.

6 Deborah L. Rhode, "Letting the Law Catch Up," in *Brown at 50: A Collection of Essays*, ed. Deborah L. Rhode and Charles J. Ogletree, Jr. (Chicago: American Bar Association, 2004), p. 51.

7 A. W. B. Simpson, *An Invitation to Law* (Oxford: Blackwell, 1988), p. 23.

8 *The Writings and Speeches of Edmund Burke*, ed. Paul Langford, 9 vols. in 10 (Oxford: Clarendon Press, 1981–2000), 8:215.

9 Robert Chambers, *A Course of Lectures on the English Law: Delivered at the University of Oxford, 1767–1773: By Sir Robert Chambers, and Composed in Association with Samuel Johnson*, ed. Thomas M. Curley, 2 vols. (Madison: University of Wisconsin Press, 1986).

10 John H. Langbein, *The Origins of Adversary Criminal Trial* (Oxford: Oxford University Press, 2003), p. 253.

11 Howard Gardner, *Five Minds for the Future* (Boston: Harvard Business Press, 2008), p. 47.

CHAPTER 27

Literary criticism

Philip Smallwood

> CRI'TICISM. *n.s.* [from *critick.*]
> 1. *Criticism*, as it was first instituted by Aristotle, was meant a standard of judging well. *Dryden's Innocence, Pref.*

Johnson's criticism has many sources: in seventeenth-century French critical accomplishments and their contemporary English translations, in Renaissance interpretive scholarship, and in classical Greek and Roman criticism. But it is shaped in no slight measure by the inspirational critical writings, in both verse and prose, of Johnson's immediate predecessors, John Dryden and Alexander Pope. Johnson called Dryden "the father of English criticism" (*Lives*, 2:118), and described *An Essay on Criticism* (1711) as one of Pope's most dazzling effusions (*Lives*, 4:68–70). And while Johnson made no personal addition to the established tradition of poetical works on critical subjects, the couplet wisdom of Pope's poem constructs an idea, and an ideal, of criticism that artistically transcends what can be expressed in simple propositions, and provides Johnson with an articulation of the critic's role. Many of the attributes of the critical writings of Dryden and of Pope are, at the same time, echoed in the formal properties of Johnson's criticism, and they presage these properties.

PREFACES AND ESSAYS

Johnson's critical writing has roots deep in the tradition of literary-critical "short views" such as Pope had both celebrated and enacted in his *Essay*.[1] For all its variety – biographical, essayistic, anecdotal, emotional, comedic, closely analytical – his critical work contains no extended treatise or lengthy theoretical excursion.

As the "father of English criticism," Dryden produced almost all his criticism in the form of essays; these served as prefaces to his own poetical and dramatic works, and Dryden wrote most of his essays to support the creative practice of his poems and plays. Johnson did not introduce his own creative writings in this way, but the majority of his most influential criticism – that of Shakespeare, for example – takes prefatory form, as do the *Prefaces Biographical and Critical to Works of the English Poets*, better known as the *Lives of the Poets*. Pope, too, was a master of the genre: his *Preface to the Iliad* (1717) and the preface to his edition of Shakespeare (1725) together constitute some of his best criticism in prose. Dryden, at a similar level of formal influence and importance, offers a vehicle for criticism, both theoretical and practical, in his prose writings. By furnishing both Pope and Johnson with a prose "character" of each of the old or ancient authors he selected to translate, or of the dramatists he valued, Dryden conveys the sense of a modern criticism that is defined not by reference to an a priori authority, but in response to the stimulus of its literary occasion.

Next to the preface is the form of the essay, and Pope and Dryden anticipate an emergent Johnsonian performance in this mode too. The elegant and socially conscious essays on critical topics in the *Tatler* (1709–11) and the *Spectator* (1711–12), composed by Joseph Addison and Sir Richard Steele, also play their part (see chapter 22, "Essays"). There are more distant sources of this essay form, in its relation of social reflection to the reading life, in the seventeenth-century critic and poet Abraham Cowley, whose "critical abilities have not been sufficiently observed" (*Lives*, 1:215), as in the essays of Francis Bacon and Michel de Montaigne. A great deal of Johnson's earlier critical work – in the *Rambler*, the *Idler*, and the *Adventurer* – finds expression in the periodical essay. Johnson's essays, like Montaigne's and Addison's, harness literary criticism to the purposes of acute social and human observation, and offer a moral and philosophical commentary on the conduct of both public and private life. Johnson's criticism speaks from the moral world at large, rather than the scholar's study or the closet – or, as with most criticism written today, as a tangential consequence of specialized research.

COMPARATIVE CRITICISM

A characteristic aspect of the criticism of Dryden and Pope is the critical judgment that is expressed not in absolute but in comparative terms. Dryden, for example, makes eloquently poised comparisons of Shakespeare and Jonson, Horace and Juvenal, Homer and Virgil, or Chaucer and Ovid. Johnson was able to bring these comparisons to mind in his own efforts to measure out the relative merits and limits of Dryden and Pope (*Lives*, 4:64–6), or when writing of Shakespeare's "observation impregnated by genius" on the one hand, as compared with the "easy, elevated and harmonious" art of Joseph Addison on the other (*Works*, 7:84). Behind this sort of English criticism stands a tradition of French critical *comparaisons* evidenced by the writings of the seventeenth-century critic René Rapin. In his studies of Homer and Virgil, Cicero and Demosthenes, Thucydides and Livy, Rapin clarified the procedures that Johnson employed in his own work with strong historical support.

The critical method made current by Rapin, which Dryden adopts, is to balance critical defects and strengths that can be discerned across all the works of an author, so that merits are not ranked in order but summarily weighed. The entire body of that achievement is appraised not in the success and failure of the parts only, but as one and a whole, according to the author's temperament, quintessential spirit, or presiding genius. Thus Dryden's famous paragraph on Shakespeare in his first great critical work, his *Essay of Dramatick Poesie* (1669), affords both Pope and Johnson a template for their own attempts to characterize a "comprehensive" mind, within the paradox of a perspective that is at once precise and general. Dryden marked out in this way for Johnson a concept of criticism that brought a rational equilibrium to an Augustan critical voice, and was able to civilize contemporary satire, partisanship, polemic, sarcasm, or lampoon. Pope placed a concept of judgment at the center of his *Essay on Criticism* to enhance the credibility of criticism, its principled disinterest, and rational worth. "Regard not then if Wit be *Old* or *New*," was Pope's famous dictum, as was the imprecation that is relevant to Johnson's own characteristic method in criticism: "Survey the *Whole*" (lines 406, 235).

There are clear differences between Johnson and his major predecessors. In the performing of judgment, what Pope called the "graceful Negligence" of Dryden's critical prose – the quality that Pope had also attributed to the critical poetry of the Roman Horace – seems distant from Johnson's early style, which is graver and more deliberative. Dryden's gaiety and levity of wit as a prose artist differs from Johnson's wry and sardonic personality. But Dryden, like Pope, also prepares the ground for the variety and range of Johnson's critical voices. "Nor in the *Critick* let the *Man* be lost," wrote Pope in his *Essay on Criticism* (line 523), and Dryden's infusion of his intellectual personality into the manners of his critical writing links critical formality and conversational informality, bonding criticism to the Johnsonian conversations on literary matters and on life that James Boswell famously reported.

THEORY

Johnson's critical environment was well supplied with monumental works of theory by the French, of which the most prominent and influential example was René le Bossu's *Traité du poème épique* (1675). The type of this "neoclassical" text is a target of Pope's satirical "Receipt to Make an Epic Poem" (1728) in the Scriblerian manner, and it serves to reenact the Aristotelian definition of epic Johnson adopted to tackle *Paradise Lost.* The context for Johnson's critical achievement, however, is not confined to the system of Bossu's *Traité*, but includes the bond between critical writing and artistic pleasure articulated in Boileau's *Art poétique* (1674) and its English reenactment, Pope's *Essay*. Rapin's prose *Reflections on Aristotle* (also 1674) takes its meaning, in part, from its comparative succinctness, and its many exemplifications of taste and judgment. Nuanced by a similar *delicatesse* and *politesse*, and by dialogues rather than doctrines, are the French critical discourses of Dominique Bouhours, especially his *Entretiens d'Ariste et d'Eugene* (1671) and *Manière de bien penser dans les ouvrages d'esprit* (1687).

THE SUBLIME

One triumph of the positive, open-minded, and full-hearted critical culture that Dryden, Pope, and their French predecessors and contemporaries performed was achieved by a language expressing the distinctive qualities and characteristic effects of the very greatest literature. Here Boileau's *Traité du sublime ou du merveilleux dans le Discours traduit du Grec de Longin* (1674) – his translation with preface of the ancient Greek critic known as Longinus – provides an inspirational precedent for understanding what it means to be transported out of oneself by an artistic and literary experience. The *Oxford English Dictionary* offers a definition for the sublime: "Affecting the mind with a sense of overwhelming grandeur or irresistible power; calculated to inspire awe, deep reverence, or lofty emotion, by reason of its beauty, vastness, or grandeur." In its combination of preface, main text, and associated "Reflexions," Boileau's *Longin* mediates a relationship between the enduring masterpieces of classical literature, especially Homer, and the new works of a modern French literary civilization, in the shape of its most recent tragedians.

In its commitment to a full-out emotional enthusiasm, Longinus's text lies behind some of Johnson's most strongly emotive reactions to native literary greatness. This is evident from Johnson's passage on the compelling power of Shakespearean drama in *King Lear*:

> The artful involutions of distinct interests, the striking opposition of contrary characters, the sudden changes of fortune, and the quick succession of events, fill the mind with a perpetual tumult of indignation, pity, and hope. There is no scene which does not contribute to the aggravation of the distress or conduct of the action, and scarce a line which does not conduce to the progress of the scene. So powerful is the current of the poet's imagination, that the mind, which once ventures within it, is hurried irresistibly along. (*Works*, 8:702–3)

For Pope, the text of the "bold *Longinus*!" (*Essay on Criticism*, line 675) had taught the skillful literary critic to "enact his precepts," and to justify his literary judgments by the eloquence he brought to their expression. The art of Johnson's criticism, and the fact that this criticism places Johnson as firmly in the history of creative literature as the history of criticism, shows how fully this lesson had been absorbed.

THE PROSE TREATISE

We turn now from Johnson's critical predecessors to his contemporaries. Here the singularity of Johnson's judgments is set against a world in which the criteria of consensus are beginning to fragment, and where the forms of criticism are subject to greater rhetorical and generic diversification. The process was encouraged by what might be called the "de-metropolitanization" of literary society in eighteenth-century Britain.

We have seen that the essay (in prose or verse) and the preface were major forms of Dryden's and Pope's critical work. But these "parasitic" varieties of criticism, in which the commentary is subordinate to the literature it comments upon, are supplemented or replaced in the middle years of the eighteenth century by the growing prestige of the long theoretical treatise in prose. This category of criticism, now broadly embraced by the history of philosophical "aesthetics," includes works by eighteenth-century critics such as Edward Young, Lord Shaftesbury, Lord Kames, Richard Hurd, Hugh Blair, Edmund Burke, Alexander Gerard, and James Beattie. Essays on many topics – originality, imagination, sublimity, genius, and taste – helped to round out the context of theory in which Johnson's practice of criticism was first conceived. And although his criticism bears a different relation to creative work and implies a different audience and set of intentions, Johnson sometimes exploits a language and a critical terminology he holds in common with theorists in this vein.

Lord Kames's repudiation of Aristotle's supposed "dramatic unities" of time and place in the *Elements of Criticism* (1764), for example, corresponds with the arguments Johnson expressed in his preface to Shakespeare (*Works*, 7:75–80). The growth of critical annotations in contemporary editions of Spenser, Milton, and Shakespeare is likewise replicated by Johnson's critical practice in his extensive notes to Shakespeare's plays. Both the textual work of the Shakespeare edition and the biographical researches of the *Lives of the Poets* immersed Johnson in scholarly inquiries which tap into the currents of antiquarian research. The researches of Edmond Malone and Thomas Warton offer celebrated examples of this trend.

RESPONSES TO JOHNSON'S CRITICISM

Johnson's independence of spirit over these years may be defined in relation to this critical, scholarly, and theoretical environment, but his outspoken criticism also required that his detailed opinions should be resisted and denied from every quarter, and should therefore be often represented as stubborn prejudice. The dialectical partnership between Johnson and his critical age can be found in his intellectual commerce with personal friends.

The artist Sir Joshua Reynolds, for instance, was an admirer of Johnson, as Johnson was an admirer, and an occasional subject, of Reynold's portrait work: the celebrated Johnsonian notion of "general nature" (*Works*, 7:61–2), developed in the preface to Shakespeare, is also a grounding concept of Reynolds's *Discourses on Art* (1769–91; see chapter 45, "Visual arts"). Johnson's critical interactions with his fellow literary critic Joseph Warton – Thomas's brother and, like Reynolds, a member of the Literary Club – seem less consistently harmonious. In regarding Warton as part of the milieu in which Johnson conceived his literary criticism, and to which it was addressed, one can invoke here a certain historical association between the imaginary characters in Dryden's *Essay of Dramatick Poesie* and the period's real-life dialogic exchanges. Such exchanges not only recall the subtly developed critical conversations of Dominique Bouhours, but also validate English literary criticism on Socratic and Platonic terms, once again marking off the Johnsonian practice of criticism from ambitions to theoretical finality.

Warton's first volume of the *Essay on the Genius and Writings of Pope* was published in 1756, and Johnson reviewed the work for the *Literary Magazine*. The two critics became friends and shared many fundamental tastes and ideas, including an admiration for the poetry of Milton, Dryden, Pope, and Shakespeare. But as time went by, and taste in the mid-eighteenth century broadened, their thinking diverged. Warton seems to have been profoundly offended by the publication of Johnson's *Lives of the Poets*, and he was not alone in this aversion (see chapter 6, "Critical reception to 1900"). Two trenchantly satirical cartoons by James Gillray – *Old Wisdom Blinking at the Stars* (1782) and *Apollo and the Muses; Inflicting Penance on Dr. Pomposo, round Parnassus* (1783) – capture the protest at Johnson's seeming lack of generosity to the eighteenth century's favorites (see figs. 23 and 24). Johnson's downbeat estimate of certain types of poetry (such as pastoral) came in for particular criticism, as did his consistently derogatory comments on poetical figures such as mythology. Warton seems to have felt himself provoked by Johnson, and was inspired to publish the long-delayed second volume of his *Essay on Pope* (1782). This book took issue with many judgments in the *Lives* and records a note of exasperation and dismay at Johnson's apparent insensitivity, as Warton experienced it, to such modern classics as Dryden's *Fables, Ancient and Modern* (1700) and a long list of lesser eighteenth-century poems. The growing disparity with Warton reveals an aspect of the *deflective* context of Johnson's criticism. It is the background against which Johnson stands out in relief.

Johnson's critical world, then, is a community of aesthetic evaluation that is both inspiration and audience. In this his work expresses the boldness of Longinus – that quality advocated by the Roman poet Horace in his *Ars Poetica* – as the essence of critical judgment, and here he is an alien, and even a solitary, spirit. His criticism is more than a mere *consequence* of the writings of Dryden and Pope, and more than a *reflection* of the context available from contemporary critical form, taste, and literary ideology. Cause-and-effect relationships in literary history are never simple, and Johnson's critical independence ensures that the networks of seventeenth- and eighteenth-century critical writing will always constitute too narrow a perspective on his historical role. At the same time, critical historians have tended to underplay the durable merits of that critical world, and some later commentators, emulating Romantic condescension to Johnson, have attributed his alleged critical shortcomings to the prison of neoclassical concepts, to Enlightenment rationalism, or to the cultural lockdown of an "Age of Reason."

HEIRS AND SUCCESSORS

It would therefore be simplistic to sketch Johnson's criticism even briefly without reference to his context of reception. The extent to which his critical work released the flow of inspiration for a new generation of creative genius is the historical verification of his enduring moral courage as a literary critic.

Jane Austen's admiration for, and allusions to, Johnson have become increasingly visible to literary historians. The creative *effects* of Johnson's criticism, immanent within literature, can be traced through the writings of Frances Burney, George Crabbe, George Eliot, and the *Lyrical Ballads* of William Wordsworth (if we think of their common commitment to the "language of men," which Johnson admired in Shakespeare).[2] But the consequences for the "Muses' handmaid" – critical composition – are also wide. Sir Walter Scott's *Life of Dryden* (1818), which introduced his monumental edition of Dryden's *Works*, runs within the critical and rhetorical channels of Johnson's biography of the same poet. Wordsworth's critical essays echo Johnson in the invocation of "our common nature," and register a comparable resistance to the distortions of poetical diction.

For Samuel Taylor Coleridge, Johnson's Shakespearean criticism, advocating the appreciation of Shakespeare's characters as a "species," prompts disagreement on the topic of character-creation. But Coleridge is in unconscious sympathy with Johnsonian criticism in other ways, especially where he does justice to the mingled tragic and comic nature of the plays or responds warmly to their supernatural elements, as in his "Lectures on Shakespeare." Very similar ironies of correspondence can be found in the Shakespearean criticism of William Hazlitt (in his *Characters of Shakespeare's Plays*, 1817) and of A. W. Schlegel (in his *Lectures on Dramatic Art*, 1808). Both professed hostility to Johnson as the critic most needful to resist, but their work suggests some uncanny resemblances and unacknowledged debts. The French journalist, critic, and novelist Stendhal even silently plagiarized his preface to Shakespeare and called Johnson the "father of romanticism."[3]

Through the wide dissemination of a principled taste for Shakespeare, Johnson's context embraces the evolving European tradition that had inspired his criticism. But if a contextual circle is closed by such foreign links, it ought not to exclude the context of Johnson's literary criticism to which all else is subordinate – the English dramatic and poetic works his criticism exists to discriminate among. That we still read the authors on whom Johnson wrote, and react with admiration or dissent to his opinions upon them, makes us part of the context, and even when we disagree, a "consequence" of Johnson.

NOTES

1 Alexander Pope, *The Twickenham Edition of the Poems of Alexander Pope*, ed. John Butt *et al.*, 11 vols. in 12 (New Haven, CT: Yale University Press, 1939–69), 1:197–326, line 222.
2 Preface to *Lyrical Ballads*, in *The Prose Works of William Wordsworth*, ed. J. B. Owen and J. W. Smyser, 3 vols. (Oxford: Clarendon Press, 1974), 1:131.
3 Stendhal (Henri Beyle), *Œuvres complètes*, ed. Pierre Martino, 35 vols. (Paris and Geneva: Champion, 1970), 3:152.

CHAPTER 28

London

Cynthia Wall

CI'TY. *n.s.* [*cité*, French, *civitas*, Latin.]
1. A large collection of houses and inhabitants.

> Men seek their safety from number better united, and from walls and other fortifications; the use whereof is to make the few a match for the many, and this is the original of *cities*. *Temple*.

"For who would leave, unbrib'd, *Hibernia*'s Land, / Or change the Rocks of *Scotland* for the *Strand*?" asks the speaker in Samuel Johnson's first major poem, *London*. As this work was published by Richard Dodsley and printed by Edward Cave at Tully's Head in Pall Mall in 1738, when Johnson was twenty-nine, it marks his first literary entry into London. Famously, the author of this poem would later answer the rhetorical question flatly: "No, Sir, when a man is tired of London, he is tired of life; for there is in London all that life can afford" (Boswell, *Life*, 3:178).

Johnson's first use of the Strand is a fitting emblem of the city itself. "In former Times it was an Highway leading from *London* to *Westminster*," writes John Strype in 1720 in his survey of London, curving along the Thames between Charing Cross and the Inns of Court.[1] In the eighteenth century it remained the most direct connection between the City (the old medieval center, and still the financial center) and the Court (Westminster, parks and palaces, Piccadilly and Pall Mall), passing through the Town (theatre and law, fashion and dissolution). The borough of Southwark lies south of the River Thames, a sort of suburb of town houses and retreats of more dubious sorts. To understand eighteenth-century London, one must understand these regions, their relations, and their associations.

By the mid-eighteenth century, London was one of the largest cities in Europe; at over 700,000 people, it rivaled Paris in cultural importance – in "all that life can afford." Johnson's love of London was not an idiosyncratic obsession. Among his various lodgings and wanderings, Johnson's own life brings us literally and literarily inside both the centers and the corners of London.

THE CITY

"The City" of London is the medieval center inscribed by the original Roman walls and eight gates (Posterngate, Aldgate, Bishopsgate, Moorgate, Cripplegate, Aldersgate, Newgate, Ludgate). It is a tangled warren of alleys and courtyards, bisected by a few great thoroughfares: west to east, Newgate Street leads into Cheapside and Poultry, which branch out to Threadneedle, Cornhill, and Lombard Streets; and north to south run Aldersgate, Bishopsgate, and Gracechurch Streets. The names of the streets reflect their original functions: Fish Street Hill runs up from the river and the Billingsgate fish market; Pudding Lane was where "the butchers of Eastcheap have their scalding house for hogs … and their puddings, with other filth of beasts, are voided down that way to their dung boats on the Thames";[2] Cornhill once held a corn market, and later the Royal Exchange for merchants and tradesmen. St. Paul's Cathedral anchors the center; the Tower of London broods over the eastern border; the thirteenth-century London Bridge, itself a small village of houses and shops, linked London to Southwark across the Thames – the only bridge in London until 1750 (when Johnson was forty-one). The City historically governed itself, its trade guilds fiercely independent of king and court in Westminster. The Lord Mayor of London lived in the City, and the Royal Society for the Improvement of Natural Knowledge began there.

In 1665 an outbreak of plague ravaged the City; in September 1666 the Great Fire virtually destroyed it. New buildings of brick and slate replaced the old wooden, thatched structures, and some streets were widened; indigenous businesses relocated, sometimes permanently, and the street names lost much of their denotative status. Still the City remained essentially itself: busy, tangled, a mixture of vast prosperity and devastating poverty.

When Johnson first came to London in 1737, he entered its literary portals through a medieval gate. Edward Cave, under the name Sylvanus Urban, published the *Gentleman's Magazine* in St. John's Gate, Clerkenwell, and Johnson began reporting on the proceedings of the Houses of Parliament for Cave's magazine in the early 1740s (see chapter 25, "Journalism"). Business in the City flourished; large-windowed shops crowded the streets, and their well-lit, well-displayed interiors impressed foreign visitors. Public markets such as Leadenhall and Newgate, for the sale of fruits, vegetables, dairy, and meat, or Billingsgate for fish, clustered at its center. The East India House in Leadenhall Street was an imposing symbol of international trade, with its docks on the Thames. The Bank

Figure 33 South view of St. John's Gate, in Clerkenwell, 1720, where Edward Cave would begin publishing the *Gentleman's Magazine* in 1731.

of England, in Threadneedle Street, was founded in 1694 (when the king needed a big loan). The Guildhall housed "the Courts for the City … The Hall itself is very spacious and stately," writes Strype, "suited to the Greatness and Magnificence of the City."[3]

But the City also had its crowded, dark, dubious corners, its "rookeries" of slums, its warrens of crime, its prisons. In *The Life of Savage*, Johnson follows his friend, the profligate poet Richard Savage, into the inhospitalities of poverty:

> He lodged as much by accident as he dined, and passed the night sometimes in mean houses, which are set open at night to any casual wanderers, sometimes in cellars, among the riot and filth of the meanest and most profligate of the rabble; and sometimes, when he had not money to support even the expences of these receptacles, walked about the streets till he was weary, and lay down in the summer upon a bulk, or in the winter, with his associates in poverty, among the ashes of a glass-house. (*Lives*, 3:165)

What Johnson does not say in the biography is that he was often there with Savage on these homeless roamings. Savage – without Johnson – spent time in Newgate Prison. In *London*, Johnson nostalgically notes that "A single Jail, in ALFRED's golden Reign, / Could half the Nation's Criminals contain" (*London*, lines 248–9); by the 1720s, Daniel Defoe would count over twenty "publick Gaols" and over one hundred "Tolerated Prisons" or private houses of confinement.[4]

As Boswell noted, "one end of London is like a different country from the other in look and manners" (*London Journal*, p. 153). But even within the ends of London, the disparities could be startling: the Bank of England, the Royal Exchange, the East India House, and St. Paul's Cathedral stood cheek by jowl with prisons and hovels, edging into Whitechapel, "encroached upon by building of filthy cottages, and with other purpressors, inclosures, and laystalls"[5] – where "falling Houses thunder on your Head" (*London*, line 17, in *Works*, 6:48).

THE TOWN

In 1724, Defoe remarked on the rapid expansion of London to the west of the City, tracing the buildup of "the Town," as it was called, between the City and Westminster:

> From hence we go on still *West*, and beginning at *Gray's Inn*, and going on to those formerly called *Red Lyon* Fields, and *Lamb's Conduit* Fields, we see there a prodigious Pile of Buildings … 'tis built quite to *Lamb's Conduit* Fields, *North*, including a great Range of Buildings yet unfinish'd, reaching to … the great New Square at the *West* end of it … this Pile of Buildings is very great, the Houses so magnificent and large, that abundance of Persons of Quality, and some of the Nobility are found among them.[6]

Instead of the tangled web of the City, the by-now central London patterned geometrical lines and open squares, a magnet for theater and opera, the home of barristers and other professionals. Drury Lane Theatre, managed from 1747 to 1776 by Johnson's friend and former pupil David Garrick, was an enormous, imposing structure, famous for Shakespearean revivals, and Johnson's only play, *Irene*, debuted there in 1749. Covent Garden, the most luxurious theater in London, opened in 1732; Oliver Goldsmith's play *She Stoops to Conquer* premiered there in 1773 (see chapter 43, "Theatre"). The legal profession, too, found a home in the Town. The Inns of Court, Lincoln's Inn and Gray's Inn, and the Middle and Inner Temples, all housing barristers and law students, lie on either side of the Strand – elegant squares of buildings surrounding contemplative green space (see chapter 26, "Law"). In 1763 Johnson had chambers at No. 1, Inner Temple Lane ("Dr. Johnson's Buildings" were erected on the site in 1857).

But, like the City, the Town was also a demographic ménage. The theater district bristled with brothels. A tradesman might rent rooms to a starving poet, as in Frances Burney's novel *Evelina* (1778). Somerset House, on the Strand, designed by William Chambers in 1770, accommodated a representative world of English spheres: the Royal Academy of Art, founded by Sir Joshua Reynolds in 1768; the Royal Society, from 1780 to 1857; the Society of Antiquaries, from 1781 to 1873; Navy headquarters; the Stamp Office; and miscellaneous smaller offices (such as the Hackney Coach and Barge Master).

Over the course of his London life, Johnson lodged all over the Town. He first entered London "*aetat.* 28" and lived "at the house of Mr. Norris, a staymaker, in Exeter-street, adjoining Catherine-street, in the Strand" (Boswell, *Life*, 1:103). At one point he lodged in an "upper room" in Holborn, where he set up shop for the *Dictionary* (and where Burney's heroine Evelina unhappily found herself at "Mr. Dawkins's, a hosier in High Holborn" – a "desart," she said, compared to the fashionable West End she had inhabited earlier). Holborn was once a principal highway into the City "for the cartage of wool and hides, corn, cheese and wood," and it remained a center for trade – busy, prosperous, and known for silversmiths.[7] And in No. 17 Gough Square, just off Fleet Street, Johnson compiled most of his *Dictionary*. The house – the only one of his London houses still standing – is now a museum to him.

Central London was central to Londoners in the eighteenth century; its network of taverns and coffee shops constituted what the philosopher and sociologist Jürgen Habermas has called the "public sphere," where people would mingle to drink, dine, and discuss. Johnson's social life was very much inclined towards the public sphere of taverns. His early meals were "at the Pine Apple in New-street, just by ... I had a cut of meat for six-pence, and bread for a penny, and gave the waiter a penny; so that I was quite well served" (Boswell, *Life*, 1:103). He and Sir Joshua Reynolds began their famous Literary Club at the Turk's Head in Gerrard Street. He called a chair in a tavern "the throne of human felicity":

> "As soon," said he, "as I enter the door of a tavern, I experience an oblivion of care, and a freedom from solicitude: when I am seated, I find the master courteous, and the servants obsequious to my call; anxious to know and ready to supply my wants: wine there exhilarates my spirits, and prompts me to free conversation and an interchange of discourse with those whom I most love: I dogmatise and am contradicted, and in this conflict of opinion and sentiments I find delight." (Hawkins, *Life*, pp. 55–6)

Coffee houses were equally warm, hospitable, convivial places, each with its own character and clientele: Will's Coffee House, in Russell Street,

Covent Garden, for the poets (John Dryden, William Wycherley, Joseph Addison, and Alexander Pope variously presiding), others for political persuasions and various professions. And the center of London proved central for Boswell's life and *Life*: he met Johnson for the first time on May 16, 1763, in the bookseller Tom Davies's shop in Russell Street, "a fine broad street, well inhabited by tradesmen."[8]

SOUTHWARK

Just across the river, in Southwark, was Vauxhall Gardens, where "the main walks were lit at night by hundreds of lamps, but there were also dark walks with windings and turnings so intricate that 'the most experienced mothers often lost themselves in looking for their daughters'."[9] (Burney's Evelina found herself uncomfortably, even dangerously, lost in those dark walks.) Georg Frideric Handel performed here; his *Music for the Royal Fireworks* was rehearsed on April 21, 1749, by one hundred musicians in front of an audience of over twelve thousand. Johnson, along with Boswell, Goldsmith, Hester Thrale, and the Prince of Wales, is pictured in a supper box at Vauxhall in a watercolor by Thomas Rowlandson, exhibited at the Royal Academy in 1784. Boswell considered Vauxhall Gardens as "peculiarly adapted to the taste of the English nation; there being a mixture of curious show, – gay exhibition, musick, vocal and instrumental, not too refined for the general ear; – for all which only a shilling is paid. And, though last, not least, good eating and drinking for those who wish to purchase that regale" (Boswell, *Life*, 3:308).

WESTMINSTER

Westminster – lying to the west of both the Town and the City – was home of king and court, and is steeped in history. St. James's Palace was built there by Henry VIII; the Banqueting Hall at Whitehall Palace witnessed the execution of Charles I; the Houses of Parliament, or Palace of Westminster, were originally built for Edward the Confessor, and the original Westminster Hall still survives (the rest of the buildings were rebuilt after a fire in 1837). Hyde Park, Green Park, and St. James's Park were originally mapped out by kings, and were opened to the public in the late seventeenth and eighteenth centuries. The fashionable and wealthy walked or rode in carriages in the parks, in Restoration comedies and eighteenth-century novels as well as real life. But the West End could be as demographically salted as the east; going home one night, Boswell "felt carnal inclinations raging through [his] frame," and he "determined to gratify them":

> I went to St. James's Park, and, like Sir John Brute [in Sir John Vanbrugh's play *The Provoked Wife*], picked up a whore. For the first time did I engage in armour [a condom], which I found but a dull satisfaction. She who submitted to my lusty embraces was a young Shropshire girl, only seventeen, very well-looked, her name Elizabeth Parker. Poor being, she has a sad time of it! (Boswell, *London Journal*, p. 227)

Boswell's early lodgings were in Westminster, in Downing Street: "a genteel street, within a few steps of the Parade; near the House of Commons, and very healthful" (*London Journal*, p. 50). Buckingham House (or the Queen's House), on the west end of St. James's Park, was described as "one of the great Beauties of *London*," with "rows of goodly Elms on one hand, and gay flourishing Limes on the other."[10] Here Johnson met King George III in its library in 1767.

NEVER TIRED OF LONDON

Johnson, having lived most of his life in central London, with dark nights in the City and glimpses of aristocratic life in the west, chose to die in London as well. He had been ill in Lichfield but, as Boswell records,

> such was his love of London, so high a relish had he of its magnificent extent, and variety of intellectual entertainment, that he languished when absent from it, his mind having become quite luxurious from the long habit of enjoying the metropolis; and, therefore, although at Lichfield, surrounded with friends, who loved and revered him, and for whom he had a very sincere affection, he still found that such conversation as London affords, could be found no where else. (Boswell, *Life*, 4:374–5)

"The town is my element," he told his doctor. "I am not afraid either of a journey to London or a residence in it." (Boswell, *Life*, 4:358)

He returned and died, and a monument was erected to him in Westminster Abbey, where he joined Ben Jonson, John Milton, John Dryden, William Congreve, Matthew Prior, Joseph Addison, David Garrick, Oliver Goldsmith, Thomas Gray, and (thanks to David Garrick's efforts in 1740) William Shakespeare. This city, to which none would go "unbrib'd," had become for Johnson and for the literary world of the mid-eighteenth century, the center of all that life can afford.

NOTES

1 John Stow, *A Survey of the Cities of London and Westminster: Containing the Original, Antiquity, Increase, Modern Estate and Government of Those Cities*, 2 vols. (London, 1720), 2:101.
2 Stow, *Survey*, 1:189.
3 Stow, *Survey*, 1:558.
4 Daniel Defoe, *A Tour thro' the Whole Island of Great Britain, Divided into Circuits or Journies*, 3 vols. (London, 1724–6), 2:155.
5 Stow, *Survey*, 1:376.
6 Defoe, *Tour*, 2:117.
7 Ben Weinreb *et al.* (eds.), *The London Encyclopaedia*, 3rd edn. (London: Macmillan, 2008), p. 395.
8 Stow, *Survey*, 2:93.
9 Weinreb *et al.*, *London Encyclopaedia*, p. 936.
10 John Macky, *A Journey through England: In Familiar Letters from a Gentleman Here, to His Friend Abroad* (London, 1714), p. 125; *The Works of John Sheffield, Earl of Mulgrave, Marquis of Normanby, and Duke of Buckingham*, 2 vols. (London, 1723), 2:279.

CHAPTER 29

Medicine

T. Jock Murray

ME'DICINE. *n.s.* [*medicine*, Fr. *medicina*, Latin. It is generally pronounced as if only of two syllables, *med'cine.*] Physick; any remedy administered by a physician.

I wish to die, yet dare not death endure;
Detest the *medicine*, yet desire the cure. *Dryden.*

The history of medicine in the eighteenth century can be viewed either as a period of stagnation and confused beliefs between the ancient and the new, or as the adolescence of modern medicine. The present generation may look back with a mixture of amusement and disdain on the physician's complex medications containing arsenic, strychnine, turpentine, and beetroot, and with revulsion – even horror – at the harsh purging, bleeding, cupping, blistering, and application of leeches. But the physicians of the past, functioning in their belief systems, were no less clever than those of today, and, as Lester King notes, no more or less muddle-headed, obtuse, grasping, prejudiced, or contentious.[1]

Although sometimes called a "lost age in medicine,"[2] and "interesting, but not *very* interesting,"[3] this period ushered in new ideas about medical education, professionalism, medical ethics, the care of the mentally ill, public health, occupational illness, hospital care, and advances against smallpox, scurvy, and heart failure. It was the springboard for many more momentous changes in the next century.

THE PATIENT

Most histories of medicine begin with the physician, but I would like to start this brief overview with the patient – and not with Samuel Johnson as patient, although he suffered from many ailments, as Johnson was not a typical patient. From the letters and diaries of those dealing with illness we hear of the distress and also the complaints about the doctors and their treatments. But even this view omits the poor folk who were illiterate or unable to afford pens, paper, and ink.

Life in the eighteenth century was threatening to those housed in squalid, cold, dim, damp, and crowded rooms. A trivial cut or infected ear could easily progress to a more serious state, even death. Polluted water, decaying food, gin drinking, injuries, and violence in the streets all added to the risks. Parents regarded themselves fortunate if a child survived to age five. Hester Thrale, for example, had thirteen pregnancies over fourteen years, delivering twelve children, only four of whom survived to adulthood. Children of the poor, even if they survived infection and malnutrition, might be abandoned by their parents who could not afford to feed them.

Some diseases were particularly feared. Smallpox killed a third of those infected, and left many of the survivors, like Lady Mary Wortley Montagu, scarred for life. Bubonic and pneumonic plague epidemics were less frequent, but the memory and fear remained. Typhus was especially common in crowded London, spread by lice and fleas, and typhoid fever, spread through contaminated food, milk, or water, also caused many deaths. Influenza occurred every autumn and winter, with five major epidemics between 1762 and 1788. Syphilis, known as the "great pox," had been spreading across Europe since the sixteenth century, causing each country to blame another for the origin. As the diaries of Boswell and the caricatures of William Hogarth show, promiscuity and the resultant sexually transmitted diseases were widespread in England. Tuberculosis, the "white plague," was increasing also in frequency. Scrofula – a more superficial lymphatic form of tuberculosis – affected young Samuel Johnson. When he was unresponsive to a suppurating seton, or drain, weeping pus on his neck for years, the physician Sir John Floyer recommended he attend the peculiar ceremony of the "Royal Touch," from the even more peculiar Queen Anne. It was believed by many that the touch of the monarch could cure scrofula, and this was the last of these ceremonies that attested to the divine nature of the monarchs.

Although mortality rates declined during the century, medicine probably played only a small part. Perhaps the propaganda from the medical profession about hygiene, public health measures, diet, ventilation, and other aspects of healthy living played some part, but medical therapies altered few, if any, diseases. Employment, improved economy, and a better standard of living were more significant factors. Even simple innovations helped, such as cheap cotton that could be boiled and washed, thereby reducing the contamination by lice.

ILLNESSES

The cause of conditions such as injuries and toothaches seemed evident, but serious acute illnesses and chronic conditions were more mysterious. Older beliefs, fostered by the Church, suggested illness was often related to sinful acts and moral weakness. The role of the planets and the orientation of the stars was fading as a belief, replaced by the concern about invisible environmental causes – putrid gases and other miasmas from the polluted air, believed to be emanating from sick people, spoiled food, damp and fetid material, decaying vegetation, and dead animals. It was known that there was a contagious nature associated with smallpox, plague, malaria, syphilis, influenza, and some of the more nonspecific fevers, even if it was not known what exactly it was that was contagious.

When illness occurred in a family, the first step would be to use the home remedies kept in the cupboard, or to mix one from the medical recipes in the back of cookbooks or from one of the 153 home medical books circulating in the eighteenth century. Physicians generally saw home remedy books, with their exaggerated claims, as an intrusion into their newly acquired professional status and privilege – even though physicians, sometimes writing under pseudonyms, often authored them.

Educated people had more resources at hand, as they knew the language of the arts, science, and medicine. Medical texts were being written in English rather than Latin, and the latest medical theory, discovery, or fad would be discussed in the literary and scientific clubs of the day. Johnson had an interest in medicine, and argued fine points of medicine and therapy with his many physician friends. Hester Thrale said he made a study of all branches of medicine, and may have been "tempted no little to the sin of Quackery" (*Thraliana*, 1:197), indicating he had more than an intellectual interest as he often offered medical advice to his friends, and wrote prescriptions in Latin that were filled by the apothecaries.

MEDICAL PRACTITIONERS

Most sick people would not likely seek the attention of a physician except in dire circumstances. Physicians, moreover, were not to be found in many rural areas. It is likely that a person with a symptom or a sick child would, after trying the usual home remedies, seek the help of a local healer. There were the respected and well-meaning wise women offering a service, and others in the town attempting to make a living offering a single nostrum

Figure 34 Woodcut after William Hogarth, *The Four Stages of Cruelty*, no. 4, *The Reward of Cruelty*, 1751.

or skill, such as tooth-pulling, boil-lancing, bone-setting, or a cure-all for scurvy, indigestion, or whatever ails you.

Others providing services were non-physician humanitarians who saw needs in the communities and filled them. The Rev. John Wesley was one of these: he noted the absence of physicians in most villages and towns and believed that, even if they were available, their therapies were too complex, harmful, and expensive for ordinary folk. He therefore collected folk remedies, published as *Primitive Physick; or, An Easy and Natural Method of Curing Most Diseases* (1747). It was the most popular home remedy book of the century, and Wesley opened dispensaries to provide medicine and the new electrical therapy to as many as fifty patients a day.

The hierarchy of physicians, surgeons, and apothecaries in this era is very complex, as there were many forms of practitioners. Physicians separated themselves from other practitioners by the cloak of science, a university education in Latin, and being "learned" rather than practicing a simple skill. These were the elitist group of qualified physicians, graduates of Oxford and Cambridge (open only to Anglicans), who would be admitted to the Fellowship of the Royal College of Physicians of London. There were qualified graduates of the Continental and Scottish schools who were gaining in prominence, but who could only be licentiates, not fellows, of the College, and who rankled at their classification as second-class. There were also apprenticeship physicians, who applied to universities for a degree in medicine based on their experience.

Then there were "irregular physicians," who practiced without any formal recognition. One such was Dr. Robert Levet, who lived in Johnson's house for twenty years. Levet obtained his medical and surgical skills by attending lectures and demonstrations, and by walking the wards of Paris hospitals to observe physicians caring for patients. As Johnson said, Levet learned medicine by the ear rather than from books, and even waited tables in establishments frequented by surgeons to listen to their talk. Each day he went into the poor areas of London to care for people who had little to pay him, except perhaps a glass of gin. Johnson, who admired Levet's dedication, said that only Levet became drunk for the right reasons. In his moving elegy, "On the Death of Dr. Robert Levet," Johnson needled the College physicians who would not give Levet his due respect.

The surgeon – in the usual eighteenth-century spelling, *chirurgeon*, defined in the *Dictionary* as "One that cures ailments, not by internal medicines, but outward applications" – gained increasing respect by separating his profession from that of the barber in 1745. The surgeons were now becoming more "learned," like the physicians, experimenting, writing books, and advancing the study of anatomy. Even more numerous were surgeon-apothecaries, who provided an array of medical and surgical services and are probably the origin of our modern general practitioners. The apothecaries were providers of medicines, and were restricted by the physicians from charging for medical advice. In any community there were various remedy-sellers and quacks. The artist William Hogarth saw little difference between the elite physicians and the quacks, bone-setters, tooth-pullers, and midwives. In his caricature *The Undertakers*, the bewigged physicians sniffing on their pomander canes were accompanied by three well-known quacks. Overall, there were a lot of medical practitioners in this era, about the same ratio of one for every 850 people that we see in many countries today.

Practice was not always easy or remunerative, and hospital appointments difficult without the right training and prominent supporters. A reasonable annual income was usually a few hundred pounds (see chapter 31, "Money"). Acquiring paying patients was slow, and many caregivers became beholden to their more wealthy patients. Others improved their income by fee-splitting with the apothecaries, writing popular home medical books, or taking paying positions with local administrations. A few earned money by selling their special remedies; one of the most successful was Johnson's friend and coauthor, Dr. Robert James, whose famous "Dr. James' Fever Powder" was widely used and available for over a century.

CONCEPTS OF DISEASE

In the early eighteenth century there was no uniform concept of disease. The predominant medical belief was still based on the ancient concept of the humors – blood, phlegm, choler (yellow bile), and melancholy (black bile) – and the elements of air (blood was warm and moist), water (phlegm was cold and moist), fire (yellow bile was warm and dry), and earth (black bile was cold and dry). The healthy constitution was a balance of these elements, and in the face of illness, therapy was aimed at reestablishing a balance: removing the offending humors by bleeding, blistering, purging, applying leeches, or administering drugs to encourage vomiting and sweating.

Although therapies were slow to change, the views of illness and health were widely debated. The "iatro-mathematicians" thought the future was in measurement and careful notations of weight, time, numbers, shapes, and sizes. Sir John Floyer invented a special watch with a second hand to measure the pulse with unprecedented precision, and the Rev. Stephen Hales devised a method of recording the blood pressure in a horse. Isaac Newton's experimental natural philosophy encouraged physicians to think of the body as a machine, and leaders such as Herman Boerhaave of Leyden believed in a model based on physics. Hydraulic concepts would allow bodily function and disease to be understood by measurement of weight, forces, fluid pressures, and physical influences.

Other theories were circulating at the same time. John Brown of Edinburgh expounded his view that there were only two forms of disease – *sthenic* (strong) and *asthenic* (weak) – and two treatments, sedative and stimulant. Others followed the more orthodox William Cullen, who encouraged commonsense observation, assessment of the environment, and classification of disease. John Hunter advocated putting all theory aside and just doing experiments. Other cults fostered beliefs in the cure-all benefits of mesmerism, homeopathy, unusual diets, spas and water, and electricity.

There was criticism about the harsh remedies of the doctors, with their purging medications, bleeding, leeches, enema syringes, cupping, and vile-tasting remedies, and without the benefit of anesthesia. The caricatures of Hogarth, George Cruikshank, and James Gillray show the dangers of falling into the hands of the doctors, depicting them as cruel buffoons, more interested in money, status, and the patient's daughter than the care of the sick person. As Roy Porter noted on his evaluation of the reports on medicine in the *Gentleman's Magazine*, however, the public attitude towards the profession was generally positive, and was improving.[4] The physician was better equipped than his predecessors, with new surgical techniques and instruments, and promising medications such as laudanum (opium dissolved in alcohol), mercury oxide, cinchona (Jesuit's bark), a form of quinine, calomel, ipecacuanha, and, at end of the century, digitalis.

MEDICAL ADVANCES

Dating advances in medicine is often misleading, since the practical impact of a discovery may occur decades, even a century, after the supposed breakthrough took place. The invisible world made visible by the microscope, the clinical wisdom of Dr. Thomas Sydenham, and the physiological revelations about the heart and circulation of William Harvey – all from the seventeenth century – became fully influential only in the eighteenth. Likewise, the promise of smallpox vaccination, digitalis therapy, and anatomical and physiological discoveries of the eighteenth century would be fulfilled only in the nineteenth. Lady Mary Wortley Montagu, wife of the ambassador to Constantinople, later campaigned for inoculation against smallpox, a procedure that was replaced only at the end of the century by the more benign cowpox vaccination popularized by Edward Jenner.

Because of the superior medical education offered in Scotland, Scottish doctors were becoming the leaders in surgery and obstetrics. John Hunter conducted extensive researches in comparative anatomy and physiology, founded surgical pathology, and raised surgery to the level of a respectable branch of science. His brother William Hunter, an eminent teacher of anatomy, became famous as an obstetrician. The leading obstetrician in London, William Smellie, published a three-volume work that outlined the safe use of obstetrical forceps, putting obstetrics on a sound scientific footing as a medical discipline.

James Lind, a British naval surgeon from Edinburgh, did a trial experiment showing the benefits of lime juice in preventing and curing scurvy, a disease that killed thousands of men in armies and navies roaming the new world. Although the Royal Navy was slow to officially adopt the preventative, it eventually saved innumerable lives, and provided the British with the nickname "limeys."

Perhaps the most important change in this era was the redirection of focus from mysterious external forces to changes within the body and its organs. The seventy-nine-year-old Giovanni Battista Morgagni, a professor of anatomy at Padua, applied the concepts of iatro-physics as a pathological basis for disease, recording the clinical and pathological changes in almost seven hundred cases to show the basis of their disease. To many this is the beginning of modern medicine. In the same year a small tract published in Vienna by Leopold Auenbrugger described the diagnostic technique of percussion – tapping – that would show the pathological changes in the organs such as the lungs, again focusing on the internal changes in disease, beginning the art of physical examination. The son of a wine merchant, Auenbrugger noted his father could tell how much wine remained in a barrel by tapping the sides, listening for the change in sound.

Medical journals, too, were beginning to appear in this era. Medical education was advancing with the innovations of the Scottish schools. Dr. John Gregory of Edinburgh published his lectures to medical students as *Lectures on the Duties and Qualifications of a Physician* (1773), which laid the foundation for a formal code of medical ethics. He discussed the important question of whether medicine is to be regarded as an art or a trade. He addressed the standards of decorum in the life of a physician, appropriate behavior and dress, breaking bad news to patients, truth-telling, commitment to patients, comforting as well as curing, physician interactions, and recognizing when a physician is beyond his level of competence.

Public health, population statistics, and health legislation were all getting more attention. Samuel Johnson's friend Dr. Robert James translated a work of Bernard Ramazzini from 1706, which documented the occupational health risks of forty-three occupations, including blacksmith, baker, saddler, and carpenter.

There was growing governmental and civic responsibility for providing for the infirm and new hospitals were built including the Westminster General Infirmary (1719), Guy's Hospital in Southwark (1725), St. George's Hospital at Hyde Park (1737), Middlesex Infirmary in Soho (1745), and the

London Hospital in Whitechapel (1752). Smaller illness-specific hospitals were initiated for venereal disease, cancer, and specific sufferers such as penitent prostitutes. Philanthropy and community support were growing and allowed hospitals and provincial dispensaries (but not asylums) to provide free services. Only the poor would go to hospitals for their care, however, as the middle and upper classes were treated at home. Friendly Societies were created to provide fee-paying members with benefits and support when they became ill or aged.

In summary, it was a distressing age to be ill, as most treatments were unlikely to alter the outcome of the disease. But significant advances were being made in the understanding of health and disease, and in recognition of a social responsibility for the health of the population. The developments of this era would provide the groundwork for even more dramatic changes in the nineteenth century.

NOTES

1 L. King, *The Medical World of the Eighteenth Century* (Chicago: University of Chicago Press, 1958), p. xv.

2 W. R. Le Fanu, "The Lost Half Century in English Medicine, 1700–1750," *Bulletin of the History of Medicine*, 46 (1972), 319–48.

3 Roy Porter, *The Greatest Benefit to Mankind: A History of Humanity from Antiquity to the Present* (London: HarperCollins, 1997), p. 247.

4 Roy Porter, "Lay Medical Knowledge in the Eighteenth Century: The Evidence of the *Gentleman's Magazine*," *Medical History*, 29 (1985), 138–68.

CHAPTER 30

Mental health

Allan Ingram

SA'NITY. *n.s.* [*sanitas*, Latin.] Soundness of mind.

How pregnant, sometimes, his replies are?
A happiness that often madness hits on,
Which *sanity* and reason could not be
So prosp'rously delivered of. *Shakesp. Hamlet.*

The long eighteenth century was the period in Britain and Western Europe when the mind came into its own. Thought – including progress in science and medicine and in the understanding of the mind itself – was at last, after the religious and civic turmoils of the seventeenth century, deriving the full benefit of those decisive breaks with the past that had occurred during the European Renaissance. Increasingly liberated from the remaining pockets of medievalism, such as humoral theory in understanding the body, and from strict religious oversight of what might be thought and written, scientists were able, probably for the first time, to give full rein to those fundamentals of modern science, free thought and factual observation. William Harvey, early in the seventeenth century, identified and demonstrated the circulation of the blood; Isaac Newton, half a century later, discovered the movements and orbits of lunar and planetary bodies. In the same way, the celebrated physician Thomas Willis argued in his *Cerebri anatome* (1664) that the human brain operated through a series of nervous impulses and reactions, basing his conclusions on clinical observation and experiment. The whole human organism was being recognized as more dynamic, more mechanical, and far more surprising than earlier generations of scientists had dared to think, and the most exciting faculty of all in the new body was the mind itself. There was more to thought, it began to appear, than we thought.

PHILOSOPHY AND THE MIND

While some were observing the brain and the nervous system, other thinkers and medical men were turning their attention to issues concerning the mind – to what was being thought and why. Here the key figure was John Locke, the philosopher and physician. *An Essay concerning Human Understanding* (1690) was probably the single most influential philosophical work upon the study of mind for the century that followed (see chapter 33, "Philosophy"). By denying the existence of innate ideas and deriving all knowledge from sense or sensation, Locke separated thought from any residual traces of what might have been a divine template, and positioned it instead firmly within the individual organism, its species characteristics, and its distinctive quirks and malfunctions. In doing so, he set the agenda for attitudes towards issues of identity, of mental normality and abnormality, of popular as well as philosophical understanding of sanity and insanity, and of education for a chain of thinkers who followed.

One of these followers, David Hume, makes clear the debt owed by moral philosophy to scientific rationalism in adding a subtitle to his *Treatise of Human Nature* (1739–40): "An Attempt to introduce the experimental Method of Reasoning into Moral Subjects." Hume argued, like Locke, for the experiential basis of all ideas, but he went further in denying the existence of a self. For Hume, all sense of self derived from habit. In this context, the role of a divinity retreats out of sight. Thirty years earlier, Bishop George Berkeley had argued in his *Essay towards a New Theory of Vision* that ideas were simply what we became accustomed to associate with repeated sense impressions, while the philosopher and physician David Hartley, ten years after Hume's *Treatise*, held in the *Observations on Man* that our mental life proceeds almost entirely upon the basis of the association of ideas.

Many people, of course, found such theories deeply shocking. Hume's reputation as an atheist kept him from securing chairs at the leading Scottish universities, and Johnson famously described him "and other sceptical innovators" as "vain men" who had "gone to milk the bull" (Boswell, *London Journal*, p. 343). Boswell, too, who like Johnson suffered periodically from crippling lowness of spirits, found such ideas intensely disturbing. As he records in his journal for 1775: "My state of mind today was still affected by Hartley and Priestley's metaphysics," adding, "and was continually trying to perceive my faculties operating as machinery."[1] On one hand, it was distressing to think of oneself as no more than a set of mechanical or nervous reactions, moving with minimal control from one supposed idea to a second that was in some way associated with it. On the other, people were threatened by the implied absence of the need for God in relation to the new mind, particularly as the advance of Newtonian science could be seen as implying that God was an unnecessary concept in the physical universe.

MANIA AND MELANCHOLY

While concepts of mind were changing dramatically during the period, medical ideas on diagnosing and treating the mind, on what constituted mental health and mental illness, changed more slowly. Here religion had traditionally had a strong hold, and it continued to do so.

Mental illness, for the whole of this period, tended to be divided into two broad categories: mania and melancholy. The former arose from undue excitement of the mental faculties, whether through emotions such as anger or passion, or uncontrolled ambition, or even religious exaltation. The latter was marked by continual lowness of spirits deriving from any one of a number of causes – from the very human ones of boredom, loneliness, bereavement, or disappointment in love or fortune, through to religious despair and a loss of faith in God or man, and even, in the most perplexing cases, arising and persisting for no apparent reason at all. There were also some conditions, first identified by Thomas Willis, that involved an alternation between mania and melancholy, a version of what twenty-first-century practitioners would refer to as bipolar disorder.

Standard treatments existed for mania, and most doctors and establishments were content to relieve the vital spirits by bloodletting and various kinds of purging, and then waiting for nature to take its course. More violent maniacs might be confined and chained, some in private "madhouses," others in London's most notorious asylum, the Hospital of St. Mary Bethlehem – better known in the abbreviated form of its name, Bedlam. Some physicians, such as Patrick Blair in the 1720s and Joseph Mason Cox in the last decades of the period, developed various kinds of shock therapy designed to render the body even more disordered than the mind supposedly was, and thus to induce in the mind a comparative calmness, with mixed success.

With melancholy patients, however, physicians found a good deal to work with, and here the influence of religion was most decisively felt. For even the most devout of believers, particularly those of the Protestant nonconformist groups, doubts about divine intentions and ultimately

Figure 35 Thomas Rowlandson, *The Hypochondriac.*

about the fate of one's own soul were part of the religious experience, even a kind of rite of passage. Nonconformist divines therefore had a ready role in counseling such people through their "trouble of mind," and bringing them to a truer understanding of God. John Bolton, Richard Baxter, and Timothy Rogers at the end of the seventeenth century and into the eighteenth, and their inheritors throughout the eighteenth century, including John Wesley, repeatedly stressed the importance of talk, of taking such problems seriously. Many first-person narratives describe the kinds of distressing madness that could break out in these melancholy periods, including self-harm and suicide attempts. Above all, in these circumstances, they stress the supportive role of the religious community in keeping faith with their stricken brother or sister.

TALKING AND WRITING CURES

Treatment for melancholy never lost touch with this important current. While the force of religion diminished during the period, and physicians, apothecaries, and quacks energetically developed manual and chemical therapies, from cold baths and electric shocks to concoctions of potentially lethal (or just plain disgusting) substances, the mainstream therapists simply kept talking to their patients, albeit often in combination with a series of purges, vomits, or unusual dietary arrangements. Correspondence between doctor and patient – given a patient who was middle class, literate, and capable of living outside a madhouse – was a perfectly usual and acceptable form of counseling. Letters between physicians, such as Locke, George Cheyne, and Erasmus Darwin, and patients, such as Samuel Richardson or Johnson himself, indicate both the importance of the advice and of the line of contact.

From here it was a short step to dispensing with the doctor altogether and exchanging correspondence instead with a relative or a friend, as Thomas Gray did with Richard West and Horace Walpole, and William Cowper with John Newton. Some, like Smollett's fictitious Matthew Bramble with Dr. Lewis in *Humphry Clinker*, and Johnson himself with Dr. Thomas Lawrence, combined the roles of both physician and friend. A further step took one to keeping a diary or journal, like Boswell and (for parts of his life) Johnson, or even to tracking and exploring one's mental state in poems, like Anne Finch or Edward Young, or in prose narratives, like Cowper again or Mary Wollstonecraft, or even, again like Boswell, in the newspapers – in his case, under the pseudonym of "The Hypochondriack." Such kinds of therapy fall into the period's enthusiasm for self-treatment in all forms of illness and demonstrate the early effectiveness – or not – of what later became known as "the writing cure."

BE NOT SOLITARY; BE NOT IDLE

For the eighteenth century, melancholy was a major category of illness; surviving it and living with it was a serious concern that affected the texture and quality of one's everyday existence. Boswell, in a most telling image, attempts to pin down the nature of Johnson's mental problems:

> His mind resembled the vast amphitheatre, the colisæum at Rome. In the centre stood his judgement, which, like a mighty gladiator, combated those apprehensions that, like the wild beasts of the *Arena*, were all around in the cells, ready to be let out upon him. After a conflict, he drove them back into their dens; but not killing them, they were still assailing him. (Boswell, *Life*, 2:106–7)

This is a particularly appropriate figure for a man who derived so many of his models of learning from classical culture, while at the same time it places Johnson's doubts and misgivings firmly within a set of Christian values and assumptions. This man, who above all things feared being "Sent to Hell, Sir, and punished everlastingly" (Boswell, *Life*, 4:299), was operating within a strong tradition of Protestantism, and his mental health took its fluctuations – its "paroxisms and remissions," as Johnson put it in 1776 (*Works*, 1:257) – from the success or failure of his ability to deal with a lifetime of uncertainty over the fate of his immortal soul.

Johnson as gladiator is one mode of dealing with mental well-being. It captures the energy of the human mind in joining combat over and over again, and it powerfully represents the remorseless nature of the doubts that are never settled, that will always recur. In this sense, for all its strength, the mind is trapped in a cycle where the gladiator, judgment, is itself part of the circle of entrapment. Johnson, the true Christian soul under relentless persecution, like many other contemporary souls both inside and outside asylums, is condemned to rely on the same mental faculty fighting the same fight – for life, as it were.

Boswell's image, though, draws attention to only one aspect of Johnson's mental life, albeit a central one. There were other ways to manage melancholy, and in these too Johnson can be seen as part of his age. Talk, for example, while developing as a therapy, was also an effective distraction: talk brought into play a range of mental abilities within a secure and convivial social setting, and it provided the mind with other materials to set against the forces of religious doubt and personal worthlessness – against the moment, as Johnson puts it in *Rasselas*, "when solitude should deliver him to the tyranny of reflection" (*Works*, 16:66). Talk also extended to correspondence, enlarging both the circles of sociability and the spread of topics and points of view.

For Johnson especially, letters served as vehicles for the exchange of kindnesses, courtesies, and advice (see chapter 3, "Correspondence"). His words to Hester Thrale in 1774, on her disappointment following the death of a relative, give a good illustration of a mind attempting to deal with a disagreeable, and therefore threatening, topic:

> Be alone as little as you can; when you are alone, do not suffer your thoughts to dwell on what you might have done, to prevent this disappointment. You perhaps could not have done what you imagine, or might have done it without effect. But even to think in the most reasonable manner, is for the present not so useful as not to think. Remit yourself solemnly into the hands of God, and then turn your mind upon the business and amusements which lie before you. (*Letters*, 2:117–18)

In terms of self-treatment, or nonmedical therapy, this is exemplary. At a time, though, when the moral managers among mad-doctors – from

William Battie in the 1750s, through William Pargeter in the late 1780s and early 1790s, to the Tukes at the York Retreat from 1796 onwards – were stressing the importance of steering patients' minds through the crises of their conditions, and thereby enabling them eventually to steer for themselves, Johnson's remarks display a detailed and sympathetic understanding of the pitfalls of mental disturbance and of some of the means of dealing with it.

"Be not solitary; be not idle," Johnson advised Hester Thrale (*Letters*, 2:118), quoting one of his favorite authors, Robert Burton – or, as he told Boswell more expansively, "If you are idle, be not solitary; if you are solitary, be not idle" (*Letters*, 3:201). For Johnson, the ultimate management of the mind came through books, both the reading of them and the writing. Fearing that his fundamental faults were "waste of time, and general sluggishness" (*Works*, 1:257), Johnson found that books provided the one constant corrective: being "not idle," and thereby attempting to close one avenue to the charge of moral worthlessness, could always involve reading, while the labor of composition, even the drudgery of compiling a dictionary, had not only an ultimate social benefit but, equally important, a personal spiritual one.

BALEFUL INFLUENCE

Boswell describes the beginnings of Johnson's mental troubles early in the *Life*. He became, in the summer of 1729, "overwhelmed with an horrible hypochondria, with perpetual irritation, fretfulness and impatience; and with a dejection, gloom, and despair, which made existence misery": thereafter, "all his labours, and all his enjoyments, were but temporary interruptions of its baleful influence" (Boswell, *Life*, 1:63–4). Boswell then quotes a prayer, from Johnson's own diary some years later: "I have this day entered upon my twenty-eighth year. 'Mayest thou, O God, enable me, for JESUS CHRIST's sake, to spend this in such a manner that I may receive comfort from it at the hour of death, and in the day of judgement! Amen'" (1:70).

Johnson's melancholy was situated firmly within the traditions and experiences of his time: he was strongly influenced by the inheritance of Protestantism, yet convinced that the individual held it in his own power to rectify and amend for his faults and omissions; resistant to newer, skeptical philosophies, yet aware that the human mind took much of its tone from personal idiosyncrasies and abnormalities; respectful of the authority of the Church and of the medical profession, yet resolute, even stubborn, in his reliance on mental self-therapy and the responsibility of the individual to handle his own doubts, misgivings, and despairs, either through lonely battle or by a lifetime's devotion to moral self-management. The "labours" and "enjoyments" that Boswell saw as "interruptions" of the "baleful influence" of melancholy were also, crucially, the activities and exertions, the managing of the mind, that enabled Johnson to live with it. In this respect, as in so many others, Johnson himself is an exemplification of the human mind of the eighteenth century truly coming into its own.

NOTES

1 James Boswell, *Boswell: The Ominous Years, 1774–1777*, ed. Charles Ryskamp and F. A. Pottle (London: William Heinemann, 1963), p. 212.

CHAPTER 31

Money

D'Maris Coffman

> MO'NEY. *n.s.* [*monnoye*, French; *moneta*, Latin. It has properly no plural except when money is taken for a single piece; but monies was formerly used for sums.] Metal coined for the purposes of commerce.
>
> *Money* differs from uncoined silver, in that the quantity of silver in each piece of *money* is ascertained by the stamp it bears, which is a publick voucher. *Locke.*

"The dearness of every thing," wrote philosopher and historian David Hume, "from plenty of money, is a disadvantage, which attends to an established commerce, and sets bounds to it in every country, by enabling the poorer states to undersell the richer in all foreign markets." New forms of money were prompting anxiety:

> This had made me entertain a doubt concerning the benefit of *banks* and *paper credit*, which are so generally esteemed advantageous to every nation. That provisions and labour should become dear by the encrease of trade and money, is, in many respects, an inconvenience; but an inconvenience that is unavoidable, and the effect of that public wealth and prosperity which are the ends of all our wishes.[1]

THE MONETARY ECONOMY

Many of David Hume's compatriots shared his skepticism of banks, paper money, and credit, though few identified them so strongly with inflation. Those antiquarians who concerned themselves with long-term price trends more often focused their attention on the debasement of the coinage. Hume was one of the few to notice the importance of "paper money" and credit to the growth of the eighteenth-century economy. While few contemporaries would disagree with the notion that they were living in an era of rapid economic and social change, the tendency of modern historians to emphasize that change rather than the continuities with earlier periods obscures the reality that many of the salient features of the eighteenth-century economy had roots that stretched back to the Middle Ages.

Two important events, however, define the eighteenth-century experience of money and the monetary economy. The de facto switch to the gold standard, and with it the disappearance of familiar silver coins, could not have escaped attention, as pounds, shillings, and pence remained the unit of account. Likewise the Financial Revolution, with its unprecedented scale of securitization and monetization of government debt, introduced unfamiliar financial instruments into the public's consciousness. While the early English stock market was emblematic of this trend, more mundane lottery tickets, seamen's tickets, Exchequer bills, and promissory notes were ubiquitous features of eighteenth-century life. These bewildering new forms of paper money and credit fed the moral anxieties of a reading public, but most of the chief innovations were extensions of well-established practices. It may have been the growth of print culture that not only brought the public finances under increasing scrutiny, but also offered opportunities for contemporaries to comment on the desirability of new practices. Samuel Johnson, David Hume, and Adam Smith were all participants in those debates. What kind of money, then, might eighteenth-century Englishmen know?

POUNDS, SHILLINGS, PENCE

The origins of pre-decimal English money – the system of pounds (*l.* or £), shillings (*s.*), and pence (*d.*) – can be traced to antiquity; these abbreviations correspond to the Latin *librae*, *solidi*, *denarii*. This system was adopted by the Franks and introduced to England at the Norman Conquest. In the twelfth century King Henry II established the silver standard of a "pennyweight" as 1/20 of a troy ounce, or 1/240 of a troy pound of sterling silver. There were thus twelve pence to the shilling and twenty shillings to the pound. A crown was five shillings, a half-crown two shillings and sixpence. Farthings were a quarter of a penny.

It is notoriously difficult to translate these amounts into modern terms, but the prices of some common expenditures in the eighteenth century will give a rough idea of the purchasing power of different amounts of money. In 1755, for instance, a live chicken cost 1*s.* 6*d.* "Coarse beef" in 1779 sold for 3*s.* 5*d.* per pound, salt butter 8*d.* per pound, and coal 14*d.* per bushel. Seven pence purchased a pound of sugar in 1779; a pound of good tea went for 12*s.* The price of pound of wheat flour in 1786 was 1¾*d.* One shilling bought admission to the Vauxhall pleasure gardens, or, in 1763, to Mrs. Salmon's, the best waxworks in London. A typical two-volume novel sold for 5*s.*

Annual amounts offer another perspective. Early in Johnson's lifetime, an unskilled day laborer might make a shilling a day, six days a week, for a total of just over £15 12*s.* a year. Rents seem comparatively inexpensive – an average laborer's annual rent in 1771 was £1 8*s.* 2*d.* with an additional charge for "firing" (coal fires) of £1 3*s.* 11*d.* – but food and clothing accounted for a large portion of a family's income. A poor friend advised Johnson that "thirty pounds a year was enough to enable a man to live [in London] without being contemptible," though a middle-class family at mid-century would not consider itself comfortable with less than fifty pounds a year. The very wealthy might have incomes in the tens of thousands of pounds per annum.[2]

METALLIC COINS

Because early English coins were hammered rather than milled – a manufacturing process that produces the telltale serrated edges of modern coins – counterfeiting and coin clipping, or scraping off bits of precious metal to melt into bullion, bedeviled the authorities. Gold and silver are softer than the base metals used by modern mints; coins experienced wear and tear from circulation. The supply of precious metals, relative to each other and to other commodities, changed over time, forcing periodic adjustments. As a consequence, regular recoinages were a recurring and frustrating feature of English life.

After 1660 the crown began to produce milled coins, which soon replaced the older hammered coins. The guinea, first minted in 1663, was a gold coin equivalent to one pound sterling (i.e., twenty shillings) but, after fluctuating for decades, its value was fixed at twenty-one shillings in 1717. This seemingly innocuous adjustment accounts for much of the novelty of eighteenth-century English money, as silver coins all but disappeared from circulation in the eighteenth century. Whenever it was profitable to do so, enterprising subjects ignored the laws against defacing coins. Silver coins were melted down, disguised as Spanish bullion, and shipped abroad. A fuller description of the mechanics of these arbitrage operations reveals the importance of "paper money" to the early modern English economy. The changing physical composition of the coinage was just the most obvious material consequence of bimetallism and the gradual shift to a de facto gold standard in the wake of Sir Isaac Newton's "Great Recoinage" of 1696–9.

RETAIL CREDIT

Metallic coins made up only part of what modern economists call the "money supply." By some estimates, paper money constituted 40 percent of the total money or monetary equivalents in circulation. Contemporary "political arithmeticians" offered competing estimates of the amount of coin and paper in circulation, as well as other measures (of national wealth, income, and expenditure), which today are called "national accounts." Although they did not perceive the role of these instruments in causing inflation or affording economic growth, there was general agreement that paper money played a significant role in economic life.

Even without formal paper money, which often involved sums larger than the public would encounter in daily life, the English economy operated on an elaborate system of retail credit. Up and down the social order, economic actors encountered what modern finance has termed "cash flow" difficulties: they received payments for goods and services only once or twice a year, but incurred expenditure constantly. In practice, this meant that shopkeepers kept ledgers of their patrons' purchases, and they would present their customers with bills to be paid in full every six to twelve months. Maintaining reputation and creditworthiness required the regular settlement of debts, but few customers paid for purchases with cash.

Although the scale of this activity increased over the course of the sixteenth, seventeenth, and eighteenth centuries, investigation of medieval manorial court and Chancery records has revealed the extent to which these economic practices existed even in the Middle Ages. One of the most striking findings of this research is the relatively constant proportion of bad debts. Much eighteenth-century moral anxiety around indebtedness had less to do with the presumed novelty of extending retail credit to customers than with the increasing "arms-length" nature of these transactions. Studies of internal migration in the seventeenth century suggest that as much as 80 percent of the population lived outside their counties of origin in the period before the Civil Wars. Although rates of migration between rural counties declined afterwards because of the operation of the Poor Laws, significant migration to London remained a feature of economic and social life. English shopkeepers and their customers were no longer connected by the traditional ties that bound rural communities together.

Retail credit contributes to the "velocity" of money – the rate with which it circulates in an economy – but it adds to the "money supply" only when it assumes the form of a negotiable instrument that circulates in lieu of cash until redeemed. For ease of discussion, contemporary negotiable instruments may be divided into those that originated in private debts, and those that represented the debts of the state. Monetization of state debt was one of the defining features of the Financial Revolution.

BILLS OF EXCHANGE AND PROMISSORY NOTES

Bills of exchange were the earliest form of paper money. First introduced in England in 1307, they were primarily used to handle international transactions between merchant houses. Transporting specie (gold and silver) across oceans to settle trading debts among merchant houses meant confronting grave danger and high transaction costs. From antiquity, bills of exchange were used to manage these risks.

Modern readers would recognize a bill of exchange as a check. If a merchant (the *drawee* of a bill) wanted to import goods, he would deposit money with a merchant banker (*drawer*), who in turn would sell him a bill. The merchant would then offer the bill to the exporter, usually a foreign merchant (*payee*), who could safely travel with it across open waters to his port of origin. Once back home (or, increasingly, in any trading center), he would present the bill to another merchant banker (the *accepter*), who would in turn settle it against the account he held with the original merchant banker (drawer). Most European bills took sixty to ninety days to mature, and were often negotiated at a discount. They were also subject to fluctuations in foreign exchange markets, as merchants found themselves with larger balances in one currency than in another or as they grew skeptical of the safety of the coinage of another realm.

Although early bills of exchange were not conceived as negotiable instruments (nor would they count in modern definitions of the money supply), they became negotiable in practice as entrepot (reexport) trade increased. Rather than returning to their home ports, merchants might well cash them in their next port of call, via the services of other merchant bankers or an exchange bank, such as the Wisselbank established in Amsterdam in 1609. By the seventeenth century, most merchant banks held substantial sums in all major currencies, and settled transactions with offsetting credits and debits.

Goldsmith bankers and scriveners, meanwhile, whether or not they served merchant communities, had issued receipts (known formally as "running cash notes") since the sixteenth century for the value of coins and metals left on deposit. These were promissory notes (promising repayment upon demand), of which the "bill of exchange" was simply the first commonly used and most sophisticated of these instruments. Ordinary promissory notes were also used in domestic transactions. While the majority of these instruments functioned like a check (made out to a specific individual), which entitled the drawer to redeem them for the value of gold or silver specified, increasingly they were written as "bearer" instruments and circulated until redeemed. In some instances, the drawer could partially redeem them, leaving it to the cashier to denote the residual value of the note. Although the circulation of promissory notes is most commonly associated with the seventeenth century, recent scholarship has confirmed their widespread presence in sixteenth-century economic life. In 1704, Parliament passed a statute confirming the negotiability of promissory notes – they were assumed to be negotiable without recourse to previous parties in the chain of endorsements – which had already been accepted in the common law. Henceforth even common laborers and domestic servants were often paid their wages in promissory notes, which increased the portion of the population that had contact with paper money. Even those who did not handle paper instruments could see the material consequences of their growth in the changing composition of the metallic coinage.

The size of the bills market was sufficient to throw the English monetary system into crisis in the 1690s. Military spending to fight the Nine Years War (1688–97) drove down the value of the English pound sterling on foreign exchanges by increasing the supply of pounds in London seeking corresponding bills of exchange payable in Amsterdam or Paris. Once the exchange rate differentials exceeded the transaction costs of transporting bullion, economic actors had an incentive to export silver from England. Some of this was accomplished by melting coin, but clipping soon proved rampant. By 1695, scholars estimate the average silver content of coins in circulation to be less than half the original mint weight. Gold had, in turn, risen in value by 40 percent, making the par conversion of gold guineas and pounds sterling unrealistic. Even after the recoinage, which introduced a bimetallic standard, the ratio of gold to silver prices in London was higher than in Paris or Amsterdam.

When Isaac Newton fixed the guinea at twenty-one shillings in 1717, he ensured that gold would continue to flow into England and silver out of it. The result, from the perspective of the ordinary Englishmen, was that silver coinage disappeared in the eighteenth century. Gold guineas remained in circulation, as did copper farthings, but silver shillings and silver pence became scarce. Pounds, shilling, and pence remained the "unit of account," so merchants' ledgers, family account books, and state revenue, expenditure, and debt remained denominated this way. Yet it was not until England's return to the gold standard after the Napoleonic Wars of the early nineteenth century that the traditional pre-decimal coinage returned to ordinary pocketbooks.

The most common paper money today, the banknote, represented the smallest portion of the money supply. The Bank of England, founded in 1694, was a joint-stock company with a royal charter. From the beginning, the Bank of England issued banknotes, which were promissory notes, pledging to pay the bearer on demand. The initial aim had been to help the Mint retire clipped coin, but the exigencies of war finance meant they were unable procure good coin from Treasury and were instead forced to redeem many of their notes for interest-bearing bills. From 1696 to 1759, the Bank issued banknotes only in denominations larger than £50. After 1759, the minimum was lowered to £10, and then to just £5 in 1793. It was not until the nineteenth century that the Bank would obtain a virtual monopoly on note issuance.

STATE DEBT, PAPER MONEY, AND THE STOCK MARKET

Other forms of paper money and paper credit were negotiable forms of state debt. Some of these dated from the Civil Wars and Interregnum, others even earlier, but an increasing number of new instruments appeared during the Financial Revolution of the early eighteenth century. Some of these, Exchequer bills and government tallies, represented large sums of money. Others, from lottery tickets to seamen's tickets, were for small sums.

Exchequer tallies, which had existed since the mid-twelfth century, were the most expensive way for the government to borrow. They represented receipts for advances made by cashiers and receivers of the various tax revenues, and paid the standard rate of interest (6 percent) initially and a gratuity (2 percent) to cover transaction costs. They were, in effect, the Treasury's equivalent of payday loans, as those making the advances were also in receipt of the eventual revenues and so could repay themselves. The Restoration Treasury Secretary, George Downing, had ensured that they were recorded numerically, which guaranteed some level of probity in their repayment. Before the gradual abolition of tax farming in the late seventeenth century, repayments of advances to smaller tax farmers had been subordinated to those of the cashiers, who often cashed the bills at a discount out of their own funds. In effect, Exchequer tallies were a relic from an earlier era of court borrowing. The Seven Years' War marked the end of this practice.

A related but distinct form of borrowing was the Exchequer bill (not to be confused with modern Treasury bills), which was introduced in 1696. Unlike banknotes, they were interest-bearing, but paid less than the 6–8 percent paid on tallies. Those who redeemed banknotes from the Bank of England in the wake of the recoinage received these bills instead. Over time, the Bank of England achieved a monopoly on their issuance and made a considerable profit on their sale and administration. They were negotiable and circulated widely; by 1738, the total value of Exchequer bills outstanding was over £2 million.

To establish the Bank of England in 1694 and to raise monies to finance the War of the Spanish Succession (1701–14), Parliament created life annuities (secured by the excise revenues) and inaugurated a series of lottery schemes. Unlike modern lotteries, the earliest English lotteries were far more analogous to a government loan than a gambling operation. Prizes were comparatively small and the cost of the blank tickets was refunded over a fixed period by redeeming coupons attached to them. Lottery tickets, including the detachable coupons, circulated widely and could be used in commercial transactions or as payment of wages. By the same token, seamen's tickets (for wages earned at sea) circulated in port towns as paper money.

Parliament realized quickly that "negotiability" – the ability to trade or redeem annuities or the ease or difficulty with which interest on Exchequer bills could be assigned and collected – carried a premium, which could, in turn, reduce interest payments. The Bank of England began to manage these "conversions" to redeemable debt instruments after 1717. It was only a matter of time before the directors of the bank saw the opportunity to convert government debt directly into equity in the company.

JOINT-STOCK COMPANIES AND THE GOVERNMENT DEBT

The English stock market dated from the 1680s, when it functioned chiefly to attract venture capital. Over time, the Bank of England and its two principal competitors, the East India Company and the South Sea Company, came to manage the state debt as they negotiated deals to convert redeemable annuities and other long-term debt instruments into stock. The Bank and the two rival trading companies needed cash (the interest payment on the debts) to conduct their operations and to pay dividends, while Parliament needed a convenient mechanism for retiring expensive debts as interest rates fell after 1710. The terms of the deals were so favorable that they helped to prime the South Sea Bubble of 1720 (see chapter 35, "Politics").

One somewhat perverse outcome of the crisis was the Bubble Act of 1720, which prevented firms without royal charters from organizing themselves as joint-stock companies. Until its repeal in 1825, this legislation effectively limited the English stock market to the Bank of England, South Sea Company, East India Company, Royal African Company, Royal Exchange Assurance Corporation, London Assurance Corporation, and a handful of other companies. One consequence, however, was that after 1720, a wide segment of the population (including widows) owned shares.

UNPRECEDENTED SCRUTINY

Not all contemporaries welcomed the new species of paper money, nor did they uncritically accept that financial innovation and the expansion of paper credit were beneficial to society. The lapse of the Restoration Licensing Acts in 1695 meant that government policy, especially the management of the public finances, was open to comment in a way that it had not been since the Civil Wars and Interregnum. Fiscal and financial innovation was subject to unprecedented scrutiny by polemicists working for both political parties, by essayists and novelists (many of whom had well-known political affiliations), and by wider members of the reading public. Far more than the structural changes – the failure of bimetallism and with it the ultimate adoption of a de facto gold standard and the growth of paper money – it was that scrutiny, awareness, and self-reflection, in which David Hume himself participated, that gave eighteenth-century money and the monetary economy its distinctive stamp. Traditional money was, in effect, less often seen than heard.

NOTES

1 David Hume, *Political Essays*, ed. Knud Hakkonssen (Cambridge: Cambridge University Press, 1994), pp. 116–17.

2 The figures in this section were kindly provided by Michael F. Suarez, S.J.

CHAPTER 32

Nationalism

Clement Hawes

> NA'TION. *n.s.* [*nation*, Fr. *natio*, Latin.] A people distinguished from another people; generally by their language, original, or government.
>
> A *nation* properly signifies a great number of families derived from the same blood, born in the same country, and living under the same government. *Temple.*

"Patriotism," Samuel Johnson famously observed in 1775, "is the last refuge of a scoundrel" (Boswell, *Life*, 2:348). No wonder that this remark is among his most widely quoted one-liners: elective politics continues to provide an endless parade of con men wrapped in the sanctifying flag of one nation or another. Specialists in the British eighteenth century will recognize that "Patriotism" here refers not merely to a professed love for country as such, but to a particular brand of oppositional politics during the 1770s. In this case, however, abstracting Johnson's quip from its original context does not badly distort his views. Although Boswell insists that Johnson's target was "false patriotism" only (Boswell, *Life*, 1:424), the observation resonates tellingly with his broader engagement with the politics of nationalism. For Johnson, the politics of national self-love was an opportunity for something potentially more disturbing than the rise of a cynical politico: a mobilization of "the people" that risked shrinking universal moral horizons to the boundaries of a single nation. In resisting this nationalist tendency Johnson often embraced cosmopolitanism: though the word was not used in the eighteenth century, the notion is captured in the title of Oliver Goldsmith's work of 1762, *The Citizen of the World.*

ENGLISH LITERARY CULTURE

Johnson's relation to nationalism is, at best, wary and ambiguous. His most notable achievements are linked to the development of a vernacular culture in eighteenth-century Britain. His most famous works are formidable contributions to English literary culture: English lexicography (*A Dictionary of the English Language*); the English periodical essay (the *Rambler*, *Idler*, and *Adventurer* essays); English scholarship (his Shakespeare edition); and the history of English literature (*Lives of the Poets*). Along with journalism, the novel is the genre of print culture that scholar Benedict Anderson describes as having enabled the creation of nationhood by its *imagining* for its readers a vast social organism – a national community – synchronized according to a shared and secular calendar. Johnson, who excelled in the new genres that print culture generated, likewise wrote a short novel, *Rasselas*.

In each of the examples above, however, Johnson severely qualifies the specifically *national* importance of the genre. He always acknowledges both the faults and the international borrowings of even the best English poets. Appalling and enraging some of his contemporaries, he pointedly balances praise of Shakespeare with a sharp-edged account of his failures. *Rasselas* is set in Abyssinia, and features Coptic Christian characters aware of European depredations: a resetting, as it were, of what Anderson calls the "imagined community" as global. Johnson's essays, moreover, often argue against imperialism as well as subtler modes of national aggrandizement. Both "An Introduction to the Political State of Great-Britain" and "Observations on the Present State of Affairs" (1756) – powerful essays published in the *Literary Magazine* – give a scathing account of recent British imperial history at the beginning of the Seven Years' War (1756–63; see chapter 46, "War"). And Johnson, despite expressing concern in the preface to the *Dictionary* about the encroachment of French syntax among the fashionable, was after all no linguistic xenophobe: he ultimately welcomes, as so many naturalized citizens, the many foreign loanwords that English has absorbed. His dig about modish indulgence in a Frenchified English syntax is a jab at the Grand-Tour ethos of Francophilia, still widespread among the elite across Europe and Russia. Among Johnson's definitions of *national* in the *Dictionary*, after all, is "Bigotted to one's country." Johnson was not thus bigoted.

This level of political foresight is remarkable. Johnson, however, often manages a further balancing act: to *combine* cosmopolitan values with some of the internally progressive and egalitarian tendencies of nationalism as regards the common people. In his first definition of *national*, he picks up precisely this angle: "Publick; general; not private; not particular." In "The Bravery of the English Common Soldiers" (1760) – a topic open to a sentimental treatment – Johnson attributes the bravery in battle of English commoners to their uppity insubordination: "insolence in peace is bravery in war" (*Works*, 10:284). Johnson has no truck with the exceptionalist theme of "English liberty" as an explanation: "liberty" for the English poor, as he notes, amounts merely to "the choice of working or starving," a choice to be found among the poor in every country (*Works*, 10:431, 283).

Taking the full measure of Johnson's political and intellectual achievement requires a better sense of the specific ways in which eighteenth-century nationalism had been articulated. A full-blown ethnic nationalism was not yet a major force in the eighteenth century. Nationalism as populism – in the form of British nativism – was usually opposed, not very productively, to a cosmopolitanism that was aloof and elitist. Against the background of this conceptual deadlock we get Johnson's attempt to elaborate the potential of each simultaneously. Johnson's cosmopolitan nationalism – a hard-earned paradox – comes into focus as the simultaneous critique of actually existing forms of nationalism on the one hand and cosmopolitanism on the other.

JOHNSON'S CRITICAL COSMOPOLITANISM

We see Johnson's political breadth and acuity first in his stringently minimal universalism, one of his signature themes. At the very beginning of his career, for instance, he stakes out a universalist position in the preface to his translation of Father Jerome Lobo's *Voyage to Abyssinia*. There Johnson writes, "wherever human nature is found, there is a mixture of vice and virtue, a contest of passion and reason; and … the Creator doth not appear partial in his distributions" (*Works*, 15:3–4). This attention to the universal does not in any way deny wide variations in local manners. Conceding such differences, it nevertheless assumes a stable range of human potential and motives. Johnson insists on a worldwide capacity for basic rationality, a capacity realized only in the struggle with an equally universal tendency to succumb to passion. This always precarious rationality is explicitly not limited to "Western" horizons. As late as 1775, in *Taxation No Tyranny*, Johnson continued to maintain that "Humanity is very uniform" (*Works*, 10:429).

Johnson's finely shaded engagement with an often elitist cosmopolitanism can likewise be seen in his approach to appropriating the Greek and Roman classics. During the eighteenth century, a gentleman's education was designed to provide a knowledge of the classics (see chapter 20,

"Education"). This persistent cultivation of social distinction played out, predictably enough, as a denigration of local and vernacular cultures everywhere in relation to the classics: the cultures of ancient Greece and Rome were held to be superior to the cultures of modern England and France. As a middle-class student, young Johnson was unable to complete his baccalaureate degree at Oxford. He nevertheless knew the classics intimately – he eventually received an honorary doctorate from Oxford – and, like John Milton, Alexander Pope, Thomas Gray, Christopher Smart, and many others, he himself wrote several poems in Latin. Johnson's two most famous poems, *London* (1738) and *The Vanity of Human Wishes* (1749), are both brilliant rewritings of poems by the Roman satirist Juvenal.

The Roman classics had constituted a shared European culture throughout the medieval period, when the empire of Christendom tied the continent together – the classics did not belong to any nation. The clerisy had made up a creamy layer of medieval Christendom, an empire based on religious community, and ecclesiastical Latin had served to unify an international elite. As Ernst Robert Curtius shows in *European Literature and the Latin Middle Ages* (1948), a cultural cohesion had also been constructed around the *topoi* – the commonplaces that linked medieval literature throughout Europe back to the classics. When the Protestant Reformation shattered this continent-wide community of faith, the conflicts between laity and clergy over Latin, and translations thereof, established the Protestant and proto-nationalist ramifications of vernacular print culture. And as much as he appreciated the literary value of classical literature, Johnson had little use for its social role as so much fossilized cultural capital. A bookseller's son, Johnson enthusiastically embraced Britain's eighteenth-century bourgeois public sphere. In addition to allowing various forms of vernacular culture to thrive, this vibrant public sphere constituted alert public opinion, empowered by its own literate rationality, as a political force to be reckoned with. Johnson attempted to leaven this vernacular and antielitist culture with the historical perspective that came from his knowledge of the classics.

JOHNSON'S CRITICAL NATIONALISM

What exactly one meant by "the nation" in Johnson's lifetime was surprisingly complex. Was it England? Did it include Wales, which had been conquered by England in the Middle Ages? Was it all of Great Britain, incorporating England, Wales, and Scotland, brought into being with the union of the Scottish and English Parliaments in 1707?

Johnson came of age as his country made its rugged transition from the dynastic state of England to the increasingly "national" state of Hanoverian Great Britain. Among the choices demanded by the times was the question of Jacobitism: Should one be loyal to the exiled Stuart family? Or to Parliament, the House of Hanover it established on the throne, and so to the nation as such? (See chapter 35, "Politics.") And if to the nation, which version of it? The ever-expanding national state? The reactionary absolutist dynasty? Those who remained loyal to James II and his Stuart heirs after 1688 were "Jacobites" (from Latin for James, *Jacobus*). Their political aims were illegal and so necessarily underground. There was a regional dimension to the conflict as well, a struggle over the Celtic (or "British") peripheries. Jacobites, who instigated major rebellions in 1715 and 1745, were especially strong in the Catholic redoubts of Ireland and in the Episcopalian Highlands of Scotland. Although Johnson has been suspected in a few quarters of having been a Jacobite, that view belies almost all of his written work. His obvious disaffection – especially his political and intellectual distance from the Hanoverian court and the Whig ministries before the 1760s – has fueled this dubious speculation.

Although Johnson does seem to flirt with Jacobite rhetoric in his early satire, *Marmor Norfolciense* (1739), he does so in a way consistent with his usual misgivings about the military-fiscal state – capable, through deficit financing, of sustained warfare – and the drawbacks of its standing professional army. Even this piece, moreover, mocks monarchs in general (and not George II only) as fundamentally committed to neglecting the welfare and good opinion of posterity. *Marmor Norfolciense* likewise lists "pretenders" – Stuart claimants to the throne – in a catalogue of absurd trivia with which the sitting monarch is preoccupied: hardly a Jacobite talking point, if one is hoping for political momentum. A clear distance from absolutist politics can be seen in Johnson's stinging emphasis on public accountability in the following ironic passage, also written in 1739: "Unhappy would it be for men in power, were they always obliged to publish the motives of their conduct. What is power but the liberty of acting without being accountable?" (*Works*, 10:63). Johnson's point in *A Compleat Vindication of the Licensers of the Stage* is that the prevailing Whig court and ministry, by suppressing politically unfriendly stage plays, are behaving like the absolutist governments to which they are the supposed alternative. From this progressive angle, Johnson hammers Prime Minister Robert Walpole and the Hanoverian court without in any way enhancing the essentially charismatic appeal of a Stuart dynasty known, above all, for its stiff-necked absolutism.

FOLKLORIC NATIONALISM

We see Johnson's effort to clarify the "which nation?" problem a decade later, as he responded to the stirring of folkloric nationalism among his contemporaries. Thomas Gray, William Collins, William Blake, and Johnson's friend Oliver Goldsmith were some of the famous poets who participated in this trend. This emerging cultural nationalism, often discussed as an aspect of early Romanticism, depended on rounding up detritus from the past – popular antiquities now discovered (or sometimes invented) as "national." Hence the widespread antiquarian collection of local artifacts and their recasting – however plural or mixed their provenance – as purified national symbols: ballads, folk tales, superstitions, proverbs, legends, and so on. In the examples of Gray's "Elegy Written in a Country Church-Yard" and Goldsmith's "Deserted Village" there is also a marked turn to the rural countryside, and so to the illiterate and normally invisible common people. That "heterogeneous" thing, *the people* (as Johnson said), was being invoked as a unitary bearer of an essentialized national identity and character: for him, a bridge too far.

As various writers began to celebrate all things folkish over and against the classics, an equation was made between folk culture and literary authenticity. That which was strictly homegrown – such was the argument – was not mediated by, or dependent on, the classics. In this sense there was a powerful desire for a specifically national brand of "originality." *Unchosen* limitations in particular became romanticized, producing a fad of lionizing uneducated "peasant poets." After the Union of 1707, the Celtic peripheries, especially Scotland, were likewise mined for antiquities that were simultaneously Celtic and "British" in a newly inclusive sense. Gray arrives at a robust celebration of Britishness in his poem "The Bard" (1757), in which a defiant Welsh bard, though defeated by the army of Edward II, prophesies a glorious cultural future for "Britannia's issue," starting with the Welsh Elizabeth Tudor – better known as Queen Elizabeth.

THE INVENTION OF TRADITION

An investment in all things Gothic began to prevail in certain cultural domains. Anything primitive – pitted against the theme of "progress" – could thus be celebrated as "original." In fact, one could simply *make up* primitive origins: hence the pattern of a nationalist "invention of tradition." If an early rival to the classical epic poets did not exist – a British Homer – then he would have to be invented. James Macpherson, starting in 1760, obliged with the famous "Ossian" hoax, in which he published supposed translations of ancient epic poems and credited them to the third-century Scottish bard Ossian. Macpherson published English "translations" of two epics and a host of poetic fragments. Johnson's debunking of Macpherson in *A Journey to the Western Islands of Scotland* (1775) – "I believe [the poems] never existed in any other form than that which we have seen. The editor, or author, never could shew the original" (*Works*, 9:118) – was not an expression of anti-Scots bigotry. Johnson was extremely critical, across the board, of trafficking in supposed folkloric essences, and he remained aloof from the sentimental overestimation of ballads during the ballad revival. He stakes out a deliberately cosmopolitan nationalism that remains profoundly resistant to the xenophobia, ethnocentrism, essentialism, and sheer bad faith so often accompanying bourgeois mythmaking around the *folk*.

PATRIOTISM

Johnson knew that such national mythmaking tended to promote irrational feelings on a dangerous scale, often of organic connection or kinship, which potentially sets the stage for an equally xenophobic reaction to those deemed "outside" the national brotherhood. In *The Patriot* (1774), Johnson attempted to reclaim the term *patriotism* from the Wilkites. Johnson was critical of the radical John Wilkes – the "scoundrel" of our point of departure – for, among other things, equating patriotism with his own venomous rabble-rousing against immigrant Scots in England and French settlers in Quebec. Johnson disliked Wilkes's libertine character, but his central disagreement with him revolved around Britain's escalating conflict with the rebelling American colonists. Of them – George Washington, Thomas Jefferson, and the rest – Johnson, an early critic of British involvement in the slave trade, writes unforgettably that "we hear the loudest yelps for liberty among the drivers of negroes" (*Works*, 10:454).

Samuel Johnson – once both celebrated and disparaged as the definitive little-Englander – appears in the *Dictionary of Global Culture* edited by Kwame Anthony Appiah and Henry Louis Gates, Jr. (1997); the figure once embraced by nationalists is now claimed by the cosmopolitans. Certainly his literary achievements alone warrant attention in such an enlarged arena, but it must be recognized as well that he self-consciously contributed to the development of a vernacular culture with global rather than merely national horizons of concern.

CHAPTER 33

Philosophy

Fred Parker

PHILO'SOPHY. *n.s.* [*philosophie*, Fr. *philosophia*, Latin.]
1. Knowledge natural or moral.

> I had never read, heard nor seen any thing, I had never any taste of *philosophy* nor inward feeling in myself, which for a while I did not call to my succour. *Sidney.*

Samuel Johnson was no systematic philosopher but, like many of the writers and thinkers of his age, he was inevitably engaged in discussions that make sense in a philosophical context. The questions that exercised eighteenth-century British philosophers – especially regarding the basis of our knowledge and the foundation of our moral sense – echoed throughout the culture as a whole. Two figures above all, John Locke and David Hume, provide a starting point for any discussion of philosophy in the eighteenth century.

LOCKE

John Locke published *An Essay concerning Human Understanding* in 1690, and for the next hundred years this work provided the dominant framework in Britain for thinking about knowledge and the mind. This was true not only of intellectuals who read Locke's work firsthand, but also of the more general readership: the principles of his thinking became the common currency of essays and of novels. Locke's influence was great, but to speak only of *influence* may be misleading. Lockean thought was widely diffused and assimilated because it synthesized ways of thinking that meshed with the wider culture. Among these were the gradual erosion of religious certainties, the rise of scientific inquiry, the conception of society as an aggregate of individuals, and the wish to understand and accommodate conflicts of opinion rather than fighting them out.

What Locke did was to ask *how* we know what we think we know, and to make that epistemological question the foundation of all further inquiry. Locke argued that the mind does not come hardwired with "innate ideas" or truths self-evident to reason – otherwise young children would know much more than they appear to, and beliefs would not differ between individuals and across cultures as widely as they do. Instead, he insisted, all our knowledge is based on nothing other than the data of sense-experience and our reflections on those data. The mind is a "dark room," or *camera obscura*, with "some little openings" through which "*Ideas* of things without" enter to become the building blocks of our experience.[1] Or, to use Locke's more famous metaphor, the mind is "white paper" (2.1.2), or a *tabula rasa*, which must be written on by our senses. The emphasis on *experience* – in Greek, *empeiria* – has led many to call Locke's philosophy *empiricism*.

This attention to experience, as Locke recognized, opens a gap between the mind and the world. Our knowledge concerns our *ideas* of things, rather than things themselves. (Lockean philosophy was sometimes called "the way of ideas.") This distinction matters, because most of our ideas do not directly resemble anything in the object to which they refer, but have what we would now call a large subjective component. Our ideas of color, for example, are conditioned by our organs of vision, and a person with jaundice or with color blindness sees *differently*, but not necessarily inaccurately. Moreover, ideas get connected together in the mind; these connections become habitual; and, although they may correspond to connections that often appear out in the world, they may also be accidental, freakish, and random. In his chapter on "the association of ideas," Locke calls this a form of madness, but he thinks it occurs very commonly.

Locke further problematized knowledge by focusing on the role of language. If the link between the world and our ideas is not straightforward, neither is the further link between our ideas and the words we use. Words *should* stand for "clear and distinct ideas" (3.10.2) in the mind of the person using them, but Locke gives a powerful account of the many forces that make this difficult. Some thinkers, for instance, adopt mystifying jargon, and many others use words in a vague or empty way, without really possessing the ideas that they stand for. Then there is the messily metaphorical tendency of language itself, as well as my too-hasty assumption that my words stand for the same ideas in your mind as they do in mine. And words for general ideas – *man*, say – easily mislead us into imagining that we have some knowledge of the real essence of man, when in truth our ideas *never* reach to the essences or substances that (we may suppose) underlie the phenomena of experience.

Locke's work influenced and reinforced various tendencies in eighteenth-century thought. It set firm limits to the powers of understanding, and gave reasons to believe that deep philosophical speculations about ultimate realities were necessarily fruitless or empty: the proper sphere of understanding was the world of experience and practice. This harmonized perfectly with the new experimental emphasis in modern science (see chapter 37, "Science and technology"). Newton had discovered the laws that governed what gravity *did*, without, he insisted, needing any hypothesis as to what gravity *was*. It also accorded with the attitude famously epitomized at the end of Voltaire's *Candide* (1759), where Candide puts metaphysics aside in favor of more immediate and practical claims: "that's all very well said, but we must cultivate our garden."

But this could also be seen as emphasizing the material and practical against the claims of imaginative speculation or ideal value in a way that was reductive or philistine – or, at least, as underwriting eighteenth-century individualism, with its assumption that the bonds connecting discrete individuals were likely to be contractual or commercial. A new emphasis on the individual could readily be drawn from Locke's alertness to the particularity and subjectivity of experience. Laurence Sterne's famously eccentric novel *Tristram Shandy* (1759–67), where individual experience is often so singular as scarcely to be communicable in language, takes this to one extreme, and invokes Locke as its intellectual godfather with a teasing irony that hovers between tribute and critique. Individualism was fostered in a different but related way by Locke's political theory in the *Second Treatise of Government* (1690), which makes the legitimacy of government conditional on its ability to protect the individual's natural rights to life, liberty, and property.

Johnson engaged with many of these various tendencies, some potentially conflicting, in Lockean thought. He loathed "Whiggism," which he aggressively declared to be the "*negation of all principle*" (Boswell, *Life*, 1:431). Yet, like many of his contemporaries, he shared Locke's mistrust of "enthusiasm," where the warmth or intensity of a conviction becomes a reason for maintaining it. The great project of Johnson's *Dictionary* is Lockean in its perception of how crucially language is the instrument of thought, as also in its attempt to fix the precise meanings of words – yet Johnson sees much more clearly than Locke how the fluid fertility of language resists that attempt, and Johnson affirms the vitality of that resistance even as he deplores it. His prose style, too, insists on structure and discrimination, and yet also advertises its own discursive excess, its energetic activity of mind. Where Locke locates real knowledge in the world of particulars, Johnson regularly seeks generality – in language, in thought, and in literature. Yet he characteristically brings ambitious ideas and expansive formulations to the test of actual, lived, particular experience, often with destructive, debunking intent. At his most interesting, however, he generates a dynamic tension, an ongoing dialectic, from the difficult, unstable, imperfect fit between the world and the mind.

Not until Immanuel Kant's *Critique of Pure Reason* (1780) and the writings that followed – mediated in Britain by Samuel Taylor Coleridge in particular – was there a philosophically substantial challenge to Locke's model of the mind. Kant argued that the mind was not a blank slate but an *active* partner with the world in the construction of experience and knowledge. Such a view was naturally congenial to those Romantic writers who emphasized the *creativity* of the mind – something most clearly evident in the creative arts and in the notion of original "genius," a word that acquired new meanings during the period. This stood opposed to the more usual eighteenth-century emphasis, largely shared by Johnson, on the artwork as representational or mimetic, grounded in and referring itself to experience of the world.

HUME

In his *Treatise of Human Nature* (1739–40), and again in his more widely read *Enquiry concerning Human Understanding* (1748), David Hume developed Lockean empiricism into a radical skepticism about the rationality of our beliefs – not skepticism in the layman's sense of doubting improbable stories, but a philosophical skepticism, which questions the grounds on which we presume to know anything at all.

I believe that fire warms, Hume argues, or that there is an external world, because previous experiences have habituated me to expect more experiences of the same kind – but, he maintains, there is nothing rational in such expectation. It is not knowledge, strictly speaking, but a *feeling* induced by habit. Causal connections are never apparent in experience, only what Hume calls "constant conjunctions" of events – such as the perception of fire followed by the sensation of warmth. The world of experience is structured and held together by contingent associations of ideas that we do not know to be grounded in the nature of things, although their familiarity often disguises this truth from us.

Hume also applied a version of this skepticism to moral perceptions. My belief that murder is bad is not *knowledge* – for where in the objective act or fact of killing is this badness to be found? – but is an expression of the *feeling* that murder produces in me. Morality, according to Hume, lies in the eye of the beholder, and that many people agree in seeing murder the same way is useful but does not alter the case. It is a matter of feeling or *sentiment*, not cognition.

Hume argued this position with a brilliance that exercises professional philosophers to this day. He also teased his readers with the question of how much this theoretically radical skepticism matters. In one sense it leaves everything as it was: to discover that my beliefs about fire or murder are not rational does not mean I need to give them up. The more rational Hume demonstrates skepticism to be, the less, he cheerfully acknowledges, it can influence belief or practice. Yet his writings also suggest that an understanding that there can be no justification for how we live may lead us to live our lives with a difference – more lightly, tolerantly, sociably, and ultimately pleasurably – since reason can offer no legitimate bar to our desires.

This implication opposes itself to many versions of Christian doctrine. Hume's notorious essay "Of Miracles" (section 10 of *An Enquiry concerning Human Understanding*) set out to destroy the rationality of belief in testimony to miraculous events – and so, by implication, the rationality of belief in crucial parts of the Bible. He also advanced devastating arguments against the rationality of inferring an ordering Providence from the traces of order in the world as we experience it, and offered instead a *Natural History of Religion* (1757), which finds the origin of belief in Providence in the fears of primitive mankind.

Here Hume did seem to be writing polemically, and it was often as an antireligious writer that his contemporaries either vilified or applauded him. His work pressed acutely on two pressure points of eighteenth-century thought: is rational argument the potential support or the inevitable enemy of religious belief? And how much of common moral decency will remain if religious sanctions and rational justifications are stripped away?

Johnson's sensitivity to these pressure points was the greater for the strong skeptical tendency in his own thought, as witnessed in *Rasselas* (1759), where no rational basis can be found for preferring one form of life over another. Johnson attacked Hume, however, on every possible occasion. One large element in these attacks was the belief that Hume – "a vain man" (Boswell, *Life*, 1:444) – took too flattering a view of human nature, and in particular of human *sentiment*. Hume's argument that morality was a matter of sentiment, arising from our natural, involuntary sympathy with the feelings of others, allied itself with more overtly "sentimental" strains in eighteenth-century thought and literature that placed virtue primarily in natural feeling, especially sympathetic feeling, rather than in principled, deliberate action. These strains of thought went far beyond Hume in questioning the value of (modern) civilization, affirming the childlike and "primitive," promoting a new-modeled culture of sensibility, or cultivating forms of lament over, or retreat from, the corrupting world of action. All these tendencies come together, for example, in the explosively influential writings of Jean-Jacques Rousseau. Johnson vigorously opposed such ideas. No man is naturally good, no more than a wolf, he insisted (Boswell, *Life*, 5:211) – polemically associating himself with an alternative, tough-minded tradition of moral thought that was deeply suspicious about purity of motive and natural goodness. He urged instead a disillusioned knowledge of the dark recesses of the heart, and the corresponding importance of civilization and education.

ENLIGHTENMENT?

The eighteenth century is often described as the age of the "Enlightenment." There was no single coherent school of thought or group of thinkers to whom this term applies, and its borders are exceptionally fuzzy; nevertheless, it is hard to do without it, and it corresponds to something fundamental about how philosophy in this period was perceived and how it perceived itself. In his essay "What Is Enlightenment?" (1784), Kant saw its motto as *sapere aude* – "dare to think" – and described it as the intellect's coming-of-age. Those are helpful pointers. Enlightenment thinking affirms the exercise of a free critical intelligence, unprejudiced by any received wisdom on religion, morality, or society. (The status of such "prejudice" was a key question in contemporary debate; "freethinking" or "free inquiry" was often code for an attack on Christianity.) There are exceptions, but in its main tendencies it was humanist, emancipatory, rationalist, incisive, implicitly democratic, and – especially in France, the land of the *philosophes*, of Voltaire – sharply critical of the political and religious establishment. It partly drew on the model of scientific inquiry, "natural philosophy," which was itself often regarded as an aspect of the Enlightenment, and it shared with science the sense of a confident modernity, emerging from the benighted past into the new republic of light and reason.

Johnson, like Jonathan Swift and Alexander Pope before him, mistrusted such a stance. He spoke of contemporary French intellectuals with a calculated dismissiveness. Instead of building their thought "upon the discoveries of a great many minds," he said, they "proceed upon the mere power of their own minds; and we see how very little power they have" (Boswell, *Life*, 1:454). This is the most important objection: a *philosophe* presumes to think for himself, starting with a clean slate, as a free, confident, individual intelligence. For Johnson, by contrast, philosophical thinking is a more collaborative enterprise, generative of complexity rather than clarity, counterbalancing one partial truth against another, and working with convictions that need to be recalled afresh and reconnected with practice rather than newly discovered. This describes the manner of his own periodical essays, which typically travel across different points of view, and where the reader is more likely to feel exercised than enlightened.

The counter-Enlightenment tendencies in this manner of thinking were to be urgently promoted by Edmund Burke – in this respect Johnson's pupil – in his *Reflections on the Revolution in France* (1790). Burke there mounts an eloquent defense of "prejudice" against the dangerously self-confident, freethinking rationalism of such radicals as Tom Paine, who in *The Rights of Man* (1791) replied to Burke with what he presented as a straightforward, demystifying common sense. This sharp polarity between Burke and Paine, intensified by political crisis, reveals a fault line that had run right through the century, beginning with Swift's satirical parodies of "modern" rationalism.

It would be wrong, however, to see Johnson as simply entrenched, like the reactionary Burke of the 1790s, on one side of this line. In *Rasselas* (1759) – in one sense Johnson's most philosophical work – the prince sets out like a child of the Enlightenment, an unprejudiced free intelligence, to survey the world and make an impeccably rational choice of the best way of living, the form of life that will be most conducive to happiness. That his quest proves to be an impossible one – "the more we inquire, the less we can resolve" (*Works*, 16:99) – reflects ironically on the naiveté of such aspiration, the dream of a final, authoritative understanding that would underwrite a rational autonomy. Yet Johnson has too much sympathy with his hero's aspiration to be wholly amused by its failure. Rasselas sets out on his quest because "he thought it unsuitable to a reasonable being to act without a plan, and to be sad or chearful only by chance" (*Works*, 16:69), and this position is never repudiated, even though the quest it inspires is hopeless of success. Johnson acknowledges the real vacuum created by the spirit of free inquiry, insofar as it looked for rational justifications which it could not provide, even while it decisively abandoned received wisdoms or "prejudices." There is something peculiarly modern in the way that Rasselas starts from nowhere, with no "given" way of life or beliefs, a consumer in the supermarket of life, free to choose, and therefore without grounds for choice. Both the freedom and the insecurity speak of Johnson's responsiveness to the ground broken, and the earth scorched, by Enlightenment inquiry.

Such *responsiveness* – often antagonistic, always dialogic – is intrinsic to Johnson's philosophical thinking, as we have seen. It was the debates and conversations of the eighteenth-century club or salon that provided both occasion and model for a practice of philosophy far removed from the academic treatise (see chapter 16, "Clubs"). To see Johnson in the context of these wider debates is therefore often crucial to understanding.

NOTE

1 John Locke, *An Essay concerning Human Understanding*, ed. Peter H. Nidditch (Oxford: Oxford University Press, 1975), 2.11.17.

CHAPTER 34

Poetry

David F. Venturo

PO'EM. *n.s.* [*poema*, Lat. ποίημα.] The work of a poet; a metrical composition.

A *poem* is not alone any work, or composition of the poets in many or few verses; but even one alone verse sometimes makes a perfect *poem*. *Benj. Johnson*.

Samuel Johnson never resolved his ambivalence to poetry, repeatedly evinced in his poems and criticism over a career spanning almost fifty years. Exquisitely sensitive to the medium, Johnson could be jarred by metrical irregularities, delighted by rhetorical grace, and gripped and enchained by imaginative power – what he tellingly calls "the force of poetry" (*Works*, 5:127) – such as when, as a boy, "he suddenly hurried upstairs to the street door that he might see people about him" after reading the ghost scene in *Hamlet* (*Miscellanies*, 1:158).

EXALTATION AND CONTEMPT

Poetry perplexed and divided Johnson. It could be the noblest of arts: "*Rhetoric* and *Poetry*," as he observed in the preface to *The Preceptor*, "supply Life with its highest intellectual Pleasures; and in the hands of Virtue are of great Use for the Impression of just Sentiments and illustrious Examples" (*Prefaces & Dedications*, p. 183). In the *Life of Milton*, the great lexicographer loftily defined poetry as "the art of uniting pleasure with truth, by calling imagination to the help of reason" (*Lives*, 1:282). And in the preface to his edition of Shakespeare, Johnson explained how the best poetry could "instruct by pleasing," whetting *and* sating "that hunger of imagination which preys incessantly upon life" by "exciting restless and unquenchable curiosity, and compelling him that reads [it] to read it through" (*Works*, 7:67, 83; 16:118).

By contrast, Johnson could – almost as peremptorily as the utilitarian philosopher Jeremy Bentham – dismiss poetry. Its purpose, he once told

Boswell, was purely aesthetic: "merely a luxury, an instrument of pleasure" (Boswell, *Life*, 2:351). If it could capture truth, it could also mire itself in "trifling fictions," as Johnson complained in his criticism of Milton's *Lycidas*, incongruously mingle fact and fiction, as in Alexander Pope's *Imitations of Horace*, and lose its bearings in tired "descriptions copied from descriptions ... traditional imagery, and hereditary similes" (*Lives*, 1:201). But the purely aesthetic nature of poetry could also cause Johnson to freight it with the highest expectations. If it is in fact "merely a luxury, an instrument of pleasure," then "it can have no value, unless when exquisite in its kind" (Boswell, *Life*, 2:351–2). In other words, practically useless, poetry had better delight supremely.

This extraordinary combination of exaltation and contempt, admiration and suspicion, helps account for the unusually high quality of Johnson's own verse, the relatively small quantity he wrote (enough to fill one volume in the Oxford and Yale editions) despite his remarkable fluency, and the demanding standards to which he subjected poetry in the moral essays, his edition of Shakespeare, and the *Lives of the Poets*. Furthermore, Johnson's criticism and poetic practice often conflict, as he says one thing and does another; his criticism itself sometimes asserts in one essay what it rethinks, reformulates, and even rejects, in another. In *Rambler* 168, for example, he criticizes Shakespeare for violating neoclassical standards of decorum; fourteen years later, in the preface to his edition of Shakespeare, he repeatedly rebuts such attacks by John Dennis, Thomas Rymer, Voltaire, and Pierre Corneille as "the petty cavils of petty minds" (*Works*, 7:65–6).

NEITHER AUGUSTAN NOR NEOCLASSICAL

In literary histories Johnson's poetry and criticism are typically classified as "Augustan" or "neoclassical," along with Jonathan Swift's, John Gay's, Alexander Pope's, and – to a degree – John Dryden's, but this is not entirely appropriate. In the *Lives of the Poets*, Johnson celebrates the rise of a couplet poetics that combines strength with grace and regularity, beginning in the work of the mid-seventeenth-century poets John Denham and Edmund Waller and reaching its perfection in Dryden. Johnson praises Dryden's contribution to English poetry by echoing the Roman biographer Suetonius: Dryden found the English literary Rome "brick, and he left it marble" (*Lives*, 2:155). Johnson closes his history of the couplet with Pope, any "further improvement of [whose] versification," Johnson warns, "will be dangerous," perhaps because it might lead to mannerism or metrical enervation (*Lives*, 4:79). Both Dryden and Pope are praised for "Genius" (*Lives*, 4:65–6), what we might now call imagination or creativity: Johnson pointedly concludes Pope's *Life* with the word (4:80).

But despite repeatedly celebrating the more predictable, harmonious returns afforded by the rhymes and caesuras of heroic couplets – iambic pentameter verses, rhyming *aabbcc* and so on – Johnson reserves his highest praise for the genius of the two English poets who wrote mostly in blank verse – unrhymed iambic pentameter – and before the advent of the vogue for correctness: Milton and Shakespeare. Of *Paradise Lost*, Johnson marvels, "Here is a full display of the united force of study and genius; of a great accumulation of materials, with judgement to digest, and fancy to combine them" (*Lives*, 1:289). And of Shakespeare he simply observes that he is "above all writers, at least above all modern writers, the poet of nature; the poet that holds up to his readers a faithful mirrour of manners and of life" (*Works*, 7:62). Johnson admits that, despite his strong preference for rhyme (without which "the musick of the English heroick line strikes the ear so faintly that it is easily lost"), he "cannot … wish that Milton had been a rhymer" (*Lives*, 1:294), and he commends Shakespeare's dialogue (mostly blank verse) as "level with life" and "scarcely … claim[ing] the merit of fiction" (*Works*, 7:64, 63). Johnson admires Milton and Shakespeare for avoiding – despite being poets, and thus writers of fiction – the "licentiousness of fiction" (*Lives*, 1:289), and esteems them as creative biographers or historians.

JOHNSON'S POETRY

Johnson tried his hand at a wide variety of poetic genres. In addition to his juvenilia, much of which is indebted to Dryden more than to Pope (his early couplet poems are varied with triplets and alexandrines), he wrote formal verse imitations (the political *London* and philosophical *Vanity of Human Wishes*); a neoclassical verse tragedy, *Irene*, in the manner of Joseph Addison's *Cato*; some excellent theatre prologues and one epilogue; a group of beautiful elegies and epitaphs; much drawing-room verse, mostly playful, some satiric; a substantial number of fine neo-Latin lyrics, including a series of poignant, deeply personal metrical prayers composed as his health worsened and his spirits flagged in his last years; and a handful of clean, terse, eloquent translations of Horace's odes, the earliest done in adolescence, the last less than a month before he died.

The Vanity of Human Wishes, his best-known and most accomplished poem, epitomizes the complexity of his poetry and poetics, and demonstrates why applying simple labels to him is dangerous. The poem is a neoclassical "imitation," a term Johnson defined as "A manner of translating looser than paraphrase, in which modern examples and illustrations are used for ancient, or domestick for foreign." This sort of imitation flourished in the late seventeenth and early eighteenth centuries. Johnson's *Vanity* imitates and updates Juvenal's Tenth Satire so that the Roman poet speaks as Johnson imagines he would were he living in mid-eighteenth-century England.

Johnson takes Juvenal's admonition, *When the gods wish to punish us, they grant our prayers*, and rewrites it, dialogically wringing from it a surprising new conclusion. Moreover, always an uneasy neoclassicist, he draws on other sources and inspirations, including the Hebrew book of Ecclesiastes, Boethius's late classical, quasi-Christian *Consolatio Philosophiae* (*c.* 524), and William Law's evangelical *Serious Call to a Devout and Holy Life* (1728). In addition, the poem's Augustan verse form (the heroic couplet) and metrics (scrupulously end-stopped with mostly medial caesuras, i.e., pauses after the fourth, fifth, and sixth syllables) mask decidedly un-Augustan technical features. Neoclassical or Augustan poetry, for example, is usually loosely organized into verse paragraphs connected by logical, rhetorical transitions similar to those in a prose essay. Dryden's *Religio Laici*, Swift's *Verses on the Death of Dr. Swift*, Gay's *Trivia*, and Pope's *Essay on Criticism* all follow this pattern. In Johnson, though, we see a shift from "marbles-in-a-bag" accretion to more organic structures which, by looking backward to the analogical conceits and recurring images of seventeenth-century Baroque and Metaphysical poetry, participate in the new "literature of sensibility," and look ahead to Romanticism. In *The Vanity*, for example, Johnson repeatedly uses images of fire and heat to emphasize the futility of extinguishing humanity's fervent desires. These ligaments are unlike anything found in the poetry of Swift, Gay, and Pope.

With such conceits Johnson also makes the "Drury-Lane Prologue" and the elegy "On the Death of Dr. Robert Levet" more structurally cohesive. The prologue, sixty-two lines long, repeatedly likens the history of English theatre from Shakespeare's time to David Garrick's to a series of dynasties or "Reign[s]" (lines 5, 26, 35, and 57), each more decadent than the last.[1] At the close, Johnson turns the tables by declaring the theatergoers to whom Garrick recited these lines the real "Tyrants" who rule over hapless playwrights, who are merely "Tools of Guilt," subject to the marketplace demands of fickle audiences (line 56).

The nine unpretentious quatrains of the Levet elegy are also organized around an extended, analogical conceit. Its first stanza grimly depicts humanity as prisoners sentenced to hard labor for life in a mine of hopeful self-deception, while their friends ("social comforts") die abruptly or gradually:

Condemn'd to hope's delusive mine,
As on we toil from day to day,
By sudden blasts, or slow decline,
Our social comforts drop away.
(lines 1–4)

Throughout this biographical and mythic poem, its hero, the dead Robert Levet, imaginatively restored to life by "affection's eye" (line 9), is both humble physician and questing knight, working in "misery's darkest caverns" (line 17), battling against disease and death. At the end of the poem, Johnson startlingly reverses its moral compass: death, the supposed enemy, suddenly, mercifully liberates Levet's enslaved soul from its bodily prison:

Then with no throbbing fiery pain,
No cold gradations of decay,
Death broke at once the vital chain,
And free'd his soul the nearest way.
(lines 33–6)

METAPHYSICS

The Vanity and the Levet elegy share another un-Augustan feature. Each is informed by a metaphysics, something regularly absent from the skeptical, empirical poetry of Swift and Pope ("What can we reason, but from what we know?")[2] but commonly present in the verse of later poets such as Edward Young, Christopher Smart, William Blake, William Wordsworth, and Samuel Taylor Coleridge. The skeptical finitude of the philosophers Thomas Hobbes and John Locke, reflected in their hostility to metaphysics – which they regarded as an intellectual Petri dish for the cultivation of personal madness, religious enthusiasm, and civil discord – was giving way by the 1740s to a philosophy that encouraged a new poetics of infinitude, vision, and expressionism, and endorsed the reality of a realm beyond the tangible. *The Vanity* and "Levet," both of which embody the religious and philosophical perspective of fideism, characterized by God's absence from humanity's perpetual dissatisfaction with the mundane world, and pointing toward God's presence in another, reflect this new poetics.

Finally, in *The Vanity of Human Wishes*, Johnson writes an imitation to end all Augustan imitations by dialogically refuting Juvenal. The answer to *What then should we ask for?* is not the combination of Stoic and Epicurean dispassion that the original Tenth Satire recommends. To Johnson, this goal is horrifying: "Must helpless Man, in Ignorance sedate, / Roll darkling down the Torrent of his Fate?" (lines 345–6). Rather, he proposes a Pauline pursuit of tempered emotions, of "Hope and Fear" (line 343) transmuted into something salubrious by "Love," "Patience," and "Faith" (lines 361–3). *The Vanity of Human Wishes* anticipates by a few years Bishop Robert Lowth's call in his *Lectures on the Sacred Poetry of the Hebrews* for a new poetics of passion. When Johnson's "Enquirer" (line 349) fervently asks what to pray for, the voice of "celestial Wisdom" (line 367) replies, *Pray passionately for the strength and insight wisely to regulate your passions.*

THE END OF IMITATION

Curiously, Johnson published no further neoclassical imitations after *The Vanity*, despite Boswell's observation that "he had them all in his head" (Boswell, *Life*, 1:193). Why not?

We can discover part of the answer in the *Life of Pope*, which reflects important changes in Johnson's poetics as he grew older. Imitation, he decided, violates canons of truth and authenticity: "Between Roman images and English manners there will be an irreconcilable dissimilitude, and the work will be generally uncouth and party-coloured; neither original nor translated, neither ancient nor modern" (*Lives*, 4:78). Imitations disturbingly mingle fact and fiction like John Milton's pastoral elegy *Lycidas* (1638), although Johnson finds Milton's poem worse because it confounds fiction with *sacred* truth. Tellingly, Johnson loved Pope's *Eloisa to Abelard* (1717) because it is domestic and biographical, and therefore immediately useful to readers in its truthfulness. If Pope in his imitations distances truth by mixing it with fiction, Shakespeare makes his plays, especially his romances, seem more real by "approximat[ing] the remote, and familiariz[ing] the wonderful" (*Works*, 7:65) – *approximating* here has its Latinate, etymological meaning of "bringing closer."

Johnson's demand for truth in poetry also clarifies his objections to the verse of his friends Thomas Warton and Thomas Percy, who participated in a "medieval revival":

Wheresoe'er I turn my View,
All is strange, yet nothing new;
Endless Labour all along,
Endless Labour to be wrong;
Phrase that Time has flung away,
Uncouth Words in Disarray:
Trickt in Antique Ruff and Bonnet,
Ode and Elegy and Sonnet.
("Lines on Thomas
Warton's Poems")

Johnson pronounces it *uncouth*, which he defines in the *Dictionary* as "odd; strange; unusual," one of the same adjectives he applies to Pope's *Imitations of Horace*. Thus Johnson, the supposed Augustan, shares concerns for authenticity with the German Romantic Friedrich von Schiller, who distinguished "sentimental" from "naive" poets – that is, sophisticated strivers after naturalness from those who, born to a tradition, cleanly, unself-consciously work within it. Unlike Pope, Johnson understood that, as historian J. G. A. Pocock observes, in the first age of self-conscious historicism, "the more thoroughly and accurately the process of [neoclassical] resurrection was carried out, the more evident it became that copying and imitation were impossible – or could never be anything more than copying and imitation."[3]

Finally, Johnson's reservations about imitations increased because, although they sometimes delighted the "man of learning" who could compare imitation and original, they could not appeal to the "common reader" who, unfamiliar with the original, judged poetry only by her or his "common sense … uncorrupted with literary prejudices" (*Lives*, 4:78, 184). This ideal common reader, who trusted his or her own responses instead of acquiescing to critics' preferences, became more important to Johnson as he grew older – for example, in his defense of Shakespeare's mingled dramas and his rejection of the neoclassical unities. Johnson tried to empower his readers by assuring them, "there is always an appeal open from criticism to nature" (*Works*, 7:67). Most famously, the common reader gave him a vehicle for raising objections to the irregular rhythms and rhyme schemes, closed idiom, complicated syntax, and sublime obscurity of William Collins's and Thomas Gray's Pindaric odes.

POETIC IDIOM

From the time he wrote his *Essay on Epitaphs* (1740), Johnson preferred an open idiom in elegies and epitaphs (classical epitaphs were usually written in elegiac meter, so he regularly conflated the two genres). Because epitaphs and elegies combine biography and theology by providing moral exempla and mourning the dead, their style, Johnson argued, should be simple, both to appeal to a broad audience and to avoid rhetorical embellishment. By the time of the *Life of Waller* (1779), he had decided that *all* religious poetry should be plain and unpretentious, since finite poetry can neither adequately praise nor describe by analogy an infinite and unknowable God: "The ideas of Christian Theology are too simple for eloquence, too sacred for fiction, and too majestick for ornament; to recommend them by tropes and figures, is to magnify by a concave mirror the sidereal hemisphere" (*Lives*, 2:53–4). Canons of truth are *never* to be violated by rhetorical decoration in sacred verse.

Late in life, Johnson favored a clean, open idiom for virtually *all* poetry. This explains his praise of Gray's "Elegy Written in a Country Church-Yard" and his dislike of Gray's and Collins's odes (despite his friendship with Collins). He repeatedly finds the odes affected, "laboured" (a favorite Johnsonian criticism), and hence unpleasing – and, for Johnson, "the end of poetry is to instruct by pleasing" (*Lives*, 4:122, 183; *Works*, 7:67). Gray writes like a man who is "tall by walking on tiptoe"; his poems have "too little appearance of ease and nature" (*Lives*, 4:183). Collins's "diction [is] often harsh, unskillfully laboured, and injudiciously selected" (*Lives*, 4:122). Like Thomas Warton, Collins "affected the obsolete when it was not worthy of revival," and indulged in syntax "out of the common order" (*Lives*, 4:122). Behind Collins's and Gray's practice lay their conviction (with which the Johnson of the *Lives* disagreed) that the language of poetry should be different from – that is, more elaborate and more complicated than – the language of prose. This debate over the language of poetry and prose would be renewed by Wordsworth and Coleridge a generation later in the preface to the second edition of *Lyrical Ballads* and in *Biographia Literaria*.

Many of Johnson's contemporaries, especially among the literati, were offended by his criticism of Gray and Collins. James Gillray's satiric cartoon, *Apollo and the Muses; Inflicting Penance on Dr. Pomposo, round Parnassus* (1783), epitomizes their outrage (see figure 24). In the long run, though, the consensus is with Johnson. The odes of Wordsworth, Coleridge, Keats, and Shelley have been judged better poems – more open in their diction, more relaxed in their style and syntax, and more philosophically interesting – than those of their eighteenth-century precursors. The directness and simplicity of Johnson's Levet elegy anticipate the Romantic poetry of Blake, Wordsworth, and Coleridge better than anything by Collins and Gray except "Elegy Written in a Country Church-Yard." Johnson's poems and literary criticism reveal a vigorous, engaged writer and honest, nuanced, occasionally contradictory thinker who relished the literary disputes of his age and contributed, sometimes surprisingly, to new directions in poetry and poetics.

NOTES

1 For text of Johnson's poems I have used Samuel Johnson, *The Complete English Poems*, ed. J. D. Fleeman, The English Poets Series (Baltimore, MD: Penguin Books, 1971. Reprint, New Haven, CT: Yale University Press, 1982), because the editor retains eighteenth-century spelling, punctuation, and capitalization.

2 Alexander Pope, *An Essay on Man*, in *The Twickenham Edition of the Poems of Alexander Pope*, ed. John Butt *et al.*, 11 vols. in 12. (New Haven, CT: Yale University Press, 1939–69), 3.1, epistle 1, line 18.

3 J. G. A. Pocock, *The Ancient Constitution and the Feudal Law: A Study in English Historical Thought in the Seventeenth Century: A Reissue with a Retrospect* (Cambridge: Cambridge University Press, 1987), p. 4.

CHAPTER 35

Politics

Steven Scherwatzky

PO'LITICKS. *n.s.* [*politique*, Fr. πολιτική.] The science of government; the art or practice of administring publick affairs.

Be pleas'd your *politicks* to spare,
I'm old enough, and can myself take care. *Dryden.*

When it comes to the study of eighteenth-century British politics, the barrier to entry can seem either deceptively simple or surprisingly difficult. At first glance an understanding of the period appears to be a straightforward matter of defining the terms *Whig* and *Tory*, the names of the two political parties through the eighteenth century. Yet definitions are hardly straightforward, especially considering there is good reason to wonder if the terms define anything at all; and if they do, their meaning changes significantly over the course of the era. In his essay "Of the Parties of Great Britain," David Hume admits that "to determine the nature of these parties is, perhaps, one of the most difficult problems that can be met with, and is a proof that history may contain questions as uncertain as any to be found in the most abstract sciences."[1]

Hume was not alone in struggling with this problem, which continues to frustrate students of the period today. These terms do not have exact modern equivalents, and it can be anachronistic, even misleading, to link them with current categories such as "liberal" or "conservative." But the frustration posed by Whig and Tory is only the beginning, as the terms permutate into *Hanoverian* and *Jacobite*, *Court* and *Country*, and the ever-vexatious *Patriot*, which can be applied, for good or ill, to all or none. Complicated twists and turns of policy, as new monarchs and ministries followed old, and supporters of one war opposed the next, make it difficult to figure out what the parties stood for.

THE EXCLUSION CRISIS

The terms *Whig* and *Tory* first came into prominence during the Exclusion Crisis of 1679–81, which involved a series of parliamentary efforts to block

James, Duke of York and brother to King Charles II, as the Stuart dynasty's heir to the throne. The motivation behind this attempt to alter the line of succession was largely religious: England was a Protestant country, where the king was the putative head of the Anglican state Church. The Stuarts had long been tainted by their association with Roman Catholicism, to which James converted in the 1660s. If James were to become king, said his critics, England would fall prey to papist influence (see chapter 11, "Anglicanism").

This is the controversy that gave rise to the two parties that would last long after the Exclusion Crisis had passed. *Whig*, derived from the word *Whiggamore*, which in the 1640s denoted rebellious Scottish covenanters (populist supporters of Presbyterianism over state-sanctioned Episcopacy), described those who supported the attempt to exclude James, Duke of York, in favor of James Scott, Duke of Monmouth, the illegitimate son of Charles II. *Tory*, which comes from an epithet applied in the 1640s to scurrilous Irish Roman Catholics, signaled those who supported the Duke of York's hereditary right to the throne. The origin of each word is significant, though derogatory and simplistic: Whigs challenge centralized state and religious authority; Tories embrace it. Though the effort to exclude the Duke of York from the throne ultimately failed, the terms *Whig* and *Tory* lived on.

THE GLORIOUS REVOLUTION

After the Exclusion Crisis passed and the Duke of York became King James II in 1685, the meanings of the terms shifted to reflect the new political situation. Now supporters of James II and the idea of a strong hereditary monarch were called Tories, and those who sought to limit the king's prerogative and grant greater authority to Parliament were called Whigs. When James worked to promote the Roman Catholic interest in England, parliamentary pressure forced him to abdicate the throne. The deal brokered by Parliament that brought William of Orange and his wife Mary, the Protestant daughter of James II, to the throne of England came to be known as the Glorious Revolution (1688). The revolution was deemed glorious because no blood was shed, and James II fled to exile in France. Despite the fact that there were Tories as well as Whigs who were unhappy with the king, the Glorious Revolution was not so glorious for Tories, who rightly saw it as a victory for Whig principles of limited monarchy.

The Glorious Revolution led to the passage of two landmark pieces of legislation, the Bill of Rights and the Toleration Act (1689), which respectively limited the king's power and provided greater religious freedom. But there were other important – some would say Whiggish – consequences as well, such as the establishment of the Bank of England (1694) and, eventually, the Act of Settlement (1701). These two developments would resonate throughout the eighteenth century. The Bank of England made possible the transition to a credit economy that helped finance foreign wars and manage the national debt (see chapter 31, "Money"), and the Act of Settlement would determine which family would sit on the English throne.

With the death of William III in 1702 came the accession of Queen Anne, the last of the Stuart monarchs. Unlike her Catholic father, James II, Anne was a devout Anglican and supporter of the Revolution. But her shifting party preferences eventually settled on firm Tory principles, celebrated most notably by Alexander Pope in his poem *Windsor-Forest* (1713): "Rich Industry sits smiling on the plains / And peace and plenty tell a Stuart reigns."[2] Yet the Tory celebration would not last long, as the death of Anne in 1714 led to a drastic change that brought the first of the Hanoverian monarchs to the throne of England.

THE HANOVERIANS

The Act of Settlement ensured that the Protestant succession – secured by the Bill of Rights – would go to the Hanoverian line, which produced the first three Georges. Now partisanship hardened and the ideas of Whig and Tory came into clearer focus, with still newer meanings. Whigs celebrated the Hanoverian succession along with the commercial opportunities and prospect of social mobility the Bank of England made possible. Many Tories, in contrast, remained devoted to the Stuarts, as well as to an older agrarian ideal and paternal social structure. Hume ventured a definition:

> A Tory, therefore, since the *revolution*, may be defined, in a few words, to be *a lover of monarchy, without abandoning liberty; and a partisan of the family of STUART*: as a Whig may be defined to be *a lover of liberty, though without renouncing monarchy; and a friend to the settlement of the PROTESTANT line.*[3]

George I, Elector of Hanover (a territory in Germany) and entirely unskilled and uninterested in English language and culture, became king of England upon Anne's death in 1714.

With George's accession also came the onset of Whig domination that would last forty-six years. During this time the Tories found themselves proscribed from political place and privilege. Various Whig ministries, especially that of Robert Walpole, sought to equate Tories with another group known as Jacobites (from the Latin *Jacobus*, or James). Jacobites sought to restore the exiled Stuart king James II and his heirs, James Edward Stuart, known as the Old Pretender, and Charles Edward Stuart, the Young Pretender (or Bonnie Prince Charlie), to the throne.

The Jacobite threat was more than just talk. The first major Jacobite uprisings occurred in 1715, and they continued intermittently until the defeat of Charles Edward Stuart at the Battle of Culloden in 1746. Perhaps because of his Toryism, Samuel Johnson has occasionally been linked with Jacobitism, but the evidence is scanty at best. Though a staunch monarchist, he thought as little of James II as he did of George II, and often expressed fear of the kind of civic upheaval any rebellion, Jacobite or otherwise, would produce.

THE RISE AND FALL OF WALPOLE

When Johnson first arrived in London in 1737, Robert Walpole had been the dominant political figure in the country for sixteen years, but he was beginning to lose his grip on power. As First Lord of the Treasury, he was the equivalent of a prime minister today. Walpole had been a Whig Member of Parliament since 1701, and enjoyed the confidence of both George I and George II. His greatest success had come in the wake of the South Sea Bubble crisis (1720), which involved the South Sea Company assuming a large portion of the national debt only to see the inflated value of its shares burst. Walpole's salvaging of the economy in the early 1720s gave him unprecedented political power. By the late 1730s, though, his Whig administration had come under fire from an energized opposition. Walpole found himself accused of corruption, beginning with protecting those responsible for the South Sea Bubble crisis with a range of financial improprieties; the alleged manipulation of elections; and an unwillingness to protect English interests against Spain in what became known as the War of Jenkins's Ear.

Walpole sought to consolidate his power by equating Tories with disloyal Jacobites, but the charges of corruption directed at Walpole produced a reconfiguration of interests. In his *Dissertation upon Parties* (1735), Henry St. John, first Viscount Bolingbroke, announced the death of party: politics, he argued, had become a question of virtue versus corruption. An opposition "Country party," composed of Tories and discontented Whigs and also known as the "Patriot" coalition, pitted itself against a "Court party," consisting largely of those who enjoyed the fruits of Walpole's patronage system. Johnson entered the fray as a Tory Patriot, contributing the anti-Court poem *London* (1738) as well as two political pamphlets, *Marmor Norfolciense* (1739) and *A Compleat Vindication of the Licensers of the Stage* (1739), which challenged, respectively, Walpole's pacifist foreign policy and Court censorship of political drama (see chapter 43, "Theatre").

As Walpole's grip on power loosened, the House of Commons lost confidence in him, and he resigned in 1742. Yet what might have seemed a victory for the Country party or the Patriot coalition was bittersweet. Leading Patriots such as John Carteret and William Pulteney soon defected to the Court, their virtuous ideals apparently neglected in favor of personal ambition. As the 1740s unfolded, the political world seemed little changed from Walpole's administration. Henry Pelham became the First Lord of the Treasury and pursued policies similar to his predecessor. Walpole was not necessarily viewed as a villain, nor was his legacy entirely villainous. Johnson rarely missed an opportunity to insult a Whig – "I have always said, the first Whig was the Devil" (Boswell, *Life*, 3:326) – but even he ultimately held Walpole in "high opinion," and he "honoured his memory for having kept this country in peace many years" (Hawkins, *Life*, p. 308).

THE 1750S

The peace and political stability engineered by Walpole would continue into the early 1750s, as the Pelham ministry worked to reduce the national debt. But after Pelham's death in 1754, England soon found itself on the path to war. Newcastle formed an administration and, in May 1756, England entered a conflict with France that would eventually be known as the Seven Years' War or the Great War for Empire (see chapter 46, "War"). Though the conflict would largely involve disputed territorial claims in North America, England's loss of Minorca in June triggered widespread public outrage. Admiral John Byng, selected by Newcastle to protect England's interest in Minorca, was arrested, tried for treason, and executed ("to encourage the others," as Voltaire remarked). Samuel Johnson, writing for the *Literary Magazine*, believed Byng had been treated with "the utmost malevolence" (*Works*, 10:258). Public opinion soon shifted towards sympathy for Byng and criticism of the how the war had been handled.

By late 1756, both Newcastle and Henry Fox, his secretary of state, had resigned. A new joint administration formed under the leadership of the

Duke of Devonshire and William Pitt the Elder. Pitt in particular enjoyed widespread popular support, styling himself as a new Patriot who favored virtue over corruption, principles over power. As John Brewer states, Pitt "constantly emphasized the way in which he and others ought to place country before self, and liberty and honour before the profits of office and the fruits of corruption."[4] The king, however, remained wary of Pitt, who aligned himself with dissident Whigs and, at times, Tories. Yet Pitt pursued the war with France vigorously, promoting England's imperial interests but alienating some of his Tory supporters, most of whom, like Samuel Johnson, favored an isolationist "Little England" ideal. Johnson's contributions to the *Literary Magazine* assailed Pitt's pursuit of empire, arguing that England's much-vaunted political stability would be compromised by entanglements in foreign territories (see chapter 21, "Empire").

GEORGE III, BUTE, AND WILKES

While Pitt pursued his war, George II died on October 25, 1760. His twenty-two-year-old grandson would be crowned George III, the first of the Hanoverians to have been born in England and the first to speak English as a native. Not only was George III a "born Briton," as he proudly proclaimed, but, having been raised by his tutor, John Stuart, the third Earl of Bute, on Bolingbroke's "Country" principles of a "Patriot King," he announced that he would rule without regard to party. For the first time since the accession of George I in 1714, the Tories would be welcomed back to the corridors of power.

Johnson, who had spent his life in opposition to the various Whig administrations, found himself the recipient of a government pension for his literary achievement (though his wicked *Dictionary* definition of *pension* as "pay given to a state hireling for treason to his country" would come back to haunt him). Yet within a year of George III's accession and the end of Tory proscription, Pitt would resign amidst disputes over the war. By May 1762 Bute had become First Lord of the Treasury, or prime minister, and his diplomatic skills helped engineer the Peace of Paris that ended the war in 1763. Even those Tories who had initially supported the war had returned, as historian Linda Colley puts it, to their "habitual insularity"[5] and were happy to see the end of conflict.

Despite the success of the peace treaty, the Bute administration had been under fire from the start. Within a month of its formation, the ever-controversial John Wilkes launched an attack in a periodical called *The North Briton* – its title a not-so-subtle jibe at Bute's Scottish heritage.

Figure 36 Hogarth, *John Wilkes Esqr.*

Wilkes, a Member of Parliament since 1757, was an outspoken critic of Bute and George III. In 1763 he was arrested on libel charges after publishing a critique of the king. As an MP, Wilkes successfully challenged the warrant, but soon found himself in legal trouble again over the printing of an obscene parody of Pope's *Essay on Man* called *Essay on Woman* (1764). He fled to the Continent, and, while in exile, was expelled from Parliament, but he became something of a *cause célèbre* at home. Despite, or perhaps because of, his notoriety, Wilkes prevailed in the 1768 election, though Parliament refused to seat him. Populist support for the charismatic Wilkes led to the cry of "Wilkes and Liberty" and the establishment of the Society for the Supporters of the Bill of Rights (1769). Samuel Johnson, for one, would have none of it. In *The False Alarm* (1770) he offered a defense of Parliament in its action against Wilkes. Still Wilkes remained a popular and iconic public figure, though his status as a political radical would eventually be compromised by his participation in the anti-Catholic Gordon Riots (1780) and his opposition to the French Revolution (1789).

THE AMERICAN COLONIES

The question of "liberty," however, did not subside with the Wilkes controversy. The expulsion of Wilkes from Parliament led to vigorous debate regarding whether voters or the Members of Parliament held ultimate authority in political decisions.

Debates over political authority and representation were brewing in the American colonies as well (see chapter 10, "America"). Many colonists had been restive since the passage of the Stamp Act in 1765, and were unhappy with the subsequent decisions to retain duties on tea. The protests that resulted from these measures, culminating in the Boston Tea Party of 1773, set the stage for the American Revolution. Some of the most eloquent attempts at conciliation with the colonies, including the best efforts of MP Edmund Burke, failed. The administration of Frederick, Lord North, formed in 1770, enjoyed the confidence of the king, who was determined to maintain the colonies that England had expended vast resources defending during the Seven Years' War. Samuel Johnson entered the fray in support of the North ministry with a pamphlet opposing the rebellious colonists in North America, *Taxation No Tyranny* (1775), in which he famously asks, "How is it that we hear the loudest yelps for liberty among the drivers of negroes?" (*Works*, 10:454). But, for the most part, Johnson seemed on the wrong side of history in *Taxation No Tyranny*, his own history included. Where he once reliably resisted the pursuit of empire, Johnson now vigorously defended its maintenance.

Despite the initial promise of a nonpartisan government in George III's reign, party politics flourished, though not necessarily in ways that brought into definition what each party represented. As historian John Cannon has observed, the Tories remained split on many important issues, from the Stamp Act to the Wilkes controversy, and the Whigs continued to break down into factions as well. Burke, a strong party man himself, admitted that it seemed "a Tory was the best species of Whig."[6] The old confusions persisted, and the public perception of party seemed at times more coordinated than any specific parliamentary alignment. As the conduct of the American Revolution came increasingly under fire, Johnson had begun to wonder if England would once more turn against itself, as it had during the 1640s: "I am afraid of a civil war," he admitted in 1783 (*Letters*, 4:109).

UNRESOLVED QUESTIONS

Johnson's fears of civil war would be unfounded, though he would surely have been troubled by the support for the French Revolution that simmered in England had he lived a few years longer to see it. But many of the political controversies of eighteenth-century England would not be resolved in his lifetime. Questions regarding the foundations of political authority, the relationship between king and Parliament, the rights of citizens, the idea of patriotism, and the nature of party itself – all would persist well into the next century. The terms *Whig* and *Tory* would continue to define the political imagination beyond any exact configuration in government. Why, then, did these party labels persist? To what extent did they denote strict ideological preferences, clear parliamentary divisions, or simply matters of public perception? Very early in his career, Johnson had written that "Political truth is of very great importance, and they who honestly endeavor after it, are doubtless engaged in a laudable pursuit."[7] But when it comes to eighteenth-century party politics, the relationship between the pursuit of truth and the competing claims of political partisanship remains as difficult to untangle today as it was then.

NOTES

1 David Hume, *Selected Essays* (Oxford: Oxford University Press, 1993), p. 36.
2 Alexander Pope, *The Twickenham Edition of the Poems of Alexander Pope*, ed. John Butt *et al.*, 11 vols. in 12 (New Haven, CT: Yale University Press, 1939–69), 1:152 (lines 41–2).
3 Hume, *Selected Essays*, p. 37.
4 John Brewer, *Party Ideology and Popular Politics at the Accession of George III* (Cambridge: Cambridge University Press, 1976), p. 97.
5 Linda Colley, *In Defiance of Oligarchy: The Tory Party, 1714–1760* (Cambridge: Cambridge University Press, 1982), p. 94.
6 John Cannon, *Samuel Johnson and the Politics of Hanoverian England* (Oxford: Oxford University Press, 1994), p. 87.
7 *Gentleman's Magazine*, 9 (Jan. 1739).

CHAPTER 36

Scholarship

Barry Baldwin

SCHO'LARSHIP. *n.s.* [from *scholar*]
1. Learning; literature; knowledge.

> It pitied my heart to think that a man of my master's understanding, and great *scholarship*, who had a book of his own in print, should talk so outrageously. *Pope.*

When Samuel Johnson left Lichfield for London in 1737, he dreamed not of fame and fortune but of a reputation as a scholar. As Robert DeMaria writes, the young Johnson chose "his heroes from the ... European scholar-poets," including "Buchanan, Scaliger, Erasmus, Heinsius, and Burman"[1] – all distinguished classicists of the sixteenth and seventeenth centuries – and he longed to join their ranks.

In the eighteenth century, the word *scholarship* meant proficiency in Greek and Latin – the modern languages were only just beginning to receive serious attention. But Johnson was well prepared for a career in classical studies. Sir John Hawkins noted that he "had through his life a propensity to Latin composition: he shewed it very early at school" (Hawkins, *Life*, p. 9). When he went to Pembroke College, Oxford, for a kind of admissions interview, his father "seemed very full of the merits of his son, and told the company he was a good scholar, and a poet, and wrote Latin verses." But Johnson himself sat silent and failed to impress. In the course of conversation, though, "he suddenly struck in and quoted Macrobius" – a fairly obscure fifth-century grammarian – and the tutor knew at once he was dealing with a serious young man. "Thus," writes Boswell, "he gave the first impression of that more extensive reading in which he had indulged himself" (Boswell, *Life*, 1:59).

Although Boswell called him "undoubtedly one of the first Latin scholars in modern times" (Boswell, *Life*, 4:385), Johnson never did become the kind of scholar he had hoped to be. He was forced to leave Oxford after just thirteen months, and his planned projects on Latin and Greek authors came to nothing. But his background in the classics stayed with him and informed many of the works he did publish: the *Dictionary*, the edition of Shakespeare, and the *Lives of the Poets* all drew on classical precedents. This background deserves attention, especially in an age in which the classics are little known.

RICHARD BENTLEY

It is a truth universally acknowledged that modern classical scholarship began with Richard Bentley's *Epistola ad Millium* (*Epistle to Mill*), a far-ranging commentary, written in Latin in 1691, on the *Chronicle* of the sixth-century Byzantine writer John Malalas. Bentley – a Cambridge professor and a notoriously pugnacious Master of Trinity College – secured his textual revolution with the *Dissertation on the Epistles of Phalaris* (1699), editions of the Roman writers Horace (1711) and Terence (1726), and, most remarkably, the discovery of a lost letter from the Greek alphabet, the digamma, which had fallen out of the language by the seventh century BCE.

The most important job facing the editor of any old work is to establish the text as the author wrote it. What may seem obvious often proves surprisingly difficult. Before the fifteenth-century invention of printing, all texts were copied by hand, and with each new copy new errors were introduced. To complicate matters further, all the earliest versions of most classical texts had been long since lost, leaving readers with only imperfect copies of imperfect copies. The editor was charged with sorting through the surviving evidence and establishing the proper readings.

Combining philological precision with historical research, Bentley's greatest innovative virtue was his insistence upon the personal collation of manuscripts – seeking out readings from different manuscripts, rather than depending on the so-called *textus receptus*. Few critics could match his diligence in comparing surviving versions and working out the lines of transmission. With his patience for "collation," as the examination of variants is known, he was able to correct many improper readings in the works of major authors.

Sometimes, though, none of the surviving manuscripts is correct. In these cases, an editor is forced to resort to "conjectural emendation" – proposing a reading that appears in none of the sources. In this, too, Bentley was a master. As one of the great classical scholars of the twentieth century describes Bentley's achievement in the *Epistola ad Millium*,

> Nothing like it had ever been seen before. Not only was it packed with emendations such as no one else could have produced at that time, it contained a

collection of the fragments of Ion of Chios, revealed an unprecedented familiarity with the ancient grammarians, including the formidable Hesychius, and, finally, established the completely unknown fact that synapheia prevails in Greek anapaestic systems right through to the catalexis. Actually, in this maiden effort we already have the whole of Bentley – the happy knack of the emender, the exact observation which enabled him to arrive at fixed rules, the vision that showed him what the great tasks of scholarship were.[2]

Bentley's most famous proposal for the text of the Latin poet Horace occurs in his passionate note on *Epistles* 1.7.29. The text reads (in English translation), "a pinched little fox had crept through a narrow chink into a bin of corn, and when well fed was trying with stuffed stomach to get out again, but in vain." Bentley found the text nonsensical: foxes do not eat corn, he reasoned, and cannot slip through granary chinks. He therefore insisted that the word in the received text, *volpecula* ("little fox"), must be a corruption, and he proposed instead *nitedula* ("little mouse"). Many were convinced. Even Alexander Pope, who would later ridicule Bentley as one of the chief dunces, originally accepted this when he came to imitate Horace's poem.

WORMWOOD STYLE

But Bentley was not universally praised. He quarreled with a number of prominent writers, most famously Sir William Temple, patron of the young Jonathan Swift. He also took aim at one of Swift's friends, Alexander Pope, who had produced a translation of Homer's *Iliad*: "A very pretty poem," he told Pope, "but you must not call it Homer."[3]

For presuming to criticize his social betters, Bentley was derided as an arrogant and boorish pedant: "The first and surest Mark of a *Pedant*," wrote one of Temple's defenders, "is, to write without observing the receiv'd Rules of Civility, and Common Decency: and without distinguishing the Characters of Those he writes to, or against: For Pedantry in the Pen, is what Clownishness is in Conversation; it is *Written Ill-Breeding*."[4] Bentley's arrogance also provoked satirical abuse. His methods and personality – he was called "The great and absolute critick" – were deftly caricatured in Swift's *Battle of the Books* and *Tale of a Tub* (1705) and Henry Fielding's *Vernoniad* (1741). Most famously, Pope's *Dunciad* (1728–43) turned Bentley into "Aristarchus" – a proverbially severe Greek editor – with his "wormwood style" and "slashing hook," whose "Digamma … o'er-tops them all."[5]

Most of this satirical abuse heaped on Bentley was purely personal, but at least some of the attacks were warranted. When Pope wrote that

Bentley "made Horace dull, and humbled Milton's strains," he was alluding to Bentley's notorious edition of *Paradise Lost* (1733), which was based on the assumption that Milton's text was both innocently corrupted by the blind poet's amanuensis and deliberately so by a rogue editor. This authorized him to apply the same sorts of conjectural emendations to a modern poem that he had applied so successfully to ancient texts – but this time the result was disastrous. Bentley made hundreds of reckless changes to the text of *Paradise Lost*, not one of which is widely accepted by Miltonists today. When his edition appeared, Pope was ready with an epigram ending, "While he but sought his Author's Fame to further, / The murd'rous Critic has aveng'd thy Murder."[6]

JOHNSON'S SCHOLARSHIP

Johnson knew Bentley's works, both the good and the bad. He agreed with Bentley's strictures on the poor Greek of Joshua Barnes, and he hailed Bentley's Greek and Latin expertise as unrivaled. He admired Bentley's edition of Horace, advising Boswell, "You will admire Bentley more when wrong, than Jason [de Nores] when right" (Boswell, *Life*, 2:444). Johnson also mocked the *Dunciad*'s satirical attacks on the great scholar, which "dropped impotent from Bentley, like the javelin of Priam" (*Lives*, 4:75).

At the same time, though, Johnson recognized the dangers to which scholars were prone. He excoriated Bentley's phantom Milton editor theory as "a supposition rash and groundless, if he thought it true; vile and pernicious, if, as is said, he allowed it to be false," also deprecating both his efforts to excuse Miltonian "equivocations" by ancient parallels, and the countless rewritings, in general and particular terms, albeit commending his verbal analysis (*Lives*, 1:288). In *Adventurer* 85 he writes, "He that buries himself among his manuscripts 'besprent,' as Pope expresses it, 'with learned dust,' and wears out his days and nights in perpetual research and solitary meditation, is too apt to lose in his elocution what he adds to his wisdom" (*Works*, 2:413–14). The more classically learned of his readers may well have spotted Johnson's allusion to, or parody of, Horace's advice in *Ars Poetica*: "Exemplaria Graeca / nocturna versate manu, versate diurna" – "Pore over Greek models by night and day alike" (lines 268–9).

Johnson's *Life* and his *Lives* disclose a range of attitudes to a number of classical scholars other than Bentley. Johnson's admiration for the Bluestocking Elizabeth Carter, translator of the Greek philosopher Epictetus, is well known (see chapter 47, "Women writers"). He also praised "Poor old [Thomas] Morell ... a good scholar, and an acquaintance of mine" (Boswell, *Life*, 5:350). Johnson, moreover, impressed his scholarly standards on others. From his frequent appeals to procure William Baxter's edition of the Greek poet Anacreon, Boswell learned to discriminate between editors. Reporting on a discussion between Johnson and Wilkes about Horace's *Ars Poetica*, line 128 – widely regarded today as the most difficult passage in Latin literature – Boswell appends his own long note (Boswell, *Life*, 3:73–4). It is described as "tedious" even by Boswell's editors, but Johnson had taught him the importance of attention to detail. Johnson even quizzed Boswell on his ability to correct a faulty text:

> Dr. Johnson pointed out a paragraph beginning with *Aristotle*, and told me there was an error in the text, which he bade me try to discover. I was lucky enough to hit it at once. As the passage is printed, it is said that the devil answers *even* in *engines*. I corrected it to – *ever* in *ænigmas*. "Sir, (said he,) you are a good critick. This would have been a great thing to do in the text of an ancient authour." (Boswell, *Life*, 5:214)

Friends who failed his tests earned his scorn. When Richard Brocklesby recited a passage from the Roman poet Juvenal, and inadvertently replaced the word *extremum* with *supremum*, "Johnson's critical ear instantly took offence, and discoursing vehemently on the unmetrical effect of such a lapse, he shewed himself as full as ever of the spirit of the grammarian" (Boswell, *Life*, 4:401).

NO DULL DUTY

In "An Essay on the Origin and Importance of Small Tracts and Fugitive Pieces" (1744), based on his extensive reading as he catalogued the library of Edward Harley, Johnson revealed a continuing interest in classical scholarship. The penultimate paragraph of that essay reads: "It may be added, in Vindication of our intended Practice, that it is the same with that of *Photius*, whose Collections are no less Miscellaneous than ours, and who declares, that he leaves it to his Reader, to reduce his Extracts under their proper Heads" (*Prefaces & Dedications*, p. 59).

Classical scholarship was on his mind, too, when he began his first great literary labor, the *Dictionary*: "I have endeavoured to proceed with a scholar's reverence for antiquity," he wrote in the preface, "and a grammarian's regard to the genius of our tongue" (*Works*, 18:78). Johnson has been widely praised for two innovations in English lexicography: providing illustrative quotations and minutely distinguishing the nuances of each word's meanings. It is true that these were novelties in English, but there were important classical models. Johnson learned much about the lexicographical tradition from classical dictionaries, which he would have come across while he was compiling the Harleian catalogue. He knew, for instance, Robert Estienne's *Thesaurus linguae latinae* (1532), as well as the vast Byzantine lexicon-cum-encyclopedia known then as Suidas, now as Suda.

This scholarly net may be more widely cast. Johnson would not relish being paired with Voltaire, whose morals he found scandalous and whose "minute and slender criticism" he castigated (*Works*, 7:80). But they agreed on this: "Un dictionnaire sans citations," wrote Voltaire, "est un squelette" – "a dictionary without quotations is mere bones." And when he published the revised fourth edition of his *Dictionary* in 1773, he composed a Latin poem about his long labors, "ΓΝΩΘΙ ΣΕΑΥΤΟΝ: Post Lexicon Anglicanum Auctum et Emendatum" ("Know Yourself: After Revising and Enlarging the English Dictionary," *Works*, 6:271–4). The poem opens with a reference to Joseph Justus Scaliger, one of the greatest classicists of the sixteenth century, and, like Johnson, a lexicographer.

After finishing the *Dictionary*, Johnson turned his attention to Shakespeare. In the preface to his eight-volume edition of the plays, he chastised an earlier editor, Alexander Pope, for dismissing textual criticism as a "dull duty." Johnson insisted that Pope "understood but half his undertaking." Comparing manuscripts, Johnson admits, is indeed dull, however necessary. Still,

> an emendatory critick would ill discharge his duty, without qualities very different from dulness. In perusing a corrupted piece, he must have before him all possibilities of meaning, with all possibilities of expression. Such must be his comprehension of thought, and such his copiousness of language. Out of many readings possible, he must be able to select that which best suits with the state, opinions, and modes of language prevailing in every age, and with his authour's particular cast of thought, and turn of expression. Such must be his knowledge, and such his taste. Conjectural criticism demands more than humanity possesses, and he that exercises it with most praise has very frequent need of indulgence. Let us now be told no more of the dull duty of an editor. (*Works*, 7:95–6)

With his own edition of Shakespeare imminent, Johnson observed, "Only four hours between me and criticism" (*Miscellanies*, 2:30) – shades of awaiting first-night reviews at Sardi's! But here, too, his work was firmly grounded in the tradition of classical scholarship. He knew "that some liberty of conjecture must be allowed in the revisal of works so inaccurately printed and so long neglected" (*Works*, 7:151). But he also noted the strong appeal of the kind of conjectural emendation that so many scholars had practiced in classical texts: "The allurements of emendation are scarcely resistible. Conjecture has all the joy and all the pride of invention, and he that has once started a happy change, is too much delighted to consider what objections may rise against it" (*Works*, 7:110).

Johnson often pontificated over editorial principles in his preface to Shakespeare, in which Bentley is invoked as one of the masters of conjectural criticism. His own view of corruption – by actors, by manuscript copiers, and by printers' errors – is quite in keeping with the traditional view of Shakespeare's text. Predecessors are variously blamed and commended for their diligent collation and conjectural restraint. Though confining them to his commentary, Johnson often expressed his own emendations with Bentley-like confidence.

THE INSTINCTS OF A SCHOLAR

The entry on Johnson in the *Dictionary of British Classicists* concludes that his Latin and Greek poems "show the importance of the classics to him, if not his importance to classics"[7] – a verdict less than just, one that could not have been returned had Johnson achieved even one of his multifarious editing ambitions.

The history of classical scholarship is filled with unrealized projects. Like other great scholars – the eighteenth-century Hellenist Richard Porson, for example, and Richard Bentley – Johnson left many classical projects unrealized, including an edition of Politian and translations of Herodian, Aristotle, and Cicero. Nor did he always live up to his own high-minded principles of collation, most notoriously ignoring Garrick's collection of materials: "Johnson had the instincts of a scholar," writes biographer Christopher Hibbert, "but neither the patience nor the application."[8]

And yet scholarship is an essential context for Johnson's works. The man who said, "The only way to preserve knowledge is to increase it,"[9] and "There is nothing so minute or inconsiderable, that I would not rather know it than not" (Boswell, *Life*, 2:357), was to the manner born. The classical scholar Samuel Parr put it best: "Dr. Johnson was an admirable scholar … The classical scholar was forgotten in the great original contributor to the literature of his country" (Boswell, *Life*, 4:385 n. 3).

NOTES

1 Robert DeMaria, Jr., *The Life of Samuel Johnson: A Critical Biography* (Oxford: Blackwell, 1993), p. xi.

2 Ulrich von Wilamowitz-Moellendorff, *History of Classical Scholarship*, trans. Alan Harris, ed. Hugh Lloyd-Jones (London: Duckworth, 1982), p. 79.

3 Steven Shankman, "Pope's Homer and His Poetic Career," in *The Cambridge Companion to Alexander Pope*, ed. Pat Rogers (Cambridge: Cambridge University Press, 2007), pp. 63–76, at p. 72.

4 Charles Boyle, *Dr. Bentley's Dissertations on the Epistles of Phalaris, and the Fables of Æsop, Examin'd* (London, 1699), p. 93.

5 Alexander Pope, *The Dunciad*, 4:201–74, in *The Twickenham Edition of the Poems of Alexander Pope*, ed. John Butt *et al.*, 11 vols. in 12 (New Haven, CT: Yale University Press, 1939–69), 5:363–4.

6 Pope, *Twickenham Edition*, 6:328.

7 Jack Lynch, "Samuel Johnson," in Robert B. Todd, ed., *The Dictionary of British Classicists*, 3 vols. (Bristol: Thoemmes Continuum, 2004), *s.v.* Johnson, Samuel.

8 Christopher Hibbert, *The Personal History of Samuel Johnson* (New York: Harper & Row, 1971), p. 157.

9 *Some Remarks on the Progress of Learning*, ed. O M Brack, Jr., & Robert DeMaria, Jr. (Tempe, AZ: Almond Tree Press, 2001), p. 9.

CHAPTER 37

Science and technology

Dahlia Porter

SCI'ENCE. *n.s.* [*science*, French; *scientia*, Latin.]
1. Knowledge.

> If we conceive God's sight or *science*, before the creation of the world, to be extended to all and every part of the world, seeing every thing as it is, his prescience or foresight of any action of mine, or rather his *science* or sight, from all eternity, lays no necessity on any thing to come to pass, any more than my seeing the sun move hath to do in the moving of it. *Hamm.*

In July 1774, Johnson embarked on a tour of North Wales with his close friends, Henry and Hester Thrale. Johnson organized the first segment of the trip, and their first stop was his birthplace, Lichfield. While in Lichfield, the group visited apothecary Richard Greene's museum of antiquities and natural curiosities; had lunch with one of the founding members of the Lunar Society, Erasmus Darwin; called on the "Swan of Lichfield," the poet Anna Seward, Darwin's friend and first biographer; and visited Andrew Newton's collection of East Indian rarities. After an eventful three days, the group set out for an eleven-day stay with Johnson's schoolmate and close friend, Dr. John Taylor. During their visit, they made excursions to view country seats (the Duke of Devonshire demonstrated his mechanical fountain for them), examined hot springs, explored underground rivers and caves, and inspected a silk mill, where Johnson "remarked a particular manner of propagating motion from a horizontal to a vertical wheel" (*Works*, 1:163–70). Add electricity and chemistry – made familiar to the Thrales by way of Johnson's experiments in the laboratory they set up at Streatham – and these two weeks constitute a Grand Tour of eighteenth-century science and its practical applications.

SCIENTIFIC DEVELOPMENTS

Their immersion in science and technology at Lichfield was far from coincidental: by the 1770s, Johnson's birthplace had become a hotbed of experimentation and technological development. Situated in the English West Midlands just north of the industrial center of Birmingham, Lichfield emblematized the eighteenth-century drive to harness scientific knowledge for practical purposes. A group of the most important figures in "applied science" had gathered there and formed the Lunar Society: James Watt, inventor of the first commercially viable steam engine to power foundries and ironworks; silversmith Matthew Boulton, founder of the Soho Mint and manufacturer of Watt's steam engine; potter Josiah Wedgwood, producer of the first bone china in Britain and inventor of the pyrometer (a thermometer used to measure extreme temperatures inside a kiln or furnace); clockmaker turned geologist John Whitehurst; natural philosopher and theologian Joseph Priestley, who wrote extensively on electricity, optics, theology, rhetoric, and, most famously, "dephlogisticated air," now known as oxygen; Erasmus Darwin, physician, botanical poet, proponent of evolutionary theory, and grandfather of Charles Darwin; and physician William Withering, an amateur geologist, author of a botanical guide to British flora, and discoverer of digitalis, a medicine for the treatment of congestive heart failure. As the wide array of pursuits in this small group of men indicates, science had yet to fragment into the specialized disciplines we know today: chemists studied physics, mechanical engineers dabbled in mineralogy, and doctors were as likely to invent a device for predicting the weather as to discover a new medicine.

In part through its practical applications, scientific knowledge gained unprecedented public standing in the eighteenth century, and like many educated men – and, to a lesser degree, women – of his generation, Johnson followed scientific developments closely. Early in his career, he wrote a long biography of Dutch physician and botanist Herman Boerhaave, and he read extensively in seventeenth-century science while compiling quotations for his *Dictionary*. Well versed in the monumental discoveries of the previous century, Johnson also kept up with current developments: as editor of the *Literary Magazine* in 1756, he reviewed several natural histories, two new works on electricity, Stephen Hales's description of his ventilation machines, Isaac Newton's letters, Francis Home's *Experiments on Bleaching*, and the current issue of the *Philosophical Transactions of the Royal Society*. Johnson's reviews cover many of the major developments in eighteenth-century science: Carolus Linnaeus's taxonomic system of plant identification transformed botany and natural history (and made it available to women); the Leyden jar and galvanic pile advanced the study of electrical current; chemical experiments revealed air to be a mixture of different gases; and new techniques and machines (arising from developments in chemistry and mechanical physics) revolutionized everything from textile manufacture to air quality in prisons. The Royal Society's flagship journal, *Philosophical Transactions*, was a clearinghouse for these developments, cataloguing and disseminating a rapidly growing heap of observations and experiments.

Scientific culture was not, however, constrained to the world of books. As the Thrales's tour indicates, it was quite the fashion to visit collections of natural history specimens and other "curiosities," whether mechanical or cultural. Once a mark of vulgar superstition, curiosity had become associated with the legitimate pursuit of scientific knowledge by the eighteenth century, which in turn authorized the public thirst for the strange and beautiful. Private collections were often open to wealthy travelers, but the formation of the British Museum initiated a trend towards public access: when he willed his collections to form the museum in 1753, Sir Hans Sloane dictated it be available to be "visited and seen by all persons ... for the improvement, knowledge and information of all."[1] Commercial museums sprouted up everywhere from London and Edinburgh to Philadelphia and Boston, and admission prices were often justified by the museum's educational value: as Charles Wilson Peale argued, his Philadelphia museum should be a "national concern since it is a national good," comprising "a *collection* of everything useful or curious – a world in miniature!"[2] Curiosity also buoyed public attendance at scientific lectures and demonstrations, such as Benjamin Franklin's spectacular experiments with electricity (which included setting Philadelphia's Schuylkill River on fire and roasting a turkey with an electrical jack) and Humphry Davy's illustration of the effects of nitrous oxide (by dosing himself and members of the audience). By the early nineteenth century, Davy had achieved celebrity status, drawing huge crowds to his London lectures on "chemical philosophy."

THE CALCULATING SPIRIT

Always curious, Johnson took every opportunity to visit museums and mills, but like many of his contemporaries, he also liked to dabble in science himself. As Boswell recorded in the *Tour of the Hebrides*, Johnson was an astute observer of mechanical processes:

> I have often been astonished with what exactness and perspicuity [Johnson] will explain the process of any art. He this morning explained to us all the operation of coining, and, at night, all the operations of brewing, so very clearly, that

Mr. M'Queen said, when he heard the first, he thought he had been bred in the Mint; when he heard the second, that he had been bred a brewer. (Boswell, *Life*, 5:215)

Beyond minute and careful observation, Johnson engaged in "small experiments" (Boswell, *Life*, 3:398) sometimes on his own body, as when he measured a pared fingernail to ascertain its rate of growth (*Works*, 1:118–19). From counting steps to weighing leaves to keeping minute records of expenses (even when he was not paying), Johnson's diaries and letters record a penchant for exactitude and accuracy. He liked, in short, to count. As Boswell renders Johnson's pronouncement: "That, Sir, is the good of counting. It brings every thing to a certainty, which before floated in the mind indefinitely" (Boswell, *Life*, 4:204).

Johnson's proclivity for measurement reveals a particular cast of mind, but one not unique to him: the "calculating spirit" was characteristic of the age. The renowned prison reformer John Howard, for example, made 1,441 visits to 224 different prisons in England and Wales between 1773 and his death in 1790, meticulously recording his observations and collating them in the extensive tables appended to successive editions of *The State of the Prisons*. Reform movements from abolition to animal rights followed Howard's lead, mounting pressure for legal change on indisputable heaps of data. Often the work of single individuals, these fact-collecting projects changed the character of scientific inquiry: as Jan Golinski suggests, the scrupulous daily records of meteorological conditions kept by educated middle- or upper-class men such as John Rutty and Thomas Baker "exemplify the emerging modern construct of scientific objectivity."[3] Likewise, ships' captains and surgeons – any travelers with basic knowledge of new instruments – were encouraged by the Royal Society to replace narrative accounts with systematic, tabular observations of atmospheric and geomagnetic conditions. Much of the raw data collected in the *Philosophical Transactions* came from the letters and accounts of these amateur fact collectors, the workforce of eighteenth-century science.

FROM COLLECTION TO SYNTHESIS

Johnson did not contribute to the *Philosophical Transactions*, nor was he created a Fellow of the Royal Society. He made no lasting contributions to the increase of scientific knowledge. Science, however, left its mark on him, specifically through what Pat Rogers calls "its revelation of a mode of enquiry, a logic of demonstration, and a conceptual framework."[4] Johnson's love of measurement and precise observation marks him as a proponent of Francis Bacon's inductive method, outlined in the *Novum Organum* (1620) and heralded as the hallmark of "legitimate" science in Britain well into the nineteenth century. For Bacon, the steps of method – observation and collection, arrangement, comparison, connection, distinction and separation, and finally composition – would lead to the discovery and expression of "laws and determinations of absolute actuality," revealing finally "the unity of nature in substances the most unlike." In response to Bacon's insistence on sweeping away all theories to enable "the fresh examination of particulars," seventeenth-century practitioners purposefully eschewed broad claims to concentrate on collecting facts.[5]

By the mid-eighteenth century, however, the wealth of data had become a burden, and natural historians saw the need for something beyond accumulation and arrangement. In his monumental *Histoire naturelle* (1748), for example, the Comte de Buffon insisted that accurate description was an essential beginning, but it was also "necessary to elevate ourselves to something grander and more dignified … the combination of observations, the generalization of facts, linking them together by the power of analogies."[6] Buffon sought to move his science from the compilation of particular instances to a sweeping and comprehensive overview of knowledge. In this new formulation, Baconian induction promised to turn the rapidly expanding heap of facts into general principles; it was the path (one of Bacon's favorite metaphors) that would lead natural philosophy out "woods of experience" into the realm of universal laws (Bacon, *Works*, 4:18).

The shift from collection to synthesis fueled the massive encyclopedic projects of the second half of the eighteenth century. Following Buffon's lead, Jean le Rond d'Alembert – mathematician, physicist, and coeditor of the great *Encyclopédie* with Denis Diderot – claimed that encyclopedic arrangement "consists of collecting knowledge into the smallest area possible and of placing the philosopher at a vantage point, so to speak, high above this vast labyrinth."[7] For all his preoccupation with facts, Johnson clearly recognized the necessity of a synthetic approach; *The Vanity of Human Wishes* opens with a version of d'Alembert's encyclopedic prospect: "Let observation with extensive view, / Survey mankind from China to Peru" (lines 1–2, in *Works*, 6:91–2). After this opening, the poet pleads with Democritus (a Greek philosopher of science) to "pierce each scene with philosophic eye" (line 64), which in turn generates the poem's movement between particular instances and general principles. Johnson offers an empirically established catalogue of human frailties, but in striving for moral resolution in the final stanza – a resolution that ironically rejects the poem's empirical evidence in favor of an appeal to heaven and faith – he follows his scientific contemporaries in aspiring to something "grander and more dignified" than a mere compilation of facts. The poem's wide prospect and final movement to transcend observation replicates the new mandate of the descriptive sciences, effectively transferring the methods of natural history to the examination of the human condition.

SCIENTIFIC LANGUAGE

It is no surprise that Bacon's method was applied to everything from determining the character of heat to locating the seat of virtue or taste: empiricist science had, from its inception, encoded an analogy between the physical and the moral worlds. Works ranging from Alexander Pope's long philosophical poem *An Essay on Man* (1734) to William Wordsworth's mock-Gothic ballad "The Thorn" (1798) recognized and traded on this deeply ingrained analogy.

Johnson's writing is stocked with such analogies; as William Wimsatt argues, a characteristic feature of Johnson's style is to redeploy "philosophic words" – words used in scientific works to describe chemical processes, physical laws, and new technologies – as figures for social or psychological conditions.[8] In the preface to the *Dictionary*, Johnson explicitly comments on this process as a larger historical phenomenon:

> As by the cultivation of various sciences, a language is amplified, it will be furnished with words deflected from their original sense; the geometrician will talk of a courtier's zenith, or the excentrick virtue of a wild hero, and the physician of sanguine expectations and phlegmatick delays … vicissitudes of fashion will enforce the use of new, or extend the signification of known terms. The tropes of poetry will make hourly encroachments, and the metaphorical will become the current sense. (*Works*, 18:107)

In the *Dictionary* entry for the word *amplify*, Johnson marks out two distinct ways that new scientific developments might "amplify" language. First, science increases the material substance of language, the sheer number of words, and thus may "improve [language] by new additions." It also, however, has the opposite effect, leading one to "speak largely in many words," and as a consequence to "form large or pompous representations." Johnson's characteristically dense prose garnered precisely this critique: some of his contemporaries thought that, instead of "*enriching* our tongue" with the introduction of "*Latinisms*, and other vicious modes of expression," Johnson had ended up "corrupting" it – "his diction was too monotonous, too obviously artificial, and now and then turgid even to absurdity."[9] This criticism of Johnson's inflated, bombastic style relies on precisely the same extension of signification it denigrates: the seventeenth-century medical definition of *turgid* was applied figuratively to literary style only in the eighteenth century.

Johnson's definitions often underscore how scientific language enters figurative usage by way of specific scientific debates. Turning to the entry for *eccentrick*, for example, we find the second definition – "not having the same center with another circle" – refers to planetary orbits in Ptolemaic philosophy, which relied on a complicated two-sphere model to explain why the planets' movements around the earth were not uniform. The fourth definition – "Irregular; anomalous; deviating from stated and constant methods" – suggests how the word has been "deflected." Johnson quotes Dryden's claim that "a character of *eccentrick* virtue, is the more exact image of human life, because it is not wholly exempted from its frailties." The astronomical issue of eccentric orbits has been translated into the deviation of human character from an imagined ideal. Dryden's point about character thus contains an analogical shift in worldview – just as we no longer believe the earth is the center of the solar system, so we no longer accept perfect virtue as the true standard of human behavior. In the progression of definitions, Johnson conveys how advances in science – in this case, the shift to heliocentrism fomented by Copernicus, Galileo, and Kepler in the sixteenth and seventeenth centuries – promoted "the metaphoric growth of meaning" in the seventeenth and eighteenth centuries.[10]

The heat of the geocentric–heliocentric debate had died down long before, but Johnson's exemplifying quotations in the *Dictionary* often engage current problems in science. For example, the central verb in the passage above, *deflect*, specifically refers to an eighteenth-century navigational problem: as Johnson puts it in his definition of that word, at various places on the globe, the compass needle would "deviate from a true course, or right line" towards true north. As we know today, compass declination is caused by the earth's magnetic field, but in the eighteenth century the science of geomagnetism was still in its youth: natural philosophers were beginning to discard the idea of two opposed magnetic poles (north and south), but were still far from imagining a fluid, multidirectional geodynamo. An imperfect understanding of causes, however, did not stop writers from proposing magnetic variation as a way of solving a pressing practical problem, the lack of a reliable way of determining longitude at sea. In 1755, in fact, Johnson wrote a pamphlet for Dr. Zachariah

Williams that put forward a method of calculating longitude by tracking magnetic variation.

The entries in the *Dictionary* invoke this debate, while also using it as a byway to other larger concerns about empiricist science. Johnson's first exemplary quotation for *deflect* comes from Sir Thomas Browne's *Pseudodoxia Epidemica* (1646, commonly known as *Brown's Vulgar Errors*), and establishes the standard scientific usage of the verb through a description of the compass variation at the Azores. The second quotation, also from Browne, appears to describe the same magnetic phenomenon, but actually refers to another subject altogether, the course of the River Nile. The definitions thus show Browne borrowing a technical term from one science (magnetism) and applying it to a distinctly different problem (mapping). The third quotation shifts practical concerns into a philosophical register. Johnson draws the passage from book 4 of Richard Blackmore's *Creation, a Philosophical Poem* (1712), a work that sought to prove the existence of a divine creator against the tenets of philosophical materialism (which argued that the principles of matter were the only paradigm necessary to explain all aspects of life). To controvert materialism, Blackmore suggests the reader try to follow the logic of those who seek to "reer the World without the Power Divine."[11] If we begin with "unbounded matter, in unbounded space," the poet reasons, it would be necessary for some atoms of matter "from a straight course [to] *deflect*" because, otherwise, "they could not meet, they could no World erect" (lines 190, 195–6). Blackmore aims to make materialism appear ridiculous by rhyming a misapplied technical term with its desired, if unlikely, effect. With this illustrative quotation, Johnson shifts attention from a practical navigational issue to the far-reaching religious and philosophical implications of empiricist science and its methods of determining truth.

Johnson's life and work reflect the broad spectrum of scientific developments, technological innovations, and methodological debates current in the eighteenth century. Whether recording the operation of new machines, experimenting on his own body, or describing how scientific ideas enter and change language, Johnson illustrates the mutually productive relationship between science and technology in the period, as well as the larger philosophical and critical paradigms that arose with them. A dabbler with broad rather than deep knowledge, Johnson also embodies the predisciplinary condition of eighteenth-century science and the diffusion of scientific ideas, language, and methods into every realm of eighteenth-century culture.

NOTES

1 Hans Sloane, *The Will of Sir Hans Sloane* (London, 1753), pp. 28–9.
2 Charles Wilson Peale, *The Selected Papers of Charles Wilson Peale*, vol. 2, ed. L. B. Miller (New Haven, CT: Yale University Press, 1983), pp. 265, 274.
3 Jan Golinski, *British Weather and the Climate of Enlightenment* (Chicago: University of Chicago Press, 2007), p. 90.
4 Pat Rogers, *The Samuel Johnson Encyclopedia* (Westport, CT: Greenwood Press, 1996), p. 351.
5 Francis Bacon, *The Works of Francis Bacon*, ed. James Spedding, Robert Leslie Ellis, and Douglas Denton Heath, 15 vols. (Boston, 1860–4), 4:146, 120, 93.
6 George Louis LeClerk, Comte de Buffon, *L'Histoire naturelle, générale et particulière*, 1744–88, 1:51. Available online, edited by Thierry Hocquet and Pietro Corsi: http://www.buffon.cnrs.fr/. My translation.
7 Jean le Rond d'Alembert, *Preliminary Discourse to the Encyclopedia of Diderot*, trans. Richard Schwab (Chicago: University of Chicago Press, 1995), p. 47.
8 William Wimsatt, *Philosophic Words* (Hamden, CT: Archon Books, 1968), pp. 56–65.
9 W. V. Reynolds, "The Reception of Johnson's Prose Style," *Review of English Studies* 11, no. 42 (April 1935), 145–6.
10 Wimsatt, *Philosophic Words*, p. 42.
11 Richard Blackmore, *Creation, a Philosophical Poem* (London, 1712), line 188.

CHAPTER 38

Scotland

Murray Pittock

> OATS. *n.s.* [*aten*, Saxon.] A grain, which in England is generally given to horses, but in Scotland supports the people.
>
> The *oats* have eaten the horses. *Shakespeare.*

Samuel Johnson's view of Scotland and the Scots has usually been seen in negative terms: the focus has been on what Boswell calls his "prejudice against both the country and people of Scotland" (Boswell, *Life*, 2:300). Boswell sought to hide his own Scottish identity when he was first introduced to Johnson in 1763, in deference to the Englishman's perceived Scotophobia:

> recollecting his prejudice against the Scotch, of which I had heard much, I said to Davies, "Don't tell where I come from." – "From Scotland," cried Davies, roguishly. "Mr. Johnson, (said I) I do indeed come from Scotland, but I cannot help it." … I meant this as light pleasantry to sooth and conciliate him, and not as an humiliating abasement at the expence of my country. But … he seized the expression "come from Scotland," which I used in the sense of being of that country; and, as if I had said that I had come away from it, or left it, retorted, "That, Sir, I find, is what a very great many of your countrymen cannot help." (Boswell, *Life*, 1:392)

The taunts aimed at Scotland continued throughout their twenty-year acquaintance. In 1769, Johnson told Boswell, "Sir, you have desart enough in Scotland" (2:75); in 1775, he expressed himself on "the extreme jealousy of the Scotch" (2:306), and his infamous gibing definitions of terms like *oats* in the *Dictionary* are well known. His declaration that "The impudence of an Irishman is the impudence of a fly … The impudence of a Scotsman is the impudence of a leech, that fixes and sucks your blood" (*Miscellanies*, 1:427) seems to be confirmation of Johnson's insularity and prejudice bordering on racism.

AFFECTIONATE CARICATURE?

At the same time, there are problems with this traditional account. First, there is the question of how far Boswell's Johnson was more an "affectionate caricature" than a piece of biographical fidelity. Traditional accounts that minimize Boswell's "organizational and interpretive power"[1] have become increasingly marginalized over the last forty years, and this has been reflected in controversies over both Boswell's artistry and his accuracy in reporting Johnson's sentiments, particularly in the field of Johnson's alleged Jacobitism, his loyalty to the exiled Stuart dynasty (see chapter 35, "Politics"). Second, there is the question of how far Johnson's anti-Scottishness was directed at a particular *kind* of Scotland – the Presbyterian, pro-Hanoverian, and Unionist Scotland of the eighteenth-century Scotsman on the make. Johnson, as historian J. C. D. Clark notes, thought "that the decline of learning went together with the advance of Presbyterianism,"[2] and Johnson "pointedly refused to enter a Presbyterian church in Scotland."[3]

In reflecting "the culture of an age" in his construction of Johnson, Boswell arguably also sought to record the general nature of contemporary English prejudices against the Scots, in which Johnson could be the "*true-born englishman*" (Boswell, *Life*, 2:300). Johnson's role as a sage, an epigrammatist, and a grand version of the typical Englishman of his day can be seen repeatedly in Boswell's portrayal, which is intended in part at least as the dramatic rendition of a specifically English type to a broader British audience, one that also places Johnson in situations where Boswell's superior social background and the Great Cham's occasional ridiculousness will be shown up, allowing his apparent amanuensis "to be almost humouring the older man's stubbornly narrow horizons."[4] Far from being a "Boswell" in the modern sense – someone who will present a faithful picture of a great man to posterity – the real Boswell repeatedly tinkered with Johnson's sometimes lumbering epigrams to render them sharp and balanced, as the recently published manuscript version of the *Life* has demonstrated.[5]

What has long been identified as his "Flemish picture" of Johnson, with its use of "unvarnished surfaces as a means of suggesting inspirational depths,"[6] is itself a tribute to Boswell's cunning slant, his talent for selection and his fictive recreation of his source materials. Johnson's harshness and crudity are not revealed as the surface of a rough diamond; they are instead toned down to give the representation of coarse, direct English decency without the corresponding degree of offensiveness sometimes present in the originals. Johnson's attitudes toward Scots as recorded in the *Life* are thus not always to be trusted, while Boswell's triumphal record of the Scottish tour on which he took Johnson in 1773 is arguably a way of presenting the education of the typical Englishman: it was a tour, Boswell observes, that led to Johnson's prejudices becoming "much lessened" (Boswell, *Life*, 5:20). The tour, in other words, was portrayed as a triumph for Boswell's perspicacious cosmopolitanism over Johnson's insular prejudice, an opposition not without implicit reference to the social divisions between the men: in Scotland, Boswell – a nobleman and heir to a barony – presents himself as knowing people everywhere whom Johnson has never met.

A SOCIETY IN DECAY

Outside the pages of Boswell, however, one of the things about Johnson that most clearly differentiates him from this construction of insular prejudice is the fact that he in fact knew a good deal about Scotland, far more than most Englishmen: he was interested in the country. On his journey there in 1773, Johnson was not learning so much as he was measuring what he saw against his existing knowledge of Scotland's history, society, and, above all, religion. One of the things that is clear about Johnson from his own writings, though, is his tendency to see Scotland as a "society in decay."[7] His recorded lament over the loss of Scots learning in the seventeenth century, and his exclamations over two old churches altered in the Scottish Reformation – St. Giles in Edinburgh ("what was once a church!") and Holyrood Palace ("that deserted mansion of royalty") (Boswell, *Life*, 5:41, 43) – reinforce the sense that Scots Presbyterianism was guilty of simony, a word Johnson defines bluntly as "The crime of buying or selling church preferment." The simoniac character of Scots Presbyterianism was the chief denominator of Johnson's surliness towards the country: from his point of view, Scotland began by selling out its queen (Mary, Queen of Scots, captured in 1567–8, to be executed on the orders of Queen Elizabeth in 1587), continued by selling its king (Charles I, delivered to the English Parliament in 1647, to be executed two years later), and crowned it all by selling its very nationality (the Union of 1707 dissolved the Scottish Parliament and integrated it into the new nation, Great Britain).

To understand Johnson's views as well as Boswell's characterization of them, we must try to see the Scotland of their day as they would have understood it. Much had changed in Anglo-Scots relations since the sixteenth century. England and Scotland had long been separate countries, with separate kings and separate parliaments. But after centuries of independence, a party among the leaders of the Scottish state had become more pro-English in the period between the English (1533–9) and Scottish (1560) Reformations, seeing England as their ally in the Protestant cause. The Catholic Mary, Queen of Scots, managed to rule for a few years over the newly Protestant country before a civil war between her supporters and Protestant opponents took place in 1567–73. The situation looked promising for the Scots in 1603, when Queen Elizabeth of England died without an heir, and her cousin, James VI of Scotland, became James I of England in the so-called Union of the Crowns. But, even with a Scottish monarch ruling both Scotland and England, Scotland did not flourish in the seventeenth century.

The Scottish Reformation, unlike its English counterpart, was not initiated by the crown: it was mounted in opposition to it, and was far more destructive of the fabric of the Church and its churches than was the case in the south. In 1637–8, the supposed Catholicizing policies of Charles I (in fact aimed at uniformity of Anglican and Episcopalian worship) led to a Protestant rebellion, the National Covenant of 1638, and in the end to civil war throughout the British kingdoms. The Stuart dynasty were ever after suspected by the Presbyterian party, who sold Charles into the English Parliament's custody in 1647. Divisions in Scotland helped the leader of the English Republic, Oliver Cromwell, to rule it from the beginning of the 1650s, but although Charles II was welcomed home in 1660, the reestablishing of Episcopalianism which followed led to further armed rebellion by the Covenanting Protestants. After the Stuarts were deposed in 1688–9, Presbyterianism became the established Church of Scotland; but while the supporters of the Stuarts – the Jacobites – were initially in a minority, after the Union of 1707 they were seen by many as the supporters of Scottish national rights, and thousands fought under their banner in successive risings, until their final defeat at Culloden in 1746 and their suppression in the British army occupation of Scotland that followed.

THE 1760S

By the early 1760s, largely Presbyterian Scots were causing resentment in England, as they arrived in London in pursuit of career enhancement. Their whole country was still under suspicion because of the Jacobite episode, while the ability of these Scots to focus on opportunities down south was itself a product of the defeat of the Jacobites. Nonetheless, their clannish organization was seen by many as redolent of Jacobitism, and that is how Scots in London were often portrayed by the political cartoons. The Jacobite cause had long represented itself as selfless, concerned with honor and the national rights of Scotland, rather than careerism and greed. It had portrayed Presbyterians as hypocrites who would sell sacred things – even their own king and country – to gain position and opportunity, while the Jacobites saw themselves as sacrificing everything they had to defend their country and their king. It was in this context that Johnson and Boswell first met in 1763, and in which many of Johnson's views were written or recorded.

Boswell's own sympathies were often nationalist (with a smallish "n") and crypto-Jacobite: he "hankered after the reign of the Stuarts," so was a suitable companion for Johnson's prejudices.[8] But he was by no means Johnson's only Scots friend of that hue. In 1738–40, shortly after he arrived in London, Johnson had been closely associated with William Guthrie, a Scot with Jacobite connections and the son of an Episcopalian priest. He was also friendly not only with Englishmen with Jacobite leanings, such as Edward Cave and Richard Savage, but also with a prominent Jacobite Scot, William Drummond, bookseller and possibly sometime Gentleman Volunteer in Major John Haldane's troop in Strathallan's Perthshire Horse squadron (or Captain in the Duke of Perth's Regiment), who fought for Charles Edward in 1745–6. Drummond was the publisher for the *Scottish Communion Office* of 1764, a key text of Nonjuring Episcopalians (those Episcopal clergy who would not take the oaths to support those who had succeeded the Stuarts on the throne). The third edition of 1765 was produced with the help of Bishop Forbes, an ardent Jacobite patriot and the compiler of *The Lyon in Mourning*. Johnson supported Drummond's efforts to publish a Gaelic New Testament, and also admired Thomas Ruddiman, Jacobite cultural leader and Arthur Johnston, the Latin poet and supporter of High-Church Episcopalianism. Moreover, Johnson was fond of Johnston and Ruddiman's city, Old Aberdeen, seat of King's College, the environs of which were still an Episcopalian and to some extent Catholic stronghold. If this were not enough, it was Alexander Wedderburn, a Scot from a Jacobite family, who promoted Johnson's pension, which was granted under the Scottish Earl of Bute's administration in 1762.

Lichfield Cathedral in Johnson's home city had suffered very badly in the War of the Three Kingdoms in the 1640s – the complicated series of conflicts of which the English Civil Wars were the most familiar component. For Johnson, Scotland was an example of what might happen in England should Protestant zealotry gain the upper hand. Almost all of Scotland's cathedrals had been ruined or severely damaged, and Johnson saw a clear link between such ruins and "the intellectual and religious decay of society."[9] When such decay is avoided, cultural value survives: in the chapel at Inch Kenneth, Johnson remarked approvingly of the survival of the image of the "bas-relief of the Virgin with her child" and the "handbell" which once rang for the elevation of the Host (*Letters*, 2:105). For Johnson, Scottish Presbyterianism is a force that insults women (Mary, Queen of Scots), overthrows kings (Charles I), and sells its churches (stripped of their decorations), its kings, and its country (Charles I in 1647; the Union of 1707). For good measure, it also destroys learning. In Johnson's view, Scots Presbyterianism is the simoniac religion of a Knoxian mob: the Scottish leader of the Protestant Reformation, John Knox, "set on a mob," Johnson said, "without knowing where it would end" (Boswell, *Life*, 5:62). And Knox's successors in London in the era of Bute, he was convinced, pursued places, perquisities, and pelf with the unprincipled greed of their forebears.

Johnson angrily thought that those who wished to "melt the lead of an English cathedral" should be forced to swallow their "cargo of sacrilege" (*Works*, 9:xxxiv, 20), as he describes the lead stolen from Aberdeen and Elgin cathedrals. The "poor remains of a stately cathedral" at St. Andrews are the concomitant of a wider decay, manifest in its small and struggling university (*Letters*, 1:55). In likening Knox to Alaric the Visigoth, whose sack of Rome in 410 CE foreshadowed both the end of empire and the successful defense of Rome against a second sack forty years later, when Pope Gregory talked Attila the Hun out of it, Johnson makes a comparison between St. Andrews and Rome, and perhaps implicitly aligns its patriot Cardinal Beaton, Primate of Scotland, murdered by the Reformers in 1546, with the papacy.

GAELIC SYMPATHIES

Johnson's sympathetic interest in the Scottish Highlands and its inhabitants – and, in fact, in the Gaelic languages – may come as a surprise to those more familiar with his vituperation of Macpherson's Ossian (see chapter 32, "Nationalism"). In 1757 Johnson had encouraged the study of Irish Gaelic, and in 1766 he defended the Scottish version of the language; his "Last Word on Ossian" was a "ghost-written piece for the Gaelic scholar William Shaw."[10] Johnson shows sympathy for the economic decline of the Gàidhealtachd – the Highlands culture – in Scotland, as well as its ancient patriarchal loyalties and martial traditions. His sympathies, though, are underpinned by the fact that, whereas Presbyterian Scotland brought its ills on itself by its own vice and destructiveness, the decline of the Gàidhealtachd was a consequence of its oppression from outside: "where there was formerly an insurrection, there is now a wilderness" (*Works*, 9:97), he says, in unmistakable allusion to Tacitus's speech, put in the mouth of the Scottish martial hero Calgacus: "solitudinem faciunt, pacem appellant," or "they make a wilderness and call it peace." The "desart" of Scotland mentioned at the beginning of this essay turns out to be one not only of native viciousness, but (as in pre-Union Scottish patriotic discourse) also the result of imperial oppression. Tacitus's speech praises republican virtue (Calgacus as a Caledonian Horatio) against imperial corruption. Given that this is a discourse which, in his comments on Canada, the Falkland Islands, and elsewhere, is strongly present in Johnson's writing, it is more than likely that he is using it here. The Highlanders are the victims of powerful trends in modernity of which their Presbyterian neighbors (who have colluded in their oppression where they have not initiated it) are among the basest examples.

This vehemence in Johnson – a vehement sympathy with Scotland, as well as a vehement despising of it – comes to some degree from the fact that he saw in it an awful warning of what England might become. Already England was a society with "so many churches sinking into ruins" (*Works*, 10:114–15), and Johnson's commentary on his own country satirizes – via Juvenal as well as Tacitus – the inner decay of an imperial society, laced with notes of Jacobitical disappointment. In this assessment, Scotland's place in the Union was not just as England's resented junior partner on the make, but rather itself an epitaph on the integrity of a governing Presbyterian class whose greed, hypocrisy, and anti-intellectualism made the cause of the making of Scotland a great lost opportunity, emblematic of the final decline of learning and "the vanity of human wishes." Johnson's assessment of Scotland was corrosive, negative, and final – but not out of insular prejudice, but rather well-informed disappointment at what the country had become. If Boswell is to be trusted, in 1773 Johnson congratulated Lord Monboddo's son on his Latin by saying, "When King James comes back, you shall be in the 'Muses Welcome!'" (Boswell, *Life*, 5:81), referring to a collection of 1617 for James VI, which Johnson saw as evidence of Scottish learning in an earlier, Episcopalian, era. The last "King James," to whom Johnson or Boswell is slyly referring, the Jacobite heir, had died in 1766. He would never come back now; nor would that independent Scotland of secular learning, selfless loyalty, and religious order which Johnson mourned, while despising those who had sold its birthright.

NOTES

1 William R. Siebenschuch, *Form and Purpose in Boswell's Biographical Works* (Berkeley and Los Angeles: University of California Press, 1972), p. 4.

2 J. C. D. Clark, *Samuel Johnson: Literature, Religion and English Cultural Politics from the Restoration to Romanticism* (Cambridge: Cambridge University Press, 1994), pp. 36, 239.

3 John Cannon, *Samuel Johnson and the Politics of Hanoverian England* (Oxford: Oxford University Press, 1994), p. 22.

4 Murray Pittock, *James Boswell* (Aberdeen: AHRC Centre for Irish and Scottish Studies, 2007), p. 99.

5 James Boswell, *James Boswell's Life of Johnson: An Edition of the Original Manuscript*, ed. Marshall Waingrow *et al.*, 2 vols. to date (New Haven, CT: Yale University Press, 1994–).

6 Bruce Redford, *Designing the Life of Johnson* (Oxford: Oxford University Press, 2002), p. 53.

7 Clark, *Johnson*, p. 239.

8 *The Correspondence of James Boswell and William Johnson Temple, 1756–1795*, ed. Thomas Crawford, 2 vols. (Edinburgh: Edinburgh University Press; New Haven, CT: Yale University Press, 1997–), 1:liv.

9 John A. Vance, *Samuel Johnson and the Sense of History* (Athens: University of Georgia Press, 1984), p. 80.

10 Thomas M. Curley, "Johnson's Last Word on Ossian," in *Aberdeen and the Enlightenment*, ed. J. J. Carter and Joan Pittock (Aberdeen: Aberdeen University Press, 1987), pp. 375–431.

CHAPTER 39

Sermons

Jennifer Ellis Snead

> SE'RMON. *n.s.* [*sermon*, Fr. *sermo*, Lat.] A discourse of instruction pronounced by a divine for the edification of the people.
>
> His preaching much, but more his practice wrought;
> A living *sermon* of the truths he taught. *Dryden*.

Samuel Johnson's sermons have received the least attention of any of the categories of his writing, despite the fact that his religious beliefs and moral philosophy are perennial topics of scholarship. My observation is not new; James Gray opened *Johnson's Sermons: A Study* (1972) with two reasons for "this apparent lacuna in Johnsonian scholarship": doubt, dating back to Johnson's lifetime, as to the authorship of the sermons themselves, and a bias against homiletic writings on the part of literary scholars.[1] Gray's account of the status of Johnson's sermons in Johnsonian scholarship of the first half of the twentieth century holds true for their status in the opening years of the twenty-first as well; *Johnson's Sermons: A Study* is still the only book-length treatment of Johnson's homiletic writing. I believe this is because of the same pair of reasons: (1) we cannot be completely sure that the sermons were authored solely by Samuel Johnson, and (2) homiletic writing, despite its popularity during the eighteenth century, remains unpopular in eighteenth-century literary scholarship. Placing Johnson's sermons in their eighteenth-century context thus involves taking ourselves out of our twenty-first-century contexts, specifically of how we value homiletic writing and of how we think of authorship. In the eighteenth century, both of these topics were thought of quite differently than they are now.

SERMONS AS LITERATURE

When Johnson remarked to John Wilkes in 1781 that sermons "make a considerable branch of English literature" (Boswell, *Life*, 4:105), he was commenting on more than their aesthetic literary value. A major shift in homiletic writing had occurred over the first fifty or so years of the eighteenth century. Sermons were increasingly written for the bookshelf and the hearthside, as well as for use in the pulpit. Sermon literature became popular outside the church among lay readers who purchased individually published sermons and collections of homiletic writings for private devotional reading, for family prayers, or for meetings of pious societies for the reformation of manners. In parishes where Sunday services did not always include a sermon – often the case if the incumbent preacher had multiple livings – or where the preaching was deemed dull and uninspiring, members of those congregations could make up the lack at home by reading published sermons out loud. The market for printed sermons burgeoned; even so inveterate a preacher as John Wesley began writing sermons specifically for publication, works that differed vastly in tone and style from those we are told he actually preached. Booksellers capitalized on this demand by publishing large numbers of sermons, in collections or by individual authors, so much so that by 1742 Henry Fielding's *Joseph Andrews* could feature a bookseller complaining about how the trade was "so vastly stocked" with sermons that his shelves had room for no more.[2]

The purchasers of printed sermons would already have been accustomed to marking important occasions with some kind of homiletic experience. Sermons punctuated the weekly round of the layperson's year. Exegeses of passages from Scripture were preached during Sunday worship services, but sermons also marked public religious and political occasions during the week. Saints' days, feast days, fast days; consecrations, ordinations, baptisms, weddings, funerals; public prayers of thanksgiving or atonement for political crises, military victories, or natural disasters – each event called for an appropriate sermon. In the wake of the evangelical revivals of the 1720s and 1730s, sermons calling for repentance and conversion were regular features of weekday early mornings and late evenings (so as not to interfere with the schedule of Anglican worship or the daily labors of their working-class audiences) in those communities where revivalism took hold. Gray has written that "for eighteenth-century readers [sermons] had something of the interest of present-day manuals of popular psychology, as well as the status of a model of English prose."[3]

REASON AND RESTRAINT

The "model of English prose" that eighteenth-century sermons represented for their reading audiences had also undergone many changes during the late seventeenth and early eighteenth centuries. From the 1610s to the Restoration of 1660 the pendulum of sermon writing had swung from one extreme to another, from the Baroque or Metaphysical style of the first half of the seventeenth century, exemplified by the elaborate metaphors of preachers such as John Donne and Lancelot Andrewes, to the austere plain speaking of the Puritan Commonwealth. In the aftermath of the seventeenth-century political and religious upheavals that culminated in the Glorious Revolution of 1688 (see chapter 35, "Politics"), the Church sought an alternative to both High Anglican wit and Puritan zealotry, a homiletic style that would both reflect and shape an ecclesiology that viewed itself as a moderate path between extremes (see chapter 11, "Anglicanism").

This centrist orientation, or Latitudinarianism, was guided by the work of philosopher John Locke and the theology of John Tillotson, Archbishop of Canterbury from 1691 to 1694, both informed by the dictates of reason, moderation, and tolerance. Latitudinarian sermons focused on morality rather than metaphor, on directives for good behavior in this life rather than diatribes on avoiding hellfire in the next. Their arguments were founded on reason, restraint, and ethical conduct. Throughout the first three decades of the eighteenth century, Anglican homiletics was dominated by an emphasis on simplicity, moderation, and practical piety – the reasoned application of belief to everyday life, eschewing the niceties of theological debate and doctrinal polemics.

THE EVANGELICAL REVIVAL

The morality and moderation of Latitudinarian preaching was challenged by the evangelical revival of the late 1730s and early 1740s. Leaders of the revival – founding figures in the development of Methodism such as George Whitefield, John Wesley, and Howell Harris – dismissed traditional preaching as ineffective in encouraging lay piety. Evangelical sermons aimed for a heightened awareness of humanity's helplessly sinful state. Their audiences were often driven into frenzies of terror at the idea that there was absolutely nothing on earth one could *do* to save oneself from eternal damnation. Such terrors could be allayed, argued the evangelical sermon, only by faith in Christ's saving grace: this was the first step along the road to conversion.

Working outside of Anglican institutional organization – most were not affiliated with a parish, and they were often banned from preaching from established pulpits on Sundays – evangelicals preached wherever and whenever they could draw a crowd, often in fields in the predawn darkness or in barns, lent by sympathetic followers, in the late evenings. They also printed and distributed their sermons outside of traditional channels and formats, as cheap tracts and broadsides carried in the saddlebags of itinerant preachers. For its detractors, evangelical preaching was old wine in new bottles – the specter of seventeenth-century Puritan fanaticism, threatening the established religious and social order. Still these sermons were effective and converted thousands, and by the 1780s the Church of England had its own evangelical wing, whose members incorporated the preaching style and pious practices of the earlier revivalists into established Anglican worship.

FAITH AND WORKS

The challenge to Anglican centrism represented by evangelical preaching was one of content as well as style: what, especially given the expansion of reading audiences for homiletic writings during the first half of the eighteenth century, should sermons be for? Should they, as the Latitudinarian tradition insisted, encourage ethical and moral outward behavior through reasoned appeals to moderation and rationality? Or should they rather inculcate inner belief through simple appeals to feeling and emotion? Were humans agents in their own salvation, able through individual, daily actions to influence their eternal fate? Or were they powerless to counteract their own sinful natures and utterly reliant on belief in divine mercy? In other words, eighteenth-century homiletic traditions in preaching and print split over the old Protestant debate of faith versus works, or what Isabel Rivers has called "the tension between the languages of reason and grace."[4]

While Johnson's sermons have been stylistically characterized as "learned," "elegant," and "reasoned," the spiritual offspring of Tillotson and other late seventeenth-century Latitudinarians, they also reflect this mid-century tension between faith and works in their invocation of what Johnson calls "a holy fear," which "implicitly condemns all self-confidence, all presumptuous security; and enjoins a constant state of vigilance and caution, a perpetual distrust of our own hearts, a full conviction of our natural weakness, and an earnest solicitude for divine assistance" (*Works*, 14:29). This doubt of human efficacy, however, supplies a greater incentive to good works as the surest way to assuage, or at least hold in abeyance, fears of eternal damnation. In their sturdy, reasoned insistence on man's active participation in his own salvation and their unflinching acknowledgment of doubt, Johnson's sermons demonstrate Johnson's characteristic blend of devotion and pragmatism.

JOHNSON'S SERMONS

In terms of their style and content, Johnson's sermons navigate the homiletic currents that swirl through the first half of the eighteenth century, Anglican and evangelical, reasoned and feeling, pious and pragmatic. In terms of their authorship, they are no less the products of the historical moment in which they were produced. Although it has been estimated from contemporary accounts – his own diaries and Boswell's *Life* – that Johnson wrote more than forty sermons, only a little over half of that number have been identified as his.

Johnson composed and sold his sermons for others to preach. This was a common and acceptable process for the dissemination of eighteenth-century British homiletic writing: clergymen regularly bought or borrowed the sermons of others for use in their own pulpits, sometimes in their entirety, and sometimes in part, rarely with full attribution to their original composers. Johnson himself wrote most of his sermons for John Taylor, a childhood friend and the Prebend of Westminster, who collaborated with him on the composition of several, and who may have made significant changes on his own to several more. After Taylor's death in 1788, these sermons were found among his papers and published in two volumes as *Sermons on Different Subjects, Left for Publication by John Taylor, LL.D.* The second volume advertised that it contained, in addition, "A Sermon written by Samuel Johnson, LL.D., for the funeral of his wife," but the rest of the sermons were not acknowledged as Johnson's. This apparent disregard for textual property was part and parcel of more general attitudes towards authorship throughout the eighteenth century. Writers of all genres usually relinquished all right to their works to the booksellers who printed and sold them, before copyright laws and ideals of individual creative genius developed and shaped concepts of proprietary authorship in the late eighteenth century (see chapter 13, "Authorship").

The convoluted tale of the attribution and composition of the sermons is told in full in the editors' introduction to the Yale edition of the sermons, which carefully attempts to distinguish those that are "flawlessly Johnsonian" from those "where the touch of Taylor seems to have obscured but not obliterated Johnson's image" (*Works*, 14:ix–xxix, lii–lix). In its insistence on discriminating between the pure products of Johnson's homiletic genius and those muddied by Taylor's additions or modifications, the Yale edition follows in the footsteps of Johnson's earliest editors and biographers of the late eighteenth and early nineteenth centuries, whose delineation of Johnson's genuine works was a crucial part of their attempts to establish him posthumously as a literary giant. None of the sermons associated with Taylor were included in any edition of Johnson's collected works until 1825. The role played by Johnson's sermons in the story of the establishment of the Johnsonian canon overall reflects changing attitudes towards authorship and textual ownership, and the development of an ideal of individual literary genius, at the beginning of the nineteenth century; as the introduction to the Yale edition suggests, this ideal of literary genius continues to have an impact on critical attitudes towards the sermons.

Gray has argued that the sermons are best appreciated as collaborative or cowritten texts, albeit with Johnson's influence, in style and ideas, being the stronger, but interwoven with Taylor's sense of his own particular pulpit and audience.[5] As collaborations that resist definitive individual attribution, the sermons might also be considered as what John Bryant terms "fluid texts," registering "the evolution of authorship, the pressures of production, and the power of readers."[6] In other words, the circumstances of their composition need to be placed as fully into the fluid context of eighteenth-century authorship and ownership just as their style and ideas are usually placed into the context of eighteenth-century homiletics, or the context of Johnson's thought. Doing so would make Johnson's sermons works of value in their own right, rather than relatively minor probationers within the Johnsonian canon.

NOTES

1 James Gray, *Johnson's Sermons: A Study* (Oxford: Clarendon Press, 1972), p. 1.

2 Henry Fielding, *Joseph Andrews*, ed. Martin Battestin (Middletown, CT: Wesleyan University Press, 1969), p. 79.

3 Gray, *Johnson's Sermons*, pp. 1–2.

4 Isabel Rivers, *Reason, Grace, and Sentiment: A Study in the Language of Religion and Ethics in England, 1660–1780*, vol. 1, *Whichcote to Wesley* (Cambridge: Cambridge University Press, 1991), pp. 1, 9–10.

5 Gray, *Johnson's Sermons*, p. 36.

6 John Bryant, "The Uses of the Fluid Text," *Textual Cultures* 2, no. 1 (2007), 16–42, at p. 21.

CHAPTER 40

Shakespeare

Fiona Ritchie

> DRA'MA. *n.s.* [δρᾶμα.] A poem accommodated to action; a poem in which the action is not related, but represented; and in which therefore such rules are to be observed as make the representation probable.
>
> Many rules of imitating nature Aristotle drew from Homer, which he fitted to the *drama*; furnishing himself also with observations from the theatre, when it flourished under Eschylus, Euripides, and Sophocles. *Dryden's Æn. Dedicat.*

The year of Johnson's birth saw the publication of the first modern edition of Shakespeare's works. The plays had been collected into an imposing folio volume in 1623, seven years after Shakespeare's death, and this had been reprinted in 1632, 1663, and 1685. But not until Nicholas Rowe's six-volume edition of 1709 did what could be considered an edited version of Shakespeare appear.

Rowe, a popular dramatist of the period, concentrated on the theatrical presentation of the plays: he introduced act and scene divisions, noted the location of the action, regularized entrances and exits, and included the *dramatis personae* for each play – all features included in virtually all modern editions of Shakespeare, and unavailable before Rowe. His editorial labor also included modernizing some of the spelling and punctuation of Shakespeare's text and producing an account of Shakespeare's life which was to become the standard biography of the playwright for much of the eighteenth century.

Rowe's project marks the starting point of an important era of Shakespeare editing. His work was followed by editions from other eminent men of letters: Alexander Pope (1723–5), Lewis Theobald (1733), Thomas Hanmer (1744), William Warburton (1747), Edward Capell (1768), Isaac Reed (1785), and Edmond Malone (1790). Johnson was born in the year in which this illustrious tradition was inaugurated, and his own edition of Shakespeare (1765) falls in the middle of this succession of scholarly texts of the Bard. And his work, as expanded by his sometime collaborator George Steevens (1773 and 1778), formed the basis of subsequent editions by Malone, Reed (1803), and James Boswell, Jr. (1821), which became the standard versions of Shakespeare for decades to come. Shakespeare was a crucial part of the literary landscape.

THE GENUINE TEXT

Pope's attitude to Shakespeare, as described in the preface to his edition, is somewhat typical of the age. "Of all *English* Poets," writes Pope, "*Shakespeare* must be confessed to be the fairest and fullest subject for Criticism, and to afford the most numerous as well as most conspicuous instances both of Beauties and Faults of all sorts."[1] There is a sense that Shakespeare affords a rich object of study, but also that, as a writer, he is far from perfect. This is echoed in Pope's editorial method, in which "Some suspected passages which are excessively bad … are degraded to the bottom of the page, with an Asterisk referring to the places of their insertion," while "Some of the most shining passages are distinguish'd by comma's in the margin, and where the beauty lay not in particulars but in the whole a star is prefix'd to the scene."[2] Pope's personal appreciation of the works clearly influenced his presentation of Shakespeare: what he liked must be genuine, and what he found "excessively bad" clearly did not belong in Shakespeare's text.

Other editors took a less subjective approach. Theobald rejected Pope's aesthetic response, and sought instead to adhere closely to what he called Shakespeare's "genuine Text," collating the old copies of the plays, both quartos and folios, in order to find the meaning of obscure passages. Theobald claimed that his edition was more methodical: "Nothing is alter'd but what by the clearest Reasoning can be proved a Corruption of the true Text, and the Alteration a real Restoration of the genuine Reading."[3] Nevertheless, the editor's input is sometimes required in instances where all the surviving texts appear to be corrupt – in which case a judicious revision of the text, known as "conjectural emendation," must be employed (see chapter 36, "Scholarship"). Warburton for one seems to have taken the concept of conjecture too far in his edition, proposing numerous readings that strain the bounds of credibility. In *As You Like It*, for example, Rosalind says Orlando's kissing "is as full of sanctity as the touch of holy bread," referring to the sacrament of the Church. Warburton, though, changes the end of the line to "holy beard," justifying his emendation thus: "We should read *beard*, that is, as the kiss of an holy saint or hermit, called the *kiss of charity*: This makes the comparison just and decent; the other impious and absurd."[4]

Warburton was roundly mocked for emendations such as this one, and Johnson famously declared his distrust of this type of editorial practice: "As I practised conjecture more, I learned to trust it less" (*Works*, 7:108). Johnson did, however, recognize the need for occasional conjectural emendation, but insisted it should be employed only when a "passage appeared inextricably perplexed," in which case he attempted "to discover how it may be recalled to sense, with least violence" (7:106). Johnson also established the authority of the First Folio of 1623 as a base text, trying to find a way to make the original make sense before imposing his own reading: "But my first labour is, always to turn the old text on every side, and try if there be any interstice, through which light can find its way" (7:106).

CRITICISM

Johnson echoes many of his predecessors' pronouncements on Shakespeare. The playwright had been criticized for his neglect of the neoclassical unities of time, place, and action, which dictated that a play must take place within a single day, in a single location, and be composed of one main plot. Pope, however, claimed that "To judge … of *Shakespeare* by *Aristotle*'s rules is like trying a man by the Laws of one Country, who acted under those of another."[5] Johnson similarly declares, "Whether Shakespeare knew the unities, and rejected them by design, or deviated from them by happy ignorance, it is, I think, impossible to decide, and useless to inquire" (*Works*, 7:79). Both claim that Shakespeare wrote without the influence of learning and to please his audience, Pope noting that "He writ to the *People* … without assistance or advice from the Learned,"[6] and Johnson asserting that "Shakespeare engaged in dramatick poetry with the world open before him; the rules of the ancients were yet known to few; the publick judgment was unformed" (*Works*, 7:69). Similarly, just as Pope had described Shakespeare as "not so much an Imitator, as an Instrument of Nature"[7] and Theobald referred to his "grand Touches of Nature,"[8] Johnson famously claimed that "Shakespeare is above all writers, at least above all modern writers, the poet of nature; the poet that holds up to his readers a faithful mirrour of manners and of life" (*Works*, 7:62).

CHARACTER

Johnson goes on to praise Shakespeare's characterization, and so it seems that for him Shakespeare's "naturalness" is bound up with human nature, with the way in which he depicts people. Johnson values Shakespeare's characters for the ways in which they are like us: "His persons act and speak by the influence of those general passions and principles by which all minds are agitated, and the whole system of life is continued in motion. In the writings of other poets a character is too often an individual; in those of Shakespeare it is commonly a species" (*Works*, 7:62). He also recognizes that many of Shakespeare's characters are startlingly original: for example, he proclaims Falstaff "unimitated" and "unimitable." His analysis, however, concentrates on what is familiar and recognizable in the character: "Thou compound of sense and vice," he calls Falstaff; "of sense which may be admired but not esteemed, of vice which may be despised, but hardly detested." Notable here is also Johnson's emotional response to the character: his sense is admired and his vice despised, his faults "naturally produce contempt," but "his licentiousness is not so offensive but that it may be borne for his mirth" (*Works*, 7:523).

In his interest in the emotions provoked by character, Johnson is very much in line with the theatrical practices of the period. Performers were increasingly known for the characters they portrayed, and their ability to move the audience was highly prized. As the most famous actor of his day, Johnson's friend David Garrick was at the forefront of this movement, and descriptions of the emotional impact he had on playgoers abound (see chapter 43, "Theatre"). In *Hamlet*, for example, Thomas Davies described how, "When Mr. Garrick first saw the ghost, the terror he seemed to be impressed with, was instantaneously communicated to the audience."[9] Leading actors of the day became particularly associated with some of the Shakespearean roles in which they performed: Susannah Cibber was "the only Cordelia of excellence,"[10] and was painted in the role by Peter Van Bleeck (1755); Hannah Pritchard was considered the greatest Lady Macbeth of her day, and was depicted in the play (opposite Garrick) by Johann Zoffany (1768); and James Quin was a celebrated Falstaff, immortalized in porcelain figurines that could be purchased by his fans.

ADAPTATIONS

Shakespeare's characters were certainly popular on the stage, but it is important to know that his plays were not necessarily performed in the

Figure 37 Peter van Bleeck, *Mrs. Cibber in the Character of Cordelia*, 1755.

ways in which he wrote them. Beginning in the Restoration, the plays were altered – sometimes substantially rewritten – for a variety of reasons, and many of these adaptations held the stage well into the nineteenth century.

Often the changes had to do with altering the audience's emotional response to the play. Most famously, *King Lear* was given a happy ending by Nahum Tate in 1681: Cordelia and her father are allowed to live, and a love story is introduced between Cordelia and Edgar. The concept of "poetic justice" dictated that good characters must prosper and the bad must be punished. Tate's ending preserved this dictum. The ending may strike us as a perversion of Shakespeare, but it proved so popular with playgoers that the tragic ending was not restored until 1838.

And it was not just audiences who felt this way: as a reader, Johnson too struggled with the emotional impact of the play's conclusion, writing, "I was many years ago so shocked by Cordelia's death, that I know not whether I ever endured to read again the last scenes of the play till I undertook to revise them as an editor" (*Works*, 8:704). In his notes to the play, Johnson is troubled by the cruel blow that Shakespeare has dealt the virtuous Cordelia, and seems to favor Tate's ending over Shakespeare's:

> A play in which the wicked prosper, and the virtuous miscarry, may doubtless be good, because it is a just representation of the common events of human life: but since all reasonable beings naturally love justice, I cannot easily be persuaded, that the observation of justice makes a play worse; or, that if other excellencies are equal, the audience will not always rise better pleased from the final triumph of persecuted virtue. (*Works*, 8:704)

MORAL PURPOSE

The morality of art was a central concern of the period, and Johnson appears skeptical about Shakespeare's ethics: "He sacrifices virtue to convenience, and is so much more careful to please than to instruct, that he seems to write without any moral purpose" (*Works*, 7:71). Eighteenth-century aesthetic theory held that art should both delight and teach, but Johnson implies that Shakespeare privileges the former at the expense of the latter. Johnson does not claim that Shakespeare is immoral per se, but he does express anxiety that readers and playgoers must construct his moral code for themselves: "From his writings indeed a system of social duty may be selected, for he that thinks reasonably must think morally" (7:71). Shakespeare's approach to morality is simply too haphazard for Johnson: "his precepts and axioms drop casually from him; he makes no just distribution of good or evil, nor is always careful to shew in the virtuous a disapprobation of the wicked; he carries his persons indifferently through right and wrong, and at the close dismisses them without further care, and leaves their examples to operate by chance" (7:71). Thus Tate's revision of *King Lear* is not just designed to be more emotionally satisfying to the audience; it also rectifies Shakespeare's casual approach to morality in his treatment of the characters.

Other Restoration and eighteenth-century Shakespeare adaptations altered the plays to give them a clearer moral message. William Davenant's version of *Macbeth* (1664) gives the protagonist a dying line to allow him to demonstrate some remorse for his crimes: "Farewell vain World, and what's most vain in it, Ambition."[11] This was subsequently expanded by Garrick in his version of the play to provide an entire death speech for the character, which showcased the actor's talents in such scenes. Garrick produced his version of the play in 1744, and the following year Johnson published his *Miscellaneous Observations on the Tragedy of Macbeth*. This was intended as a specimen of his editorial ability; Johnson attached to it proposals for a complete edition of Shakespeare's plays.

PAGE AND STAGE

It is interesting that both Johnson and Garrick, who were old friends, chose to focus on the same play. We might see their works as two different approaches to Shakespeare, Johnson dealing with his work on the page, and Garrick with how the play should be performed on the stage. But this obscures how closely the two methods of presentation were linked in the eighteenth century.

Johnson does concentrate on textual matters, offering notes that elucidate the meaning of various passages. But he opens with a long discussion of witchcraft which, while it is clearly designed to provide historical context on the supernatural beliefs of Shakespeare's day, also chimes with contemporary stage practice: ever since Davenant's version, the witches had played a greatly expanded part in the play as they sang, danced, and swooped about the stage on flying machinery, and were one of the main draws for the audience. Johnson's interest in the witches is therefore unsurprising if we consider how the play was being staged at this time. Garrick's adaptation of *Macbeth*, on the other hand, certainly focuses on making the protagonist a suitable vehicle for himself as an actor, but it also engages with the editorial work being conducted on Shakespeare at this time: Garrick chooses between readings of certain lines that had been proposed by editors and scholars, including Johnson, with whom he presumably discussed the play.

Johnson's proposed edition was stalled by a copyright dispute: the publisher Jacob Tonson threatened Johnson's printer, Edward Cave, with legal action, claiming that he owned the texts of Shakespeare's plays (see chapter 15, "Book trade"). The validity of his claim was questionable, but the mere threat of a lawsuit was enough to make Cave back down and abandon the project. But Johnson tried again in 1756, issuing a new set of proposals for the printing of an edition, which he would eventually publish in 1765 in eight volumes. This proposal was perhaps inspired by the success of his

Dictionary, which had appeared in 1755 to much acclaim: the proposals of 1756 concentrate on Johnson's plans to fix Shakespeare's language and elucidate his meaning, which had in many cases become obscure, just as he had attempted to do for the English language in his lexicographical work.

The *Dictionary* is also relevant here since Shakespeare is one of the most frequently cited authorities in that text: Johnson included illustrative quotations for each definition, showing each word in use, and many of the examples are from Shakespeare. In many cases Johnson begins his textual criticism of Shakespeare in the *Dictionary*, working to clarify the language in the Shakespearean passages he cites.

The prominence of Shakespeare in the *Dictionary* also shows Shakespeare's position in eighteenth-century culture at large. As the number of editions increased, his work became known to more and more people through the increased accessibility in print, not just in the costly multivolume editions but also in the cheap, individual copies of the plays that proliferated in the 1730s. The plays were also frequently performed: Shakespeare made up about a quarter of the entire eighteenth-century theatre repertory (see chapter 43, "Theatre"). And although the Restoration adaptations remained popular, a new reverence towards Shakespeare developed over the course of the eighteenth century. The word *bardolatry* was not coined until 1901, but the phenomenon was in full bloom as Johnson's edition was published: Shakespeare had been commemorated with a statue placed in Poets' Corner, Westminster Abbey, in 1741, and Garrick's celebratory Shakespeare Jubilee at Stratford-upon-Avon in 1769 firmly entrenched Shakespeare's place in English culture. Johnson's edition of Shakespeare constitutes a part of this eighteenth-century movement, and is significant for its enduring influence on the way that Shakespeare was perceived from 1765 onwards.

NOTES

1 *The Prose Works of Alexander Pope*, vol. 2, ed. Rosemary Cowler (Oxford: Blackwell, 1986), p. 13.

2 Pope, *Prose Works*, 2:25.

3 Lewis Theobald (ed.), *The Works of Shakespeare: in Seven Volumes: Collated with the Oldest Copies, and Corrected; with Notes, Explanatory, and Critical*, 7 vols. (London, 1733), 1:xl.

4 William Warburton (ed.), *The Works of Shakespear*, 8 vols. (London, 1747), 2:349.

5 Pope, *Prose Works*, 2:16.

6 Pope, *Prose Works*, 2:16.

7 Pope, *Prose Works*, 2:13.
8 Theobald, *Works of Shakespeare*, 1:xx.
9 Thomas Davies, *Memoirs of the Life of David Garrick, Esq.*, 2 vols. (London, 1780), 1:56.
10 Thomas Davies, *Dramatic Micellanies* [*sic*], 3 vols. (London, 1783–4), 2:320.
11 William Davenant, *Macbeth*, in *Five Restoration Adaptations of Shakespeare*, ed. Christopher Spencer (Urbana: University of Illinois Press, 1965), pp. 33–107 (5.8.42).

CHAPTER 41

Slavery and abolition

Brycchan Carey

> SLAVE. *n.s.* [*esclave*, French. It is said to have its original from *Slavi*, or *Sclavonians*, subdued and sold by the *Venetians*.] One mancipated to a master; not a freeman; a dependant.
>
> The condition of servants was different from what it is now, they being generally *slaves*, and such as were bought and sold for money. *South.*

Johnson's lifetime coincided almost exactly with the rise and fall of the British slave trade. Some Britons had been involved in slave trading as early as the sixteenth century, but for most of the sixteenth and seventeenth centuries Great Britain was a relatively minor participant. Britain signaled its intention to make serious money from slave trading with the establishment of the Royal Adventurers into Africa in 1660. This company, which genuinely was led by members of the restored royal family, shortly after became the Royal African Company.

THE *ASIENTO*

It was not until the early eighteenth century, however, that Britain wrested control of the slave trade from the Spanish, who had dominated slave trading throughout the seventeenth century. The turning point was the War of the Spanish Succession (1701–14). On the face of it this was a dynastic conflict, which contemporaries knew would determine the balance of power in Europe, but in the event it would also determine the relationship between Europe, Africa, and the New World for the rest of the eighteenth century and, arguably, for much longer. The war was concluded with the Peace of Utrecht (1713). As part of the negotiations towards this treaty, Spain granted Britain the right to supply its colonies in the New World with slaves, an agreement known as the *asiento*. From this point onwards, Britain became the foremost slave-trading nation, a position it continued to occupy until it voluntarily abolished its slave trade in 1807.

In the early eighteenth century, many Britons were enthusiastic about the opportunities offered by the country's new role as the world's primary slave trader. Although the Royal African Company continued to trade in slaves, the trade after 1712 was effectively privatized, and from that point onwards almost anyone with sufficient start-up capital could legally trade in slaves. Presupposing the *asiento* and the reforms to the Royal African Company, the new South Sea Company was set up in 1711 to capitalize on the profits of slave trading to the Spanish empire in the South Atlantic. So successful was the slave trade, and so large were the expected profits, that the company undertook to pay the nation's war debts.

Speculation in the company was intense and led to an economic bubble. The South Sea Bubble burst in 1720, producing one of the first great financial panics of the modern age, and many British investors faced financial ruin. The company itself, nevertheless, was restructured and traded in slaves for many years alongside other slave-trading companies and captains. Investors continued to sink money into the trade, and most of them met with handsome returns. Throughout Johnson's life, most of the wealthy individuals he encountered would have derived at least some of their wealth either from slave trading or from the produce of colonial plantations worked by slaves. While claims that the labor of slaves provided the economic impetus for the British Industrial Revolution of the later eighteenth century are probably exaggerated, it is nevertheless true that the work done by the enslaved very considerably enriched the British economy, and made some individuals spectacularly rich.

THE SLAVE TRADE

The slave trade and the system of plantation slavery that it supported may have been business as usual during Johnson's lifetime, but it is important not to lose sight of what that meant for the individuals caught up in the system.

Before Europeans intervened in the market, Africa, like most regions in the world, had a limited internal slave trade. The arrival of Europeans on the coast of Africa provided a bonanza for unscrupulous Africans and Europeans alike. African businessmen cashed in on the (to them) high prices offered for slaves by European slave traders, while Europeans took the opportunity to buy slaves at (to them) low prices unimaginable, or illegal, in Europe. European traders distorted African markets and, in some cases, made African technologies economically unviable. Traditional West African industries such as weaving and pottery, technologically equal to European industries, were rendered uneconomic in the face of the slave trade and the superior technologies of European metalworking. By the time Johnson had reached middle age, many West African economies had been effectively destroyed by European slave trading. The result in Africa was lasting poverty, social dislocation, and conflict; throughout the eighteenth century, some African nations waged war on others purely to provide the European market with slaves.

Those individuals unlucky enough to be caught up in the slave trade faced a bleak future. Eighteenth-century European slave traders knew little of what went on in the interior of Africa, but it is now known that many enslaved people spent months, even years, being transported to the coast. It will never be known how many died on the journey, but the figure is certainly in the millions. Once at the coast, the enslaved may have been imprisoned in one of the many forts constructed for the purpose by European slave traders, or they may have been held captive by African slave traders. Eventually they would be sold and put aboard a slave ship. Such ships would sometimes take months to purchase a full complement of slaves, adding a few to the ship's hold each day while sailing along the African coast in the full glare of the equatorial sun.

Eventually the ship would be full and would set sail for the New World in the infamous "middle passage." This transatlantic crossing could take between two and six months, depending on the weather and destination, and was well known throughout the eighteenth century as being the cause of considerable suffering. The enslaved were packed into crowded holds in tropical heat and with little ventilation. They were shackled for long periods, fed rotten food, and beaten for minor "offenses." Needless to say, disease was both rife and color-blind: European sailors died in similar proportions to African slaves. Having crossed the Atlantic, the survivors would be put up for sale in slave markets across the Americas and then, for most, set to work on plantations growing a variety of tropical goods. Chief among these was sugar, a lucrative crop which requires intensive cultivation and backbreaking labor. Slaves who for any reason were unable or unwilling to work would be beaten, whipped, and sometimes murdered. From the start, and throughout the eighteenth century, plantation slavery depended both on the brutal coercion of plantation slaves and the willingness of European consumers to ignore that brutality.

LONDON'S BLACK POPULATION

While the vast majority of the enslaved remained in the New World colonies, a small number were brought to Europe, where most worked as domestic servants. By the middle of the eighteenth century, London had a black population of several thousand slaves and former slaves, most of whom lived in the fashionable homes whose masters they served.

One such was Francis Barber. Barber had been born a slave in Jamaica around 1735 and was brought to England in 1750 by his owner, Colonel Richard Bathurst. Two years later, Bathurst's son (also Richard) sent the young slave to Johnson to help Johnson adapt to life after the death of his wife. Thus, Johnson briefly became responsible for overseeing a slave. In 1754, the elder Bathurst died, emancipating Barber in his will. Barber continued to work for Johnson as a paid manservant, although in the early years he was not often present: Johnson sent him to school for five years at a cost of £300, while on two other occasions Barber disappeared, once to sea. Nevertheless, Barber ultimately returned to work in Johnson's household. Johnson was evidently fond of Barber, and in his will he left Barber the substantial sum of £70 a year for life.

Another former slave who may have been known to Johnson was Ignatius Sancho, who had been brought to England as a child slave in the 1730s. Freed as a young man, Sancho had for some time been butler to the Duke of Montagu but, in 1773, he was set up as a shopkeeper in Westminster. He spent this semi-retirement socializing with second-tier artists and writers and writing witty letters, which were collected and published two years after his death in 1780. As a preface to this collection, the young MP Joseph Jekyll wrote a short biography of Sancho in Johnson's style (even claiming in a note that Johnson himself had planned to write it). Jekyll claimed that Sancho was friends with several of Johnson's circle, not least David Garrick, and as one of the tiny group of educated Africans in London that included Francis Barber, Sancho may well have been known in the Johnson household.

ANTISLAVERY MOVEMENTS

The proximity of educated Africans such as Barber and Sancho no doubt hardened Johnson's opposition to slavery. In the mid-eighteenth century, it was not difficult to find people who, like Johnson, thought that slavery was objectionable. Nevertheless, few of these people had any clear views on how the institution might be abolished, even though some were starting to argue publicly for its reformation.

The growing black population in London focused the minds of some writers, politicians, and lawyers. One of the latter was Granville Sharp, who was horrified to find that runaway slaves were being kidnapped, beaten up, and either left for dead on the streets of London or shipped out to the plantations to a life of forced labor. In the late 1760s, Sharp began a series of legal actions against the owners of these slaves, which culminated in the celebrated Mansfield decision of 1772. This landmark legal case was brought by Sharp against the owner of a slave, James Somersett, who had escaped, been recaptured, and was about to be shipped against his will to Jamaica. The case attracted a great deal of attention in the press and was heard by no less a person than the Lord Chief Justice, Lord Mansfield. Eventually Mansfield ruled that no person, whether slave or free, could be compelled to leave the country against his or her will. This verdict was not the end of slavery in England, as many historians have erroneously thought. It did, however, mean that, because slaves could emancipate themselves with little fear of recapture, slavery very shortly became for all practical purposes unenforceable in England.

Crucially, the publicity surrounding the case had brought slavery and the British slave trade into the open, and it is from about this time that we can see the beginnings of an informal antislavery movement marked by the publication of occasional pamphlets and poems. One such was *The Dying Negro*, a long poem coauthored by John Bicknell and Thomas Day in 1773. Imaginatively recreating the true story of a slave who had killed himself after being forced on board a ship bound for the plantations, the poem reminded the reading public both of the brutality of slavery and of the inefficacy of Mansfield's decision a year after the case. The poem was widely read, and a second edition followed in 1774. In this, Day added a long introduction in which he attacked the colonial slaveholders, who at that moment were mobilizing their forces in revolution. Though slaveholders, he argued, "these are the men whose clamours for LIBERTY are heard across the Atlantic Ocean."[1] Whether Johnson read the second edition of *The Dying Negro* is unknown, but he certainly shared the sentiment. In his pamphlet *Taxation No Tyranny*, published in March 1775, he famously asked, "How is it that we hear the loudest yelps for liberty among the drivers of negroes?" (*Works*, 10:454). Between them, Day and Johnson were at least partially responsible for bringing into view a problem with American liberty, one that would remain unsolved long into the twentieth century.

THE

DYING NEGRO,

Written by Mr Bicknel & Mr Day (named in the life of Edgeworth)

A

P O E M.

To you this unpolluted blood I pour,
To you that Spirit which ye gave restore.

The THIRD EDITION, Corrected and Enlarged.

LONDON:

Printed for W. FLEXNEY, opposite Gray's-Inn-Gate, Holborn; J. WILKIE, in St. Paul's Church-Yard; and J. ROBSON, in New Bond-Street.

M.DCC.LXXV.

[PRICE ONE SHILLING AND SIX-PENCE.]

Figure 38 J. Bicknell and T. Day, *The Dying Negro, a Poem*, 3rd edn.

If the British public had ever shared any complacency about their nation's imperial project, the war with the American colonists brought it to an end. Whether one thought the founders of the United States of America were dangerous traitors or inspired visionaries, it was clear to all that something had gone very wrong with the British colonial model. Across the Atlantic, some of the newly founded states, including Vermont, Massachusetts, and Pennsylvania, had abolished slavery. What had once seemed a legislative pipe dream had now been positively enacted by English-speaking assemblies. On the other hand, the newly independent plantation colonies in the American South seemed unlikely to relinquish slavery. To many in Britain, it seemed that, either way, slavery was at the heart of the problem. What better way to secure the future compliance of the remaining British American colonies, some reasoned, than by reforming and regulating the slave trade? Almost immediately after the end of the American War, therefore, the British colonists in the West Indies came under intense scrutiny from the British public – notwithstanding their howls of protest that they had remained loyal throughout the war and thus did not deserve such treatment.

Nevertheless, it is clear that in the early 1780s the tide of public opinion was beginning to turn against the slave trade. News reached England of the massacre on board the slave ship *Zong* in 1781, and the public was briefly outraged. The captain of the ship, fearing that his water supplies might run short, had thrown 133 slaves overboard. This act of mass murder meant that, on the pretext of ensuring the ship's safety, he could claim the value of the slaves back on the ship's insurance, which he would be unable to do had they merely died of thirst. Again, Granville Sharp and others pursued this through the courts, but the murderers escaped justice. Nonetheless, the scene was now set for a full-scale public debate about slavery and the slave trade. In 1784, James Ramsay's *Essay on the Treatment and Conversion of African Slaves in the British Sugar Colonies*, a long-awaited book by a British clergyman who had had firsthand experience of plantation slavery, effectively began the mass movement for the abolition of the slave trade. It was, however, a movement in which Johnson, who died in December that year, would play no part.

Johnson's life, then, coincided almost exactly with the rise and fall of the British slave trade. The Society for the Abolition of the African Slave Trade was founded three years after his death; within months it had mobilized public opinion across the country. Between 1787 and 1792, there was a great outpouring of national sentiment against the slave trade. Hundreds of poems, plays, novels, pamphlets, treatises, and sermons poured forth from the press in support of abolition. A much smaller number of publications supported the slave trade, including the poem *No Abolition of Slavery; or, The Universal Empire of Love*, written by James Boswell in 1791. Boswell's intervention, though, does not seem to have profoundly affected the course of the abolition debate.

More serious were developments across the English Channel. By 1793, it was clear that the French Revolution would not diffuse liberty throughout the globe and that war with France was impending. The national mood shifted abruptly, and abolition of slavery moved to the bottom of most people's agenda for a decade. The fortuitous coincidence of victory over the French at Trafalgar (October 1805), which buoyed the national mood, and the short-lived unity "Ministry of All the Talents" (February 1806–March 1807) meant that a window of opportunity opened for abolitionists in 1806. After a few months of frenetic campaigning and politicking, the British slave trade was abolished by law in the spring of 1807. But it would be another thirty years before the existing slaves in the British empire would achieve their emancipation, and decades more before Britain's former colonies in North America would abolish slavery. Johnson may not have lived to see these events, but his unvarying opposition to slavery throughout his lifetime no doubt played at least a small part in bringing them about.

NOTE

1 John Bicknell and Thomas Day, *The Dying Negro: A Poetical Epistle*, 2nd edn. (London, 1774), p. vii.

CHAPTER 42

Social hierarchy

Nicholas Hudson

> RANK. *n.s.* [*rang*, Fr.]
> 4. Class; order.
>
> The enchanting power of prosperity over private persons is remarkable in relation to great kingdoms, where all *ranks* and orders of men, being equally concerned in publick blessings, equally join in spreading the infection. *Atterbury.*

The enormous changes that occurred in the British social hierarchy during the eighteenth century may be illustrated by the example of Johnson himself: he was the son of a failed Lichfield bookseller who came to London in 1737 with very little money and without any connections with the nobility or with the wealthy. By the end of his life, he was a revered public figure who counted people of great wealth and eminence among his personal acquaintance. Such a rise from poverty to fame was almost unknown a century before, except in a few cases when talented people attracted the regard of rich patrons. Johnson, on the contrary, famously spurned the vaunted "patronage" of the powerful Lord Chesterfield, making a virtue of his isolation from the court and "polite" circles. What had happened in Britain to make such a rise possible – not only for Johnson, but for many low-born writers, public figures, and men of business?

BACKGROUNDS

Particularly after the Glorious Revolution of 1688, Britain began to make great strides towards being a modern capitalist nation. The traditional aristocracy and the great landowners continued to wield political power, but their ascendancy was increasingly challenged and limited by self-made merchants, tradesmen, and bankers. This change resulted partly from Britain's widening domination of international trade by virtue of its well-organized chartered companies, its large and efficient navy, and its colonies in America and the Caribbean, as well as its commercial outposts in India (see chapter 21, "Empire"). Britain had the world's greatest banking system, centered on Bank of England, founded in 1694, providing an almost unlimited source of funds for investment and for the creation of a formidable war machine to protect the nation's interests. The aristocracy itself did not remain an insular, distant class, as it did in France and other European nations; instead it actively involved itself in trade and commerce, becoming deeply indebted to financiers in the City of London. Led by this commercialized elite, agriculture became highly competitive and commercial, as farms became larger and more efficient, and land was mined for coal to fire factories and manufactures. The "Industrial Revolution" had really begun long before the 1780s, where it is usually placed.

This steady growth of the economy had many effects on the social order. There were actually only limited opportunities for social mobility into the aristocracy: the nobility remained protective of its titles and political power, and very few new lords and ladies were created, even among the newly rich. But with new access to wealth, people in the "middling-ranks" – what later became the middle class – could emulate the fashions and lifestyle of the nobility, and even mix with their betters at many social occasions and entertainments. The titles "gentleman" and "lady," traditionally the preserve of those with sufficient land, were seized by every man who could afford a fine wig and sword, and by every lady who wore an elegant dress and accompanied her family to the playhouse or opera. Moralists of the time found this trend deeply distressing: it became difficult to tell who was truly from the upper ranks and who was not. Even people well down the social scale – even shopkeepers and apprentices – could have the wherewithal to purchase fashionable clothes and strut about like lords. The danger that a young lady might run away with a sailor or footman in fancy clothes became a prominent theme in conduct literature, and provisions were made in 1753 to give the state and parents greater control over marriage (see chapter 19, "Domestic life"). More generally, complaints about the luxury that had invaded England, weakening or "effeminizing" a formerly hardy people, became one of the standard refrains in moralistic books and pamphlets.

THE LOWER RANKS

Nearer the bottom of the social scale, improvements in lifestyle were less considerable and, in many ways, even negligible. By far the largest group in Johnson's England consisted of laborers, domestic servants, and people in service jobs. The threshold for a modestly comfortable life was about £50 a year, but most working people earned much less (see chapter 31, "Money"). Though wages remained stagnant throughout the century, the increased purchasing power of the middle and upper ranks, along with the increasing population, created a steady inflation on all commodities. The capitalization of agriculture inflated the price of grain and basic food, for producers often hoarded and monopolized, leading to serious bread riots, particularly during times of bad harvests (as in the 1760s). The eighteenth-century state had not caught up with the need to provide an efficient safety net for the severely poor and the destitute. The desperately poor and starving remained reliant on parish relief, obligatory charity organized by the Church. The well-off often despised this relief, and viewed the poor with disdain as freeloaders impoverished by idleness and vice.

On the other hand, the plight of workers and the poor in the eighteenth century should be put into perspective. Recent research has revealed that even families who scraped by from year to year participated modestly in the pursuit of fashion, prizing an old gold watch or a fancy hat to wear at the local fair. European visitors often remarked on the relative wholesomeness of lower-rank life in England. In addition, Johnson's contemporaries, and notably Johnson himself, can be credited with instigating a concern for the poor, and the creation of charitable foundations such as charity schools and foundling hospitals. It remains true, nonetheless, that the mass of the working poor did not participate proportionately in the general enrichment of eighteenth-century society: Johnson's England, while it allowed increased opportunities for the lucky and the talented, remained unsympathetic and unpropitious among those who desired only a living wage through work or service.

POLITENESS

Another result of the increasing wealth of eighteenth-century Britain bears a special relation to Johnson: the age witnessed the creation of a highly profitable publishing industry (see chapter 15, "Book trade"). The reasons for this economic expansion remain controversial, for this age actually witnessed a concentration of the publishing industry in the hands of very few people, some of whom (such as Johnson's friends the Dodsley brothers and William Strahan) became exceedingly rich. This concentration has suggested to some scholars that eighteenth-century literature had become elitist and antagonistic to change. But this inference is clearly mistaken: Johnson's era witnessed an unprecedented outburst of popular literature, often with themes profoundly antagonistic to the ruling order, the dominance of the rich, and even the authority of Christianity. If literacy rose only modestly (staying in the region of about 50 percent of men and 40 percent of women), increased incomes and a widening desire to be "polite" inspired those who could read to consume a diverse range of the printed material pouring from a newly profitable press. To read not just the Bible but also newspapers, periodicals, pamphlets, novels, printed plays, and all kinds of writing became a mark of respectable status.

In a multitude of coffee houses and parlors, middle-rank people exhibited their politeness by chatting about the latest news, a popular new novel, or the latest poem by Alexander Pope, John Gay, James Thomson, or Johnson. This material characteristically taught them how to be "polite": the spectacular success of the periodical the *Spectator* (1711–12), mostly written by Joseph Addison and Sir Richard Steele, can be attributed to the intention of these authors to train middle-rank readers about the basics of good taste and respectable lifestyle. Those who produced this plethora of literary modeling may have emulated aristocratic ideals, but they were very seldom upper-rank themselves. Addison, for instance, came from a respectable clerical family, but not the aristocracy; Steele was the son of an Irish attorney.

Other great writers of the time derived from even more modest origins. John Gay felt deep humiliation that he had once served as an apprentice to a silk merchant. The father of novelist Samuel Richardson was a Derbyshire joiner (roughly, a carpenter). Johnson's friend Oliver Goldsmith was son of an Irish curate. What these men shared was a relatively modest background combined with hard-earned literacy and an unusual access to books and education. They were nonetheless outsiders with no claim to social prestige or great financial backing. They wrote for a living, and did not expect to become rich or prestigious because they wrote (see chapter 13, "Authorship"). Of all the authors of the eighteenth century, only Alexander Pope, son of a Catholic linen-draper, could claim to have become truly rich through writing, the fruit of his ingenious grasp of the publishing business.

BRIDGING HIGH AND LOW

These authors nonetheless became social arbiters, for they had mastered upper-rank styles while exhibiting an intimate knowledge of middle-rank, and even lower-rank, experience. It is this bridging that distinguishes the best writing of the eighteenth century, including Johnson's. The unique flavor of eighteenth-century literature derives from its distinctive combinations of "high" and "low" – its mastery of classical forms previously accessible only to the upper ranks with an appreciation for what occurred in the middle-rank parlor, the roadside inn, and even the kitchen. The mock-heroic, that uniquely eighteenth-century literary form, exemplifies this controlled tension between "high" language and "low" subjects. Pope's *Dunciad* (1728 and 1742) exhibits both the poet's mastery of classical forms, previously the preserve of upper-rank people, and his knowledge of the often squalid and impoverished world of eighteenth-century publishing. Gay's *Beggar's Opera* (1728) uses the conventions of the high heroic world of opera to portray jailers, criminals, and prostitutes.

In a different and more serious way, Johnson also combines classical learning with his deep knowledge of ordinary life in the streets of London. Particularly in his first series of periodical essays, the *Rambler*, Johnson's prose style is marked by lofty formality and a learned, Latinate vocabulary. But the subjects of these essays are often the struggles of middle-rank people: tailors seeking acceptance in polite circles, women forced by circumstance into domestic service or prostitution, and writers like himself whose ornate language masks their humble lives. In contrast with writers of the mock-heroic, Johnson used dignified language not to laugh at the struggles of ordinary people and the poor, but to reveal their lives as intensely and universally "human" – as, in fact, no less significant than the lives of the rich. Viewed in this context of a liberalized social hierarchy, Johnson emerges as a man preoccupied with the trials of people who, for the first time in history, had opportunities for advancement towards respectability and even power. Many of the main characters depicted in *The Vanity of Human Wishes* (1749) – Thomas Wolsey, George Villiers, William Laud, Thomas Wentworth, Edward Hyde – shared the characteristic of being men of relatively modest origins raised to power, and then tumbling to a disgraceful end.

SUBORDINATION

Such a characterization of Johnson as an ally of common people will seem at odds with the common impression that he was an elitist conservative obsessed with the need for social "subordination." Yet the image of Johnson as an elitist derives largely from statements recorded in the *Life of Johnson* by Boswell, who did not meet him until 1763, when Johnson was fifty-three. Son of a Scots laird, heir to a great estate, Boswell resented people of less fortunate background who called themselves "gentlemen," and preferred to call even his great friend "Dr. Johnson" (signaling Johnson's learning rather than his rank). The 1760s marked a considerable shift in England's political and social life. The new king, the young George III, strove to be, as Johnson wrote, "father of the people": he toured English farms and manufactures, and maintained a virtuous royal household, only to be scorned as "Farmer George." So far from winning over the "people," George found himself outflanked by popular politicians like John Wilkes, a man of polite social standing who nonetheless mobilized a voluble movement of tradesmen and shopkeepers against the king. Oddly enough, the king and the rabble-rouser had something in common: Wilkes felt, like George, that the route to influence lay in the need to connect with common people.

But George III lost the battle, at least until the 1780s. The times when Boswell knew Johnson, 1763 to 1784, are remarkable for political commotion exemplified by terrible riots (particularly the St. George's Fields Massacre in 1768 and the Gordon Riots in 1780), along with a level of hostility to the king in Parliament that led George himself to consider abdication. As Johnson's friend and political star Edmund Burke wrote in 1770, "there is something particularly alarming in the present conjuncture. There is hardly a man, in or out of power, who holds any other language."[1] Such rumblings of "revolution" continued to roll into the 1790s, the era of the French Revolution, after Johnson's death.

For all his own mobility "up" the social scale, Johnson hated this disorder. His own rise had been made possible by the continuation of a legally strong monarchy and a relatively liberal aristocracy, elitist but open to the opportunities of an emergent capitalist economy. Like many people in the emergent "middle class," Johnson wanted stability rather than upheaval, and feared the signs of restlessness and even rebellion among the common masses. Between 1770 and 1775, he produced a remarkably cogent and eloquent series of political essays – *The False Alarm*, *The Patriot*, *Taxation No Tyranny*, and others – which have in common a defense of the king, and generally an unease with the agitation of "pedlars" and lower-rank malcontents. For him, the American Revolution epitomized growing popular defiance of political authorities and social betters (see chapter 10, "America").

Curiously, the conservatism of Johnson's later years helped to make him a hero for a generation of readers after his death. After the outbreak of the French Revolution in 1789, an increasing number of people began to identify themselves as "middle class," meaning the solid bedrock of

English society, neither very rich or poor, the guardians of strong patriotic values and moral decency. Many of this class reacted with alarm to news of pike-wielding mobs marching in Paris, especially as English radicals declared their intention of fomenting a similar revolution in Britain. With the publication of Boswell's *Life of Johnson* in 1791, these readers identified closely with Johnson's support for "subordination," his loyalty to the monarch, and the staunch Englishness of such major works as the *Dictionary*, his edition of Shakespeare, and *Lives of the English Poets*. In the nineteenth century, Johnson's conservatism was exaggerated. It was often ignored that he himself had risen from impoverished origins and that he remained deeply sympathetic to the sufferings of the poor. Throughout his life, Johnson refused to pander to the aristocracy and the rich, remaining proudly independent and indignant at upper-rank snobs like Lord Chesterfield, who disguised low cunning and self-interest beneath a fashionable veneer. While concerned to maintain social order in a time of growing turmoil, Johnson was no elitist, and he hated real repression of all kinds.

Understanding the changing social hierarchy of the eighteenth century is thus necessary to a just reading of Johnson's life and works. This is no easy task, for Johnson's attitudes transformed throughout his life in response to a rapidly evolving social landscape. What holds together Johnson's opinions at all stages, however, was his status as a "new man" in a liberalized, and increasingly capitalist nation.

NOTE

1 Edmund Burke, "Thoughts on the Present Discontents," in *The Writings and Speeches of Edmund Burke*, ed. Paul Langford, 9 vols. in 10 (Oxford: Clarendon Press, 1981–2000), 2:253.

CHAPTER 43

Theatre

Nora Nachumi

THE'ATRE. *n.s.* [*theatre*, Fr. *theatrum*, Lat.]
1. A place in which shews are exhibited; a playhouse.

This wise and universal *theatre*,
Presents more woful pageants than the scene
Wherein we play. *Shakesp. As you like it.*

When Samuel Johnson set out for London in March 1737 he did so in the company of his former student, David Garrick. To say that Johnson's choice of traveling companion was fortunate is an understatement. Not only would Garrick be remembered as the foremost actor of his age but, as manager of the Theatre Royal at Drury Lane, he would, in 1749, stage Johnson's only play, *Irene*. In 1737, however, Johnson was the one determined to brave London's theater world. His plan was to finish *Irene*, to see it acted and published, and, in doing so, to establish himself as a man of letters. His timing could hardly have been worse.

THE LICENSING ACT

On June 21, 1737 – before Johnson finished *Irene* –Parliament passed the Licensing Act, a law which changed the face of London's theater world. Since the Restoration of the monarchy in 1660, only two theaters had been authorized by royal patent to present plays, giving them an effective duopoly. These "patent theaters," as they were called, enjoyed a fair amount of freedom. But the Licensing Act was designed to prevent the production of plays critical of Walpole's government, and it reinforced the prohibition of plays being performed in anything other than the patent theaters. All new plays, additions to old plays, prologues, and epilogues had to be approved by the Examiner of Plays, a subordinate of the Lord Chamberlain.

In response to the act, many of the unlicensed theaters that had flourished during the early 1730s shut down, at least temporarily. Other small theaters focused on different forms of entertainment, such as pantomime and musical revues. By the mid-1750s, however, additional legislation requiring all sorts of entertainments to be licensed, and prohibiting shows at fairs, reinforced the duopoly of London's two patent houses, the Theatres Royal at Drury Lane and Covent Garden, whose season ran from mid-September through May. With the addition of the Little Theatre in the Haymarket – whose manager, Samuel Foote, received a patent in 1766 to hold a summer season – London's legitimate theaters totaled three through the end of the century.

Johnson's opposition to the Licensing Act is a matter of record. In 1739, with *Irene* on the shelf, he expressed his disgust in a pamphlet titled *A Compleat Vindication of the Licensers of the Stage*. In it, his narrator ironically defends the government's attempt to ensure the ignorance of its people by the suppression of plays, recommends that the act be extended to cover the press, and suggests that people no longer be taught how to read. Johnson was clearly troubled by the government's power to limit expression. His failure to get *Irene* produced, however, almost certainly added fuel to his fire. After all, the Licensing Act reduced the number of theater managers to whom novice playwrights like Johnson could submit work.

THE REPERTORY SYSTEM

These theater managers wielded enormous power in the selection and casting of plays for their companies. Deluged by scripts, they were more likely to look at plays recommended by people they knew. In Johnson's case, Garrick's older brother, Peter, encouraged him to submit *Irene* to Charles Fleetwood, then manager of Drury Lane, who rejected it. Johnson blamed the verdict on his lack of connections with men of high rank, but the revisions Garrick recommended Johnson make to the play before its performance in 1749 suggest that Fleetwood's decision may have been motivated by more practical concerns. After all, theater managers always had to ensure that a season's profits were greater than its expenses. In reading and accepting a new play managers had to evaluate "the quality of the writing, and the capacities of the acting company to perform the piece so as to give it a profitable run of six to nine nights, with some hope of its taking a place in the repertory thereafter." At stake was the "continuance of the theatre and the livelihood of all those from sceneshifter to premiere ballerina employed by the company, as well as profit to the author and manager. Failure put the whole business in jeopardy."[1]

Adaptations of old plays were a much safer bet. William Shakespeare, dead for more than a century, remained the most popular playwright on the London stage throughout the century, and his contemporaries Ben Jonson, Francis Beaumont, and John Fletcher were also popular. But their plays were rarely presented without significant alterations (see chapter 40, "Shakespeare"). Alterations kept the plays fresh and playgoers interested. These alterations could be radical, as when tragedies received happy endings. Even when endings were not completely rewritten, more subtle alterations and shifts in emphasis attuned the text to contemporary events and ideas. The period also saw an increase in propriety: the racy, even bawdy, language that marked so many plays during the Restoration was toned down and the plays renamed. William Wycherley's *Country Wife* (1675), for example, was transformed by David Garrick into *The Country Girl* (1766).

Under the repertory system people went to the theater to see specific performers interpret particular parts – Garrick *as* Lear, for instance, or Mary Ann Yates *as* Lady Macbeth. Actors became stars, and novel acting styles helped to keep playgoers interested. By the time Johnson arrived in London, the formal, declamatory style and measured cadences of Restoration performers such as Thomas Betterton and Anne Bracegirdle had evolved into something more emphatic. By the mid-1740s, Charles Macklin and Garrick had popularized a new style characterized with a more natural manner of moving and method of phrasing. An emphasis on psychological realism – at least as it was understood at the time – is a hallmark of performances during the period. Thus the *Hamlet* of Garrick's era was not the same play as it was in Betterton's time; both the text and the method of performing the play had been altered in significant ways. Moreover, as George Winchester Stone reminds us, "to talk in terms of one style [of acting], or two or three, is pretty much nonsense, because although a common denominator in this period was a certain psychological realism both for tragedy and comedy, the styles of communicating it varied with the individual actors."[2]

The popularity of familiar actors in familiar roles meant that adaptations of old plays continued to sell tickets and made up a large portion of the plays produced during the season. New plays, nevertheless, were produced on occasion. Between 1747 and 1776 Drury Lane, under Garrick, averaged sixteen tragedies, thirty comedies, and twenty-two plays that cannot be categorized per season. Covent Garden, which operated under four different management regimes during this period, produced an average of sixteen tragedies, thirty comedies, and twenty-four plays that cannot be categorized each year. Only a small number of these plays, however, were new. At Drury Lane, Garrick produced two to four new plays, or "mainpieces," a year, while Covent Garden produced an average of only one and a half during the season. Although tragedy had the critical cachet, audiences seemed to prefer new comedies. Two types of comedy were particularly in vogue during Johnson's lifetime, "laughing" and "sentimental" comedy. The laughing comedy was an older form, and included what have been called "comedies of wit" and "comedies of humors." The newer sentimental comedy was noteworthy for its emphasis on virtue, sensibility, and sentiment. Despite their differences, however, both types of comedy resembled adaptations of older plays in their cultivation of a more polished and genteel style than their Restoration predecessors.

AT THE THEATER

An evening at the theater usually lasted from three to five hours and was, by all accounts, both a spectacle and a communal event. At the two patent houses, the performance started at six o'clock. Prior to the play, or the mainpiece, there might be a prologue spoken in verse by one of the leading performers. Composed for new plays, adaptations of old ones, and special events, prologues varied in tone and topic. Most, however, concluded by asking the audience to approve the forthcoming play or performance or to rejoice in a special occasion. At Garrick's request, for example, Johnson wrote the prologue for the opening night of Garrick's tenure as manager at Drury Lane. In it, Johnson describes the English stage in decline, until it is restored to its former glory by Garrick. Epilogues, which followed mainpieces, did similar duty. Both were usually retired once a play became part of the repertory. Between the acts of the mainpiece came dances, music, or songs. Afterpieces followed epilogues; shorter than mainpieces, they varied in type, including farce, ballad opera, burletta, pantomime, and procession. Sometimes the tone of the afterpiece resembled that of the play and sometimes it differed, as when a tragedy was followed by a burletta or farce. Concluding the evening was an announcement of the next evening's performances, followed, beginning in the 1740s, by a rousing rendition of "God Save the King" sung by performers and spectators alike.

During the period, London's theater audiences grew in both number and diversity. Harry William Pedicord estimates that, from 1740 to 1742, about 8,460 people attended the theater each week; by 1758–60, that number had risen to 11,874. At mid-century, then, approximately "seventeen out of every thousand attended either of the patent houses."[3] Some of this increase in audience came from increasingly large theaters. Drury Lane, for instance, seems to have held about 1,000 people after Garrick's interior renovations in 1747; by 1762, that number had climbed to about 1,800. Between 1732 and 1782, Covent Garden held about 2,000 people at capacity. That audience was not composed primarily of the upper classes, as it had been during the Restoration, but also included those from the middling and even working classes.

Social distinctions were manifested by seating location. Persons of the first quality sat in the boxes which lined the side walls of the theater, or in the row of front boxes that lined the auditorium wall facing the stage. Wealthy tradesmen and their families sat in the first gallery above the front boxes. Above them, the second gallery was reserved for servants and others from the working classes. Extending from the front boxes to the orchestra pit in front of the stage was the pit. Raked to improve acoustics and visibility, the pit was typically occupied by a mixture of minor gentlemen and intellectuals. Seating was tight; writing in 1790, the architect George Saunders noted of Covent Garden that "1 foot 9 inches is the whole space … allowed for seat and void."[4] Except for the boxes, seating was unreserved, which often led to chaos when the doors finally opened. The theater was noisy; prostitutes frequented the upper gallery, and pickpockets were plentiful. Nevertheless, during Johnson's lifetime, the patent theaters were small enough so that "all could see the facial expressions of the actors, judge the appropriateness of their slightest gestures, and hear, when the house was quiet, their well modulated speech."[5]

The structure of the stage helped generate intimacy between the audience and the performers. Restoration stages, in general, were designed with a large forestage that extended past the proscenium into the auditorium. This design not only enabled "forward movement on the part of the actors," Allardyce Nicoll writes, but also encouraged a "corresponding forward movement on the part of the spectators – the two groups, as it were, meeting in one location."[6] In front of the curtain line, on both sides of this platform, were stage doors through which the performers made most of their entrances and exits. Above these doors, and next to them on the stage, were stage boxes so that persons of the first quality actually sat on the stage (a practice ended by Garrick in 1762). Behind the proscenium arch, the stage was raked so to improve visibility and acoustics. Candles placed near tin reflectors at the base of the stage (footlights) and in chandeliers above it illuminated the actors and scenery.

Over the next 150 years, as Colin Visser explains, "the action moved from the forestage to the scenic area behind the proscenium. Lighting was increased in the scenic area, the proscenium doors that led onto the forestage were reduced in number, and eventually the doors and the forestage itself were eliminated."[7] In Johnson's day, however, no invisible "fourth wall" separated the audience from the performance: much of the action still occurred on the forestage. Moreover, lights in the auditorium were not dimmed for performances. Consequently, the theater was a place where spectators observed not only the play but each other as well.

THE BUSINESS OF THE THEATER

To produce a new play in this arena was risky business. Although they seem to have quieted down quite a bit by the 1760s, theater audiences were still extremely loud and opinionated by modern standards. Every ten years or so, riots forced the patent houses to redecorate. In addition to quarrels among literary and political factions, spectators clearly expressed their likes and dislikes about theater policies, plays, and performers. On the opening night of *Irene*, for example, the audience loudly protested the fact that the heroine was to be strangled on stage. As a result, Garrick, who had already revised Johnson's text for performance, was forced to alter the play again; on the second night, Irene was more decorously strangled offstage, as Johnson had intended. A hostile audience could easily close a play on opening night, and negative reviews in the papers could affect attendance and curtail a play's run.

If a play managed to survive its debut, the rewards could compensate for a great deal of anxiety. During the season, theaters held "benefit nights" for performers and house servants, for authors, and for charities. Four forms of financial arrangements were possible for these benefits: a "clear" or free benefit was one in which the beneficiary was awarded every penny of the evening's proceeds; a "house charge" benefit meant that the beneficiary paid the managers a fixed sum and for special services such as extra lighting; a "partial benefit" was one in which two or more individuals shared the profits and the house charges; and a "half-value-of-tickets" benefit was one in which "as many as twenty-one house employees were given tickets to dispose of."[8] Author's benefits, the main source of income for playwrights, generally occurred on the third, sixth, and – if the playwright should be so lucky – on the ninth nights of a play's initial run. Although the response to *Irene* was only lukewarm,

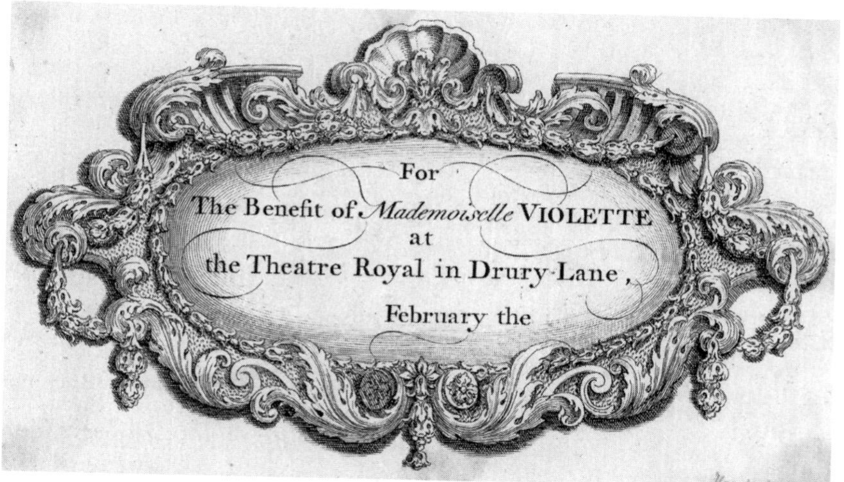

Figure 39 Admission ticket for the benefit performance of Eva Marie Veigel at Drury Lane, 1747.

Garrick kept the play going for nine nights – a long run at a time when most new plays had only a few performances – so that his friend could reap almost £200 in profits. Though not as lucrative an option, playwrights also could sell their plays for publication (publishers generally bought the copyright directly from the author, so playwrights stood to gain little after selling their rights). A successful first run clearly influenced the price a publisher would be willing to pay. Robert Dodsley bought the copyright to *Irene* for £100. Never before had Johnson earned so much over the course of an entire year.

Nevertheless, *Irene* was Johnson's first and last play. According to Boswell, Johnson himself was no fan of the theatre – for this he blamed his poor eyesight and vision; he did, however, attend plays and, for a time, amused himself backstage at Drury Lane. Perhaps he found the process too difficult – and the risks too great – to warrant potential future rewards. Perhaps, as Peter Martin speculates, Johnson's ambiguous relationship to the stage reflected a belief that the contemporary theatre was a slave to fashion, and thus made a mockery of the "great national theatrical tradition."[9] Whether or not Johnson was correct in this belief, his efforts to see *Irene* produced suggest that the theatre held a significant place in Johnson's imagination as it did in England itself.

NOTES

1 George Winchester Stone, Jr., "The Making of the Repertory," in *The London Theatre World, 1660–1800*, ed. Robert D. Hume (Carbondale: Southern Illinois University Press, 1980), pp. 185, 194.

2 *The London Stage, 1660–1800: A Calendar of Plays, Entertainments and Afterpieces, Together with Casts, Box-Receipts and Contemporary Comment: Compiled from the Playbills, Newspapers and Theatrical Diaries of the Period*, ed. G. W. Stone, C. B. Hogan, E. L. Avery, W. van Lennep, and A. H. Scouten, 6 vols. in 12 (Carbondale: Southern Illinois University Press, 1960–79), 4:xciii.

3 *The London Stage*, 4:cxci.

4 Edward Langhans, "The Theatres," in *The London Theatre World*, p. 48.

5 *The London Stage*, 4:xxx.

6 Allardyce Nicoll, *The Garrick Stage: Theatres and Audience in the Eighteenth Century* (Manchester: Manchester University Press, 1980), p. 25.

7 Colin Visser, "Scenery and Technical Design," in *The London Theatre World*, p. 67.

8 *The London Stage*, 4:ci.

9 Peter Martin, *Samuel Johnson: A Biography* (London: Weidenfeld & Nicolson, 2008), p. 212.

CHAPTER 44

Travel

Paula McDowell

> To TRA'VEL. *v.n.* [This word is generally supposed originally the same with *travail*, and to differ only as particular from general: in some writers the word is written alike in all its senses; but it is more convenient to write *travail* for *labour*, and *travel* for *journey*.]
>
> 1. To make journeys: it is used for sea as well as land, though sometimes we distinguish it from *voyage*, a word appropriated to the sea.
>
> Fain wou'd I *travel* to some foreign shore,
> So might I to myself myself restore. *Dryden*.

In 1725, the novelist, poet, and playwright Mary Davys declared that the novel was dead. "'Tis now for some time, that those Sort of Writings call'd *Novels* have been a great deal out of Use and Fashion," she observed, "and that the Ladies (for whose Service they were chiefly design'd) have been taken up with Amusements of more Use and Improvement; I mean History and Travels."[1] Davys's assertion that "Novels" and "Travels" are distinct kinds belies their actual overlap in the 1720s. Jonathan Swift satirized the gullible readers of travel books in *Travels into Several Remote Nations of the World, by Lemuel Gulliver* (1726), and travel would remain a staple structural device of the eighteenth-century novel. Many eighteenth-century authors whom we now classify as novelists – including Henry Fielding, Tobias Smollett, Laurence Sterne, and Ann Radcliffe – also published accounts of their travels.

But Davys was right that "Travels" – by which she meant travel books – were wildly popular. "Travels" constituted a major category of the British book trade from the first century of printing, and travel writing had an impact on almost every other genre of writing and area of knowledge. Thousands of individual accounts were published, and the seventeenth century saw a proliferation of collections. By the eighteenth century, travel books were so numerous as to need their own bibliography: in 1704, the brothers Awnsham and John Churchill published a *Collection of Voyages and Travels* (1704), which includes a lengthy "Catalogue of most Books of Travels" in English, Latin, Italian, Spanish, and French. The category of "travel writing," as distinct from "Books of Travels," encompasses an even broader variety of forms, from personal correspondence to official reports.

Because most of our knowledge comes from written records, we know far more about the travels of elites than we do about the customary travels of the poor or the forced travel of slaves. Nonetheless, it is worth keeping in mind the question asked by the editors of a valuable recent anthology of eighteenth-century travel writings: "who counts as a traveller, or a travel writer?"[2] At the height of the Grand Tour craze in the mid-eighteenth century, some 15,000 to 20,000 British Grand Tourists were abroad each year. Meanwhile, the number of enslaved Africans forced annually across the Atlantic by British traders was well over double that many.

EXPLORERS AND TRADERS

The most widely read travel books were accounts of explorers and traders, which dated back centuries. Christopher Columbus was profoundly influenced by accounts of the Venetian merchant Marco Polo, who traveled to Cathay (China) in the thirteenth century, and by the near-mythical Sir John Mandeville, whose fantastical *Travels* (1357) was one of the most popular vernacular texts of the Middle Ages. In England, Richard Eden published the first collection of translated travel narratives, *The Decades of the Newe Worlde or West India* (1555), and Richard Hakluyt rallied to the cause of English nationalism by publishing *Principle Navigations, Voiages, Traffiques and Discoveries of the English Nation* (1589; 2nd edn., 3 vols., 1598–1600). Among the most celebrated explorers were Sir Francis Drake, whose circumnavigation of the globe sparked numerous accounts after his return to England in 1580, and Sir Walter Ralegh, who described his own colonizing efforts in *Discoverie of the Large, Rich, and Beautiful Empire of Guiana* (1595).

In the seventeenth century, the writing and editing of travel accounts would become something of an industry. Thomas Coryate described his trek through Europe and India in *Coryats Crudites* (1611), and Samuel Purchas edited a series of accounts culminating in *Hakluytus Posthumus, or Purchas His Pilgrimes* (4 vols., 1625). Court poet and colonist George Sandys's *Relation of a Journey* (1615) became an influential source of information on the Near East, as did merchant and jeweler Sir John Chardin's *Travels* (10 vols., 1686–1711). Despite having been court-martialed for cruelty, the pirate and seaman William Dampier died with a popular reputation as the greatest explorer-adventurer between Drake and Captain James Cook for having published *A New Voyage Round the World* (1697). Not surprisingly, Swift critiqued the legacy of Gulliver's "cousin Dampier."

MISSIONARIES

Travel literature was second in popularity only to religious and didactic literature, and these categories overlap in the case of missionary writings. From the founding of the Society of Jesus in 1540, Jesuit missionaries began accruing an enormous body of memoirs, private correspondence, and official "Annual Letters" describing their travels to India, Africa, America, and elsewhere, and these writings had an almost incalculable influence on European ideas about the world. In England, Protestant sectarian groups such as Quakers and Methodists were especially well-organized publishers of missionary reports. The journals of Methodist leaders John Wesley and George Whitefield record their literally hundreds of thousands of miles of travels, and Quaker women, as well as men, published narratives of their journeys throughout Britain and "beyond the seas." One especially harrowing account, *This Is a Short Relation of … Katharine Evans and Sarah Chevers* (1662), describes these women's imprisonment for three years by the Inquisition in Malta. Undaunted, Evans and Chevers returned to England and continued their missionary travels throughout England, Scotland, Ireland, and Wales.

WOMEN TRAVELERS

Quaker women had relatively easy access to print via the Quaker press, but in general women travel writers were much less likely to print their works. Women colonists, domestic tourists, and others left an extensive body of correspondence, diaries, and other writings describing their travels to family and friends, and much of this material remains unpublished. One especially intrepid gentlewoman, Celia Fiennes, traveled to every county in England on horseback between 1684 and 1712. Although she prepared a memoir in 1702, it was not printed until the Victorian period, when it appeared as *Through England on a Side Saddle*, a title foregrounding her sex. Another posthumously published memoir, Mary Wortley Montagu's *Turkish Embassy Letters* (1763), was one of the greatest achievements in travel writing by an author of either sex. Recounting her travels from 1716 to 1718 as the wife of the English ambassador to the Ottoman empire, Montagu's epistolary travel book challenged Britons' assumptions about the social institutions and customs of the Turkish people, and her book was admired by Johnson, Edward Gibbon, Voltaire, and others.

Emboldened by Montagu's achievement, women travel writers began to publish in significant numbers. One year after Radcliffe published her *Journey Made in the Summer of 1794, through Holland and the Western Frontier of Germany* (1795), the feminist author Mary Wollstonecraft published her *Letters Written during a Short Residence in Sweden, Norway, and Denmark* (1796). Based on her business trip to the relative wilderness of Scandinavia, accompanied only by her infant daughter and maid, Wollstonecraft's travelogue combines Enlightenment observation of customs and manners with a new Romantic emphasis on subjectivity, and renders its descriptions of scenic landscapes in the fashionable aesthetic vocabulary of the sublime and picturesque.

GUIDEBOOKS

The most enduring category of travel writing, though, was the guidebook. Dating back to ancient Greece and still flourishing today, guidebooks ranged from itineraries for tourists to topographical surveys for politicians, merchants, and armchair travelers. One especially enduring guidebook, Daniel Defoe's *Tour thro' the Whole Island of Great Britain* (3 vols., 1724–6), was based on a series of business trips through the new sovereign territory of Great Britain (see chapter 32, "Nationalism"). It was also indebted to the works of the great Tudor and Stuart topographers and historians John Leland, John Stow, and especially William Camden, who anticipated Defoe in employing the structural device of the walking tour in *Britannia* (1586; rev. edn. by Edmund Gibson, 1695).

Even in Defoe's day, though, the best-known English guidebook for the Continent was James Howell's *Instructions for Forreine Travell* (1642). Compared to modern travel guides, Howell's *Instructions* provides little practical information; his emphasis is on the moral and civic ends of touring and the importance of careful intellectual preparation for one's travels. Howell advises prospective travelers to "reade all the Topographers that ever writ of, or anatomiz'd a Town or Countrey," and to "mingle

Discourse" with experienced travelers to "to draw and draine out of them all they possibly know."[3]

THE GRAND TOUR

Howell also reminds young travelers to bring money for expenses such as instruction in "*Riding, Dancing, [and] Fencing*" (p. 49). As this advice suggests, his guidebook was intended for the category of elite travelers known as Grand Tourists. The Grand Tour of Europe was undertaken by young men of the ruling classes upon completion of university studies, and lasted anywhere from a few months to several years. According to Thomas Nugent's guidebook, *The Grand Tour* (1749), its purpose was "to enrich the mind with knowledge, to rectify the judgment, to remove the prejudices of education, to compose the outward manners, and in a word to form the complete gentleman."[4] Grand Tourists tended to keep to a set itinerary whose indispensable highlights were Paris and the major urban centers of Italy. As Johnson observed, "A man who has not been in Italy, is always conscious of an inferiority, from his not having seen what it is expected a man should see" (Boswell, *Life*, 3:36).

The Grand Tour diaries of Joseph Addison and James Boswell established their reputations as authors. Addison's *Remarks on Several Parts of Italy* (1705), based on his five-year tour of Europe, is characteristic of early eighteenth-century accounts in focusing on history and art rather than on living people (including himself). Addison's work is filled with references to ancient authors; his classical preoccupations so color his descriptions that the Italian landscape sometimes seems void of modern life. By comparison, Boswell's *Account of Corsica, the Journal of a Tour to that Island; and Memoirs of Pascal Paoli* (1768), based on his own Tour from 1763 to 1766, exemplifies the greater personal element in later eighteenth-century travel accounts.

Critics of the Tour debated its actual educational value. As Boswell's private notes suggest, the ideology of the Tour was at odds with its real attractions for many young men. The novelist Samuel Richardson pointedly makes his corrupt rake Lovelace a well-informed graduate of the Tour, while Lady Mary Wortley Montagu, a well-informed observer of these young men, lamented that their "whole business abroad (as far as I can perceive) [is] to buy new cloaths." On another occasion she complained that "the folly of British boys and stupidity or knavery of [their] governors [i.e., tutors] have gained us the glorious title of Golden Asses all over Italy."[5]

EMPIRICAL OBSERVATION

James Howell emphasizes the importance of reading as preparation for travel. Significantly, though, he adds that "one's own Ocular view ... will still find out something new and unpointed at by any other."[6] Eighteenth-century travel writing was greatly influenced by the scientific method advanced by Sir Francis Bacon and the empiricist philosophy of John Locke (see chapter 37, "Science and technology," and chapter 33, "Philosophy"), and firsthand observation was of paramount importance. In 1666 the Royal Society for the Improvement of Natural Knowledge published Robert Boyle's "General Heads for a Natural History of a Countrey." Boyle's guidelines for recording details of a country's terrain, natural resources, flora and fauna, and inhabitants encouraged a new sense of travel as data collection. His emphasis on the importance of noting a country's trees suggests that the notorious comments of Defoe and Johnson on the shortage of forests in Scotland might be seen less as xenophobic than as exemplifying their efforts to be good systematic observers of nature.

By the eighteenth century, scientists (astronomers, geographers, botanists, mapmakers, and others) routinely accompanied sailors on official voyages of exploration. Captain James Cook's three famous voyages to the South and North Pacific between 1768 and 1779 were officially made for scientific purposes (as well as for purposes of colonization). It has been estimated that Cook's vessel the *Endeavour* cost the British crown about £13,000, and that about £4,000 of this went to the Royal Society to buy scientific instruments and to pay researchers. The information brought back by Cook and others prompted new questions about the development of human societies and animal and vegetable species, and contributed to the emergence of the modern disciplines of social research (see chapter 12, "Anthropology").

GETTING AROUND

Short of elaborately equipped research vessels, how did eighteenth-century travelers actually get about? Contemporary travel writings tend to be reticent on such issues. In his *Journey to the Western Islands*, Johnson mentions details of horses, inns, and boats and once alludes to "climbing crags, and treading bogs" (*Works*, 9:29), but for the most part we are left piecing together hints regarding the actual mechanics of travel. For all but the ruling classes, the primary method of travel was on foot. The cost of keeping a horse was prohibitive to the majority of the population, and even hiring the right to cling to the roof of a stagecoach was beyond the means of the poor. On rough roads, walking could be more comfortable and faster than traveling by coach or wagon. The eighteenth century saw important developments in carriage construction, culminating in Obadiah Elliott's patenting of the elliptical spring (1805), which made possible lighter, faster, and more comfortable carriages. Until then, though, long-distance passenger travel was exhausting.

The most important development in eighteenth-century British transportation, however, had to do not with carriage design but with shifts in the system for maintaining the kingdom's roads. At the beginning of the century, interregional traffic was limited, but population explosion and the growth of manufactures contributed to a phenomenal increase in the exchange of goods. Beginning in 1663, Parliament gave a small number of trustees authority to bar roads and charge tolls to raise money for road improvements (and personal profit). By 1800 there were more than a thousand such "turnpike trusts." As a consequence of improved roads, coach journey times were substantially reduced, especially in the later eighteenth century. In 1754, the 400-mile journey from London to Edinburgh took about ten days in summer, and twelve in winter. Twenty years later, the same trip in the other direction was advertised as taking only four days.

JOHNSON AS TRAVELER AND TRAVEL WRITER

Although he left Britain only once, for a three-month tour of northern France with the Thrales in 1775, Johnson was a lifelong armchair traveler. According to Boswell, he first grew interested in seeing Scotland when "his father put Martin's Account into his hands" (Boswell, *Life*, 5:13). It is easy to see how Martin Martin's *Description of the Western Islands of Scotland* (1703), with its vivid descriptions of animals and birds, would keep a child spellbound. Decades later, when traveling through Scotland at sixty-three, Johnson demonstrated for his astonished hosts the movements of a strange animal recently "discovered" on one of Cook's expeditions, the kangaroo: "He stood erect, put out his hands like feelers, and, gathering up the tails of his huge brown coat so as to resemble the pouch of the animal, made two or three vigorous bounds across the room" (Boswell, *Life*, 5:511).

Johnson's first printed book, *A Voyage to Abyssinia* (1735), was a translation of a travel narrative, *Relation historique d'Abissinie* (1728), by the French cleric Joachim Le Grand. Le Grand's *Relation* was in turn a translation of an unpublished manuscript by the seventeenth-century Portuguese Jesuit missionary Jerome Lobo, recounting his travels to Abyssinia (Ethiopia). In his preface, Johnson praises Abbé Le Grand for his "dar[ing] … disapprobation" of missionaries who "preach the Gospel with swords in their hands, and propagate by desolation and slaughter the true worship of the God of Peace" (*Works*, 15:4). At the same time, Johnson's translation sympathizes with the indigenous Christian Abyssinians who try to retain their particular version of Catholicism against the inroads of the Jesuits. Whereas Le Grand's translation calls the Abyssinians "hérétiques" and "schismatiques," Johnson refers to them simply as "those opposed to the Church of Rome." Johnson would go on to publish *The History of Rasselas, Prince of Abissinia* (1759) as well as the Eastern tale of "Seged, Lord of Ethiopia" in *Rambler*s 204 and 205. The conspicuous disappointment of Rasselas and Seged in their quests for meaning mirrors the disappointment of Father Lobo, who reluctantly returned to Portugal after the expulsion of the Jesuits from Abyssinia in 1633.

The same year that Johnson published *Rasselas* he also wrote an introduction to John Newbery's series, *The World Displayed; or, A Curious Collection of Voyages and Travels, Selected from the Writers of All Nations* (20 vols., 1759). Johnson's introduction provides a workmanlike overview of European exploration of and trade with Africa up to the time of Columbus; more originally, it offers a powerful critique of colonialist violence. Johnson condemns many of the conventional "heroes" of histories of travel – most notably Columbus, who "made the daring and prosperous voyage, which gave a new world to *European* curiosity and *European* cruelty" (*Prefaces & Dedications*, p. 236). But he refuses to let Britons off the hook by focusing solely on Spanish and Portuguese colonialist atrocities. Emphasizing that "all the European nations" were guilty of such crimes (see chapter 21, "Empire"), he explicitly singles out "the *English* barbarians that cultivate the southern islands of *America*" (p. 227).

HUMANIST TRAVEL

In a moment of piqued Scottish pride in *Journal of a Tour to the Hebrides* (1785), Boswell states that Johnson "allowed himself to look upon all nations but his own as barbarians" (Boswell, *Life*, 5:20). As we can see from Johnson's critique of "English barbarians," however, Boswell's statement is not correct. Johnson's *Journey to the Western Islands* is a complex generic hybrid of travel diary, ethnography, and philosophical meditation. Following both Howell and Boyle, Johnson combines older humanistic motivations with the new emphasis on scientific method. His commitment to the rules of empirical research can be seen in his remark that "no man should travel unprovided with instruments for taking heights and distances" (*Works*, 9:146). Johnson is a humanist traveler who is interested in mankind and manners but, in contrast to earlier humanists (such as Bacon, who advised focusing on courts of princes), he is most interested in what he calls "the state of common life" (*Works*, 9:22). In assessing the natural landscape, he prioritizes its potential to shelter and feed its inhabitants (hence his preference for fertile valleys over rugged mountains). He embraces the spread of a money-based economy throughout Scotland because he believes that it will help ameliorate poverty. But, unlike Defoe in the *Tour*, who celebrates commerce as "progress," Johnson struggles to determine what constitutes positive change.

Johnson initially seems to see himself as traveling not only across space but also backwards in time. He expects to see in the Hebrides a "rude" prototype of modern society, but the "antiquated manners" he expected no longer exist – in part because of England's political, legal, and economic incursions. In particular, the suppression of the Highland clans after the Jacobite uprising of 1745–6 has had devastating effects on the Highlanders' way of life. Johnson begins his travel narrative by observing how much the English do not know about Scotland (or the Lowland Scots about the Highlanders), but he ends it by emphasizing how much *he* does not know: "I cannot but be conscious that my thoughts on national manners, are the thoughts of one who has seen but little" (*Works*, 9:164). His ability to rethink his own assumptions can be seen in his successive comments on the shortage of trees. Initially, he critiques the Scots for what he sees as their moral failure to plant seedlings to provide for future generations. Later, though, he realizes with dismay and sympathy that the impoverished Highlanders face more pressing needs: "He that pines with hunger, is in little care how others shall be fed" (*Works*, 9:139). Johnson believed that "he only is a useful traveller who brings home something by which his country may be benefited; who procures some supply of want or some mitigation of evil" (*Works*, 2:300). By drawing attention to the Highlanders' plight, Johnson's travel narrative allowed him to do something "useful": in the words of critic John Glendening, not "to record a distant, static history but to enter an ongoing historical process that he could perhaps alter for the good."[7]

The year that Johnson died (1784), Scottish inventor William Murdoch built a prototype of the steam road locomotive. The opening of the Manchester and Liverpool railway in 1830, and the railway boom that followed, would mark the beginning of a new epoch in Britons' ideas and experience of travel.

NOTES

1 Mary Davys, *Works*, 2 vols. (London, 1725), 1:iii.
2 Elizabeth A. Bohls, introduction to *Travel Writing, 1700–1830: An Anthology*, ed. Elizabeth A. Bohls and Ian Duncan (Oxford: Oxford University Press, 2005), p. xvi.
3 James Howell, *Instructions for Forreine Travell* (London, 1642), p. 5.
4 Thomas Nugent, *The Grand Tour: Containing an Exact Description of Most of the Cities, Towns, and Remarkable Places of Europe* (London, 1749), p. xi.
5 *Complete Letters of Lady Mary Wortley Montagu*, ed. Robert Halsband, 3 vols. (Oxford: Clarendon Press, 1965–7), 2:177, 3:148.
6 Howell, *Instructions*, pp. 5–6.
7 John Glendening, *The High Road: Romantic Tourism, Scotland, and Literature, 1720–1820* (New York: St. Martin's Press, 1997), p. 119.

CHAPTER 45

Visual arts

Martin Postle

> PAI'NTER. *n.s.* [*peintre*, Fr. from *paint.*] One who professes the art of representing objects by colours.
>
> Beauty is only that which makes all things as they are in their proper and perfect nature; which the best *painters* always chuse by contemplating the forms of each. *Dryden.*

London was the crucible of the visual arts in eighteenth-century Britain. In order to succeed financially and socially, artists needed a foothold in the capital. Even so, the precise locus for success in the metropolis was undergoing fundamental change by the 1730s, when Johnson himself settled in the city. A generation earlier, the most successful and sought-after artists were those whose circles of patronage were centered on the court. They included, notably, Sir Godfrey Kneller, the German-born portraitist and history painter, who, from 1691 until his death, held the post of Principal Painter to the King. For the most part, those who prospered in the early decades of the eighteenth century were Continental artists, such as Louis Laguerre and Jacopo Amigoni, who were skilled in painting allegorical murals in the Baroque style for the palaces and mansions of the royalty and leading aristocracy. An exception was the Englishman James Thornhill, who by his death in 1734 had assumed the mantle of Britain's leading decorative painter. Even so, at this very time the taste for the Baroque was in decline. Nor was King George II interested in patronizing the visual arts, stating, memorably, that he had no use for "bainting or boetry." In such unpropitious circumstances, it was Thornhill's son-in-law, William Hogarth, who pioneered a new and very different art form. It is fair to state that Samuel Johnson's arrival in London in the late 1730s coincided with the rise of Hogarth to a position of preeminence in the capital's art world.

HOGARTH

During the 1730s, Hogarth, who had been trained as an engraver, began to produce a highly original and influential series of artworks that he called "modern moral subjects." The first of these, *The Harlot's Progress* (1732), was followed three years later by *The Rake's Progress*, a series of eight paintings (now in Sir John Soane's Museum, London) which Hogarth disseminated widely in the form of engravings – inexpensive black-and-white prints that made paintings available to a wide public. In these and similar works, Hogarth wished to produce a form of modern history painting which would address contemporary manners and mores, issues of social injustice, and political corruption. Hogarth also tackled mainstream subjects, based on the works of English writers, notably Milton and Shakespeare, in order to promote British history painting and the indigenous literary tradition. At the same time, Hogarth's promotion of a consciously modern and Anglophile art did not mean that he ignored the art of Continental Old Master painters. Rather, as he affirmed, it was the snobbish taste of collectors and connoisseurs that he disdained.

Hogarth's passion for the traditions of European art and the importance of artistic training were manifested in his decision in the mid-1730s to take control of an art academy in London's St. Martin's Lane. There Hogarth promoted the study of life drawing, admitting artists by subscription. As he averred, his academy was to be distinct from the "foolish parade" of the intensely hierarchical French Academy, which was based upon social rank and under state control, in the grip of an elite corps of artists, intent, it would seem, on promoting their own careers and their particular styles of painting. By the 1740s, St. Martin's Lane was the home of the academy as well as the focal point of the visual arts in London. Here, artists rubbed shoulders with collectors, art dealers, and patrons, meeting to exchange news and gossip in the myriad coffee houses, such as the celebrated Old Slaughter's, and a variety of common-interest dining clubs. The artistic community of St. Martin's Lane at this time was highly cosmopolitan, and even Hogarth – bristling with nationalistic pride – acknowledged that the influx of Continental painters, engravers, book illustrators, and sculptors was beneficial. When Hogarth wished to find craftsmen to engrave his latest, and arguably his greatest, modern moral subject, *Marriage à la Mode* (1743), he looked to Paris to find the expertise he required.

A BRITISH SCHOOL

It was during the 1740s that the visual arts in England began to witness the emergence of a homegrown generation of artists – aside from Hogarth – who can be claimed, quite legitimately, as the founders of a

British School of art. Principal among these younger artists were Thomas Gainsborough and Joshua Reynolds, who, although quite different in temperament, professional demeanor, and artistic style, were to dominate the cosmopolitan art scene for the next half-century.

Gainsborough, the son of a Suffolk wool merchant, was a product of the cosmopolitan community of St. Martin's Lane, trained by a French silversmith in the art of engraving, influenced by the example of Hogarth, and intent upon succeeding in the burgeoning art market. Gainsborough, adept at both portraiture and landscape painting, realized that financial success was allied more firmly to the former genre, and during the 1740s he promoted himself through the production of small-scale group portraits, or "conversation pieces," which had been in vogue for the past twenty years. These conversation pieces culminated in what is today regarded as his masterpiece in the genre, *Mr. and Mrs. Andrews* (National Gallery, London), which depicts a well-heeled squirarchical couple occupying their rolling rural acres. Like many cosmopolitan artists, Gainsborough kept one foot firmly in the country, for the maintenance of local and regional patrons remained as important as cultivating the court or the city. Even so, while a number of artists – notably Joseph Wright, who spent most of his life in his native Derby – managed to find commercial life outside London, most eventually made their careers in the capital.

During the time that Johnson lived in London, the artist who dominated increasingly London's artistic community, and conditioned Johnson's attitude towards the visual arts, was Sir Joshua Reynolds. Reynolds was ambitious to raise the status of the visual arts in England through a close alliance to the traditions of European painting. Following a period of training in London with the portrait painter Thomas Hudson, he spent three formative years on the Grand Tour in Italy, from 1749 to 1752, absorbing the work of Old Master painters in Rome, Florence, and Venice (see chapter 44, "Travel"). On his return to England, although he continued to pursue portraiture, Reynolds emulated the style and technique of the Old Masters, causing one elder artist to retreat in disgust from his studio, exclaiming, "Shakespeare in poetry, and Kneller in painting, damme!"

During the 1750s, Reynolds was among a group of younger painters, sculptors, and architects working in London who were increasingly dissatisfied with the existing artistic status quo and with Hogarth's perceived eccentric slant on art academies and art theory, as manifest in his treatise *The Analysis of Beauty* (1753). Already within London's artistic community there were moves to found a new academy built on the French model, supported by royal patronage, all of which was anathema to Hogarth. In 1749, the architect John Gwynn, in an *Essay on Design*, had argued for such an academy; in 1753, following the publication of Hogarth's treatise, a young artist, Paul Sandby, produced a series of vicious satirical engravings aimed at undermining Hogarth's stance. Although it was not until some fifteen years later that a Royal Academy came into being, by the end of the 1750s the lobbying artists had achieved one important goal: the establishment of the public exhibition, the first of which was held at the Society of Arts in 1760.

THE ROYAL ACADEMY

Before 1760, there had been limited opportunities for artists to show their work in public, an exception being the display of contemporary art in London's Foundling Hospital, a philanthropic institution established, in part through the efforts of Hogarth, for the provision of care for the capital's orphans. With the new round of commercial exhibitions organized by the Society of Artists, though, it was possible to show new work on an annual basis and to attract new patrons.

The display of art in the public arena could attract unwelcome attention: newspaper critics weighed in freely with their opinions, as Hogarth discovered when his history painting, *Sigismunda Mourning over the Heart of Guiscardo* (1759), was so vilified that he removed it from exhibition. Others were more fortunate. Reynolds exhibited extensively, gaining plaudits for "historical" portraits, including *Garrick between Tragedy and Comedy* (1762) and *Lady Sarah Bunbury Sacrificing to the Graces* (1765). The public exhibition also provided opportunities for the promotion of landscape painting, notably through the work of Richard Wilson, whose *Destruction of the Children of Niobe* (1760) proved a benchmark in historical landscape painting, influencing a whole generation of British artists. The success of the first public exhibition of 1760 prompted the artists to charge an admission fee the following year (one shilling, with a free catalogue). Samuel Johnson was drafted by Reynolds to write the preface to the catalogue in order to justify the fee, which he did on the grounds that it would subsidize the sale of artists' work, who might not otherwise get a fair price.

By the late 1760s the exhibitions were proving popular with artists as well as the fee-paying public, to the extent that the leading artists became increasingly keen to dissociate themselves from the rank and file, whose

Figure 40 Edward Fisher after Sir Joshua Reynolds, *Strive Not Tragedy nor Comedy to Engross a Garrick*, 1762.

work they regarded as inferior. As a result, after much Machiavellian maneuvering, an elite corps of artists broke away from the Society of Artists, and, through a direct appeal to the king for patronage, formed the Royal Academy of Arts in December 1768. Following a brief consultation with his close friends, Edmund Burke and Samuel Johnson, Reynolds consented to be president. The following year, in April 1769, Reynolds received a knighthood from the king, the first to be conferred on a painter since James Thornhill a half-century earlier.

Under the aegis of Reynolds and the patronage of George III, the Royal Academy of Arts put the visuals arts on a new footing. Now, under one roof, artists were educated in the academy's schools (drawing from the living model and from plaster casts, and studying anatomy), showed their works to the public in an annual exhibition, and, through the academy's council and general assembly, provided a legislative body. In addition to the post of president, and other related administrative positions from within the ranks of academicians, the Royal Academy made a number of honorary appointments, including Oliver Goldsmith as professor of ancient history and Johnson as professor of ancient literature.

THE *DISCOURSES*

As president, Reynolds felt it was incumbent upon himself to promote the status of the visual arts through a series of lectures, or "discourses," which he gave annually, and later biennially, at the academy to academicians, students, and invited guests. Cumulatively, Reynolds's fifteen *Discourses on Art*, delivered between 1769 and 1790, provided the most authoritative and lucid account of the role of the visual arts in Britain and their relation to the tradition of Western art since the Renaissance.

The principal inspiration for the *Discourses* was derived from the treatises written by members of the French Académie Royale a century earlier (notably Charles Le Brun, Henri Testelin, André Felibien, Jean Baptiste Du Bos, and the critic Roger de Piles). Reynolds was also in touch with contemporary French artists, and would have been keenly aware of their continuing propensity for producing theoretical treatises on the arts. The inaugural *Discourse* of January 1769 was Reynolds's first substantial literary composition since the three essays he had written for Johnson's *Idler* series in 1759. Yet, while the *Discourses* may appear at first glance to be a similar serialized narrative, they do not form a cohesive treatise, not least because they were conceived and written over a span of some twenty years. So, for example, while in the earlier *Discourses* Reynolds promoted a hierarchical framework of art, based upon the primacy of High Renaissance artists such as Raphael, and the superiority of line over color, in later *Discourses* he was more amenable to the merits of colorists of the Venetian School such as Titian and Tintoretto, and the Flemish master, Peter Paul Rubens. At the same time, the *Discourses* wove a complex web of ideas which went far beyond the boundaries of art education.

Material for the *Discourses* was garnered from a wide variety of sources, including classical authors such as Horace and Longinus, Renaissance artists, as well as contemporary treatises by Francesco Algarotti, Johann Joachim Winckelmann, and Adam Smith. Reynolds also received editorial assistance from friends, notably Johnson, Edmund Burke, and Edmond Malone. Even so, their respective contributions were unjustly exaggerated by contemporaries, who underrated Reynolds's abilities as a writer. Despite the objections of detractors, it was perfectly natural for Reynolds to have sought the advice and comments of his close friends in preparing his lectures and editing the manuscript for publication.

According to Enlightenment principles, creativity was a communal pursuit, as individual genius was molded by rules and conventions. Thus, Reynolds welcomed the contributions and comments of colleagues on his *Discourses*, just as he liberally dispensed criticism on works by authors such as Richard Brinsley Sheridan, Edmund Burke, James Beattie, and George Crabbe.

ROYAL ACADEMY EXHIBITIONS

During the 1770s, the annual exhibitions of the Royal Academy proved a great commercial and critical success. Reynolds exhibited portraits, "fancy pictures" (character studies of children in the guise of saints and deities), and history paintings, including the compositionally flawed but highly influential *Ugolino and His Children in the Dungeon* (1773). At exhibition, Reynolds's principal rival in portraiture was Thomas Gainsborough, although, because of disagreements over the hanging of his works, the latter was constantly on the verge of resigning his membership. Competition in portraiture was also provided by George Romney, although, while he poached Reynolds's patrons, he maintained his distance from the Royal Academy. Other successful artists also remained on the periphery of the academy, notably George Stubbs who, although elected a Royal Academician, did not bother much with the organization.

Some were more eager to use the academy to promote their careers and their ambitions for the visual arts in Britain. They included Reynolds's protégé, the Irish artist James Barry. In 1773, Barry joined with Reynolds, Benjamin West, Angelica Kauffmann, and several other Royal Academicians in a scheme to supply religious paintings for the decoration of the interior of St. Paul's Cathedral. Following the rejection of the scheme, Barry, frustrated at his lack of opportunity to find patronage for his history paintings, became increasingly antagonistic towards Reynolds, and his inability to promote the cause of high art. In 1782 Barry was appointed professor of painting by the Royal Academy. In addition to lecturing on the importance of history painting, he used his position to berate Reynolds for his perceived lack of leadership. His own magnum opus, a series of six history paintings titled *The Progress of Human Culture*, was displayed not at the Royal Academy but in the Great Room of the Royal Society of Arts, where it remains *in situ*.

On its foundation, the Royal Academy's business was conducted initially in a print warehouse on Pall Mall, where the annual exhibition was also held. Here a number of iconic works of the British School were exhibited, including Gainsborough's *Blue Boy* (1770), West's *Death of General Wolfe* (1771), and *Watson and the Shark* (1778) by West's young American contemporary, John Singleton Copley. In 1771 the academy's teaching component was moved to apartments in Old Somerset House in the Strand, a royal palace designed in the seventeenth century by Inigo Jones. By 1780, the palace had been rebuilt by the Royal Academician William Chambers, at which time the Royal Academy began to exhibit there, in a magnificent room on the top floor, illuminated from above by natural light. Exhibits that year included Johan Zoffany's magnificent *Tribuna of the Uffizi*, Reynolds's portrait of the historian Edward Gibbon, and an inaugural exhibit, *The Death of Earl Goodwin*, by the twenty-two-year-old painter and engraver, William Blake, who had began to attend the academy's schools the previous year.

By the 1780s the visual arts in Britain occupied a quite different niche than they had fifty years earlier. The court had continued to exercise influence and patronage through support of such favorite artists as the portraitists Allan Ramsay and Thomas Gainsborough and the history painter West. Even so, it was peripheral to the careers of the majority of British artists. Reynolds, for instance – though he was president of the Royal Academy and Principal Painter to the King – did not depend upon royal favor for his success, but rather upon a wide range of patrons from all parties and persuasions. Through Hogarth's pioneering work as an engraver, and particularly through his engineering of the Copyright Act of 1735, the print trade had flourished in the open market, both domestically and on the Continent. Similarly, collectors who had been obsessed with the acquisition of Old Master paintings and prints were increasingly willing to purchase works by contemporary British artists.

Even Johnson attempted to exercise his own patronage through the promotion of his godson, Mauritius Lowe, whose painting, *The Deluge*, though rejected by the Royal Academy's Council, was exhibited in 1783, after personal written appeals to Barry and Reynolds. In the spring of 1784, Johnson, plagued with ill health, climbed the long stone staircase at Somerset House to inspect the Royal Academy's annual exhibition for one last time. There among the exhibits he would have seen Reynolds's improbable equestrian portrait of George, Prince of Wales, as a military hero, a painting which effectively ushered in a new age of Romanticism.

CHAPTER 46

War

John Richardson

WAR. *n.s.* [*werre*, old Dutch; *guerre*, Fr.]

> *War* may be defined the exercise of violence under sovereign command against withstanders; force, authority, and resistance being the essential parts thereof. Violence, limited by authority, is sufficiently distinguished from robbery, and the like outrages; yet consisting in relation towards others, it necessarily requires a supposition of resistance, whereby the force of *war* becomes different from the violence inflicted upon slaves or yielding malefactors. *Raleigh.*

Johnson's capacity for independence, even contrariness, was diminished neither by his country's being at war nor by the patriotism which often goes with that.

THE GLORIOUS FIFTY-NINE

The Seven Years' War (1756–63) was such an extensive conflict that it has been called "the first world war." It involved all the major European powers, and its theaters included North America, Europe, and India. By the time it ended, there was a new balance of power in Europe and a new, vast British empire in the world.

The high point for Britain and its allies came in 1759. In August of that year they won a pitched battle at Minden in Germany against mainly French forces; in September, General James Wolfe led, and died in, a dramatic, cliff-scaling assault that resulted in the capture of Quebec; in November, the British navy defeated a French fleet at Quiberon Bay off France's Biscay coast. The series of successes caused the usual wartime excitement among civilians at home, and one journalist complained of the "general intoxication" that made everyone speak the language of Alexander – in other words, that made everyone gossip about strategy, battles, and killing.[1] Wolfe's victory was the most celebrated of all. The newspapers reported it in copious detail when the news finally arrived in London after the long journey across the Atlantic, and they supplemented their reports with enthusiastic poems and memorials to "immortal Wolfe." Shortly afterwards, an official proclamation announced a day of public thanksgiving for the success of "this just War."[2] Looking back, the *Gentleman's Magazine* called the year "the glorious Fifty-Nine," and Johnson's friend David Garrick referred to "this wonderful year" in his popular, ebullient, patriotic song, "Heart of Oak."[3] It was, in short, a year that provided much for bellicose British patriots to celebrate.

But the fifty-year-old Johnson refused to join the celebration. His main contribution to the discussion of the "wonderful year" came in an issue of the *Universal Chronicle* two weeks after the arrival of the news of the taking of Quebec. The newspaper was still packed with adulatory pieces about Wolfe, but, sandwiched awkwardly in among them, was an *Idler* essay. The piece presents an imagined American Indian chief watching the British army's march towards Quebec, and reports his speech to his followers. The chief complains about the European invasion, the weapons that enabled it to happen, the slaughter and slavery that accompanied it, and the fraudulent arguments by which it was justified. He goes on to contemplate the current war between Britain and France in North America, and to look without concern upon the mutual killing. He ends by urging his followers to learn how to fight with modern weapons, so that when the European invaders have worn each other down, the Native Americans can attack them, drive them away, and "reign once more in our native country" (*Works*, 2:254). The *Idler* was a remarkable intervention at a moment of high patriotic fervor. With it Johnson not only questioned the justice of the British cause, but took the extra step of wishing for his own country's defeat.

The episode demonstrates Johnson's willingness, even inclination, to adopt an independent and contrary position. But it shows more than that. His reactions, together with the journalist's complaints about war hysteria, are evidence of the variety of eighteenth-century attitudes towards war. More important still for our purposes, the trenchant words of the American Indian chief indicate Johnson's deep-seated skepticism about war. He was not opposed to every war. But he disliked the excitement that accompanies wars, the elevation of soldiers into heroes, and the use of armed force to solve any but the most intractable of problems.

AN AGE OF WAR

Johnson's views are given extra point by the fact that he lived through many wars. He was born one week after the Battle of Malplaquet of September 11, 1709, probably the bloodiest battle of the War of the Spanish Succession. He died one year after the end of the War of American Independence. The wars he lived through can be listed as follows: the tail end of the War of the Spanish Succession (1701–14), the War of the Quadruple Alliance (1718–20), the War of the Austrian Succession (1739–48), the Seven Years' War (1756–63), and the War of American Independence (1775–83). Britain fought all these wars abroad – in Europe, India, North America – and invasion scares during the Seven Years' War and the War of Independence remained nothing more than scares. Hostile armies did, however, gather and fight in Britain twice during Johnson's lifetime. People loyal to James II, the exiled Stuart claimant to the crown, and his descendants were known as Jacobites (see chapter 35, "Politics"). In 1715 and 1745–6, Jacobite forces assembled in Scotland and moved south to invade northern England before being driven back and defeated. When Johnson died, Britain had been at war for about thirty-one of his seventy-five years. For a seventy-five-year-old Briton in 2011, that figure (excluding conflicts below the status of full wars) would be more like ten years. The middle and later part of the eighteenth century truly was an age of war.

Eighteenth-century warfare was, in theory at least, tactical, limited, and disciplined. Armies and navies fought for circumscribed ends, and there was no expectation of a decisive encounter that would destroy the enemy and decide the war. The aim was advantage and eventual negotiation, not crushing victory. Fighting itself was characterized by troops moving in mass formation. Infantrymen learned through training and drill to hold their fire until close to the enemy – if possible, until the enemy had already discharged their weapons. A famous general of the War of the Austrian Succession, Maurice, Comte de Saxe, argued that the reserving of fire both terrified by its display of courage and allowed troops to cause havoc while the enemy reloaded – always a slow, cumbersome, and dangerous business with eighteenth-century muzzle-loading muskets. Such fighting required considerable discipline and courage. Prussian troops were famous for the former, but the British prided themselves on special possession of the latter. In a curious essay from the middle of the Seven Years' War, Johnson inquired into the causes of the "epidemick bravery" that characterized English soldiers, taking it for granted that this quality really existed. His answer was that the Englishman's economic independence led to his having to protect himself and his own honor, and thus practicing and developing courage (*Works*, 10:281–4).

LIFE DURING WARTIME

People living in the foreign theaters of war suffered its usual depredations: troops billeted upon them, theft or destruction of property, and sometimes terrible cruelty or death. The British civilian, however, had little direct contact with war. Battles were fought and cities taken over during the two Jacobite uprisings, but the threat of protracted war and British defeat were never very great. The occasional invasion scares in other wars swiftly became the subject of comic comment in, for instance, the farce *The Invasion* (1759) and Richard Brinsley Sheridan's play *The Critic* (1779). The experience of war for the British civilian was overwhelmingly secondhand, and came through talk or print. The oral stories of returning soldiers are lost forever, but the main sources of printed information, the newspapers, survive. These reported troop movements, skirmishes, sieges, and battles, and sometimes serialized items from the rapidly growing theoretical literature about war. Historians have touted various wars from the nineteenth and twentieth centuries as the first "media war." None of the wars of Johnson's life is quite that. Eighteenth-century war reporting lacks descriptive immediacy, personal perspective, and (of course) visual images. Nevertheless, the newspapers did provide the civilian population with a lot of information about the state of current hostilities.

As in other centuries, the soldier sometimes suffered as much away from battle as in it, and some contemporary reports acknowledged this. One pamphleteer noted bitterly that, after the victories of 1759, British troops had been given "such winter quarters as the meanest fisherman's boy upon the Thames would not have put up with," and the *Gentleman's Magazine* for 1760 claimed that, though few Prussians and Austrians had fallen in battle, 3,500 died in a single camp from disease. Johnson was aware of this aspect of war. In a pamphlet of 1771 he looked back briefly on the Seven Years' War, suggesting that the majority of deaths came from disease, with the dead eventually "whelmed in pits, or heaved into the ocean, without notice and without remembrance" (*Works*, 10:371). Like some others among his contemporaries, he extended sympathy to captured enemy soldiers as well as to those of his own side. In 1759 and 1760, he was involved in a scheme for raising relief for French prisoners of war confined in dreadful conditions in England. Responding to the argument that the money would have been better spent on British soldiers, he made a direct appeal to common human sympathy: "we know that they are poor and naked, and poor and naked without a crime" (*Works*, 10:288).

In addition to newspapers, books of various kinds offered a readily available source of information. A 1759 journal from Quebec included details of truces, maneuvers, generals' speeches, and scalpings by the American Indian allies of both sides. Another book from the same year dealt with a different theater, praising Robert Clive's campaign in India for the nobility of its motives and the moderation of its means. But one of the most remarkable and imaginatively gripping eighteenth-century accounts of a military operation occurs in Tobias Smollett's picaresque novel, *Roderick Random* (1748). Smollett had been present at the 1741 naval siege of Cartagena as a surgeon's second mate aboard the *Chichester*, and he used the experience to recreate the siege in his fiction. What he caustically described was a series of blunders and misjudgments which caused the needless deaths of hundreds of seamen and soldiers. Casualties were put on hospital ships which, according to Smollett, hardly deserved the name. The injured men were cramped in quarters where they could not sit up, and their neglected wounds became so dirty that "millions of maggots were hatched amid the corruption of their sores."[4] Johnson was later to refer to the event in his *Thoughts on the Late Transactions Respecting Falkland's Islands* (1771). Perhaps remembering Smollett's description, he wrote of the many men "poisoned by the air, and crippled by the dews" during the siege (*Works*, 10:374).

THE LAST OF REMEDIES

Alongside such information, there was much public discussion of the rights and wrongs of war. Johnson described it in his pamphlet *Thoughts on … Falkland's Islands* as "the last of remedies," an evil to be avoided except in the most extreme of circumstances (*Works*, 10:370). This is the standard stated position of most people who discuss war, but Johnson took the idea of extremity seriously, and did not call for war lightly. Of the wars in his lifetime, he broadly supported the outbreak of hostilities with Spain in 1739, was opposed to the Seven Years' War, and supported the British action against the colonists in the War of Independence (*Works*, 10:453).

His different positions for these different wars take into account both the causes and the conduct of war. War may justifiably be fought to protect territory or rights; it may not be fought for mere conquest and gain. His central objection to the Seven Years' War was that Britain and France were fighting for North American land to which neither had a legitimate claim (see chapter 10, "America"). He argued in 1756, right at the beginning of the war, that the only right each side had was "that of power," and the only means of gaining the territory "usurpation and dispossession of the natural lords and original inhabitants" (*Works*, 10:186). The dislike of taking by force of arms was a common sentiment among many contemporaries, but the extension of this principle to include the American Indians was not. Most followed the philosopher John Locke in believing that rights to land came with the cultivation of it, and since (they said) the American Indians had undertaken no cultivation, they had no such rights. Johnson's position was different. The American Indians were for him the "natural lords" of the lands they lived in, and to dispossess them was equivalent to dispossessing Europeans.

Many in the eighteenth century saw their period as one of refinement and civilization, and in keeping with that, they emphasized the desirability and possibility of moderation in warfare. Contemporary war poetry, for instance, seldom shows its heroes killing, and reserves descriptions of death and pain for the vilification of the behavior of enemies. Johnson was of his time in decrying the extremes of war. He criticized British policy in North America, which had made too little effort to befriend the natives; he urged restraint at the beginning of the War of Independence; and late in his life, during his journey to Scotland, he sadly observed the effects of the British actions against the Scottish clans that had supported the Jacobite uprising of 1745–6. The pride of the clans had, he noted, been "crushed by the heavy hand of a vindictive conqueror" (*Works*, 9:89). In similar vein, he wrote during the Seven Years' War that it was "ridiculous to imagine that the friendship of nations, whether civil or barbarous, can be kept and gained but by kind treatment" (*Works*, 10:150). If war must be fought – and he thought at times it must – it should be fought as humanely as possible.

WARS NECESSARY AND UNNECESSARY

Johnson's general moral reflections upon war and warriors mirrored his attitudes towards specific wars. An *Adventurer* essay of 1753 raised the conundrum of the different reputations of successful and unsuccessful men. In the case of soldiers, Johnson argued, success should not be a guarantee of fame, since it had come at the cost of death and desolation. Rather, successful conquerors and those who tried and failed should equally be "huddled together in obscurity or detestation" (*Works*, 2:433). He expressed similar sentiments in *The Vanity of Human Wishes*. His four examples of military greatness – Charles XII of Sweden, the fifth-century BCE Persian emperor Xerxes, the Elector Charles of Bavaria, and the Duke of Marlborough – have in common both a disappointing end to their ambitions and the flawed nature of the ambitions themselves. Charles XII neglected the works of peace to pursue the conquest of Asia, and was eventually rewarded with defeat and death in obscurity by "a dubious hand" (line 220). And Xerxes, after a series of victories, descended into madness and mounted an assault upon the ocean (lines 231–2). In articulating such views, Johnson not only echoed the satire by the Roman author Juvenal he was imitating, but placed himself firmly in an eighteenth-century tradition of conservative skeptics about war and military heroes, a tradition which includes Jonathan Swift, John Gay, and Henry Fielding.

Johnson's *Idler* essay featuring the speech of the American Indian chief is of a piece with his other comments on war. What he opposes in it is conquest through arms, and the destruction of life and property that accompanies it. The Europeans are in the wrong because they have used their superior technology to take over parts of North America and subjugate the people living there. This is far from a pacifist argument. The chief ends by looking forward to the day when he and his followers will be strong enough to drive away the war-weakened Europeans. War of the kind the chief proposes, in extreme circumstances and in defense of birthright and native soil, is justified, even necessary, in Johnson's view. Most contemporaries would have agreed with this. What distinguishes Johnson from them are the independence and courage to apply general principles to particular and current events. Few were, or are, prepared during times of war hysteria to take positions, like Johnson's, directly contrary to those of the majority.

NOTES

1 *The Universal Chronicle, or Weekly Gazette* 79 (Sept. 29–Oct. 6, 1759).
2 *The Universal Chronicle, or Weekly Gazette* 83 (Oct. 27–Nov. 3, 1759).
3 *The Gentleman's Magazine* 30 (1760), 38.
4 Tobias Smollett, *The Adventures of Roderick Random*, ed. Paul-Gabriel Boucé (Oxford: Oxford University Press, 1979), p. 187.

CHAPTER 47

Women writers

John Wiltshire

WO'MAN. [*wifman*, *wimman*, Saxon; whence we yet pronounce women in the plural, *wimmen*, *Skinner*.]
1. The female of the human race.

O *woman*, lovely *woman*, nature form'd thee
To temper man: we had been brutes without thee. *Otway*.

"I dined yesterday at Mrs. Garrick's, with Mrs. Carter, Miss Hannah More, and Miss Fanny Burney," said Samuel Johnson in 1784. "Three such women are not to be found: I know not where I could find a fourth, except Mrs. Lennox, who is superiour to them all" (Boswell, *Life*, 4:275). More remarkable than Frances Burney's chagrin at this striking remark is Boswell's neglect of the obvious leads with which it presented him. He says little in his biography about the other authoresses named here, all of whom could have filled gaps in his *Life*, especially concerning Johnson's early years.

Boswell had no interest in his subject's relations with intellectual women. The record shows, though, that Samuel Johnson was throughout his career the friend, supporter, and champion of female writers, whether they be translators, poets, playwrights, or novelists. From his first days, laboring on the *Gentleman's Magazine* and picking up whatever jobs he could, he thought of them as fellow authors, struggling like him to gain a living in a literary marketplace that was undergoing critical changes (see chapter 13, "Authorship"). Nothing, in fact, demonstrates Johnson's extraordinary freedom from the commonplace prejudices of his time more than his relationships with them. To see this is to realize that there is an alternative to Boswell's story about Johnson's life – focused on Johnson in the later, more comfortable circumstances of his life and in largely masculine company – that demands to be told.

Johnson's life coincided with a great rise in the prominence of women intellectuals. Women wrote works of imaginative literature and offered both opinions and expertise on a range of subjects, including politics, sociology, history, philosophy, linguistics, literary criticism, and classical scholarship. Johnson knew and supported many of the women involved in this revolution. "Of the female mind," reported Sir John Hawkins, "he conceived a higher opinion than many men" (Hawkins, *Life*, p. 235). "Johnson set a higher value upon female friendship than, perhaps, most men" (*Miscellanies*, 2:252), wrote one of those friends, Frances Reynolds, after his death. She was commenting on Johnson's early alliance with two women, "Miss Carter and Miss Mulso, now Mrs. Chapone," and goes on to say that he often repeated – "with very apparent delight" – some verses by Hester Mulso, cited in his *Dictionary* under *quatrain*.

CHARLOTTE LENNOX

Another prominent female mind whom Johnson complimented by including her in the *Dictionary* was Charlotte Lennox. "Mrs. Lennox" was probably the most significant of the authoresses whom Johnson championed and befriended throughout his life. She arrived in London in the 1740s, like Johnson an outsider seeking a living in the capital. Thomas Babington Macaulay in 1831 gave a vivid sketch of the state of literary affairs that met them: "Johnson came up to London precisely at the time when the condition of a man of letters was most miserable and degraded. It was a dark night between two sunny days. The age of patronage had passed away. The age of general curiosity and intelligence had not arrived."[1] Harsh for a man of letters, worse for a woman. Charlotte, born Ramsay, had unwisely married the shiftless Alexander Lennox in 1747, so her struggles, like Johnson's, were made worse by the need to support a partner (and in her case an increasing family).

With Johnson's help, Lennox published her first novel, the quasi-autobiographical *Harriot Stuart* in 1750. This was the occasion of a celebration reported by Hawkins:

> One evening at the club, Johnson proposed to us the celebrating the birth of Mrs. Lenox's first literary child, as he called her book, by a whole night spent in festivity … Our supper was elegant, and Johnson had directed that a magnificent hot apple-pye should make a part of it, and this he would have stuck with bay-leaves, because, forsooth, Mrs. Lenox was an authoress, and had written verses; and further, he had prepared for her a crown of laurel, with which, but not till he had invoked the muses by some ceremonies of his own invention, he encircled her brows. The night passed, as must be imagined, in pleasant conversation, and harmless mirth, intermingled at different periods with the refreshments of coffee

and tea. About five, Johnson's face shone with meridian splendour, though his drink had been only lemonade. (Hawkins, *Life*, p. 172)

This anecdote conjures up a quite different scene from those we find in Boswell. Here is a literary party on the very fringes of polite society. Making their own festivity, bestowing their own honors, bohemian and avant-garde before these categories were invented, this is a joyous celebration of independence from the world of patrons and booksellers, a gathering that modern readers might relate to, however remote they may feel from the forms and formalities of Johnson's later Literary Club.

Johnson was always a loyal colleague of Lennox. He introduced her to the novelist Samuel Richardson, to whom he speaks of "our Charlotte" (*Letters*, 1:56), and to Lord Orrery, both of them assisting in getting her next novel, *The Female Quixote*, published. Johnson wrote the dedication, and very possibly collaborated with her in the writing of the penultimate chapter, headed "Being in the Author's opinion, the best Chapter in this History."[2] The novel was a success – in fact, Lennox's only great success – and was translated into several European languages. The Austen family made it their "evening amusement" in the winter of 1807, "to me a very high one," Jane Austen wrote, "as I find the work quite equal to what I remembered it."[3]

Like Johnson, Lennox turned her hand to anything that might consolidate her reputation and keep the wolf from the door. She published translations; *Shakespear Illustrated*, which related Shakespeare's plots to their sources, in three volumes (1753–4) with a dedication by Johnson; and a number of novels, including *Henrietta* in 1758 ("by the author of *The Female Quixote*") and *Sophia*, serialized in 1762. She writes in 1760 of her "slavery to the Booksellers, whom I have the more mortification to see adding to their heaps by my labours, which scarce produce me a scanty and precarious subsistence."[4] Hers was a "career narrative," a consistent professional commitment to writing throughout her life. In this she was unlike many other women authors of her time, who, whether rich or poor, preferred to play down the financial rewards of publication. Though she continued to produce plays and translations, by 1781 Johnson was writing on her behalf:

I am desired by Mrs Lennox to solicite your assistance. She is in great distress; very harshly treated by her husband, and oppressed with severe illness. Do for her what you can, You were perhaps never called to the relief of a more powerful mind. She has many fopperies, but she is a great Genius, and nullum magnum ingenium sine mixtura ["never was there a great genius without some such mixture"]. (*Letters*, 3:353–4)

The quotation from his friend's novel that Johnson uses in the *Dictionary* – one of those chosen, as he wrote in the preface, through "the tenderness of friendship" (*Works*, 18:95) – illustrates *talent*: "Persons who possess the true *talent* of raillery are like comets; they are seldom seen, and all at once admired and feared." Perhaps this reveals something that Johnson and Lennox had in common: the quick wit that scared others and could make life difficult. Prickly, quick to resent slights, and self-destructive, Lennox also shared characteristics with Johnson's other great friend of the early years, Richard Savage – and, like him, died in poverty.

THE BLUESTOCKINGS

The friends Elizabeth Carter and Hester Mulso, in common with most of the genteel ladies who are sometimes called the Bluestockings, disliked and disapproved of Lennox. Friends too of Samuel Richardson, they were also colleagues of Johnson, and they closely watched his career. Mulso wrote four amusing little letters, that, along with his replies, lightened the tone of *Rambler* 10 in April 1750. She was later to become famous as Mrs. Chapone, the author of a pre-evangelical advice manual, many times reprinted, *Essays on the Improvement of the Mind* (1773).

"Mrs." Carter – she never married; the title was an honorific – was something else: in the words of Thomas Birch, "a very extraordinary Phaenomenon in the Republick of Letters,"[5] she was to publish a volume which lasted well into the twentieth century as the standard translation of the Greek Stoic philosopher Epictetus. Her father was a friend of the proprietor of the *Gentleman's Magazine*, Edward Cave, to which Elizabeth began contributing verses in 1734, when she was seventeen. Johnson published an epigram in her honor in the magazine for April 1738, and she replied, like him, in both Latin and Greek. This dialogue suggests what the later record confirms: a mutual regard based on both classical scholarship and independent character. Highly intelligent, widely read, learned in many languages, and, of the Bluestockings, the most openly feminist, Carter impressed Johnson, and their lifelong alliance is a remarkable one. She soon left London but kept in touch through regular visits to the city. In the country, encouraged by Catherine Talbot, who also contributed an essay to the *Rambler*, she began work on her translation of Epictetus, which as *All the Works* (1758) was eventually published by Richardson to consistent acclaim. Though it was expensive, Johnson was a subscriber.

ELIZABETH MONTAGU

Following the publication of Carter's Epictetus, Elizabeth Montagu – Johnson called her the "Queen of the Blues"[6] – sought Carter's friendship, and the two women became close. Montagu is a significant figure in the eighteenth-century literary scene, but her precise contribution is difficult to assess. She was the most prestigious of a number of wealthy ladies who held "conversations" or salons at their grand houses in Mayfair or thereabouts, assemblies which "mix the rank and the literature, and exclude all beside," as Frances Burney was to put it in 1782.[7] Montagu combined the roles of society hostess, amateur author, and literary patron. She subscribed, for example, to Anna Williams's *Miscellanies in Prose and Verse*, which Samuel Johnson promoted for his indigent housemate in 1759, and later allowed Williams and Carter annuities. Chapone's *Essays* acknowledged her assistance and is dedicated to her. Johnson's carefully composed complimentary letters to Montagu, often soliciting her aid, suggest how even he found it difficult to separate her charity from her style, her "Beneficence" from her "Elegance" (*Letters*, 1:186).

Johnson seems to have been, if not a regular, then a frequent guest at her assemblies, and no doubt a drawing card. Montagu was also a close friend of the statesman and man of letters, Lord Lyttelton, and contributed, anonymously, three of his *Dialogues of the Dead* (1760). She soon announced to Elizabeth Carter her zeal to become "an author in form."[8] She devoted the coming years to serious study and paid for the publication of her *Essay on the Writings and Genius of Shakespear* in May 1769. An ambitious work, this compared Shakespeare's plays to Greek and French classical models and defended the national poet against the ridicule of Voltaire. Johnson's opinion of the book was not high: he could not get through the volume, which occasioned one of his most perceptive remarks: "there is no real criticism in it: none shewing the beauty of thought, as formed on the workings of the human heart" (Boswell, *Life*, 2:88).

Offended by his treatment of Lyttelton in the *Lives of the Poets*, by 1781 Montagu had dropped Johnson, and rewarded his obsequiousness with angry contempt: "I wish his figure was put as a frontispiece to his works, his squinting look and monstrous form would well explain his character. Those disgraces which make a good mind humble and complacent, ever render a bad one envious and ferocious." Johnson's opinions no doubt "challenged her superiority – the superiority of the lettered aristocracy – in the learned world."[9]

WOMEN FRIENDS AND WRITERS

Frances Reynolds, the sister of Sir Joshua, was a recipient of Johnson's sponsorship and kindness – possibly a tricky business, since he was a close friend of her brother, with whom she did not get on. Her ambition was to publish a quasi-philosophical work, an "Enquiry concerning the principles of taste, and of the origin of our ideas of beauty, etc," a draft of which she showed to Johnson in 1781. He sent her these comments:

> There is in these such force of comprehension, and such nicety of observation as Locke or Pascal might be proud of. This I say with intention to have you think that I speak my opinion.
>
> They cannot however be printed in their present state. Many of your notions seem not very clear in your own mind, many are not sufficiently developed and expanded for the common reader; the expression almost every where wants to be made clearer and smoother. You may by revisal and improvement make it a very elegant and curious work. (*Letters*, 3:355–6)

Johnson's comments are the very model of literary mentorship: encouraging, praising, discriminating, yet completely firm about the work's limitations, and in a later letter, its ultimate unmarketability. The *Enquiry* was finally privately published in 1785.

There are many other learned ladies whom Johnson knew: Catharine Macaulay, the radical historian, for instance, or the poet Anna Seward, "Swan of Lichfield," who strongly disliked her fellow citizen. Hester Thrale, perhaps Johnson's closest friend, contributed a poem to Anna Williams's volume. Thrale was a devoted diarist, and her journals, known as *Thraliana*, provide a fascinating source of information on the literary world of her day. After Johnson's death she published a variety of interesting work: *Anecdotes of the Late Samuel Johnson, LL.D.* (1786), one of the first biographies of her friend; *Observations and Reflections Made in the Course of a Journey through France, Italy, and Germany* (1789), a travel narrative; and *British Synonymy; or, An Attempt at Regulating the Choice of Words in Familiar Conversation* (1794), a kind of forerunner of Roget's *Thesaurus*.

It was Thrale who introduced Johnson to the last important writer, a brilliant one indeed, whom he was to befriend. Frances Burney was completing her highly successful novel *Evelina* when they met in 1777, but she was also – perhaps unknown to him, as apparently to Boswell – the keeper of copious and detailed diaries. Burney had earlier seen Johnson at one of her father's musical evenings and thought him terrifyingly grotesque in appearance, but his praise of the novel and his teasing treatment of her at the Thrales's Streatham mansion were disarming. Their friendship became a strong one, made stronger by his recognition of the intellectual acumen that lay beneath her shy social demeanor. Burney's accounts of the gaieties over meals at Streatham, as well as her serious conversations with Johnson in the months before his death, offer a quite different figure from Boswell's, and her reporting may be more accurate and detailed even than his. Johnson did not need to support Burney, as he did Lennox and Reynolds, among so many others, but it is notable that it was members of his Club, including Boswell, who were to be instrumental in finally extricating her from servitude at the court of George III in 1791.

Agent, advisor, mentor, colleague, friend: Johnson filled all these roles with women writers, and with women from across the political spectrum – from the conservative Hannah More to the radical Mary Wollstonecraft, who paid him a visit in 1784. Boswell was merely the creature of his period in virtually ignoring this important aspect of his subject. Johnson, on the other hand – free from gender prejudice and, with women colleagues, freed from envy – sponsored and encouraged them, treated them as comrades, throughout his life. "My dear Dr. Johnson," Jane Austen later called him. Perhaps he was especially dear to her because of his championship of women writers like herself.

NOTES

1 *The Complete Works of Thomas Babington Macaulay*, 10 vols. (Boston and New York: Houghton Mifflin, 1910), 6:717–18.
2 Charlotte Lennox, *The Female Quixote*, ed. Margaret Dalziel (Oxford: Oxford University Press, 1970), pp. 414–15 n. and 421.
3 *Jane Austen's Letters*, ed. Deirdre Le Faye, 3rd edn. (Oxford: Oxford University Press, 1995), p. 116.
4 Miriam Rossiter Small, *Charlotte Ramsay Lennox, an Eighteenth Century Lady of Letters* (New Haven, CT: Yale University Press, 1935), p. 28.
5 Sylvia Harcstark Myers, *The Bluestocking Circle: Women, Friendship and the Life of the Mind in Eighteenth-Century England* (Oxford: Clarendon Press, 1990), p. 53.
6 *Dr. Johnson and Fanny Burney: Being the Johnsonian Passages from the Works of Mme. D'Arblay*, ed. Chauncey Brewster Tinker (New York: Moffat, Yard and Co., 1911), p. 179.
7 *The Diary and Letters of Madame d'Arblay*, ed. Austin Dobson, 6 vols. (London: Macmillan, 1905–6), 2:123.
8 Myers, *Bluestocking Circle*, p. 193.
9 Norma Clarke, *Dr. Johnson's Women* (London: Hambledon and London, 2000), p. 146.

Further reading

OVERVIEWS AND REFERENCES

Clifford, J. L., and D. J. Greene. *Samuel Johnson: A Survey and Bibliography of Critical Studies* (Minneapolis: University of Minnesota Press, 1970).

Clingham, G. (ed.). *The Cambridge Companion to Samuel Johnson* (Cambridge: Cambridge University Press, 1997).

Fleeman, J. D. *A Bibliography of the Works of Samuel Johnson, Treating His Published Works from the Beginnings to 1984*, 2 vols. (Oxford: Clarendon Press, 2000).

Greene, D. J., and J. A. Vance. *A Bibliography of Johnsonian Studies, 1970–1985* (Victoria, BC: University of Victoria, 1987).

Lynch, J. *A Bibliography of Johnsonian Studies, 1986–1998* (New York: AMS Press, 2000).

Rogers, P. *The Samuel Johnson Encyclopedia* (Westport, CT: Greenwood Press, 1996).

LIFE

Bate, W. J. *Samuel Johnson* (New York: Harcourt Brace Jovanovich, 1977).

Boswell, J. *The Life of Samuel Johnson, LL.D.*, ed. G. B. Hill, rev. L. F. Powell, 6 vols. (Oxford: Clarendon Press, 1934–64).

Clifford, J. L. *Dictionary Johnson* (New York: McGraw-Hill, 1979).

Young Sam Johnson (New York: McGraw-Hill, 1955).

DeMaria, R. *The Life of Samuel Johnson: A Critical Biography* (Oxford: Blackwell, 1993).

Hawkins, J. *The Life of Samuel Johnson, LL.D.*, ed. O M Brack, Jr. (Athens: University of Georgia Press, 2009).

Holmes, R. *Dr. Johnson and Mr. Savage* (London: Hodder & Stoughton, 1993).

Kelley, R. E., and O M Brack, Jr. (eds.). *Samuel Johnson's Early Biographers* (Iowa City: University of Iowa Press, 1971).

Martin, P. *Samuel Johnson: A Biography* (London: Weidenfeld & Nicolson, 2008).

Meyers, J. *Samuel Johnson: The Struggle* (New York: Basic Books, 2008).

Nokes, D. *Samuel Johnson: A Life* (New York: Henry Holt, 2010).

Piozzi, H. L. *Thraliana: The Diary of Mrs. Hester Lynch Thrale (Later Mrs. Piozzi)*, ed. K. C. Balderston, 2nd edn., 2 vols. (Oxford: Clarendon Press, 1951).

PUBLICATION HISTORY

Brack, O M, Jr. "The Works of Samuel Johnson and the Canon," in *Samuel Johnson after 300 Years*, ed. G. Clingham and P. Smallwood (Cambridge: Cambridge University Press, 2009), pp. 246–61.

Fleeman, J. D. "Johnson's Prospectuses and Proposals," in *Augustan Studies: Essays in Honor of Irvin Ehrenpreis*, ed. D. L. Paley and T. Keegan (Newark: University of Delaware Press, 1985), pp. 215–38.

Hanley, B. *Samuel Johnson as Book Reviewer* (Newark: University of Delaware Press, 2001).

Hazen, A. T. (ed.). *Samuel Johnson's Prefaces & Dedications* (New Haven, CT: Yale University Press, 1937).

Kaminski, T. *The Early Career of Samuel Johnson* (Oxford: Oxford University Press, 1987).

CORRESPONDENCE

Anderson, H. P., P. B. Daghlian, and I. Ehrenpreis (eds.). *The Familiar Letter in the Eighteenth Century* (Lawrence: University of Kansas Press, 1966).

Redford, B. *The Converse of the Pen: Acts of Intimacy in the Eighteenth-Century Familiar Letter* (Chicago: University of Chicago Press, 1986).

Winn, J. A. *A Window in the Bosom: The Letters of Alexander Pope* (Hamden, CT: Archon Books, 1977).

EDITIONS

Boswell, J. *The Life of Samuel Johnson, LL.D.*, ed. J. W. Croker, 5 vols. (London, 1831).

The Life of Samuel Johnson, LL.D., ed. G. B. Hill, rev. L. F. Powell, 6 vols. (Oxford: Clarendon Press, 1934–64).

Brack, O M, Jr. "The Works of Samuel Johnson and the Canon," in *Samuel Johnson after 300 Years*, ed. G. Clingham and P. Smallwood (Cambridge: Cambridge University Press, 2009), pp. 246–61.

Greene, D. J. "No Dull Duty: *The Yale Edition of the Works of Samuel Johnson*," in *Editing Eighteenth-Century Texts*, ed. D. I. B. Smith (Toronto: University of Toronto Press, 1968), pp. 92–123.

Johnson, S. *A Journey to the Western Islands of Scotland*, ed. J. D. Fleeman (Oxford: Clarendon Press, 1985).

Lives of the English Poets, ed. G. B. Hill, 3 vols. (Oxford: Clarendon Press, 1905).

The Lives of the Most Eminent English Poets: With Critical Observations on Their Works, ed. R. Lonsdale, 4 vols. (Oxford: Oxford University Press, 2006).

The Works of Samuel Johnson, ed. F. P. Walesby, 11 vols. (Oxford, 1825).

The Works of Samuel Johnson, L.L.D., ed. J. Hawkins, 15 vols. (London, 1787–9).

The Works of Samuel Johnson, L.L.D., ed. A. Murphy, 12 vols. (London, 1792).

The Works of Samuel Johnson, L.L.D., ed. A. Murphy, rev. A. Chalmers, 12 vols. (London, 1823).

The Yale Edition of the Works of Samuel Johnson, ed. J. Middendorf *et al.*, 18 vols. to date (New Haven, CT: Yale University Press, 1958–).

Johnson, S., and J. Boswell. *Johnson's Journey to the Western Islands of Scotland, and Boswell's Journal of a Tour to the Hebrides with Samuel Johnson*, ed. R. W. Chapman (Oxford: Clarendon Press, 1924).

TRANSLATIONS

Clingham, G. "A Johnsonian in Japan," *Johnsonian News Letter*, 60 (2009), 37–40.

Levin, Y. D. "English Literature in Eighteenth-Century Russia," *Modern Language Review*, 89, no. 4 (1994), xxv–xxxix.

The Perception of English Literature in Russia, trans. C. Philips (Nottingham: Astra Press, 1994).

Stone, J. "On the Trail of Early *Rambler* and *Idler* Translations in France and Spain," *Johnsonian News Letter*, 57 (2006), 34–41.

Weinbrot, H. "Johnson before Boswell in Eighteenth-Century France: Notes toward Reclaiming a Man of Letters," in *Aspects of Samuel Johnson: Essays on His Arts, Mind, Afterlife, and Politics* (Newark: University of Delaware Press, 2005), pp. 270–98.

CRITICAL RECEPTION TO 1900

Boulton, J. T. (ed.). *Johnson: The Critical Heritage* (London: Routledge & Kegan Paul, 1971).

Cafarelli, A. W. "Johnson's *Lives of the Poets* and the Romantic Canon," *The Age of Johnson*, 1 (1987), 403–35.

Carlyle, T. "The Hero as Man of Letters: Johnson, Rousseau, Burns," in *The Works of Thomas Carlyle*, 30 vols. (London, 1897), 5:154–95.

Grundy, I. "Early Women Reading Johnson," in *Johnson after 300 Years*, ed. G. Clingham and P. Smallwood (Cambridge: Cambridge University Press, 2009), pp. 207–24.

Hart, K. *Samuel Johnson and the Culture of Property* (Cambridge: Cambridge University Press, 1999).

Hay, J. *Johnson: His Characteristics and Aphorisms* (London, 1884).

Macaulay, T. B. "Boswell's Life of Johnson," *Edinburgh Review*, 54 (September 1831), 1–38.

Mason, T., and A. Rounce. "'Looking Before and After'? Reflections on the Early Reception of Johnson's Critical Judgments," in *Johnson Re-Visioned:*

Looking Before and After, ed. P. Smallwood (Lewisburg, PA: Bucknell University Press, 2001), pp. 134–66.

McGuffie, H. L. *Samuel Johnson in the British Press, 1749–1784: A Chronological Checklist* (New York and London: Garland, 1976).

Phillips, S. R. "Johnson's *Lives of the English Poets* in the Nineteenth Century," *Research Studies*, 39 (1971), 175–90.

Rounce, A. "Toil and Envy: Unsuccessful Responses to Johnson's *Lives of the Poets*," in *Johnson after 300 Years*, ed. G. Clingham and P. Smallwood (Cambridge: Cambridge University Press, 2009), pp. 186–206.

Stephen, L. "Hours in a Library, No. VIII. Dr. Johnson's Writings," *Cornhill Magazine*, 29 (March 1894), 280–94.

Samuel Johnson (London: Macmillan, 1878).

Tomarken, E. *A History of the Commentary on Selected Writings of Samuel Johnson* (Columbia, SC: Camden House, 1994).

Turner, K. "The 'Link of Transition': Samuel Johnson and the Victorians," in *The Victorians and the Eighteenth Century: Reassessing the Tradition*, ed. F. O'Gorman and K. Turner (Aldershot: Ashgate, 2004), pp. 119–43.

Weinbrot, H. "Samuel Johnson, Percival Stockdale, and 'Brickbats from Grubstreet': Some Later Responses to the *Lives of the Poets*," in *Aspects of Samuel Johnson: Essays on His Arts, Mind, Afterlife, and Politics* (Newark: University of Delaware Press, 2005), pp. 241–69.

CRITICAL RECEPTION SINCE 1900

Abrams, M. H. "Dr. Johnson's Spectacles," in *New Light on Dr. Johnson*, ed. F. W. Hilles (New Haven, CT: Yale University Press, 1959), pp. 177–88.

Alkon, P. *Samuel Johnson and Moral Discipline* (Evanston, IL: Northwestern University Press, 1967).

Basker, J. G. "Multicultural Perspectives: Johnson, Race, and Gender," in *Johnson Re-Visioned: Looking Before and After*, ed. P. Smallwood (Lewisburg, PA: Bucknell University Press, 2001), pp. 64–79.

Bate, W. J. *The Achievement of Samuel Johnson* (New York: Oxford University Press, 1955).

Battersby, J. L. *Rational Praise and Natural Lamentation: Johnson, "Lycidas," and Principles of Criticism* (Rutherford, NJ: Fairleigh Dickinson University Press, 1980).

Bloom, E. A. *Samuel Johnson in Grub Street* (Providence, RI: Brown University Press, 1957).

Brownell, M. R. *Samuel Johnson's Attitude to the Arts* (Oxford: Clarendon Press, 1989).

Chapin, C. F. *The Religious Thought of Samuel Johnson* (Ann Arbor: University of Michigan Press, 1968).

Clark, J. C. D. *Samuel Johnson: Literature, Religion and English Cultural Politics from the Restoration to Romanticism* (Cambridge: Cambridge University Press, 1994).

Clarke, N. *Dr. Johnson's Women* (London: Hambledon & London, 2000).

Clingham, G. *Johnson, Writing and Memory* (Cambridge: Cambridge University Press, 2002).

Curley, T. M. *Samuel Johnson and the Age of Travel* (Athens: University of Georgia Press, 1976).

Samuel Johnson, the Ossian Fraud, and the Celtic Revival in Great Britain and Ireland (Cambridge: Cambridge University Press, 2009).

Damrosch, L. *Fictions of Reality in the Age of Hume and Johnson* (Madison: University of Wisconsin Press, 1989).

Samuel Johnson and the Tragic Sense (Princeton, NJ: Princeton University Press, 1972).

The Uses of Johnson's Criticism (Charlottesville: University Press of Virginia, 1976).

Davis, P. *In Mind of Johnson: A Study of Johnson the Rambler* (Athens: University of Georgia Press, 1989).

DeMaria, R. *Johnson's Dictionary and the Language of Learning* (Chapel Hill: University of North Carolina Press, 1986).

Samuel Johnson and the Life of Reading (Baltimore, MD: Johns Hopkins University Press, 1997).

Deutsch, H. *Loving Dr. Johnson* (Chicago: University of Chicago Press, 2005).

Engell, J. *Forming the Critical Mind: Dryden to Coleridge* (Cambridge, MA: Harvard University Press, 1989).

Folkenflik, R. *Samuel Johnson, Biographer* (Ithaca, NY: Cornell University Press, 1978).

Fulford, T. *Landscape, Liberty, and Authority: Poetry, Criticism, and Politics from Thomson to Wordsworth* (Cambridge: Cambridge University Press, 1996).

Fussell, P. *Samuel Johnson and the Life of Writing.* (New York: Harcourt Brace Jovanovich, 1971).

Greene, D. J. *The Politics of Samuel Johnson* (New Haven, CT: Yale University Press, 1960).

Gross, G. S. *This Invisible Riot of the Mind: Samuel Johnson's Psychological Theory* (Philadelphia: University of Pennsylvania Press, 1992).

Grundy, I. *Samuel Johnson and the Scale of Greatness* (Leicester: Leicester University Press, 1986).

Hagstrum, J. *Samuel Johnson's Literary Criticism*, rev. edn. (Chicago: University of Chicago Press, 1952).

Hanley, B. *Samuel Johnson as Book Reviewer* (Newark: University of Delaware Press, 2001).

Hart, K. *Samuel Johnson and the Culture of Property* (Cambridge: Cambridge University Press, 1999).

Hawes, C. *The British Eighteenth Century and Global Critique* (New York: Palgrave Macmillan, 2005).

Henson, E. *"The Fictions of Romantick Chivalry": Samuel Johnson and Romance* (Rutherford, NJ: Fairleigh Dickinson University Press, 1992).

Hinnant, C. H. *Samuel Johnson: An Analysis* (Basingstoke: Macmillan, 1988).

"Steel for the Mind": Samuel Johnson and Critical Discourse (Newark: University of Delaware Press, 1994).

Hinnant, C. H. (ed.). *Johnson and Gender*, special issue of *South Central Review* 9, no. 4 (1992).

Hudson, N. *Samuel Johnson and Eighteenth-Century Thought* (Oxford: Clarendon Press, 1988).

Johnston, F. "Johnson and Austen," in *Johnson after 300 Years*, ed. G. Clingham and P. Smallwood (Cambridge: Cambridge University Press, 2009), pp. 224–45.

Samuel Johnson and the Art of Sinking, 1709–1791 (Oxford: Oxford University Press, 2005).

Kemmerer, K. N. *"A Neutral Being between the Sexes": Samuel Johnson's Sexual Politics* (Lewisburg, PA: Bucknell University Press, 1998).

Kernan, A. *Samuel Johnson and the Impact of Print* (Princeton, NJ: Princeton University Press, 1987).

Leavis, F. R. "Johnson and Augustanism," in *The Common Pursuit* (Harmondsworth: Penguin, 1952), pp. 97–115.

Lipking, L. *The Ordering of the Arts in Eighteenth-Century England* (Princeton, NJ: Princeton University Press, 1970).

Lynch, J. *The Age of Elizabeth in the Age of Johnson* (Cambridge: Cambridge University Press, 2003).

Lynch, J., and A. McDermott (eds.). *Anniversary Essays on Johnson's "Dictionary"* (Cambridge: Cambridge University Press, 2005).

Lynn, S. *Samuel Johnson after Deconstruction: Rhetoric and the Rambler* (Carbondale: Southern Illinois University Press, 1992).

McIntosh, C. *The Choice of Life: Samuel Johnson and the World of Fiction* (New Haven, CT: Yale University Press, 1973).

McNair, A. *Dr. Johnson and the Law* (Cambridge: Cambridge University Press, 1948).

Maner, M. *The Philosophical Biographer: Doubt and Dialectic in Johnson's "Lives of the Poets"* (Athens: University of Georgia Press, 1988).

Nagashima, D. *Johnson the Philologist* (Osaka: Kansai University of Foreign Studies, 1988).

Parke, C. N. *Samuel Johnson and Biographical Thinking* (Columbia: University of Missouri Press, 1991).

Parker, B. *The Triumph of Augustan Poetics: English Literary Culture from Butler to Johnson* (Cambridge: Cambridge University Press, 1998).

Parker, G. F. *Johnson's Shakespeare* (Oxford: Clarendon Press, 1989).

Scepticism and Literature: An Essay on Pope, Hume, Sterne, and Johnson (Oxford: Oxford University Press, 2003).

Potkay, A. *The Passion for Happiness: Samuel Johnson and David Hume* (Ithaca, NY: Cornell University Press, 2000).

Quinlan, M. J. *Samuel Johnson: A Layman's Religion* (Madison: University of Wisconsin Press, 1964).

Raleigh, W. *Six Essays on Johnson* (Oxford: Clarendon Press, 1910).

Reddick, A. *The Making of Johnson's Dictionary, 1746–1773*, rev. edn. (Cambridge: Cambridge University Press, 1996).

Reinert, T. *Regulating Confusion: Samuel Johnson and the Crowd* (Durham, NC: Duke University Press, 1996).

Schwartz, R. B. *Samuel Johnson and the New Science* (Madison: University of Wisconsin Press, 1971).

Samuel Johnson and the Problem of Evil (Madison: University of Wisconsin Press, 1975).

Smallwood, P. *Johnson's Critical Presence: Image, History, Judgment* (Aldershot: Ashgate, 2004).

Spector, R. D. *Samuel Johnson and the Essay* (Westport, CT: Greenwood Press, 1997).

Stock, R. D. *Samuel Johnson and Neoclassical Dramatic Theory* (Lincoln: University of Nebraska Press, 1973).

Tate, A. "Johnson on the Metaphysical Poets," in *Essays of Four Decades* (Chicago: Swallow Press, 1968), pp. 491–508.

Vance, J. A. *Samuel Johnson and the Sense of History* (Athens: University of Georgia Press, 1984).

Venturo, D. F. *Johnson the Poet: The Poetic Career of Samuel Johnson* (Newark: University of Delaware Press, 1999).

Voitle, R. *Samuel Johnson the Moralist* (Cambridge, MA: Harvard University Press, 1961).

Wechselblatt, M. *Bad Behavior: Samuel Johnson and Modern Cultural Authority* (Lewisburg, PA: Bucknell University Press, 1998).

Weinbrot, H. *Aspects of Samuel Johnson: Essays on His Arts, Mind, Afterlife, and Politics* (Newark: University of Delaware Press, 2005).

Wharton, T. F. *Samuel Johnson and the Theme of Hope* (New York: St. Martin's Press, 1984).

Wiltshire, J. *Samuel Johnson in the Medical World: The Doctor and the Patient* (Cambridge: Cambridge University Press, 1991).

Wimsatt, W. K., Jr. *Philosophic Words: A Study of Style and Meaning in the "Rambler" and "Dictionary" of Samuel Johnson* (New Haven, CT: Yale University Press, 1948).

The Prose Style of Samuel Johnson (New Haven, CT: Yale University Press, 1941).

Wimsatt, W. K. (ed.). *Samuel Johnson on Shakespeare* (New York: Hill and Wang, 1960).

REPRESENTATIONS

Liebert, H. W. *Lifetime Likenesses of Samuel Johnson* (Los Angeles: William Andrews Clark Memorial Library, 1974).

Smallwood, P. "The Johnsonian Monster and the *Lives of the Poets*: James Gillray, Critical History and the Eighteenth-Century Satirical Cartoon," *The British Journal for Eighteenth-Century Studies*, 25, no. 2 (2002), 217–45.

REPUTATION

Baruth, P. *The Brothers Boswell* (New York: Soho Press, 2009).
Bronson, B. H. "The Double Tradition of Dr. Johnson," in *Johnson Agonistes and Other Essays* (Berkeley: University of California Press, 1965), pp. 156–76.
Deutsch, H. *Loving Dr. Johnson* (Chicago: University of Chicago Press, 2005).
Hart, K. *Samuel Johnson and the Culture of Property* (Cambridge: Cambridge University Press, 1999).
Wiltshire, J. *The Making of Dr. Johnson: Icon of Modern Culture* (Hastings: Helm Information, 2009).

AMERICA

Clifford, J. L. "Johnson and the Americans," *The New Rambler* (January 1959), 13–18.
Curley, T. M. "Johnson and America," *The Age of Johnson*, 6 (1994), 31–73.
Greene, D. J. "Samuel Johnson and the Great War for Empire," in *English Writers of the Eighteenth Century*, ed. J. H. Middendorf (New York: Columbia University Press, 1971), pp. 37–68.
Schwandt, J. "Re-Reading *Taxation No Tyranny*: Was the United States of America a Mistake?" *Studies on Voltaire and the Eighteenth Century*, 263 (1989), 275–6.
Winans, R. B. "Works by or about Samuel Johnson in Eighteenth-Century America," *The Papers of the Bibliographical Society of America*, 62 (1968), 537–46.

ANGLICANISM

Brantley, R. "Johnson's Wesleyan Connection," *Eighteenth-Century Studies*, 9 (1976), 143–68.
Chapin, C. F. *The Religious Thought of Samuel Johnson* (Ann Arbor: University of Michigan Press, 1968).
Clark, J. C. D. "Religious Affiliation and Dynastic Allegiance in Eighteenth-Century England: Edmund Burke, Thomas Paine and Samuel Johnson," *ELH*, 64 (1997), 1029–67.
Davis, M. M. "'Ask for the Old Paths': Johnson and the Usages Controversy," *The Age of Johnson*, 17 (2006), 17–68.
Gibson, W. *The Church of England, 1688–1832: Unity and Accord* (London: Routledge, 2000).
Greene, D. "Augustinianism and Empiricism: A Note on Eighteenth-Century English Intellectual History," *Eighteenth-Century Studies*, 1 (1967), 33–68.
New, M. "Preface by Way of a Sermon" and "Introduction," in *The Sermons of Laurence Sterne: The Notes*, vol. 5, *The Florida Edition of the Works of Sterne* (Gainesville: University Press of Florida, 1996), pp. vii–xx, 1–55.

Reedy, G. *The Bible and Reason: Anglicans and Scripture in Late Seventeenth-Century England* (Philadelphia: University of Pennsylvania Press, 1985).

Rivers, I. *Grace and Sentiment: A Study of the Language of Religion and Ethics in England, 1660–1780*, 2 vols. (Cambridge: Cambridge University Press, 1991, 2000).

Rupp, G. *Religion in England, 1688–1791* (Oxford: Clarendon Press, 1986).

Scherwatzky, S. "Samuel Johnson's Augustinianism Revisited," *The Age of Johnson*, 17 (2006), 1–16.

Scholtz, G. "*Sola Fide*? Samuel Johnson and the Augustinian Doctrine of Salvation," *Philological Quarterly*, 72 (1993), 185–212.

Schwartz, R. B. *Samuel Johnson and the Problem of Evil* (Madison: University of Wisconsin Press, 1975).

Spellman, W. M. *The Latitudinarians and the Church of England, 1660–1700* (Athens: University of Georgia Press, 1993).

Suarez, M. F. "Johnson's Christian Thought," in *The Cambridge Companion to Samuel Johnson*, ed. G. Clingham (Cambridge: Cambridge University Press, 1997), pp. 192–208.

Walker, R. G. *Eighteenth-Century Arguments for Immortality and Johnson's "Rasselas"* (Victoria, BC: English Literary Studies, 1977).

Yates, N. *Eighteenth-Century Britain: Religion and Politics, 1714–1815* (London: Pearson, Longman, 2007).

Young, B. W. *Religion and Enlightenment in Eighteenth-Century England: Theological Debate from Locke to Burke* (Oxford: Clarendon Press, 1998).

ANTHROPOLOGY

Barnard, A. J. "Anthropology, Race, and Englishness: Changing Notions of Complexion and Character," *Eighteenth-Century Life*, 25 (2001), 94–102.

Cunzhong, F. "Dr. Johnson and Chinese Culture," in *The Vision of China*, ed. A. Hsia (Hong Kong: Chinese University Press, 1998), pp. 263–81.

Douthwaite, J. V. *The Wild Girl, Natural Man and the Monster* (Chicago: University of Chicago Press, 2002).

Driver, F., and J. Martins (eds.). *Tropical Visions in an Age of Empire* (Chicago: University of Chicago Press, 2005).

Fullagar, K. "'Savages That Are Come among Us': Mai, Bennelong, and British Imperial Culture, 1774–1795," *The Eighteenth Century*, 49 no. 3 (2008), 211–37.

Lamb, J. *Preserving the Self in the South Seas* (Chicago: University of Chicago Press, 2001).

McCormick, E. *Omai: Pacific Envoy* (Oxford: Oxford University Press, 1977).

Pocock, J. G. A. "Nature and History, Self and Other," in *Voyages and Beaches: Pacific Encounters 1769–1840*, ed. A. Calder, J. Lamb, and B. Orr (Honolulu: University of Hawai'i Press, 1999), pp. 25–44.

Poovey, M. *A History of the Modern Fact* (Chicago: University of Chicago Press, 1998).
Rogers, P. *Johnson and Boswell: The Transit of Caledonia* (Oxford: Oxford University Press, 1995).
Smith, B. *European Vision and the South Pacific* (Oxford: Oxford University Press, 1960).
Thomas, N. "'On the Varieties of the Human Species,' Forster's Comparative Ethnology," in *Observations Made during a Voyage Round the World*, ed. N. Thomas, H. Guest, and M. Dettelbach (Honolulu: University of Hawai'i Press, 1996), pp. xxiii–xl.
Wheeler, R. *The Complexion of Race: Categories of Difference in Eighteenth-Century British Culture* (Philadelphia: University of Pennsylvania Press, 2000).
Williams, G., and P. J. Marshall. *The Great Map of Mankind: British Perceptions of the World in the Age of Enlightenment* (London: J. M. Dent, 1982).

AUTHORSHIP

Belanger, T. "Publishers and Writers in Eighteenth-Century England," in *Books and Their Readers in Eighteenth-Century England*, ed. I. Rivers (Leicester: Leicester University Press, 1982), pp. 5–26.
Collins, A. *Authorship in the Days of Johnson* (London: R. Holden, 1929).
Fleeman, J. D. "The Revenue of a Writer: Samuel Johnson's Literary Earnings," in *Studies in the Book Trade in Honour of Graham Pollard* (Oxford: Oxford Bibliographical Society, 1975), pp. 211–30.
Griffin, D. *Literary Patronage in England, 1650–1800* (Cambridge: Cambridge University Press, 1996).
Schellenberg, B. *The Professionalization of Women Writers in Eighteenth-Century Britain* (Cambridge: Cambridge University Press, 2005).
Sher, R. *The Enlightenment and the Book: Scottish Authors and Their Publishers in Eighteenth-Century Britain, Ireland and America* (Chicago: University of Chicago Press, 2006).

BIOGRAPHY

Altick, R. D. *Lives and Letters* (New York: Knopf, 1966).
Folkenflik, R. *Samuel Johnson, Biographer* (Ithaca, NY: Cornell University Press, 1978).
Jolly, M. (ed.). *Encyclopedia of Life Writing*, 2 vols. (London: Fitzroy Dearborn, 2001).
Stauffer, D. A. *The Art of Biography in Eighteenth Century England* (Princeton, NJ: Princeton University Press, 1941).
Vance, J. A. (ed.). *Boswell's Life of Johnson: New Questions, New Answers* (Athens: University of Georgia Press, 1985).
Wheeler, D. (ed.). *Domestick Privacies: Samuel Johnson and the Art of Biography* (Lexington: University Press of Kentucky, 1987).

BOOK TRADE

Murphy, A. "The History of the Book in Britain, *c.* 1475–1800," in *The Oxford Companion to the Book*, ed. M. F. Suarez and H. R. Woudhuysen, 2 vols. (Oxford: Oxford University Press, 2010), pp. 172–9.

Raven, J. *The Business of Books: Booksellers and the English Book Trade, 1450–1850* (New Haven, CT: Yale University Press, 2007).

Rivers, I. (ed.). *Books and their Readers in Eighteenth-Century England: New Essays* (London and New York: Continuum, 2001).

Suarez, M. F., and M. L. Turner (eds.). *The Cambridge History of the Book in Britain*, vol. 5, *1695–1830* (Cambridge: Cambridge University Press, 2009).

CLUBS

Borsay, P. *A History of Leisure: The British Experience since 1500* (Basingstoke: Palgrave Macmillan, 2006).

Clark, P. *British Clubs and Societies, 1580–1800: The Origins of an Associational World* (Oxford: Oxford University Press, 2000).

Jacob, M. C. *The Radical Enlightenment: Pantheists, Freemasons, and Republicans* (London and Boston: Allen & Unwin, 1981).

McElroy, D. D. *Scotland's Age of Improvement: A Survey of Eighteenth-Century Literary Clubs and Societies* (Pullman: Washington State University Press, 1969).

Shields, D. S. *Civil Tongues and Polite Letters in British America* (Chapel Hill: University of North Carolina Press, 1997).

CONVERSATION

Burke, P. *The Art of Conversation* (Ithaca, NY: Cornell University Press, 1993).

Burke, P., B. Harrison, and P. Slack (eds.). *Civil Histories: Essays Presented to Sir Keith Thomas* (Oxford: Oxford University Press, 2000).

Miller, S. D. *Conversation: A History of a Declining Art* (New Haven, CT: Yale University Press, 2006).

Parke, C. N. "The Arts of Conversation," in *The Cambridge Companion to Samuel Johnson*, ed. G. Clingham (Cambridge: Cambridge University Press, 1997), pp. 18–33.

DICTIONARIES

Cowie, J. F. *The Oxford History of Lexicography* (Oxford: Clarendon Press, 2009).

DeMaria, R. *Johnson's Dictionary and the Language of Learning* (Chapel Hill: University of North Carolina Press, 1986).

Gurr, A. (ed.). *Eighteenth-Century Lexis and Lexicography*, special issue of *The Year Book of English Studies*, 28 (1998).

Lynch, J., and A. McDermott (eds.). *Anniversary Essays on Johnson's "Dictionary"* (Cambridge: Cambridge University Press, 2005).

Reddick, A. *The Making of Johnson's Dictionary, 1746–1773*, rev. edn. (Cambridge: Cambridge University Press, 1996).

Sledd, J. H., and G. J. Kolb. *Dr. Johnson's Dictionary* (Chicago: University of Chicago Press, 1955).

Starnes, D. T., and G. E. Noyes. *The English Dictionary from Cawdrey to Johnson, 1604–1755*, new edn. (Amsterdam: John Benjamins, 1991).

DOMESTIC LIFE

Bannet, E. T. *The Domestic Revolution: Enlightenment Feminisms and the Novel* (Baltimore, MD: Johns Hopkins University Presss, 2000).

Davidoff, L., and C. Hall. *Family Fortunes: Men and Women of the English Middle Class, 1780–1850* (Chicago: University of Chicago Press, 1987).

Gillis, J. *For Better, for Worse: British Marriages, 1600 to the Present* (Oxford: Oxford University Press, 1985).

MacFarlane, A. *Marriage and Love in England: 1300–1840* (Oxford: Basil Blackwell, 1986).

Stone, L. *The Family, Sex, and Marriage in England: 1500–1800* (New York: Harper & Row, 1977).

Road to Divorce: A History of the Making and Breaking of Marriage in England (Oxford: Oxford University Press, 1995).

Tadmor, N. *Family and Friends in Eighteenth-Century England: Household, Kinship, Patronage* (Cambridge: Cambridge University Press, 2001).

EDUCATION

Ashley Smith, J. W. *The Birth of Modern Education: The Contribution of the Dissenting Academies, 1660–1800* (London: Independent Press, 1954).

De Bellaigue, C. *Educating Women: Schooling and Identity in England and France, 1800–1867* (Oxford: Oxford University Press, 2007).

Fletcher, A. *Growing Up in England: The Experience of Childhood, 1600–1914* (New Haven, CT: Yale University Press, 2008).

Hilton, M., and J. Shefrin (eds.). *Educating the Child in Enlightenment Britain* (Aldershot: Ashgate, 2009).

Hunt, M. R. *The Middling Sort: Commerce, Gender, and the Family in England, 1680–1780* (Berkeley: University of California Press, 1996).

Jewell, H. M. *Education in Early Modern England* (Basingstoke: Macmillan, 1998).

O'Day, R. *Education and Society, 1500–1800: The Social Foundations of Education in Early Modern Britain* (London: Longman, 1982).

Searby, P. *A History of the University of Cambridge*, vol. 3, *1750–1870* (Cambridge: Cambridge University Press, 1997).

Skedd, S. "Women Teachers and the Expansion of Girls' Schooling in England, *c.* 1760–1820," in *Gender in Eighteenth Century England*, ed. H. Barker and E. Chalus (London: Longman, 1997), pp. 101–25.

Sutherland, L. S., and L. G. Mitchell (eds.). *The History of the University of Oxford*, vol. 5, *The Eighteenth Century* (Oxford: Clarendon Press, 1986).

Tompson, R. S. *Classics or Charity? The Dilemma of the 18th Century Grammar School* (Manchester: Manchester University Press, 1971).

Vickery, A. *The Gentleman's Daughter: Women's Lives in Georgian England* (New Haven, CT: Yale University Press, 1998).

Vincent, W. A. L. *The Grammar Schools: Their Continuing Tradition, 1660–1714* (London: John Murray, 1969).

EMPIRE

Augstein, H. F. (ed.). *Race: The Origins of an Idea, 1760–1850* (Bristol: Thoemmes Press, 1996).

Brown, L. *Ends of Empire: Women and Ideology in Early Eighteenth-Century English Literature* (Ithaca, NY: Cornell University Press, 1993).

Eze, E. C. (ed.). *Race and the Enlightenment: A Reader* (Oxford: Blackwell, 1997).

Ferguson, M. *Subject to Others: British Women Writers and Colonial Slavery, 1670–1834* (New York: Routledge, 1992).

Nussbaum, F. A. *Torrid Zones: Maternity, Sexuality, and Empire in Eighteenth-Century English Narratives* (Baltimore, MD: Johns Hopkins University Press, 1995).

ESSAYS

Christie, O. F. *Johnson the Essayist: His Opinions on Men, Morals, and Manners* (London: G. Richards, 1924).

Good, G. *The Observing Self: Rediscovering the Essay* (London: Routledge, 1988).

Korshin, P. J. "Johnson's *Rambler* and Its Audiences," in *Essays on the Essay: Redefining the Genre*, ed. A. J. Butrym (Athens: University of Georgia Press, 1989), pp. 92–105.

Olson, R. C. *Motto, Essay, Context: The Classical Background of Samuel Johnson's "Rambler" and "Adventurer" Essays* (Lanham, MD: University Press of America, 1984).

Rogers, P. "*The Rambler* and the Eighteenth-Century Periodical Essay: A Dissenting View," in *Telling People What to Think: Early Eighteenth-Century Periodicals from "The Review" to "The Rambler,"* ed. J. A. Downie and Thomas N. Corns (London: Cass, 1993), pp. 116–29.

Spector, R. D. *Samuel Johnson and the Essay* (Westport, CT: Greenwood Press, 1997).

Tankard, P. "A Petty Writer: Johnson and the *Rambler* Pamphlets," *The Age of Johnson*, 10 (1999), 67–87.

"The Rambler's Second Audience: Johnson and the Paratextual 'Part of Literature'," *Bulletin of the Bibliographical Society of Australia and New Zealand*, 24 (2000), 239–56.

Wiles, R. M. "The Contemporary Distribution of Johnson's *Rambler*," *Eighteenth-Century Studies*, 2 (1968), 155–71.
Woodruff, J. F. "Johnson's *Rambler* and its Contemporary Context," *Bulletin of Research in the Humanities*, 85 (1982), 27–64.

FICTION

Backscheider, P., and C. Ingrassia (eds.). *A Companion to the Eighteenth-Century English Novel and Culture* (Oxford: Blackwell, 2005).
Hunter, J. P. *Before Novels: The Cultural Contexts of Eighteenth-Century Fiction* (New York: Norton, 1990).
McKeon, M. *The Origins of the English Novel, 1600–1740* (Baltimore, MD: Johns Hopkins University Press, 1987).
Richetti, J. *Popular Fiction before Richardson: Narrative Patterns, 1700–1739* (Oxford: Clarendon Press, 1969).
Richetti, J. (ed.). *The Cambridge Companion to the Eighteenth-Century Novel* (Cambridge: Cambridge University Press, 1996).
Watt, I. *The Rise of the Novel: Studies in Defoe, Richardson, and Fielding* (Berkeley: University of California Press, 1957).

HISTORY

Breisach, E. *Historiography: Ancient, Medieval, and Modern*, 3rd edn. (Chicago: University of Chicago Press, 1997).
DeMaria, R. "Plutarch, Johnson, and Boswell: The Classical Tradition of Biography at the End of the Eighteenth Century," in *The Eighteenth-Century Novel: Essays in Honor of John Richetti*, ed. G. Justice (New York: AMS Press, 2009), pp. 77–98.
Kenyon, J. *The History Men* (London: Weidenfeld & Nicolson, 1983).
Phillips, M. S. *Society and Sentiment: Genres of Historical Writing in Britain, 1740–1820* (Princeton, NJ: Princeton University Press, 2000).

JOURNALISM

Basker, J. G. "Criticism and the Rise of Periodical Literature," in *The Cambridge History of Literary Criticism*, vol. 4, *The Eighteenth Century*, ed. H. B. Nisbet and Claude Rawson (New York and Cambridge: Cambridge University Press, 2008), pp. 316–32.
Habermas, J. *The Structural Transformation of the Public Sphere: An Inquiry into a Category of Bourgeois Society*, trans. Thoras Burger and Frederick Lawrence (Cambridge, MA: MIT Press, 1989).
Italia, I. *The Rise of Literary Journalism in the Eighteenth Century: Anxious Employment* (New York: Routledge, 2005).
Keymer, T. (ed.). *The "Gentleman's Magazine" in the Age of Samuel Johnson*, 16 vols. (London: Pickering and Chatto, 1998).

LAW

Baker, J. H. *An Introduction to English Legal History*, 3rd edn. (London: Butterworth, 1990).

Chambers, R. *A Course of Lectures on the English Law, 1767–1773*, ed. T. M. Curley, 2 vols. (Madison: University of Wisconsin Press, 1986).

Curley, T. M. "Johnson's Secret Collaboration," in *The Unknown Samuel Johnson*, ed. J. J. Burke, Jr. and D. Kay (Madison: University of Wisconsin Press, 1983), pp. 91–112.

Holdsworth, W. S. *A History of English Law*, 17 vols. (Boston, MA: Little, Brown, 1922–72).

Langbein, J. H. *The Origins of Adversary Criminal Trial* (Oxford: Oxford University Press, 2003).

Lemmings, D. *Professors of the Law: Barristers and English Legal Culture in the Eighteenth Century* (New York and Oxford: Oxford University Press, 2000).

McAdam, E. L. *Dr. Johnson and the English Law* (Syracuse, NY: Syracuse University Press, 1951).

McNair, A. *Dr. Johnson and the Law* (Cambridge: Cambridge University Press, 1948).

Scanlan, J. T. "Johnson and Pufendorf," *1650–1850: Ideas, Aesthetics, and Inquiries in the Early Modern Era*, 8 (2003), 27–59.

"Johnson's *Dictionary* and Legal Dictionaries," in *Samuel Johnson's Dictionary and the Eighteenth-Century World of Words*, ed. G. Iamartino and R. DeMaria, *Textus*, 19 (2006), 87–106.

"Samuel Johnson's Legal Thought," in *Johnson after 300 Years*, ed. G. Clingham and P. Smallwood (Cambridge: Cambridge University Press, 2009), pp. 112–30.

Simpson, A. W. B. *An Invitation to Law* (Oxford: Blackwell, 1988).

LITERARY CRITICISM

Battersby, J. L. "Life, Art, and the *Lives of the Poets*," in *Domestick Privacies: Samuel Johnson and the Art of Biography*, ed. D. Wheeler (Lexington: University Press of Kentucky, 1987), pp. 26–56.

Damrosch, L. *Samuel Johnson and the Tragic Sense* (Princeton, NJ: Princeton University Press, 1972).

The Uses of Johnson's Criticism (Charlottesville: University Press of Virginia, 1976).

Engell, J. *Forming the Critical Mind: Dryden to Coleridge* (Cambridge, MA: Harvard University Press, 1989).

Evans, S. D. *Samuel Johnson's "General Nature": Tradition and Transition in Eighteenth-Century Discourse* (Newark: University of Delaware Press, 1999).

Fix, S. "The Contexts and Motive of Johnson's *Life of Milton*," in *Domestick Privacies: Samuel Johnson and the Art of Biography*, ed. D. Wheeler (Lexington: University Press of Kentucky, 1987), pp. 107–32.

Hagstrum, Jean. *Samuel Johnson's Literary Criticism*, rev. edn. (Chicago: University of Chicago Press, 1967).
Keast, W. R. "Johnson's Criticism of the Metaphysical Poets," *ELH*, 17 (1950), 59–70.
"The Theoretical Foundations of Johnson's Criticism," in *Critics and Criticism*, ed. R. S. Crane (Chicago: University of Chicago Press, 1957), pp. 169–87.
Leavis, F. R. "Johnson as Critic," in *"Anna Karenina" and Other Essays* (London: Chatto and Windus, 1973), pp. 197–218.
Lipking, L. *The Ordering of the Arts in Eighteenth-Century England* (Princeton, NJ: Princeton University Press, 1970).
London, A. "Johnson's *Lives* and the Genealogy of Late Eighteenth-Century Literary History," in *Critical Pasts: Writing Criticism, Writing History*, ed. P. Smallwood (Lewisburg, PA: Bucknell University Press, 2004), pp. 95–113.
Parker, G. F. "Johnson and the *Lives of the Poets*," *Critical Quarterly*, 29 (2000), 323–37.
Johnson's Shakespeare (Oxford: Clarendon Press, 1989).
Scepticism and Literature: An Essay on Pope, Hume, Sterne, and Johnson (Oxford: Oxford University Press, 2003).
Smallwood, P. "The Johnsonian Monster and the *Lives of the Poets*: James Gillray, Critical History and the Eighteenth-Century Satirical Cartoon," *The British Journal for Eighteenth-Century Studies*, 25, no. 2 (2002), 217–45.
Johnson's Critical Presence: Image, History, Judgment (Aldershot: Ashgate, 2004).
"Johnson's Criticism and 'Critical Global Studies'," *The Age of Johnson*, 18 (2007), 151–72.
Snead, J. "*Disjecta Membra Poetae*: The Aesthetics of the Fragment and Johnson's Biographical Practice in the *Lives of the Poets*," *The Age of Johnson*, 15 (2004), 37–56.

LONDON

Brewer, J. *Pleasures of the Imagination: English Culture in the Eighteenth Century* (New York: Farrar, Straus, and Giroux, 1997).
Merritt, J. F. (ed.). *Imagining Early Modern London: Perceptions and Portrayals of the City from Stow to Strype, 1598–1720* (Cambridge: Cambridge University Press, 2001).
Stow, J. *The Survey of London*, ed. H. B. Wheatley (London: Dent, 1987).
Wall, C. *The Literary and Cultural Spaces of Restoration London* (Cambridge: Cambridge University Press, 1998).

MEDICINE

Bynum, W. F. "Physicians, Hospitals and Career Structures in Eighteenth-Century London," in *William Hunter and the Eighteenth-Century Medical*

World, ed. W. F. Bynum and R. Porter (Cambridge: Cambridge University Press, 1985), pp. 106–23.

Cunningham, A., and R. French (eds.). *The Medical Enlightenment of the Eighteenth Century* (Cambridge: Cambridge University Press, 1990), pp. 4–39.

Gray, J., and T. J. Murray. "Dr. Johnson and Dr. James," *The Age of Johnson*, 7 (1996), 213–45.

King, L. *The Medical World of the Eighteenth Century* (Chicago: University of Chicago Press, 1958).

Landers, J. *Death and the Metropolis: Studies in the Demographic History of London, 1670–1830* (Cambridge: Cambridge University Press, 1993).

Lane, J. *A Social History of Medicine: Health, Healing and Disease in England, 1750–1950* (London: Routledge, 2001).

Le Fanu, W. R. "The Lost Half Century in English Medicine, 1700–1750," *Bulletin of the History of Medicine*, 46 (1972), 319–48.

Murray, T. J. "Dr. Samuel Johnson's Movement Disorder," *British Medical Journal*, 1 (1979), 1610–14.

"Samuel Johnson: His Ills, His Pills and His Physician Friends," *Clinical Medicine*, 3 (2003), 368–72.

Porter, D., and R. Porter, *Patient's Progress: Doctors and Doctoring in Eighteenth-Century England* (Cambridge: Polity Press, 1989).

Porter, R. *The Greatest Benefit to Mankind: A History of Humanity from Antiquity to the Present* (London: HarperCollins, 1997).

Porter, R. (ed.). *Patients and Practitioners: Lay Perceptions of Medicine in Pre-Industrial Society* (Cambridge: Cambridge University Press, 1985).

Wiltshire, J. *Samuel Johnson in the Medical World: The Doctor and the Patient* (Cambridge: Cambridge University Press, 1991).

MENTAL HEALTH

Andrews, J., and A. Scull. *Customers and Patrons of the Mad-Trade: The Management of Lunacy in Eighteenth-Century London* (Berkeley: University of California Press, 2003).

Gilman, S. *Health and Illness: Images of Difference* (London: Reaktion Books, 1995).

Ingram, A. *The Madhouse of Language: Writing and Reading Madness in the Eighteenth Century* (London: Routledge, 1991).

Ingram, A. (ed.). *Patterns of Madness in the Eighteenth Century: A Reader* (Liverpool: Liverpool University Press, 1998).

Ingram, A., with M. Faubert. *Cultural Constructions of Madness in Eighteenth-Century Writing: Representing the Insane* (Basingstoke: Palgrave Macmillan, 2005).

Porter, R. *A Social History of Madness: Stories of the Insane* (London: Weidenfeld & Nicolson, 1987).

Radden, J. (ed.). *The Nature of Melancholy: From Aristotle to Kristeva* (Oxford: Oxford University Press, 2000).

Scull, A. *Museums of Madness: The Social Organization of Insanity in Nineteenth Century England* (London: Allen Lane, 1979).

Shorter, E. *A History of Psychiatry: From the Era of the Asylum to the Age of Prozac* (New York: John Wiley, 1997).

MONEY

Bisschop, W. R. *The Rise of the London Money Market, 1640–1826* (London: Cass, 1968).

Chandaman, C. D. *The English Public Revenue, 1660–1688* (Oxford: Oxford University Press, 1975).

Dickson, P. *The Financial Revolution in England* (New York: St. Martin's Press, 1967).

Mayhew, N. J. "Population, Money Supply, and the Velocity of Circulation in England, 1300–1700," *Economic History Review*, n.s. 48 (1995), 238–57.

McGrath, C. I., and C. Fauske (eds.). *Money, Power and Print: Interdisciplinary Studies on the Financial Revolution in the British Isles* (Newark: University of Delaware Press, 2008).

Muldrew, M. *The Economy of Obligation: The Culture of Credit and Social Relations in Early Modern England* (Basingstoke: Macmillan, 1998).

Murphy, A. L. "Lotteries in the 1690s: Investment or Gamble?" *Financial History Review*, 12 (2005), 227–46.

The Origins of English Financial Markets: Investment and Speculation before the South Sea Bubble (Cambridge: Cambridge University Press, 2009).

Neal, L. *The Rise of Financial Capitalism: International Capital Markets in the Age of Reason* (Cambridge: Cambridge University Press, 1993).

Quinn, S. "Gold, Silver and the Glorious Revolution: Arbitrage between Bills of Exchange and Bullion," *Economic History Review*, n.s. 49 (1996), 473–90.

Redish, A. "The Evolution of the Gold Standard in England," *The Journal of Economic History*, 50 (1990), 789–805.

Rogers, J. S. *The Early History of the Law of Bills and Notes: A Study of the Origins of Anglo-American Commercial Law* (Cambridge: Cambridge University Press, 1995).

Slack, P. "Measuring the National Wealth in Seventeenth-Century England," *Economic History Review*, n.s. 57 (2004), 607–35.

Valenze, D. *The Social Life of Money in the English Past* (Cambridge: Cambridge University Press, 2006).

Whitelaw, I. *A Measure of All Things: The Story of Man and Measurement* (New York: St. Martin's Press, 2007).

NATIONALISM

Anderson, B. *Imagined Communities: Reflections on the Origins and Spread of Nationalism*, 2nd edn. (London: Verso, 2008).

Colley, L. *Britons: Forging the Nation, 1688–1815* (New Haven, Conn.: Yale University Press, 1994).

Curtius, E. R. *European Literature and the Latin Middle Ages*, trans. W. R. Trask (Princeton, NJ: Princeton University Press, 1953).

Gerald, N. *The Rise of English Nationalism: A Cultural History, 1740–1830* (New York: Palgrave Macmillan, 1997).

Gerrard, C. *The Patriot Opposition to Walpole: Politics, Poetry, and National Myth, 1725–1742* (Oxford: Clarendon Press, 1994).

Griffin, D. *Patriotism and Poetry in 18th-Century Britain* (Cambridge: Cambridge University Press, 2002).

Hawes, C. *The British Eighteenth Century and Global Critique* (New York: Palgrave Macmillan, 2005).

"Johnson's Cosmopolitan Nationalism," in *Johnson Re-Visioned: Looking Before and After*, ed. P. Smallwood (Lewisburg, PA: Bucknell University Press, 2001), pp. 37–63.

Howard, H. *Britannia's Issue: The Rise of British Literature from Dryden to Ossian* (Cambridge: Cambridge University Press, 1993).

Hudson, N. *Samuel Johnson and the Making of Modern England* (Cambridge: Cambridge University Press, 2003).

Kaul, S. *Poems of Nation, Anthems of Empire* (Charlottesville: University Press of Virginia, 2000).

Pittock, M. G. H. *Inventing and Resisting Great Britain: Cultural Identities in Britain and Ireland, 1685–1789* (New York: St. Martin's Press, 1997).

Ranger, T., and E. Hobsbawm (eds.). *The Invention of Tradition* (Cambridge: Cambridge University Press, 1983).

PHILOSOPHY

Gay, P. *The Enlightenment: An Interpretation*, 2 vols. (New York: Knopf, 1966–9).

Maclean, K. *John Locke and English Literature of the Eighteenth Century* (New Haven, CT: Yale University Press, 1936).

Nadler, S. (ed.). *A Companion to Early Modern Philosophy* (Oxford: Blackwell, 2002).

Parker, G. F. *Scepticism and Literature: An Essay on Pope, Hume, Sterne, and Johnson* (Oxford: Oxford University Press, 2003).

"'We Are Perpetually Moralists': Johnson and Moral Philosophy," in *Johnson after 300 Years*, ed. G. Clingham and P. Smallwood (Cambridge: Cambridge University Press, 2009), pp. 15–32.

Potkay, A. *The Passion for Happiness: Samuel Johnson and David Hume* (Ithaca, NY: Cornell University Press, 2000).

Rutherford, D. (ed.). *The Cambridge Companion to Early Modern Philosophy* (Cambridge: Cambridge University Press, 2006).

Yolton, J. W. *Locke: An Introduction* (Oxford: Blackwell, 1985).

POETRY

Gerrard, C. (ed.). *A Companion to Eighteenth-Century Poetry* (Oxford: Blackwell, 2006).

Parker, B. *The Triumph of Augustan Poetics: English Literary Culture from Butler to Johnson* (Cambridge: Cambridge University Press, 1998).

Sitter, J. (ed.). *The Cambridge Companion to Eighteenth-Century Poetry* (Cambridge: Cambridge University Press, 2001).

Venturo, D. F. "Fideism, the Antisublime, and the Faithful Imagination in *Rasselas*," in *Johnson after 300 Years*, ed. G. Clingham and P. Smallwood (Cambridge: Cambridge University Press, 2009), pp. 95–111.

Johnson the Poet: The Poetic Career of Samuel Johnson (Newark: University of Delaware Press, 1999).

POLITICS

Brewer, J. *Party Ideology and Popular Politics at the Accession of George III* (Cambridge: Cambridge University Press, 1976).

Cannon, J. *Samuel Johnson and the Politics of Hanoverian England* (Oxford: Oxford University Press, 1994).

Cash, A. *John Wilkes: The Scandalous Father of British Liberty* (New Haven, CT: Yale University Press, 2006).

Clark, J. C. D. *English Society, 1660–1832: Religion, Ideology and Politics during the Ancien Régime*, 2nd edn. (Cambridge: Cambridge University Press, 2000).

Colley, L. *In Defiance of Oligarchy: The Tory Party, 1714–1760* (Cambridge: Cambridge University Press, 1982).

Gerrard, C. *The Patriot Opposition to Walpole: Politics, Poetry, and National Myth, 1725–1742* (Oxford: Clarendon Press, 1994).

Goldgar, B. *Walpole and the Wits: The Relation of Politics to Literature, 1722–1742* (Lincoln: University of Nebraska Press, 1976).

Greene, D. *The Politics of Samuel Johnson*, 2nd edn. (Athens: University of Georgia Press, 1990).

Hudson, N. *Samuel Johnson and the Making of Modern England* (Cambridge: Cambridge University Press, 2003).

Langford, P. *A Polite and Commercial People: England 1727–1783* (Oxford: Oxford University Press, 1989).

Monod, P. *Jacobitism and the English People, 1688–1788* (Cambridge: Cambridge University Press, 1989).

Wilson, K. *The Sense of the People: Politics, Culture, and Imperialism in England, 1715–1785* (Cambridge: Cambridge University Press, 1995).

SCHOLARSHIP

Baldwin, B. "Samuel Johnson and the Classics," *Hellas*, 2 (1991), 227–38.

Brink, C. O. *English Classical Scholarship: Historical Reflections on Bentley, Porson, and Housman* (Cambridge: James Clarke, 1986).

Clarke, M. L. *Greek Studies in England, 1700–1830* (Cambridge: Cambridge University Press, 1945).
Grafton, A. *Worlds Made by Words: Scholarship and Community in the Modern World* (Cambridge, MA: Harvard University Press, 2009).
Levine, J. M. "Bentley's Milton: Philology and Criticism in Eighteenth-Century England," *Journal of the History of Ideas*, 50 (1989), 549–68.
McKitterick, D. *A History of Cambridge University Press*, vol. 2, *Scholarship and Commerce 1698–1872* (Cambridge: Cambridge University Press, 1999).
Pfeiffer, R. *History of Classical Scholarship: From 1300 to 1850* (Oxford: Clarendon Press, 1976).

SCIENCE AND TECHNOLOGY

Davie, D. "The Language of Science and the Language of Literature, 1700–1740," in *A Traveling Man: Eighteenth-Century Bearings* (Manchester: Carcanet, 2003), pp. 47–82.
Golinski, J. *Science as Public Culture: Chemistry and Enlightenment in Britain, 1760–1820* (Cambridge: Cambridge University Press, 1992).
Porter, R. (ed.). *The Cambridge History of Science*, vol. 4, *The Eighteenth Century* (Cambridge: Cambridge University Press, 2003).
Schwartz, R. B. *Samuel Johnson and the New Science* (Madison: University of Wisconsin Press, 1971).
Uglow, J. *The Lunar Men: The Friends Who Made the Future, 1730–1810* (London: Faber & Faber, 2002).

SCOTLAND

Broadie, A. (ed.). *The Cambridge Companion to the Scottish Enlightenment* (Cambridge: Cambridge University Press, 2003).
McElroy, D. D. *Scotland's Age of Improvement: A Survey of Eighteenth-Century Literary Clubs and Societies* (Pullman: Washington State University Press, 1969).
Pittock, M. G. H. *Inventing and Resisting Britain: Cultural Identities in Britain and Ireland, 1685–1789* (New York: St. Martin's Press, 1997).
James Boswell (Aberdeen: AHRC Centre for Irish and Scottish Studies, 2007).
Rogers, P. (ed.). *Johnson and Boswell in Scotland: A Journey to the Hebrides* (New Haven, CT: Yale University Press, 1993).

SERMONS

Bowden, M. F. *Yorick's Congregation: The Church of England in the Time of Laurence Sterne* (Newark: University of Delaware Press, 2007).
Davies, H. S. *Worship and Theology in England: From Watts and Wesley to Maurice, 1690–1850* (Princeton, NJ: Princeton University Press, 1961).

Downey, J. *The Eighteenth-Century Pulpit: A Study of the Sermons of Butler, Berkeley, Secker, Sterne, Whitefield, and Wesley* (Oxford: Oxford University Press, 1969).

Edwards, O. C. "Varieties of Sermon: A Survey of Preaching in the Long Eighteenth Century," in *Preaching, Sermon, and Cultural Change in the Long Eighteenth Century*, ed. J. Van Eijnatten (Amsterdam: Brill, 2009), pp. 3–56.

Gray, J. *Johnson's Sermons: A Study* (Oxford: Clarendon Press, 1972).

Jacob, W. M. *Lay People and Religion in the Early Eighteenth Century* (Cambridge: Cambridge University Press, 1996).

Kass, T. G. "Reading the 'Religious' Language of Samuel Johnson's Sermons," *Renascence: Essays on Values in Literature*, 51 (1999), 240–51.

Noll, M. *The Rise of Evangelicalism: The Age of Edwards, Whitefield, and the Wesleys* (Downers Grove, IL: Inter-Varsity Press, 2003).

Rivers, I. *Reason, Grace, and Sentiment: A Study of the Language of Religion and Ethics in England, 1660–1780*, vol. 1, *Whichcote to Wesley* (Cambridge: Cambridge University Press, 1991).

Strom, J. "Pietism and Revival," in *Preaching, Sermon, and Cultural Change in the Long Eighteenth Century*, ed. J. Van Eijnatten (Amsterdam: Brill, 2009), pp. 172–218.

Wolffe, J. R. *The Expansion of Evangelicalism: The Age of Wilberforce, More, Chalmers and Finney* (Downers Grove, IL: Inter-Varsity Press, 2006).

SHAKESPEARE

Clark, S. (ed.). *Shakespeare Made Fit: Restoration Adaptations of Shakespeare* (London: Dent, 1997).

Cunningham, V. *Shakespeare and Garrick* (Cambridge: Cambridge University Press, 2008).

Deelman, C. *The Great Shakespeare Jubilee* (London: Michael Joseph, 1964).

Dobson, M. *The Making of the National Poet: Shakespeare, Adaptation and Authorship, 1660–1769* (Oxford: Clarendon Press, 1992).

Dugas, D.-J. *Marketing the Bard: Shakespeare in Performance and Print, 1660–1740* (Columbia: University of Missouri Press, 2006).

Parker, G. F. *Johnson's Shakespeare* (Oxford: Clarendon Press, 1989).

Rasmussen, E., and A. Santesso (eds.). *Comparative Excellence: New Essays on Shakespeare and Johnson* (New York: AMS Press, 2007).

Smallwood, P. "Shakespeare: Johnson's Poet of Nature," in *The Cambridge Companion to Samuel Johnson*, ed. G. Clingham (Cambridge: Cambridge University Press, 1997), pp. 143–60.

Walsh, M. *Shakespeare, Milton and Eighteenth-Century Literary Editing: The Beginnings of Interpretative Scholarship* (Cambridge: Cambridge University Press, 1997).

SLAVERY AND ABOLITION

Basker, J. G. (ed.). *Amazing Grace: An Anthology of Poems about Slavery, 1660–1810* (New Haven, CT: Yale University Press, 2002).

Brown, C. L. *Moral Capital: Foundations of British Abolitionism* (Chapel Hill: University of North Carolina Press, 2006).
Caretta, V. (ed.). *Letters of the Late Ignatius Sancho: An African* (London: Penguin, 1998).
Unchained Voices: An Anthology of Black Authors in the English-Speaking World of the Eighteenth Century (Lexington: University Press of Kentucky, 1996).
Carey, B. *British Abolitionism and the Rhetoric of Sensibility: Writing, Sentiment, and Slavery, 1760–1807* (Basingstoke: Palgrave Macmillan, 2005).
Chater, K. *Untold Histories: Black People in England and Wales during the Period of the British Slave Trade,* c. *1660–1807* (Manchester: Manchester University Press, 2009).
Davis, D. B. *Inhuman Bondage: The Rise and Fall of Slavery in the New World* (Oxford: Oxford University Press, 2006).
Fryer, P. *Staying Power: The History of Black People in Britain* (London: Pluto Press, 1984).
Hochschild, A. *Bury the Chains: The First International Human Rights Movement* (Basingstoke: Macmillan, 2005).
Kolchin, P. *American Slavery: 1619–1877* (London and New York: Penguin, 1995).
Thomas, H. *The Slave Trade: The History of the Atlantic Slave Trade, 1440–1870* (London: Picador, 1997).

SOCIAL HIERARCHY

Davidoff, L., and C. Hall. *Family Fortunes: Men and Women of the English Middle Class, 1780–1850* (Chicago: University of Chicago Press, 1987).
Earle, P. *The Making of the English Middle Class: Business, Society and Family Life in London, 1660–1730* (Berkeley: University of California Press, 1989).
Hudson, N. *Samuel Johnson and the Making of Modern England* (Cambridge: Cambridge University Press, 2003).

THEATRE

Hume, R. D. (ed.). *The London Theatre World, 1660–1800* (Carbondale: Southern Illinois University Press, 1980).
Moody, J., and D. O'Quinn (eds.). *The Cambridge Companion to British Theatre, 1730–1830* (Cambridge: Cambridge University Press, 2007).
Nicoll, A. *The Garrick Stage: Theatres and Audience in the Eighteenth Century* (Manchester: Manchester University Press, 1980).
Stone, G. W., C. B. Hogan, E. L. Avery, W. van Lennep, and A. H. Scouten (eds.). *The London Stage, 1660–1800: A Calendar of Plays, Entertainments and Afterpieces, Together with Casts, Box-Receipts and Contemporary Comment*, 6 vols. in 12 (Carbondale: Southern Illinois University Press, 1960–79).

TRAVEL

Black, J. *The British and the Grand Tour* (London: Croom Helm, 1985).
Curley, T. M. *Samuel Johnson and the Age of Travel* (Athens: University of Georgia Press, 1976).
Jackman, W. T. *The Development of Transportation in Modern England*, new edn. (London: Frank Cass, 1962).
Jarvis, R. *Romantic Writing and Pedestrian Travel* (New York: St. Martin's Press, 1997).
Sorrenson, R. "The Ship as Scientific Instrument in the Eighteenth Century," *Osiris*, 2nd ser., 11 (1996), 221–36.

VISUAL ARTS

Brownell, M. R. *Samuel Johnson's Attitude to the Arts* (Oxford: Clarendon Press, 1989).
Hargraves, M. *"Candidates for Fame": The Society of Artists of Great Britain, 1760–1791* (New Haven, CT: Yale University Press, 2005).
Paulson, R. *Hogarth*, 3 vols. (New Brunswick, NJ: Rutgers University Press, 1991–3).
Postle, M. *Sir Joshua Reynolds: The Subject Pictures* (Cambridge: Cambridge University Press, 1995).
Wendorf, R. *Sir Joshua Reynolds: The Painter in Society* (Cambridge, MA: Harvard University Press, 1996).

WAR

Black, J. *Britain as a Military Power, 1688–1815* (London: UCL Press, 1999).
Black, J. (ed.). *European Warfare, 1453–1815* (Basingstoke: Macmillan, 1999).
War in European History, 1660–1792 (Washington, DC: Potomac Books, 2009).
Tallett, F., and D. J. B. Trim (eds.). *European Warfare, 1350–1750* (Cambridge: Cambridge University Press, 2010).

WOMEN WRITERS

Basker, J. G. "Radical Affinities: Mary Wollstonecraft and Samuel Johnson," in *Tradition in Transition: Women Writers, Marginal Texts, and the Eighteenth-Century Canon*, ed. A. Ribeiro and J. G. Basker (Oxford: Clarendon Press, 1996), pp. 41–55.
Clarke, N. *Dr. Johnson's Women* (London: Hambledon and London, 2000).
Eger, E. *Bluestockings: Women of Reason from Enlightenment to Romanticism* (Basingstoke: Palgrave Macmillan, 2010).
Eger, E., and L. Peltz. *Brilliant Women: 18th-Century Bluestockings* (New Haven, CT: Yale University Press, 2008).

Kemmerer, K. N. *"A Neutral Being between the Sexes": Samuel Johnson's Sexual Politics* (Lewisburg, PA: Bucknell University Press, 1998).
Myers, S. H. *The Bluestocking Circle: Women, Friendship and the Life of the Mind in Eighteenth-Century England* (Oxford: Clarendon Press, 1990).
Schellenberg, B. A. *The Professionalization of Women Writers in Eighteenth-Century Britain* (Cambridge: Cambridge University Press, 2005).
Small, M. R. *Charlotte Ramsay Lennox, an Eighteenth Century Lady of Letters* (New Haven, CT: Yale University Press, 1935).
Turner, C. *Living by the Pen: Women Writers in the Eighteenth Century* (London and New York: Routledge, 1992).

Index